SOUL
WORK

We are kindred spirits

JB0-01341 © The Laurel Burch Paper Company

SOUL
WORK

A Field Guide for Spiritual Seekers

ANNE A. SIMPKINSON AND
CHARLES H. SIMPKINSON

HarperPerennial
A Division of HarperCollinsPublishers

HarperCollins books may be purchased for educational, business, or sales promotional use. For information please write: Special Markets Department, HarperCollins Publishers, Inc., 10 East 53rd Street, New York, NY 10022.

FIRST EDITION

Designed by Joseph Rutt

Library of Congress Cataloging-in-Publication Data

Simpkinson, Charles H.
    Soul Work : a field guide for spiritual seekers / Charles Simpkinson, Anne Simpkinson. — 1st. ed.
      p. cm.
    ISBN 0-06-095218-0
     1. Psychology and religion. 2. Spiritual life. 3. Soul. 4. Psychology, Religious. 5. New Age movement. I. Simpkinson, Anne Adamcewicz. II. Title.
BL624.S5343 1998
291.4'4—dc21   98-35085

98 99 00 01 02 ❖/RRD 10 9 8 7 6 5 4 3 2 1

To my grandmothers, who along
with the will to survive, brought
a piece of Poland's soul to this country.
Their legacy has served me well.

—ANNE A. SIMPKINSON

To Deany Laliotis
with deepest gratitude

—CHARLES H. SIMPKINSON

Contents

Acknowledgments

We want to begin by expressing gratitude to the late Patricia Demetrios, Ph.D., who helped us put together the prototype for the *Common Boundary Graduate Education Guide (GEG)* in 1991. Her help seeded this project.

Douglas Wengell began compiling the second edition of the GEG in the summer of 1993 as part of an internship. He worked so hard and with such diligence and intellectual astuteness that we asked him to stay on another year to complete the task as a staff member. Mary Jane Casavant also devoted much time, effort, and care to both the 1994 edition of the GEG and the current *Soul Work*.

We wish to thank our literary agent, Loretta Barrett, who encouraged us to rework the GEG into *Soul Work*.

We also value the faith Joëlle Delbourgo, editor-in-chief of the Adult Trade Division of HarperCollins, had that the process of soul work could be codified into a field guide. Thanks, too, go to Tim Duggan, who made many valuable editorial suggestions.

We also very much appreciate the help of Eugene Gendlin, Ph.D., professor of psychology and philosophy at the University of Chicago. His expert critiques and insightful feedback were extremely beneficial.

Many, many drafts of this book were carefully typed by Lisa Jackson, whose hard work, loyalty, and dedication to the project are heartfully appreciated.

There were also scores of colleagues and friends who contributed to the book either by providing information, being interviewed, writing a section or essay, or reading and reviewing what we had written. In this regard, we want to acknowledge Robin Abb, Peter Antocci, Lauren Artress, Isabella Bates, Sophy Burham, Dwight Byers, Julia Cameron, Jacqueline Carleton, Merrill Ware Carrington, Sharon Chaiklin, Esther Check, Joan Chodorow, Pamela Chubbuck, Ken Cohen, Jeri Darling, John Davis, Rosemary Dougherty, Barbara Dunn, Carl Ernst, Clarissa Pinkola Estés, James Fadiman, Georg Feurstein, Paul Fleischman, Lilias Folan, Rabbi Jacob Gabriel, Sheridan Gates, Michael Gliksohn, Belinda Gore, Elliot Greene, Michael Harner, Harville Hendricks, Joan Hickey, Robert Hilton, Virginia Wink Hilton, Helen Hunt, Sister Arlene Hynes, Sandra Ingerman, Don Hanlon Johnson, Judy Jordan, Chuck and Erica Kelley, Pir Vilayat Khan, Abi'l Khayr, Margaret Kornfeld, Jack Kornfield, Earl Koteen, Liz Lerman, John Daido Loori, Jean Matlack, Gerald May, Thomas Moore, Donald Moyner, Caroline

Myss, Belleruth Naparstek, Gregory Nicosia, Helen Palmer, Gary Peterson, Mary Pipher, Adele Pogue, Barbara Renshaw, Judy Rogers, David Rosen, Ilana Rubenfeld, Jeffrey Rubin, Sharon Salzberg, Sue Seecof, Martha Stark, Eugene Taylor Sutton, Peggy Treadwell, Lucy Abbot Tucker, Lucy R. Waletzky, Karyne B. Wilner, Peter Winkler, Steven Wirth, Marion Woodman, Roy Woodruff, and Sandra Wooten.

Common Boundary staff and associates of the magazine also worked hard writing, editing, typing, and researching. We thank Beth Baker, Susan Belchamber, Claudia Bezerra, Charles Chaplin, Kate Collins, Rachel Dumser, Sharon Fitzgerald, J. Vic Funderburk, Pat Hagan, Deborah Hughes, Livia Kent, Carolyn Knapp, Bill O'Sullivan, Mariann Payne, Vivienne Simon, Kristen Smith, Rose Solari, and Karen Strohmeyer.

And, finally, we are eternally grateful to our circle of friends who provided comfort, support, encouragement, ideas, and huge doses of empathic understanding. Our deepest thanks to Bob and Erma Caldwell, Celia Coates, Betsy and David DeRuff, Bill Dillon, Linda Fusilier, Barbara Hammer, Peggy O'Kane, Jill Raymond, Haloli Richter, Rachel Ripple, Manuel Roman, Naomi Schwiesow, and members of our centering prayer group at St. Margaret's Episcopal Church.

Preface

For more than twenty years, the two of us have been on journeys of personal discovery and growth. Individually and together, we have immersed ourselves in psychotherapy, spiritual practices, and small group activities, such as a storytelling and a centering prayer group. All of these have helped us deepen our self-knowledge and forge a relationship with the invisible mysteries that shape and give meaning to our lives. They have also allowed us to connect to kindred spirits who have encouraged and supported us and who share our commitment to bringing the sacred into the everyday. We, like so many others, were originally motivated by emotional discomfort. But we stayed involved because we became intrigued by the inner world—its rhythms, gifts, invitations, surprises, and challenges.

We have been twice blessed: not only have we been able to explore our spiritual geography, but we have also had the opportunity to make this exploration the focus of our professional lives. Starting *Common Boundary,* a magazine that investigates the powerful connections among psychology, spirituality, creativity, and ecology, and organizing annual conferences that draw 1,700 to 2,500 participants have put us in touch with remarkable men and women: pioneers and innovators, brilliant thinkers and synthesizers, dedicated healers and spiritual teachers, the best of whom communicate by example and inspire others with their generous and gentle presence. We have also been exposed to countless books, manuscripts, conferences, and publications and to representatives from myriad organizations involved in healing work.

Through the years, we've come to respect the power and beauty of soul work. We have witnessed as well as experienced profound changes to our health, relationship, friendships, work life, and sense of well-being. We've also been struck by the fact that although relief can sometimes come remarkably quickly, transformation generally involves a long and painstaking process. Over and over again we have encountered the truth behind seeing soul work as a spiral: we work a particular issue to resolution only to have it resurface again and again, usually in a less virulent form.

We have also learned that each person has a unique destiny to fulfill, so that each inner journey is different. In this vein, we thought it would be appropriate to preface this book by sharing parts of our journeys. It's not our intent to introduce ourselves by way of our wounds. Rather, we want to offer the most reliable knowledge we have acquired: what we've lived. We also thought that readers would be interested in how *Common Boundary* originated and evolved. Perhaps these stories will give you a sense of how a spiritual journey can start, and how it can move through different phases. We hope the experiences—both personal and professional—that inform this book will assist you on your journey by providing a sense of recognition, excitement, and the resources to continue on.

Chuck's Story

In the fall of 1960, I went to Yale Divinity School hoping to propitiate a demanding God. Ever since I was an altar boy, I'd had a strong but confusing relationship with the Almighty. I felt guilty because of my sexual urges. Like many of my friends growing up in the 1940s, I received the distinct message that God wanted me to ignore, if not disown, these powerful feelings that often came upon me suddenly and unexpectedly, even while serving at God's altar. I also felt that God (like my parents and grandfather) didn't think I did many things right. Preoccupation with sex was only one in a long list of "sins" that also included underachieving at school and not being popular enough with my classmates. By becoming an Episcopal priest, I hoped I would quiet this hypercritical deity.

But this unrealistic plan—my self-sacrifice—didn't work; I remained as anxious and depressed as ever. Fortunately, the school's Episcopal chaplain referred me to a psychotherapist at the student health service. After several months, the therapist convinced me that my problem was psychological in origin and that becoming a minister wasn't going to help me achieve peace of mind or self-acceptance. When he suggested further therapy, I heard him recommend a new form of salvation: psychology.

Not only did I enter therapy, but I went on to spend six years earning a Ph.D. in clinical psychology. Once I had that degree, I believed, I would understand psychological development so well that I would never have to feel so troubled again. If service to God wouldn't save me, perhaps service to the psyche could. It became my new personal religion.

When I finished my degree in 1972, I still didn't feel any better about myself, and I felt as distant as ever from God. My next strategy was to take a high-prestige faculty appointment in the Department of Psychiatry at Johns Hopkins Medical School. I worked to help organize a center for research and training in drug-abuse treatment and prevention for the state of Maryland. Needless to say, this final effort to gain self-acceptance also didn't work. When the project folded, I was utterly bereft. My blood pressure shot up, and I had the choice of going on medication or finding another way to bring it down.

In organizing the drug-abuse center, I had learned that meditation could reduce stress and lower blood pressure, so I signed up for a class in Transcendental Meditation, which was quite popular in the early 1970s. Within two months of regular meditation practice, my blood pressure had returned to normal. When I proudly announced to my physician that I had chosen meditation over medication, he completely disregarded the information; it just didn't register with him. It did, however, greatly impress me. It launched me on my spiritual journey.

The experience of lowering my blood pressure was so encouraging that I went back into psychotherapy, where I learned that my inner critic was not the voice of God but the internalized voices of my mother, father, and especially my grandfather. Ironically, although my grandfather was a juvenile-court judge who had a wide reputation for being kind and compassionate toward the young men who appeared before him, he was cold, distant, and harshly critical toward me. At the time, I believed that the discrepancy between the way he treated me and the way he treated the other boys was due to my own inadequacy. It was little consolation to me when I later learned that he had never grieved the loss of his only son, Harlan Henry Hoffman, who died at the age of seven from complications related to injuries sustained when his mother accidentally ran over him with a horse-drawn carriage. Thus I faced a major task: clearing away psychological debris so that I could hear the "still small voice" of my soul and use it, rather than my loud-mouthed inner critic, as a source of guidance.

A second milestone in my spiritual journey was my marriage to Anne in 1978. During the twenty years of our marriage, I have discovered why it is important to have a spiritual companion. All my unfinished business with my parents and grandfather surfaces in conflicts with Anne. According to family therapist Harville Hendrix and his colleague and wife, Helen Hunt (see page 101), people choose exactly the right person to help them recover lost aspects of themselves. In my case, in response to my mother's wall-to-wall criticism I had lost my exuberant spontaneity and replaced it with a demeanor appropriate for a dutiful son and mother's little helper—an inappropriate stance in an adult relationship. Issues of dependency, standing up to defend myself, and carving out time to relax and play are all areas I work on even today.

The next marker was when I began to practice Vipassana meditation after participating in a ten-day silent meditation retreat at the Insight Meditation Center in Barre, Massachusetts, in 1988. As I sat in meditation, I noted that certain negative thoughts and attitudes recurred. This was my first experience of stepping back from myself long enough to observe the way my thoughts controlled and colored my experiences of the world. In discussing this situation in therapy, I realized that these previously unconscious negative attitudes were like blinders that prevented me from paying attention to experiences that would have provided positive evidence to challenge my negativity.

At this point, I came up against the limits of talk therapy and encountered another milestone. A situation graciously presented itself in which I was able to form a collegial partnership with psychologist Eugene Gendlin. Gene had written the classic book *Focusing,* which describes a technique for listening to one's "bodily felt sense" (see page 30 for a description of the method). Taking turns listening and being listened to, we used his technique over the telephone (he in New York and I in Maryland) to help each other emotionally "digest" our life experiences and to take in the psychological nourishment of being heard by someone else, which in turn helped us hear ourselves.

During my turn as "focuser," I would describe to Gene the messages I received from my body. For example, if I experienced a sense of fear, I might locate it in my stomach. Gene would encourage me to speak reassuringly to this fear in order to hear what it had to say to me. Once I was able to listen to this concern and acknowledge that it was real, the fear would subside. I would also often address God regarding my feeling that I wasn't receiving sufficient protection from suffering. Frankly it felt pretty wild to speak with and listen to God through my body. But when you consider that our digestive and cardiovascular systems and all the autonomic processes in our bodies that occur outside of our awareness are part of the same system that regulates the movement of the earth and stars, it isn't so odd to think that I could listen to my body and thereby communicate with the life force.

Most recently, I ended my "wandering in the wilderness" by finding spiritual community in a group that meets weekly at St. Margaret's Episcopal Church for a contemplative communion service and centering prayer, a form of Christian contemplation (see page 273). Sometimes, while sitting silently in the small chapel, I think about how much has happened since my troubled and lonely days at Yale Divinity School. Although I know I had other pure and less distorted impulses behind my desire to become an Episcopal priest, I had to shed my neurotic compulsion to appease God before the young altar boy's underlying hunger to be in God's loving presence could emerge. As I gather around the altar again with this intimate group of fellow seekers, I look back upon those early days and feel a mixture of sadness and admiration for the lonely young man who was reaching out to God in the only way he knew how.

Anne's Story

The summer after graduating from Syracuse University, I moved to Washington, D.C., where I worked for Ralph Nader's Congress Project, researching and writing profiles of Senators Hubert H. Humphrey and John C. Stennis. By the fall, having been paid $100 for six weeks of work, I desperately needed a job and ended up in the production department of the *Army Times*. On the surface, things seemed to be going well. I had my own apartment on Capitol Hill and a job in my field (I had graduated with a bachelor's degree in magazine journalism and American studies), but I felt a sense of emptiness, restlessness, and depression. Today, with the proliferation of desktop graphics, it seems cumbersome and archaic to have spent eight hours a day "pasting up boards"—adhering stories that had been set in columns of type on photographic paper to boards by means of wax. But it wasn't the mechanics of the job that made it drudgery, it was my youthful chomping at the bit, my heart's desire to write—and my utter terror that I was not any good at it. Also, having grown up in a small town in southeastern Connecticut and attended a midsized university, I wasn't prepared for the sheer size and impersonality of the Big City. As a newly converted feminist, however, I wasn't about to admit even to myself how lonely, scared, and vulnerable I sometimes felt. Going to the movies or out to restaurants by myself at night became merit badges toward earning my wings of independence.

Then a former college sorority sister of mine moved to D.C. to work at a home for runaways. Having entered therapy with a psychologist who used a Bioenergetic approach, she extolled its benefits to me. Although I was too poor and probably too scared to see her therapist, I found a personal-growth center, the Community of the Whole Person, which offered individual and group Bioenergetic sessions on a sliding fee scale. For several individual sessions in the spring of 1974, I met with Barbara Brennan, who later founded the Barbara Brennan School of Healing and wrote the book *Hands of Light: A Guide Through the Human Energy Field*, and I joined a newly formed Bioenergetic therapy group.

I had no idea then what I was getting into. All I knew was that I wanted relief from the emotions that were threatening to overwhelm me. In the first group meeting, I had an unusual experience. I was lying backward over a breathing stool—affectionately called "the rack" because in opening up the body, it frequently released painful emotions—with my hands over my head. I could feel my chest muscles stretching and my breathing deepen. Suddenly, I experienced myself as a youngster standing on the toilet in the bathroom of my grandparents' home. I remembered the thrill of opening a window that looked not onto the outside but into a hallway. That memory surprised me. I hadn't thought about my grandparents' house in years. Also, I realized that if indeed it was a memory, I had been very young, as my grandparents sold that house when I was six years old.

The image in and of itself was not earth-shattering. But the fact that I had retrieved such a clear, specific, and emotionally charged scene from my distant past simply by lying backward over a stool and breathing fascinated me. Where did the image come from? Was memory locked in tissue? What about emotions? Did breathing have something to do with recalling the past? I was hooked. Not only did I continue the sessions, but eventually I earned a master's degree in counseling and body psychotherapy. I practiced massage therapy and psychotherapy for seven years before returning to writing and editing.

For many years while I was a counselor, Chuck and I were active members of the Pathwork Community in Washington, D.C. This was a spiritually oriented group originally founded by Eva Pierrakos (see page 190). But after eight or nine years of individual, group, and couples work, weekend training, and even a three-week couples intensive, I felt burned out. Not only was I giving sessions as a therapist, but I was also regularly getting them. All my friends were either on the Path or were therapists. I felt overprocessed. I escaped into the Washington world as a writer and editor for two presidential commissions. Then in 1984, when *Common Boundary*'s part-time editor decided to leave, I reluctantly took the helm.

Almost immediately I saw how the job married my intellectual interests and my passions. Over the years, I became reinvolved with alternative therapies and spiritual practice. I was Rolfed, received massages, and saw an acupuncturist regularly. I learned Vipassana meditation, received *darshan* from Mother Meera, and went on meditation retreats with Vietnamese Buddhist monk Thich Nhat Hanh.

Most recently, I have found myself returning to Christianity, a turn of events that I neither planned nor intended. It began in 1992, when I heard that the International Transpersonal Association (ITA) was to hold its biennial conference in Prague. I immediately signed up. Not only was it to be a homecoming for ITA cofounder and transpersonal psychiatrist Stanislav Grof—who had fled the Communist regime in his country and settled in the United States—but the former Czechoslovakia is located next door to Poland, the birthplace of my mother and both sets of grandparents. Because my mother had been struggling with Alzheimer's disease for several years and because my mentor had been diagnosed with breast cancer, I decided to attend the meeting, then make a pilgrimage to Czestochowa, home of the Black Madonna.

Officially crowned the Queen of Poland in the early eighteenth century, Our Lady of Czestochowa rules the hearts of the Polish people. She is venerated, celebrated, invoked, and beseeched. Upward of a million pilgrims have at times converged on her shrine in western Poland. Devotion to her in this predominantly Catholic country is palpable. In one Kraków church, a small grotto where people were praying to Our Lady noticeably radiated an energy undetected in other parts of the building. In the chapel where the Black Madonna resides, supplicants create a river of prayer. In that space, the veil between the sacred and the mundane becomes porous, and the holy makes its presence known.

After hearing Mass, I entered the tiny chancel and knelt on the hard marble floor, shoulder to shoulder with other petitioners before the icon of Our Lady. I immediately sensed a presence as cool and crystal clear as a mountain stream and as spacious and all-encompassing as the midwestern sky. I felt as if I were being asked, "Why are you here?" I responded by silently expressing my concern and love for my mother and my mentor, praying that Our Lady would hold them close to her. My petition made, I felt that my audience was over. I rose and left the chapel.

Not long afterward, I began to feel a yearning for my Catholic roots. The feeling felt foreign, as if some alien creature were now inhabiting my body. It annoyed me. I had been educated for nine years by the Sisters of Nazareth, spending untold after-school and weekend hours helping the nuns in the church and convent. Although public school opened my small universe to Protestants and Jews, it was not until college that I experienced a radical shift in world view. There's a German Renaissance woodcut by an anonymous artist that depicts the prophet Ezekiel popping his head out of the everyday world and catching a glimpse of celestial grandeur. David Miller's Religion 101 class at Syracuse University had that effect on me. His discourses on Hindu deities and Buddhist dharma opened up new intellectual vistas, and I suddenly beheld a vastly different universe, one filled with a panoply of beliefs—polytheism, karma, reincarnation, Taoist philosophy— that seismically shook the very ground of my limited life experience.

Added to this ferment were anti–Vietnam War rallies and heady women's consciousness-raising groups, the latter opening my eyes to the exclusion of women from the ministry and to the patriarchal infrastructure of the Church and the gender-biased liturgy. All that together with the necessity for decisions about sexual activity—the church's message clearly anticipated Nancy Reagan's famous dictum "Just say no!"—led me to jettison my religious practice and affiliation.

The Catholic churches I happened into over the years—for family christenings, weddings, or funerals—all seemed empty, devoid of any religious vitality. I could not imagine finding a way back. Then five years after the Czestochowa pilgrimage, I encountered centering prayer, a contemplative practice developed by Catholic monks in the mid-1970s that draws upon both the Catholic and Anglican heritage. For me, this form of prayer did not carry with it any dogmatic or political baggage. It was simply a means of "resting in God." I wholeheartedly embraced it, joining a weekly prayer group in an Episcopal church, which drew other religious refugees from the Catholic, Methodist, and Baptist churches.

Poet Derek Walcott, in his stage version of Homer's *Odyssey*, has a character observe about Odysseus that he asks "the only question the soul ever asks: Where is home?" Through the years, I have found that "coming home" involves a kind of eternal unfolding. It is as if my soul's deepest yearnings pull me into situations that at first seem painful or exciting, challenging or demanding. I dive into the situation, and only in retrospect can I see how deeper forces were at work shaping the experience. Sometimes these situations can look and feel like the Hero's Journey, a time when one must show perseverance and courage in the face of great obstacles or pain; at other times, they require dedication to decidedly unglamorous but essential physical, psychological, or spiritual discipline; and at still other times, they are as subtle, sweet, and gentle as the kiss of a breeze on an early summer day.

Soul work is a process that plants great challenges and brings forth delicious fruit. Although it can sometimes feel as dry as a drought and at other times as dizzying and breathtaking as standing on the top of Mt. Everest, it always yields experiences, connections, and wisdom far beyond my wildest dreams and expectations. In certain moments, everything that my heart desires is fulfilled; the deepest parts of me are fed. And I always feel a mixture of gratitude and awe at having had the opportunity to "do the work."

Common Boundary's Genesis

When Common Boundary began in the early 1980s, the two of us were on a journey of both psychological development and spiritual growth. Given our personalities and inclinations, we were compelled to seek out everything there was to know in the two areas and find out how they related to each other. One way to do this was to connect with others, so Chuck organized a conference in 1980. He had previously put together a panel and a workshop at the 1978 and 1979 symposia sponsored by *Family Therapy Networker* magazine, which he had founded in the mid-1970s. The response had been so enthusiastic that in the fall of 1980, with the sponsorship of a professor of pastoral counseling and the help of an ecumenical program committee, he convened a one-day event at Wesley Theological Seminary on the American University campus in Washington, D.C. More than two hundred people participated in this first conference, "Integrating Psychotherapy and Spirituality," and a group called Kindred Spirits formed to help program subsequent meetings.

As a way of staying connected to the people who attended the conference, Chuck sent out a photocopied typewritten publication known as *Kindred Spirits Newsletter*. Over time, the newsletter was typeset, and graphic illustrations and photographs were added. It grew from four to six, then from twelve to sixteen pages. By 1984 the publication had a new name, *The Common Boundary Between Spirituality and Psychotherapy*, and five hundred subscribers but no renewal system. Thus it became an expensive avocation. When Anne, who had a degree in magazine journalism, took over as editor, she began instituting simple circulation strategies, such as renewals and direct-mail promotions. Then, in January of 1989, we redesigned the publication as a magazine.

By 1990 the field had expanded substantially. The number of books published on this theme had increased tremendously, and conferences and workshops were multiplying. The Common Boundary Conference became an annual event, with the numbers of participants growing steadily. One memorable moment came during the 1990 conference when Vietnamese monk Thich Nhat Hanh led four hundred people on a peace walk to the Vietnam Veterans Memorial. Another came in 1991 at the "Sacred Stories" conference when poet and author Maya Angelou opened the conference with an entertaining and moving address and then-senator Albert Gore Jr. gave a keynote address based on his book *Earth in the Balance*. It was a thrill to hear Gore repeat parts of his keynote address when accepting the nomination as Democratic vice-presidential nominee in the summer of 1992. Then in January, Gore and Angelou were again standing near each other at the swearing-in ceremony, when Angelou read a poem she had written in honor of the inauguration.

The Common Boundary Conferences also generated two anthologies, published by HarperSanFrancisco. The first, *Sacred Stories*, was based on the 1991 conference; *Nourishing the Soul* came out of the 1993 conference. Many of the main themes of the latter book, such as body wisdom, inner and outer ecology (the relationship of nature to psychology and spirituality), and creativity, imagination, and healing, have subsequently been addressed in our annual gatherings.

Over the years we have noticed an interesting change. At first the largest number of inquiries we received at Common Boundary concerned requests for referrals to psychotherapists who were sensitive to spiritual concerns. Then people started calling not to find a spiritually sensitive psychotherapist but to find a school where they could learn to become one. This led to our publishing two editions of a resource guide, the most recent one in 1994, the *Common Boundary Graduate Education Guide: Resources Integrating Spirituality and Psychology*. Since then, yet another trend has surfaced: the integration of soul work into people's existing lives and professions. Today, many people are looking for a meaningful livelihood. Whether a secretary or a member of the diplomatic corps, a college professor, computer programmer, or caterer, people want not only to apply their skills and talents but to be nourished and engaged by their work. They want to know they are making a contribution while making a living. They also want to humanize the workplace and feel that their positive intention, focused attention, and integrity are valued. Along with bringing the soul into the workplace, there is an increasing interest in bringing soul home. Whether by initiating home-based spiritual practices, making an effort to parent consciously, creating an altar or meditation room, scheduling regular family sit-down dinners, or rearranging one's furnishings according to feng shui principles, people want to imbue daily life with meaning. To help individuals in all these areas, we conceived of *Soul Work*, a manual for identifying the resources—psychological approaches, bodywork techniques, spiritual practices, and creative arts therapies—that support, encourage, and catalyze soul work.

In assembling it, we have called upon personal experience as well as professional contacts. We have spoken with colleagues, our conference participants (in a survey at the 1996 conference), and subscribers (in a mailed survey), asking them what has been most helpful in their spiritual search. We have scoured books and the back issues of our magazine as well as other publications and journals. We made this effort because we believe no one person or organization could have provided such a wide perspective on such a large and multifaceted subject. But it is our hope that this project will not remain a one-way street. We would like to create a dialogue with you, the readers of this book. We would like to hear about your searching—what you've found helpful and worthwhile, what was not. Where did your journey begin? Where are you now? Your input and feedback will help make this book (as well as its future editions) and our work truly a collaborative effort.

Common Boundary
4905 Del Ray Avenue, Suite 210
Bethesda, MD 20814
(301) 652-9495 (phone)
(301) 652-0579 (fax)
connect@commonboundary.org (e-mail)
www.commonboundary.org (website)

Anne and Charles Simpkinson
March 1998

Introduction

Sometimes
I go about pitying myself
While I am carried by the wind
Across the sky.

—Chippewa saying

Horses, particularly magical or celestial steeds, have galloped through Tibetan folklore, mythology, and religious history since that culture's earliest beginnings. From wood-block prints that grace the colorful and ubiquitous prayer flags to legends about the King of the Horses rescuing human beings from the clutches of ogresses and earthly attachments, the image of the horse, particularly the windhorse, is a pervasive one.

At one level, the prayer-flag image of a majestic mount carrying on his back a single flaming jewel is seen as a talisman, a symbol of good fortune. But at another level, the windhorse signifies deeper realities. For example, a meditative program devised by the late Chogyam Trungpa, a lineage holder and meditation master in the Kagyu school of Tibetan Buddhism, has a practice entitled "raising the windhorse." It is a method of accessing the basic goodness that lies at the heart of life. Basic goodness, according to Trungpa, is not the idea or belief that life is good but an experience of the powerful energy of goodness that makes up the core of life. In *Shambhala: The Sacred Path of the Warrior*, Trungpa writes that raising the windhorse dispels doubt, powerlessness, depression, and fear while simultaneously actualizing fearlessness, gentleness, and a sense of humor. It also leads to developing an "authentic presence."

We find the windhorse a compelling image because it represents the relationship of personality, soul, and spirit and thus is the perfect metaphor for soul work and spiritual seeking. The horse symbolizes the physical body and personality, ego and natural instincts—in short, the self. The rider, or jewel, represents the soul, and the wind signifies the spirit, the mysterious, invisible force that is greater than we are, that animates our lives.

Soul work is the attempt to balance the knowledge and discipline of our "horse" with surrender to the flow of the spirit wind so that our soul can reach its

1

unique destiny. David Richo mentions the windhorse image in his book *When Love Meets Fear* and sums up the interaction in this way:

> Both the wind and the horse propel us
> The horse is the visible choices we make by effort;
> The wind is the invisible force we receive by grace.

Over the centuries, people have discovered and devised many ways to ride their windhorses so as to be able to flow with the invisible mysteries. This field guide is a manual for those who wish to explore the methods available today for initiating or deepening their spiritual journey. And indeed there has been an explosion of resources available in this area. Ancient texts, once the sole province of small inner circles of adepts, are now commercially published and widely available. Spiritual classics and new translations of sacred works such as the *Tibetan Book of the Dead*, the Psalms, the Song of Songs, and *Tao Te Ching* are regularly reissued. This makes access to wisdom teachings democratic and widespread.

The downside is that there's a plethora of books out there some of which are of questionable quality. We at Common Boundary are in danger of drowning in the tidal wave of new titles that arrives daily.

Additionally, workshops, training programs, and seminars are proliferating. How does one know where to begin the search? What's needed is a trusted, seasoned companion to advise, instruct, suggest, sort through, and guide. *Soul Work* was written for just this purpose. For over seventeen years, Common Boundary, through its magazine, annual conference, seminars, and book publishing projects, has been tracking developments in the psychology and spirituality fields. We have watched the evolution of transpersonal psychology, the rise and fall of the men's movement, and the increasing credibility and mainstream acceptance of mind-body studies and alternative medicine. We've reported on how feminism has changed the field of psychology and how the Twelve-Step movement is changing to accommodate the needs of minorities and women. We've explored whether spiritual community is possible in cyberspace and what effect Prozac can have on spiritual practice.

We've also profiled and interviewed leading thinkers, healers, writers, and spiritual teachers, including Buddhist monk Thich Nhat Hanh, Mother Meera, Jewish Renewal movement cofounder Rabbi Zalman Schachter-Shalomi, centering prayer cofounder Thomas Keating, medical intuitive Caroline Myss, and Jungian analyst Marion Woodman. We've talked cosmology with ecophilosopher Thomas Berry, have had Theodore Roszak explain ecopsychology, and have discussed the creative process with novelist Isabel Allende.

Common Boundary promotes no specific method or technology or branch of healing. Because of this we are perfectly poised to survey the field and identify resources that are useful to soul work. The chapters in this book present the history and context of various psychotherapeutic methods, spiritual practices, body-work approaches, and creative arts therapies. They can be used as a handy reference to currently available tools to aid one in the pursuit of a particular healing method.

Hungry for Soul

In an earlier, less secular era when philosophers, theologians, and poets had our ears and spoke to our hearts, the soul had a central place in our worldview. The idea of a nonphysical essence, a vital force, a piece of God residing deep within our beings is virtually universal and has for centuries animated notions about preexistence, immortality, heaven and hell, reincarnation, karma, and transcendence. Although not often experienced in a visible or tangible way, its reality permeated the lives of our ancestors. From shamanic journeys to Catholic plenary indulgences that provided absolution of purgatorial punishment, the soul was acknowledged, honored, and cared for. Today many view the soul as a quality of consciousness. It is, according to psychotherapist and bestselling author Thomas Moore, "a dimension of experiencing life and ourselves . . . [that] has to do with depth, value, relatedness, heart, and personal substance."

Soul is intimately connected to spirit; both are invisible aspects of our inner landscape. However, while our spirit is transcendent and takes us beyond ourselves, soul is an interior phenomenon, a silent agent deep within us that acts as a local representative of the larger life force. Spirit enjoys lofty, cloud-tipped mountain peaks; soul enjoys the low-lying tropics. Spirit lifts us out of ourselves, inspires us, and gives us vision. Soul, on the other hand, is quite content to stay at home. It connects us to people, places, and things—"life in its particulars," as Moore puts it. Without soul, we are disconnected from everything around us—family, spouse, friends, community, nature, and God.

Moore and others see the soul as a kind of mediator between spirit—representing the heavenly, vertical, eternal realms—and the material world. Moore quotes medieval philosopher Marsilio Ficino, for example, who says that the mind—and spirit—has a tendency to wander off on its own so that it loses relevance to the physical world. On the other hand, matter tends to absorb us. Soul, Ficino says, "holds together mind and body, ideas and life, spirit and the world." In this role, it signals us when we are being true to ourselves and fulfilling our life's purpose and when we are not. When we are out of alignment with our purpose, traditions tell us that we experience "soul sickness" or "loss of soul." The expression "lost soul" perfectly describes those who are detached or vacuous, who have no apparent meaning, direction, or purpose in their lives.

With the emergence of modern science, societies have placed more emphasis on the external, rational world. Many of the spiritual beliefs and rituals that once connected us to the mystical, invisible realms, which in turn infused meaning and purpose into our everyday lives and thus fed our souls, have been lost. Psychology, which in many ways has preempted philosophy and religion as the authority on how we should live, has for the most part concerned itself almost exclusively with improving the self, coping with crises, and bolstering self-esteem. Accordingly, the soul, our point of connection between spirit and self, which urges our participation in the sacred, has been neglected.

Many recent thinkers, however, are calling attention to the need to rediscover and reclaim the soul. For example, archetypal psychologist Robert Sardello points to symptoms such as addiction, alienation, loss of values, depression, emptiness, meaninglessness, and a tendency toward violence as indications that the soul is trying to get our attention.

This same malaise is mirrored at the collective level. Mother Teresa once said that in India people suffer from physical hunger; in America, they are spiritually starved. This metaphor of hunger seems to be ever-present today in discussions of contemporary life. Radio talk-show guests decry the lack of civility, the rudeness, aggression, and cynicism in society, pointing out that people are starved for a sense of values and meaning.

Workshop leaders—our contemporary circuit riders—also observe that in city after city people are craving information about healing. Literally hundreds of people attend presentations by lecturers such as Caroline Myss, the bestselling author of *Anatomy of the Spirit* and *Why People Don't Heal and How They Can*, and Andrew Weil, Harvard-educated physician, medical-school instructor, popular public-television fund-raising point man, bestselling author, and alternative medicine man. A 1993 Harvard University survey published in the *New England Journal of Medicine* found that 34 percent of Americans have used alternative medical therapies, almost none of which are eligible for insurance reimbursement. And a 1996 special issue of *Time* magazine examining "The Frontiers of Medicine" reported that $13.7 billion is spent each year on a wide array of alternative medical treatments, from acupuncture to zero balancing.

Additionally, retreat centers and monasteries nationwide maintain long waiting lists of people. The lure of silence and solitude coupled with the time to focus inward causes the sometimes rustic, always simple rooms to be booked months in advance. The popular interest in all things mythological or archetypal generated by Bill Moyers's PBS interview series with Joseph Campbell, and the return in recent years to contemplative and mystically oriented spiritual practices such as centering prayer—a Christian meditation practice with roots in the English medieval text *The Cloud of Unknowing*—Hindu chanting, and Buddhist meditation are all part of what led Moyers, in a 1994 speech to the Religion Newswriters Association, to announce that "something is happening in America that is worthy of the sharpest reporting and analysis we can bring to it." What he was referring to was an explosion of interest and participation in ways to connect with the invisible mysteries of life, to the inner world that feeds our souls.

The Return of the Invisible

The roots of this most recent soul-searching can be found in the 1960s, a time when a fascination with Eastern religions and drugs gave young people a taste of altered consciousness and unitive experiences. Suddenly there were psychedelic options to a gray-flannel existence. Ozzie and Harriet's nuclear family was replaced by communes, steak and potatoes by vegetarianism, and the corporate fast-track mentality by a laid-back, "be here now" philosophy. The peace movement had two branches: protesters who marched to stop the war in Southeast Asia and young people who flocked to ashrams and sanghas in search of enlightenment. The more staid and certainly more quiet psychoanalytic hours were replaced by primal-scream sessions, Lilly flotation tanks, and Bioenergetic sessions replete with "racks."

Then, just as the 1980s transformed many baby-boomer hippies into yuppies and dinks (dual income, no kids), so too did these years transmute spiritual, alternative medical, natural-living, and mental-health approaches. Instead of fighting for survival and respect on the cultural fringe, these methods migrated toward the mainstream, gaining increasing numbers of devoted adherents and therefore economic ground and professional credibility. The previous two decades had ushered in not only grand-scale communal be-ins and love-fests like Woodstock, but also political and social upheavals such as the assassinations of President John F. Kennedy, the Reverend Martin Luther King Jr., and Senator Robert F. Kennedy; the Vietnam War; the Watergate scandal; and the civil-rights and women's movements. These events deeply affected those coming of age, generating great disillusionment with institutions such as government and religion; insecurity and grief at the taking of life; and the demand to abolish inequalities with regard to race and gender. Political and social mechanisms that traditionally provide meaning and security lost prestige and power. The eroding sense of trust in conventional institutions fueled a more subdued but continued search for alternatives in such areas as psychology, education, and medicine. In the 1970s and 1980s, many publications, organizations, businesses, and institutions were founded—Tom's of Maine (1970), the Omega Institute for Holistic Studies (1972), New Dimensions Radio (1973), *New Age Journal* (1974), Common Boundary (1983), and the New York Open Center (1984), to name just a few—in a burst of optimism, enthusiasm, and dedication to new ways of thinking, living, and being. As they took root, their very existence stimulated further attention to newly emerging approaches to health and well-being as well as to ancient practices that had been largely abandoned as a result of technological and industrial advances.

The most obvious and clear-cut evidence of a changing consciousness is the market for books and tapes on psychological and spiritual topics, many of which have become national bestsellers. In the December 23, 1996, issue of *Time* magazine, David Gergen cited statistics from one of the nation's largest book distributors. According to his source, the demand for religious and spiritual titles jumped by more than 300 percent in just two years (June 1993 to June 1995). In a special issue of *Common Boundary* magazine, book editor Pythia Peay reported that religious books are the third largest category of books sold (behind popular fiction and cookbooks), with 1996 sales totaling $1.9 billion.

It's not a coincidence then that the all-time bestseller in the history of the *New York Times* list comes from this genre. Psychiatrist M. Scott Peck's *The Road Less Traveled* appeared week after week for a record-breaking thirteen years and sold more than six million copies. The book—which begins with the now-famous line "Life is difficult"—acknowledges the relationship of spirituality to psychotherapy and its role in our lives. Peck's medical background and professional credentials lent him a credibility that transcended denomination, sect, or creed and inspired more confidence than any member of the clergy could—except perhaps the Reverend Billy Graham. After all, who could argue with a physician prescribing spirituality? The trend of psychology professionals encouraging soul work continued with other bestselling author-therapists such as Thomas Moore (*Care of the Soul*), Clarissa Pinkola Estés (*Women Who Run with the Wolves*), and James Hillman (*The Soul's Code*).

Other books on spiritual topics have also reached bestseller status, such as Sophy Burnham's *The Book of Angels*, Betty J. Eadie's *Embraced by the Light*, Karen Armstrong's *A History of God*, Marianne Williamson's *Return to Love*, Kathleen Norris's *Dakota* and *The Cloister Walk*, and just about anything written by the prolific Deepak Chopra, M.D.

Over the past thirty years, yoga, an Eastern-based spirituality, has also sent roots deep into mainstream America. Originally introduced to the United States by Swami Vivekenanda at the 1893 World Parliament of Religions held in Chicago, yoga found fertile ground in small pockets of followers until the 1960s. Then a host of swamis arriving in America created a bumper crop of yoga practitioners. Initially accompanied by exotic accoutrements—devotional gestures to one's teacher, white drawstring pants and loose tops, incense, etc.—yoga in America bore the stamp of its Hindu origins. But gradually the asanas (postures) were transmuted into exercise routines and yoga infiltrated health and fitness regimes with promises of flexibility, longevity, and stress reduction. Today not only are health clubs and spas making yoga classes a programming mainstay, but special retreat centers like the Kripalu Center for Yoga and Health in Lenox, Massachusetts, are also successfully offering programs that draw harried urban dwellers for weekends of vegetarian fare and workshops in holistic health, personal empowerment, shamanism, and yogic exercises. A February 1994 survey commissioned by *Yoga Journal* and conducted by the prominent polling organization Roper, Starch Worldwide found that there were 6.1 million people who practiced some form of yoga either regularly or sometimes and another astonishing 16.75 million who had an interest but no experience in it.

Because traditional academic institutions move at a glacial pace, they have been less quick to integrate new approaches to psychology and spirituality into their classrooms. Into this vacuum have sprung alternative schools offering nontraditional degree programs, many with clear spiritual components. Some of the new academic institutions—such as the Institute for Transpersonal Psychology, Saybrook Institute, John F. Kennedy University, and the California Institute of Integral Studies—have received accreditation, while others are in the process of working toward that goal. According to humanistic-education advocate James Fadiman, "If you want a degree that assures you of the maximum number of job possibilities at the maximum number of institutions, then these [alternative] schools . . . won't meet your need. If, on the other hand, you are determined (while getting a degree) to develop mentally, emotionally, and spiritually, these schools will do a better job than will any traditional program, no matter how famous, endowed, or prestigious." Having done his undergraduate work at Harvard University, obtained his Ph.D. from Stanford, and helped found the Institute of Transpersonal Psychology (ITP) in Palo Alto, California, Fadiman is well qualified to compare the relative advantages and disadvantages of both. In his estimation, alternative schools offer a more holistic education; that is, one that includes mind, body, intellect, and spirit. "Conventional education," he points out, "is almost entirely mind and a little bit of competitive sports." In every class, ITP students grapple with the material as it applies to themselves, their families, their communities, their culture. Interestingly, as the school approaches its last accreditation hurdles, Fadiman reports that the student body is getting younger and that the school is attracting more international students. But the greatest area of growth is in their distant-learning program, in which students around the globe attend classes, meet with faculty, and participate in seminars on-line.

On a smaller but equally potent scale are the adult learning centers such as the Omega Institute for Holistic Studies in Rhinebeck, New York; the New York Open Center; and the granddaddy of them all, the Esalen Institute in Big Sur, California. These organizations, along with a host of national conferences, created an informal learning network through which new-paradigm thinkers, healers, and educators could disseminate their ideas and train individuals and professionals in their new healing approaches. Their longevity indicates that people are investing both time and money in learning about meditation, holistic living, body psychotherapies, creative expression through art, dance, and movement, and other psychological and spiritual tools.

Cultural Resistance

Despite all this activity, Bill Moyers points out that while the "search for meaning and the appetite to connect" is one of the most important stories of this century, it is also the most underreported. The obvious question is why?

Writers, historians, sociologists, cultural observers, and pollsters all tell us that Americans are—and always have been—deeply religious. Indeed, that early-nineteenth-century French observer of American culture Alexis de Toqueville saw the love of liberty and religion as the two defining characteristics of the residents of our young country. Puritans in New England, Quakers in Pennsylvania, Shakers in the Mid-Atlantic states, and Catholics in Maryland were only a few of the groups that sought safe haven and religious freedom in the New World. Many colonists saw this virgin land as "the New Jerusalem," as a paradise. Perhaps that's why President Ronald Reagan's image of "the shining city on the hill" worked so well for him. The phrase was not merely a distant biblical reference but an image deeply ingrained in the American psyche from Colonial times.

Today Gallup polls have found that 96 percent of Americans believe in God and that "virtually everyone prays at least in some fashion." Nearly half of those who believe in God say that God speaks directly to them through scriptures, intuitive impressions, or other people, and one-third of Americans report having had a spiritual experience that changed their lives. Additionally, those who track charitable giving say that donations to religious institutions account for the largest slice of the philanthropic pie in the United States.

However, there is a disturbing attitude that runs counter to this deep spirituality. Many have described and felt the effects of secular pressures and an implicit code that instructs: If you must have a spiritual life, keep it to yourself. As Yale University law professor Stephen L. Carter puts it in his book *The Culture of Disbelief*: "More and more our culture seems to take the position that believing deeply in the tenets of one's faith represents a kind of mystical irrationality, something that thoughtful, public-spirited American citizens would do better to avoid."

No one knows this better than First Lady Hillary Clinton, who has stepped into a buzz saw of criticism more than once when attempting to articulate her spiritual beliefs. On safe ground as long as she invokes her Methodist roots, she stirs up controversy with her leanings toward the work of author-lecturers Marianne Williamson, Jean Houston, and Michael Lerner. In a 1993 speech given at the University of Texas at Austin just after the death of her father, Mrs. Clinton unleashed the political Furies when she issued a passionate plea for bringing consciousness and compassion into the public arena. "If we ask, why is it, in a country as wealthy as we are, that there is this undercurrent of discontent, we realize that somehow economic growth and prosperity, political democracy and freedom are not enough—we lack meaning in our individual lives and meaning collectively. We lack a sense that our lives are part of some greater effort, that we are connected to one another." Describing the malaise as a "sleeping sickness of the soul," she called for a "new politics of meaning." We need to define a new world society, she said, one "that fills us up again and makes us feel that we are part of something bigger than ourselves."

Unfortunately, the media, especially Washington's corps of print, broadcast, and radio pundits, derided her for her "airy assumptions," fuzzy thinking, and her "psychobabble." *The New York Times* jumped into the fracas with a Sunday magazine cover story entitled "St. Hillary," which intoned: "The meaning of Hillary Clinton's attempts to describe a politics of meaning is hard to discuss under the gauzy and gushy wrappings of New Age jargon that blanket it."

In 1996 another flap erupted when *Washington Post* reporter Bob Woodward, in his book *The Choice*, intimated that Jean Houston, a popular workshop leader and author, was the First Lady's "spiritual advisor" because, among other things, she had facilitated Mrs. Clinton's imaginary discussions with Eleanor Roosevelt. Once again, a round of intense media criticism and derision followed.

In addition to the media's hair-trigger hostility and disdain toward spirituality, Stephen Carter sees a similar attitude in the political and legal arenas, one of "treating religious beliefs as arbitrary and unimportant, a trend supported by a rhetoric that there is something wrong with religious devotion." Sometimes it seems as if the constitutional separation of church and state is interpreted to mean that religious beliefs and values have no place in informing public policy or political debate.

Yet despite this negative climate, public figures as diverse as Czech Republic President Vaclav Havel and television producer Norman Lear have used public forums to sound a clarion call. Our disease and restlessness, our feeling of emptiness and of being disheartened in the midst of material comforts and abundance, they say, amounts to a spiritual crisis and must be addressed as such.

"We enjoy all the achievements of modern civilization that have made our physical existence in this Earth easier in so many important ways," explained

Havel in a July 1994 speech. "Yet we do not know what to do with ourselves, where to turn. The world of our experiences seems so chaotic, disconnected, confusing. . . . Experts can explain anything in the objective world to us, yet we understand our own lives less and less."

Lear, speaking to a National Press Club audience, espoused similar sentiments: "A culture that becomes a stranger to its own inner human needs—which are . . . unquantifiable, intuitive, and mysterious—is a culture that has lost touch with the best of its humanity." The consequences of such an estrangement, Lear added, are "the loss of faith in leaders and institutions—the cynicism, selfishness, and erosion of civility—and the hunger for connectedness that stalks our nation today."

Despite the pockets of skepticism, criticism, and contempt, the desire to reconnect to the inner life, to pay attention to soulful yearnings, is so strong that it is the principal impetus behind a resurgence of spiritual activity in the United States. For some of us, the quest arises because the socially sanctioned search for material success and pleasure leaves us feeling hollow. For others of us, the suffering engendered by illness, job loss, death, or divorce brings us face to face with questions about the ultimate meaning of life. Frequently these crises initiate a search for ways to alleviate physical, emotional, or psychological pain. But as we struggle to heal our bodies and our minds, we sense that our problems are also symptoms of issues related to heart, soul, and spirit. We begin to crave a connection to and realization of our deeper needs rather than the unfulfilling surface concerns that have been preoccupying us. We recognize the importance of giving and receiving love, feel a yearning for inner peace and serenity, or develop a desire to build a personal relationship with the Divine.

Often the first stage of a spiritual journey involves learning a spiritual discipline or practice, one that trains awareness and helps us overcome the compelling distractions of everyday life. Such a practice helps us to expand our awareness so that we are able to be fully conscious of the ordinary world while also experiencing it in an extraordinary way.

At this stage, if we feel a bit uneasy about our spiritual pursuits, cultural disapproval is not the only thing to blame. For many of us, the awareness that something important may be missing in our lives can be a cause of shame or embarrassment. We wonder if we are psychologically unstable or too dependent. We may be afraid that we will lose our minds by entering into inner worlds where imagination and intuitive knowledge rather than intellect guide us. We worry that we are being naive or foolish.

Despite the fears and resistance as well as the cultural disapprobation, the groundswell of interest in inner work, in spiritual growth and exploration, persists. Although one might be tempted to view this explosion of activity as a passing fad, the search is changing many lives, and the impact on the culture is evident. It is becoming apparent, for example, in the mounting interest in simple living. As we work fifty- and sixty-hour weeks in order to buy a new home, a new car, or new household gadgets, we are aware that our schedules are preempting valuable time with family and friends and even the ability to enjoy our costly possessions. Concepts such as "downsizing one's life" or "simple abundance" have gained so much attention and popularity that the winter 1997 *Trends Journal* predicted that the concept of success would increasingly be "measured by an acquisition of inner peace, spiritual growth, creative development, and a deepening respect for and commitment to family, friends, and community."

Alternative Medicine: A Portal to the Spiritual

There is no set pattern that predicts what will cause us to embark upon a spiritual search. The quest to recover one's soul or spirit is hardly ever consciously planned. Abrupt changes in circumstances or some life crisis, generally medical in nature, jolts us out of our semisomnabulent mental, emotional, and behavioral patterns. Where sickness is the key, often alternative medicine is the door that leads one to set out on a spiritual journey. Most people are introduced to alternative medicine through an injury or illness for which conventional medicine offers no relief. At their wits' end, they feel they have nothing left to lose, so they try such healing methods as herbal medicine, Therapeutic Touch, guided imagery, acupuncture, or homeopathy. When they begin to get good results, they naturally tell their friends, family, and colleagues. Enthusiastic testimonies spread by word of mouth are probably the biggest reason for the growth of alternative medicine. According to the 1997 consumer book *Five Steps to Selecting the Best Alternative Medicine: A Guide to Complementary and Integrative Health Care,* by Mary and Michael Morton, Americans in 1991 made more visits to alternative health providers (425 million) than to conventional doctors (388 million). A 1993 Harvard University survey published in the *New England Journal of Medicine* concluded that one in three Americans has used alternative medical therapies.

Most people are not seeking a spiritual experience when they call to make their first appointment with an alternative health-care practitioner. They simply want relief from a physical problem. But the holistic philosophy behind most of the alternative medical practices makes people acutely aware of the emotional, psychological, and spiritual components of their health and well-being. For the most part, conventional medicine operates under the assumption that the body, mind, and spirit work independently of one another, although there have been some advances in Western medicine in terms of acknowledging the interrelatedness of body and mind. For example, it is now well known in psychosomatic medicine that there are psychological (mental) factors involved in physical problems such as asthma. One University of Washington study found that employees who were unhappy in their jobs were more likely to injure their backs, and a study published in the *New England Journal of Medicine* concluded that people suffering from psychological stress were more susceptible to the common cold. However, despite increasing acceptance of the mind-body interaction, acknowledgment of the role of one's spirit in healing and of the complex interrelation of psyche and soma still remains largely a concern only within the alternative medicine and holistic health communities. Although studies have linked psychospiritual variables with the outcome of treatment—for example, those who feel pessimistic or "dispirited" about recovery from a serious illness will, on average, not recover as quickly or as completely as those who, because of spiritual convictions, are hopeful and optimistic about recovery—the medical profession in general remains skeptical or unaware of such links.

Nevertheless, there are countless stories about those who seek help for a physical problem from an alternative medicine practitioner only to find that the treatment eventually proves to be a gateway to a spiritual journey. This shouldn't be surprising. Physical pain grabs our attention a lot more persuasively than does some vague, hard-to-articulate spiritual yearning that may also be present. Our silent intuitions or soul promptings are easier to dismiss than the more pressing clamorings of our bodies' aches and pains, even though the former may be far more involved in our physical hurts than we suspect.

Take the example of Marty Kaplan, a former speechwriter for Vice President Walter Mondale. In a 1996 *Time* magazine essay, Kaplan describes how he was "ambushed" by spirituality. "It was tooth grinding that got me to God," he declares, and explains how, when he couldn't face the prospect of wearing a night guard to protect his teeth, he resorted to meditation, an alternative stress reduction technique he had read about in a Deepak Chopra book. As a "nice Jewish boy from Newark" who was more of a cultural than a religious Jew, Kaplan was not consciously seeking a spiritual experience. Yet taking twenty minutes each day to meditate—"a practice that has been at the heart of religious mysticism for millenniums"—awakened him to "the miracle of existence." He writes that he found God, the God "common to Moses and Muhammad, to Buddha and Jesus," who demands "not faith but continued experiences of an inexhaustible wonder at the richness of this very moment."

Stories like Kaplan's are commonplace today. A woman with a gynecological problem seeks relief in acupuncture, which leads to herbal remedies, Eye Movement Desensitization and Reprocessing (EMDR) sessions, and to books about Taoism. A young man enters therapy and takes up Buddhist meditation and vegetarianism. A woman in midcareer needing to deal with the stress of work pressures learns self-hypnosis and guided imagery, which leads her to take yoga classes at her health club. Eventually she takes up yoga as a spiritual practice. This phenomenon has been noted and studied by religious scholars, such as University of Chicago professor Martin E. Marty, who have tracked the movement away from institutionalized religion to more diffuse and individualized expressions of worship. Sociologist Wade Clark Roof calls this phenomenon the "privatization of religion," entailing a movement not only away from formal religions toward individually crafted belief systems and rituals but also from adherence to dogma toward an emphasis on trusting one's own inner experience. The philosophy behind this movement of spiritual seekers is perhaps best articulated by Washington, D.C., astrologer Caroline Casey, who advises, "Believe nothing; entertain possibilities."

For the most part, people do not join religious communities, ashrams, Zen centers, and the like because of familial roots or theological fine points. They join primarily because they feel that a particular path will help them develop an active, ongoing spiritual life. They do not want sermons about God and guilt; they want a religious experience. Practices such as chanting, contemplative prayer, *qigong*, meditation, scripture reading, Sufi dancing, tai chi, yoga—all of which derive from ancient religious traditions—provide ways to help practitioners focus attention on and develop a relationship with a force beyond themselves.

Marty sees this "craving for experience" as part of a larger "wholeness hunger." Thus, whether disappointed by their childhood faith tradition and searching for another spiritual home or wanting to stay within their tradition but desiring a deeper connection to its spiritual roots, many are pursuing a host of different avenues to the Divine. Norman Lear's name for spiritual seekers—and he considers himself one—is "gropers." In a 1993 speech at the National Press Club he said, "I am a groper, searching every step of the way for a better understanding [of the inner life]. And because I am not specifically attached to any synagogue, I suppose you can call me an 'unaffiliated groper.'" This unaffiliated groping often leads to an interesting mixture of paths. It is not unusual, for example, to encounter a Quaker yoga teacher, a shamanic Episcopalian, or a Jewish Buddhist psychotherapist.

According to a 1996 survey cosponsored by the Fetzer Institute and the Institute of Noetic Sciences, there are now twenty million "gropers," a group the researchers call "core cultural creatives." These are Americans who are "seriously concerned" with psychology, spiritual life, and self-actualization, and who are active advocates of women's issues, social concerns, and ecological sustainability. They are part of a larger group labeled cultural creatives, an American subculture made up of nearly 25 percent of the population (or 44 million people) who value spirituality, personal development, authenticity, relationships, and diversity. They are also interested in creating something new. This creative urge has resulted in a host of socially responsible businesses, ongoing attempts to reconfigure priorities and change lifestyles, educational experiments, and artistic endeavors. It has also created a community of seekers defined not so much by geographic or physical location as by the commitment to explore inner realms of dreams, archetypes, subtle energies, intuition, and the like. Once the journey of self-exploration is initiated, no matter how isolated you may feel at its outset, fellow travelers have a way of appearing to support, share in, and encourage you along the way.

Kindred Spirits Unite

Human beings are social creatures, who naturally organize into groups. Spiritual seekers are no different. Even though most of them start out on their journey alone, they frequently find kindred spirits with whom they can study or practice. According to a 1991 Gallup poll, 40 percent of Americans are engaged in small groups that meet regularly for caring and sharing. Terming this development a "quiet revolution," Princeton University sociology professor Robert Wuthnow, who directed the study for Gallup, notes that although these groups reflect an "anything-goes spirituality," many are connected to a faith tradition. Such gatherings offer support for exploring the inner landscape, for maintaining spiritual practices, and for creating a sense of community, thereby infusing the path with a dynamic vitality. A synergy builds, carrying group members with it. Meditators, for example, report that regularly practicing in a group deepens and enhances their practice. One can then go back to individual practice with a stronger resolve and an experience of the method's potential. Others in religious study-group settings, as diverse as those focused on Jewish Renewal or *A Course in Miracles*, grapple with a religious text in order both to apply its wisdom to everyday experiences and to understand how ancient texts can be imbued with contemporary relevance.

One early manifestation of this small-group phenomenon was the women's consciousness-raising groups that began meeting at the beginning of the women's movement in the 1960s. Today this tradition has expanded to include ongoing women's spirituality groups that conduct rituals like "croning" ceremonies, which acknowledge the transition a woman undergoes following menopause—physically, emotionally, psychologically, and spiritually—and which celebrate her new role as a "wise woman" (the real meaning of the word *crone*). Other groups offer support in exploring aspects of feminine spirituality such as female images of God, goddess-centered rituals, and Wicca traditions.

Men's groups, however, are not nearly as visible as they were in the 1980s and early 1990s. Sometime around 1992, sponsors of men's mythopoetic workshops and programs noticed dwindling participant numbers and responded by canceling events. Some attributed the decline to the economy, waning interest, or a blunting of the movement's cutting edge. Others believed that the grief work advocated by men's movement leader Robert Bly had been done.

In the African-American community, the men's movement took a different form. Louis Farrakhan's Million Man March, held in Washington, D.C., in October 1995, had an impact in terms of countering the negative images of African-American men. But the initial march has generated little or no organized, ongoing follow-up activities. Even the Promise Keepers, the conservative Denver-based organization founded in 1990 by former University of Colorado football coach Bill McCartney, experienced a financial contraction. At one time the organization brought in revenues of $87 million and filled entire football stadiums for its events; today it finds itself in severe financial straits. The *Washington Post* reported in February 1998 that although the group had downsized from 510 to 365 employees earlier, they were going to stop paying staff at the end of March. Although the controversial Christian men's organization had drawn over 500,000 participants to a Washington, D.C., rally the previous October, attendance had been falling off. That coupled with the switch from charging fees for events to simply accepting voluntary contributions adversely affected the organization's finances. Organization spokesman Steve Ruppe, however, was quoted as saying that the organization is simply in a "transitional period."

Despite these setbacks, a measure of success has been gained both institutionally and culturally. For example, Division 51 of the American Psychological Association is devoted to the psychological study of men and masculinity. And it is quite noticeable that in a variety of settings—weddings, funerals, college reunions—men are publicly expressing emotions, with physical embraces much more common, even de rigueur.

Another possible reason for the decline of men's groups is a shift away from men-only gatherings toward more gender-inclusive events. In a 1993 *Common Boundary* article, Bly declared that "the proper next step" is joint work between the sexes. "Things can only be solved with men and women working together, not separated," he said. The phenomenal success of John Gray's books, tapes, and lectures, all focused on aspects of his *Men Are from Mars, Women Are from Venus* theme, supports the notion that of all life's mysteries, the relationship between men and women remains one of the most fascinating and unfathomable. But the verve that surrounds women's groups, whether political or spiritual, seems to be lacking in the area of relationships.

Still another manifestation of small groups involves former couch potatoes who, bored with passively ingesting television, have organized book clubs that meet to discuss philosophical, spiritual, or psychological ideas. Study groups also listen to audiocassettes or watch videotape series, such as teacher, writer, and lecturer Brian Swimme's *Canticle of the Cosmos*, following them up with discussion.

One of the most popular types of these groups was inspired by Julia Cameron's book *The Artist's Way*, which contains exercises to allow one's creative juices to flow. Cameron links the creative process with spiritual growth. As a recovering alcoholic, she says she "learned to turn my creativity over to the only god I could believe in, the god of creativity. . . . I learned to get out of the way and let the creative force work through me." Originally, she called her study groups "sacred circles." She and her partner at the time, Mark Bryan, created such practical guidelines as avoiding self-appointed gurus, creating a place of safety and acceptance, and listening carefully to other group members. In her second book, *Vein of Gold*, she renames these groups "creative clusters" and recommends participation in them as a basic tool for supporting one's creative endeavors.

Sorting Wheat from Chaff

When Common Boundary first began in the early 1980s, most of our energy went into finding people, publications, programs, and organizations devoted to increasing consciousness and opening doors to an experience of the Divine. With our psychology backgrounds, it is not surprising that Common Boundary's initial audience for its programs and publication—then a typed and photocopied newsletter, now a fifty-six-page bimonthly magazine—were mental-health professionals including psychologists, psychiatrists, social workers, and addiction counselors, as well as a sprinkling of pastoral counselors, clergy, and members of religious orders. At the time, broaching the subject of spirituality in a professional psychology setting was a risky proposition somewhat akin to publicly discussing one's sex life. Still, enough people felt the need to bring forth their thoughts about the relationship of spirituality and psychotherapy that from the very start hundreds of therapists participated in annual Common Boundary Conferences held in the Washington, D.C., area. Over the years, because of the growth of Alcoholics Anonymous and other Twelve-Step groups, the rise (and fall) of the men's movement, women's spirituality groups, the burgeoning American Buddhist community, the mainstreaming and growth of yoga classes, and the plethora of books on psychological and spiritual topics, the field has exploded with courses, workshops, books, publications, conferences, lectures, organizations, educational programs, and the like—so much so that today Common Boundary's main function has shifted from discovering to sifting through the plethora of events, materials, and personalities, highlighting and making accessible those that we feel best assist, with integrity and depth, the work of psychological development and spiritual growth. It's a huge—at times overwhelming—undertaking, but one that is critical if soul and consciousness are to become more valued parts of our culture, and if individuals' spiritual searches are not only to be respected but actively supported by both an ever-growing community of kindred spirits and the society at large.

Because of the sheer volume of resources in the field, individuals who desire to do soul work often don't know where to turn for reliable information. The field today is enormous; the quality of classes, books, and teachers is uneven; and a comprehensive overview of how the different facets of the spiritual search relate is lacking. Therefore we have put together this handbook to guide seekers through the maze of resources available for those on an inner journey and to offer reports on what other reliable explorers have experienced and felt as they delved into the various spiritual paths. For example, you may want to know:

- How creativity is linked to spirituality
- How spirituality is being revitalized in traditional places of worship
- How marriage can be a spiritual practice
- How to distinguish among different forms of bodywork

This book will tackle these issues as well as help you identify and locate resources that may prove valuable in exploring various psychological and spiritual avenues. For example:

- The classic books that offer the best introductions to a topic
- Where to study various disciplines and techniques on a residential or nonresidential basis
- How to find retreat and education centers
- The relevant organizations, professional societies, and websites that will link you up with others who have similar interests

This book is a field guide to the vast and exciting terrain of psychological development and spiritual growth. Because it maps the entire field, it is an indispensable companion for all who are embarking upon an inner adventure. For those just starting out on an inner journey, the book's introductory materials and resources will help answer the question how and where should I begin? For those readers already embarked upon a spiritual or psychological search, the book will support, enhance, and deepen the paths they have chosen by providing information on retreat and conference centers, publications, audiotape companies, small presses, bookstores, training programs, and websites. The Resources alone are a treasure trove of valuable sources of information, seminars, and opportunities to become involved in soul work. Whatever the reader's level of involvement, *Soul Work* will help sort through the alternatives and identify hard-to-find resources.

Since 1981 Common Boundary has been tracking developments in the fields of psychology and spirituality. There is no better organization to create a clear, accessible road map for navigating the growing cultural movement that recognizes the importance of inner life. Useful as both a handy reference and an in-depth text, the book will not only feed your mind and soul but also lead you to other resources where the banquet can continue. But be forewarned: this is neither an easy path nor a superficial trend. Once you answer the call of your soul, you will be led into areas that are thrilling, challenging, difficult—sometimes tedious and exasperating. Because of the rigors of a spiritual path, it is wise to gather around you compatriots who can support you, let you know that you are not alone in your yearnings and desires, urge you on when you feel disheartened, and applaud you when you achieve a breakthrough. We hope that this book will be one of these cherished companions that offers sound advice, information, and inspiration, as well as the occasional reminder that in riding the windhorse we are indeed "carried by wind." But we must first learn how to hold the reins before letting them go.

Mind

The time will come
when, with elation,
you will greet yourself arriving
at your own door, in your own mirror,
and each will smile at the other's welcome,

and say, sit here. Eat.
You will love again the stranger who was your self.
Give wine. Give bread. Give back your heart
to itself, to the stranger who has loved you

all your life, whom you ignored
for another, who knows you by heart.
Take down the love letters from the bookshelf,

the photographs, the desperate notes,
peel your own image from the mirror.
Sit. Feast on your life.

—DEREK WALCOTT, "LOVE AFTER LOVE"

1
Lessons in Psychological Nutrition

Have you ever wondered why some conversations—even with close friends and family—are emotionally unsatisfying? Do you feel that hardly anyone is listening to you or understanding what you are saying? When you aren't heard, do you wonder if the other person cares about you? If you find yourself contemplating these things, you are not alone. As a nation, we have the technical expertise to create a vast web of communications using highly sophisticated technology, but as individuals our exchanges with each other are often primitive, unsatisfying—even unhealthy. Many people live every day of their lives in a state of chronic psychological malnourishment and don't even know it.

Such a condition results from not receiving enough recognition, validation, empathic understanding, and caring. In his 1990 bestselling book, *Dr. Dean Ornish's Program for Reversing Heart Disease*, Dean Ornish, M.D., discussed the prevention of and recovery from severe coronary heart disease. Although most people think that his program is primarily about food and diet, Ornish says that the most significant factors in healing are love, intimacy, and relationships. In his most recent book, *Love and Survival: The Scientific Basis for the Healing Power of Intimacy*, Ornish pinpoints the real epidemic in our culture: emotional and spiritual heart disease stemming from a profound and prevalent sense of loneliness, isolation, alienation, and depression.

Without adequate amounts of psychologically nutritious communications, people cannot nurture love or develop intimacy. Instead they compensate for these things by becoming overly self-centered, acquisitive, and power-hungry, among other things.

This line of reasoning usually generates several questions: Did our grandparents or great-grandparents have this same need? Isn't it self-indulgent to want validation and acknowledgement? Can't a person supply all the psychological nourishment he or she needs without relying on others? These questions reflect our suspicious and guarded attitude toward the legitimacy of people's need for psychological nourishment and are based upon an unfounded faith in individualism and a general misconception about egotism. An overblown sense of self-importance, self-centeredness, and egotistical behavior result more from a *lack* of self-acceptance, as a result of psychological malnutrition, than from a surfeit of self-esteem.

The result of these misunderstandings is that our need for adequate psychological nutrition often gets ignored or ridiculed as a form of self-indulgence. From today's perspective, our forebears were silent about these matters because their values and behavior were part and parcel of a sociological web made up of social role, status, and institutional identification. One could get along in the world without developing an awareness of one's inner self as the agent or organizer of experience because one's social grouping—one's tribe—provided the values, direction, principles, and code of behavior that formed one's identity and defined one's place in the world. Today the development of an inner self is necessary for providing direction because many of the old external supports no longer function as a compass and guide.

Psychotherapy as Food

Before the 1960s, psychotherapy and those who went to therapy carried a stigma. The average person considered psychotherapy a treatment for the insane and severely mentally imbalanced and thought that to see a psychiatrist was to be branded as crazy. Today psychotherapy is recognized not as an irrevocable sentence but as a tool for coping with distressing life situations and healing self-destructive or unhealthy patterns of behavior. Today people enter therapy because they want relief from stress, substance abuse, depression or anxiety brought on by a crisis such as the loss of a job, a divorce, or the death of a loved one, or from a pervasive sense that their lives are out of control or empty. Generally just a crack in the usual self-sufficient persona provides motivation to explore the source of the pain.

It is now commonly accepted that everyone to a greater or lesser degree has psychological difficulties that manifest as unresolved hurts and inhibitions from childhood or as vulnerabilities that prevent or undermine full functioning. With these advances in understanding, psychotherapists have not only shed much of their negative image but actually grown in numbers and stature. One reason for their increased numbers is the fragmentation of the family and the loss of our sense of geographical community. The Census Bureau indicates that we have become a highly mobile society, with 19 to 20 percent of us moving each year. Mary Pipher points out in her book, *The Shelter of Each Other*, that in 1990 "72 percent of Americans didn't know their neighbors." An extraordinary and painful loss is buried in that statistic. Gone are the days of porch-sitting and greeting neighbors on their way home from work; gone too are the days of unlocked cars and houses.

As extended family networks break apart, their members relocating geographically, and as divorce splinters nuclear families, we lose a powerful traditional support system. No longer can a child who has difficulties with one or both parents form an attachment with a grandparent, aunt, uncle, or cousin, because physical distance may prevent it. The nuclear family is under siege, and the complications of single parenthood, joint custody, and blended families stress individuals in these systems. Most of us do not remain in one community long enough to grow histories with nearby families. And managed care notwithstanding, how many physicians today dance at the weddings of babies they delivered? Torn from the fabric of family and community, we have turned to professionals for help. And although some critics may argue that we are too reliant on psychotherapy, the fact of the matter is that emotional support—talking about and having someone listen to what's really bothering us—is more important than ever.

As family and communal ties are weakened, we lose a major source of our identity. For the most part, the Depression-era and World War II generation did not need to "find themselves." They were not lost. They were for the most part securely embedded in social structures that told them who they were and where they came from. Today, however, we are forced to carve out our roles as well as to develop a set of values, a moral code, and a life purpose. The hardest part of this task is constructing a coherent, independent personality and a sense of personal worth.

What Makes a Healthy Ego?

Simply stated, if a child is responded to positively she will develop a positive evaluation of herself, which will allow her to meet life tasks and challenges with self-confidence. If, however, a child receives mostly negative responses, she will evaluate herself negatively and not feel confident in the face of life's tasks. Even where she might see the adults' faults and follies, as a child she is unable to counteract the impact of these negative messages and actions by herself. One example of this dynamic was evident in the late Princess Diana. When she failed to receive love in her marriage or support for her new role in England's royal family, she responded as if it were her fault. She struggled painfully with self-doubt, bulimia, and self-mutilation, even attempting suicide. Eventually, however (we assume with psychotherapeutic support), she was able to recognize that her lack of love and support was more a statement of Prince Charles and his family's dynamics than it was a result of a personality defect on her part. She went on to defend herself publicly, to maintain a connection with her sons, and to mature into a warm-hearted and gracious spokesperson for a variety of charitable causes.

Children form their sense of self from what they see reflected in their parents' eyes and facial expressions. For example, the British psychoanalyst D. W. Winnicott has written that a mother's face, especially in the early weeks of an infant's life, serves as a mirror for the tiny new person. It is less important for a mother to actually look at her child, and more important that she reflect the child's expressions. If the mother (or father) does not mirror back the child's expressions, the child will not receive validation of its existence. As Winnicott explains: "When I [the infant] look, I am seen, so I exist." With that basic ego groundwork in place, the child can then look out again and see the world and interact with it.

Psychologist Daniel Goleman, in his bestselling book *Emotional Intelligence*, cites the research of psychiatrist Daniel Stern, who found through the study of videotaped parent-child interactions that the small, repeated exchanges that took place between parent and child laid down the most basic lessons of emotional life. Stern discovered that the most critical moments were those in which the child's emotions were met with empathy and acceptance, indeed reciprocated in a process he labeled attunement. Attunement basically means that the mother and father accurately reflect back to the child what the child is feeling. The countless repeated movements of attunement or misattunement between parent and child form the basis for the kind of emotional relationships that adults create later in life.

Goleman goes on to observe that "prolonged absence of attunement between a parent and child takes a tremendous toll on the child" and can have devastating effects. If a parent isn't attuned to the child's emotions—to delight, sadness, distress, need for security—then the child will begin to avoid expressing, or possibly even feeling, these emotions. Thus if the parent does not reflect back a caring, valuing, accepting view of the child as she is, the child will develop a similar set of noncaring, nonvaluing eyes with which to view herself. Accordingly, the child will begin to believe she is unacceptable, unlovable, of no value, and will cover up her real self in an attempt to become whatever she believes will gain her love and acceptance, thereby reducing her fear of abandonment. She will adopt a false face or "mask" that she hopes will appear more pleasing and therefore earn more positive responses.

❋ In Conversation with Mary Pipher: ❋ How Community Builds Identity

I have always been interested in the question "How does culture affect mental health?" When I was studying anthropology, I didn't give a darn about old bones and linguistics, what I really liked was culture and personality. I loved people like the anthropologist Margaret Mead who talked about how the way social systems were organized affected how people felt and acted with each other. That's one of the things that's different about me: I look at mental-health issues with a little bit of an anthropologist's eye.

I am also very embedded in my family, my extended family, my husband's extended family, my neighborhood, and my community. One of the things that is really important to me and that informs my theories is being connected to a particular place.

Wherever I shop—whether it is a bookstore, grocery store, or restaurant—I know the people who work there. My husband and I have a joke about the Asian restaurant that we've been going to for years. If my husband orders a dish that has something in it that he doesn't like, the waitress says, "No, Jim, don't order that. You don't like broccoli."

My husband is like me in this way. We both like to have relationships with people we're dealing with. We tend to go to the same places over and over again because those are the places where we have a community of people that we like to see. I do not do my grocery shopping in a store where it's cheaper, because I know all the people in the store that I go to and I like them. I have an investment in their store staying open even though it may be more expensive than other stores in town.

If you think about it, people until recently had roots. They were rooted in communities, in extended families, in religious congregations, and so on. They had these walls of identity around them. Uniqueness tended to be played out in small ways. Of course, there were eccentrics, people who always dressed in a certain way or had funny habits. But you can only be an eccentric in a world where most people have a very homogeneous set of values. The word *eccentric* really means nothing in New York City in 1998; everyone is eccentric.

I was thinking about this last night when I was listening to National Public Radio. A man was reading a letter from his mother who'd gone back to Mexico after visiting him in San Francisco. She asked him, "Don't your neighbors like you?" She noticed that when they walked into the apartment building, people didn't talk to him. They didn't stop him in the hall and start gabbing away. She also noticed that when his children's friends came over, they didn't talk to her; they didn't call her grandmother. She thought all this meant that perhaps her son was not a well-liked person. The only way she could understand that behavior was through her experience. In her small village in Mexico, if somebody was disliked, people wouldn't talk to them; the children wouldn't call them grandfather. The idea that you would live in a place where you didn't speak to your neighbors and that children would come into the house and not address an older woman as grandmother was incomprehensible to her.

I think it's hard for children now. At one time children had many adults who knew about them, joked with them, taught them things, and stayed a part of their lives. Maybe they didn't relate with them that much but they were safely around the perimeters of their life. Children don't have that now. If they are very lucky, they have their parents' friends in their lives. Those people form the walls around their lives, a fortress to help them know who they are. But a lot of children haven't experienced these kinds of long-term relationships.

I like kids a lot and I would be much friendlier to them if I could figure out how to do it. It seems to me that one of the things we're losing as a culture is social mechanisms to connect adults and children to each other. I will see a child and think, "Oh that little kid is really cute. I'd like to talk to him," or "That little kid could use some help putting on his shoes." I'd like to move into that child's space, interact with him, teach him something, or make a joke and see if he laughs. But now, because of the culture, I stop myself. My thought is always, "Could this be misinterpreted?" I may see a child trying to get their coat buttoned and will want to stop to help them but I think, "Will their parents suspect I'm some sort of sexual pervert who likes to touch children's bodies?" So I won't do the things that I want to do and that were done for me when I was a child. This situation is bad for adults and for children. We are losing the connecting webbing between children and adults.

We all get identity from the relationships we have. In my opinion, the self is comprised of the appraisals of others. If you grow up in a community of a thousand people, you have the reflected appraisals of a thousand people with which to put together your self. That's how you know who you are. If you grow up in the suburbs and have only your parents and maybe a few neighbors that wave at you, you have a poverty of identity. You have so much less information with which to work.

It's very hard to nurture children you don't know, which means that children don't get this strong dose of love that again can translate into positive identity. The other thing that children don't get if they don't know adults is feedback. Feedback is important if you are going to develop an accurate sense of who you are. For example, if I got up from the table at my grandparents' house and didn't push my chair in, someone would say, "Push your chair in." They would also say, "Put your napkin on your lap, and don't chew with your mouth open, and say thank-you for the pie." Families still do that to a certain extent, but children used to get that everywhere—in the stores, on the street. They also got positive feedback such as "You are a good worker."

How can a person self-actualize on an island? They can't. Native Americans believed that a person banished from the tribe was not a person, because they had lost all identity under those circumstances. I believe that too, because what people who try to have an identity without connection have is only shards and fragments.

Mary Pipher is a psychologist in private practice in Lincoln, Nebraska, and the bestselling author of *Reviving Ophelia* and *The Shelter of Each Other: Rebuilding in Families*.

Introducing Psychological Nutrition

As a culture, we are all suffering from an attention deficit disorder, but not necessarily of the neurological kind. More and more frequently, our social institutions, organizations, and government are losing their responsiveness. Modern business practices eliminate "the personal touch." We shop at cavernous discount stores where there are no salespeople to direct us or answer our questions or we patronize companies that have electronic voice-mail systems that require focused attention in order to follow their rapidly delivered menu of options, which offers no promise of a response to what we originally called about.

Despite what mental-health professionals know about psychological and emotional needs, few people outside the profession recognize that the way you feel about yourself depends in part on how others respond to you. We all have a need to be acknowledged and appreciated for who we are and what we do. But our interactions with other people may be more or less nourishing to us depending upon the quality of the exchange.

Take this example: You tell a friend how excited you are that you have received a promotion. Instead of showing interest and asking what you will now be doing, your friend deflects your statement and tells you about some kudos he or she has recently received. In terms of your need for a certain amount of attention and recognition, this exchange offers neither person any nourishment.

Only recently have we recognized that we have a daily minimum requirement of psychological needs, and that the level of psychological nourishment we get has an effect on our physical and mental health. Some people downplay the fact that they have such needs, convincing themselves (and trying to convince us) that they are self-sufficient. In reality, they probably have indirect ways of getting these needs met. They may, for example, strive for fame, power, or wealth in lieu of personal connectedness. However, it is not the real person who is getting attention but his or her image, status, prestige, or money. Such indirect attention simply covers up the need.

The psychological malnutrition chart describes different styles of behavior that can lead to psychological starvation. Take the following test to see if you are doing things that prevent you from getting good psychological nutrition. If you mark yes to any of the following six indicators, you may not be getting enough direct psychological nourishment and may be relying too heavily on indirect methods, which, like artificial food, are devoid of sustenance and therefore cannot be absorbed by your psyche.

Causes of Psychological Malnutrition

Individuals who are not getting their daily minimum requirement of recognition tend to compensate by substituting superficial interactions for real contact. The following list of strategies describes the various styles of behavior through which we may try to get our needs met indirectly without admitting we have them. Note that the level of sophistication increases as you move up the scale.

1: **Doormat** You find yourself accepting abuse in a relationship because you don't feel you deserve anything better. This indirect method is not the road to sainthood; it's the road to the hell of abuse.

2: **Valiant Caretaking** You take care of everyone else as a way of never having to ask anything for yourself. You hope that someone will see your need and offer to meet it. Perhaps you are afraid that if you ask, you will meet with disappointment or rejection. If you thought better of yourself, you would realize that you deserve to get your needs met too.

3: **Eat Your Heart Out** You find yourself willing to settle for the envy of others (e.g., by bragging about your children's accomplishments, name-dropping) because you don't feel that you deserve their love. In this regard, envy compared with respect and appreciation is as satisfying as a cup of instant coffee and powdered dairy creamer compared with an aromatic, freshly prepared cup of coffee.

4: **Super Self-Absorption** You don't really listen to what others are saying unless it refers directly to you. You become irritated and bored when the conversation moves to a topic other than yourself. Others may think that your outrageous egotism is a sign that you think too well of yourself. You and they need to think again.

5: **Trumping** You view every conversation as a competitive match in which you must prove your importance. Thus you must "top" everyone's story. To make sure you are ahead, you silently keep score.

6: **Subtle Trump** Instead of seeking ways to establish direct connection or communication with another, you find yourself secretly thinking about how to promote yourself in ways that are subtle enough so that your hunger for self-importance won't be detected. This requires great imagination, and some of us have taken it to the level of an art.

Sadly, these strategies are hollow in that they really don't add to your overall sense of self-worth; indeed, they prevent you from feeling your unmet needs and confronting your feelings of inadequacy. Like drugs or alcohol, they merely cover up the problem without addressing the source of the discomfort.

If you recognize your use of any of these indirect ways of meeting your psychological needs for recognition and attention, don't be embarrassed. You are *not* selfish, egotistical, or narcissistic. You use these ploys because your interactions with others are nutritionally deficient. You are resorting to indirect means to get your needs met. Take your behavior as a message that you need more nourishment than you are getting. One way to "feed" one another is through a form of Stern's attunement. For the sake of discussion, let's say that the nutritional richness of attunement can be measured in units—minimum daily psychological nutrition requirements (MDPNRs). Though the precise number of MDPNR units has not yet been researched or established, we recommend at least one daily exchange containing six units of nutritional attention. The following scale provides you with a way of estimating the value of the attention you are receiving and giving. Remember: A person needs to be empathically "mirrored" in order to maintain a strong and healthy sense of worth. Here are some guidelines for measuring the nutritional value of the responses you give or get from others. If your score for any one day remains under six, you will no doubt find yourself resorting to indirect methods for fulfilling your needs.

Scale of Psychological Attunement

-1   **Beyond Unresponsive** The person you are talking with interrupts you in the middle of your sentence and shifts to a different topic. Subtract one unit.

0   **Unresponsive** The person obviously isn't listening, only waiting for you to stop talking. When you finish, the person shifts to an entirely different topic.

1   **Indirectly Unresponsive** The other person says or implies, "Well, you shouldn't feel that way. . . ."

2   **Self-Referential Free Association** The person says something like, "Oh, yeah, that reminds me of the time when I . . ." or "Well, you think you had it bad—listen to what happened to *me*" and makes no other reference to anything you have said.

3   **Free Association** The person responds to your statement by going off on a tangent and making only an indirect reference to what you said.

4   **Impersonal/Nonnurturing** The person indicates she has heard you but offers no sympathetic or empathic response. Basically, her stance is: "That's the way the cookie crumbles."

5   **Superficial** Although the person responds by saying, "Yeah, I know what you mean," she does not sound sincere or empathic.

6   **Adequate** The person shows evidence that he heard what you said but does not show interest or follow up your statement by encouraging you to expand upon it.

7   **Responsive** The person not only hears what you said but also inquires further so that you can elaborate. He asks questions that demonstrate interest.

8   **Resonant** The person indicates that she emotionally resonates with what you have said by responding with statements that show she is trying to imagine what you are experiencing (e.g., "I can imagine that you feel terrible about losing your favorite pair of earrings").

After reading this scale, you may be wondering if you can nourish your self-worth without depending on others. There are, of course, ways of doing so. For example, when you attend a film, play, or concert, you may sense that something is resonating with you and is satisfying. Some people who relate to nature feel nourished by contact with the outdoors. When you achieve one of your goals, you can celebrate your accomplishment. You can also give yourself attention by writing daily in a journal or diary, or by periodically reflecting on your own feelings and thoughts—in other words, listening to yourself. By giving yourself time to pursue a hobby or avocation—knitting, playing the piano, or hiking—you are recognizing the things you enjoy, choosing to spend time on them, and ultimately renewing and refreshing yourself. You may also have the satisfaction of seeing aspects of yourself reflected in what you create, whether it be a plush sweater or a three-course dinner for friends. But remember, you can't do it *all* by yourself. The positive or negative responses that you get from others affect the way you feel about yourself, whether you like it or not.

People can learn to give one another the attention they need. For example, philosopher Eugene Gendlin has developed forms of interaction that he calls nourishing partnerships and nourishing-partnership groups.

In the 1950s, clinical psychologist Carl Rogers developed a therapeutic approach entitled client-centered psychotherapy. It was different from classical Freudian analysis in that Rogers believed clients could come to know more about their problems than their therapists did. So he developed a way to encourage clients to trust what they knew about themselves, then to articulate it. He encouraged this process by repeating back to clients the gist of what they had just said so they would be able to track and go deeper into their thoughts and feelings. One of Rogers's students at the University of Chicago was Eugene Gendlin, who, after conducting research that Rogers designed, realized that the clients who made the most progress were the ones who knew how to "focus," that is, how to detect and give words to what they felt in their bodies, what Gendlin termed their "felt sense." From this research and his philosophical background came the focusing technique, which consists of small steps of bodily attention that move beyond the level of feelings that most people are aware of. By attending to the "felt sense" in the stomach or chest, we at first get only an unclear sense. But with steady attention, the body sense opens up and we find how different the information is that comes from the center of the body. We have the sense of being talked to by something deeper, something that is not infected by fears and conditioning.

A few people focus naturally; most do not. The method is not the same as being in touch with emotions or the usual gut feelings. It literally involves a body sense, feeling how your body is carrying a particular life situation, problem, or concern. Once contacted, this sense leads to small steps of physically felt change and new actions.

Gendlin combined Rogers's method of repeating the essence of what someone had said with the concept of focusing to create focusing partnerships. In this partnership, two people split a period of time, with one of them the focuser and the other the witness. The focuser can, but need not, say what the focusing is about. The witness repeats back the gist of what the focuser says. This partnership provides both support for venturing inward and a validating connection to the outer world.

Focusing Guidelines

The method usually requires some hours of training. The steps are as follows:

1. Create a clear space in the middle of your body by finding each thing that now makes your body feel heavy or tight.
2. On any one thing, wait to see what sensations, feelings, and images arise from your body.
3. Figuratively, go and sit next to what arises in the middle of your body, and let it communicate to you.
4. Say how you are sensing what comes in your body. (Your partner will then paraphrase what you have said.)
5. You'll know you have found something when you feel a sense of release in your body and a sensation akin to a breath of fresh air.
6. Remember that you cannot control whether something arises; it is a form of grace. No single step is final. More steps can change and develop what you have found.

Nourishing-Partnership Groups

Sometimes it is possible to organize a group of nourishing partnerships in a particular setting. In fact, they might provide nourishing spaces where the overall environment is not currently conducive to meaningful contact. Nourishing-partnership groups can be created by members of a family, office, or religious congregation for the express purpose of deepening communication. It's important to note that no one should expect to be heard, understood, and responded to all of

"I'm sorry, I didn't hear what you said. I was listening to my body."

the time. One can, however, regularly set aside a specific amount of time with a group of people to listen empathically and respond accordingly. Should the group continue to meet for over a year or more, that organization will surely be affected in positive ways.

When more than one set of partners meet, there are some common practices that, if followed, can encourage psychologically nutritious exchanges. They are:

1. Like Alcoholics Anonymous and other such organizations, meet in a neutral place.
2. Have all of the group business conducted by a small, separate group who want to decide on matters such as meeting time, place, and frequency and length of meeting.
3. Do not meet in the same room or space where the small group conducts its business.
4. Sit in a circle so that everyone can feel equal.
5. Begin with a two-minute check-in, in which each person gives a psychological update. Make sure not to go over the two minutes.
6. No one may express strong negative feelings about an individual in the group. Instead, if strong differences arise, a one-on-one meeting can be arranged and, failing success in that, a meeting with a mediator from the group.
7. When speaking, state the gist of what the person who spoke just before you said. Then you can contribute your own ideas, thoughts, or reactions. This keeps the fabric of the discussion from becoming frayed and creates a sense of group connection.

8. If someone who has spoken seems to have made no sense, or if everyone disagrees, it helps if someone—anyone at all—asks that person to "say more." (This might happen at that moment or after other people have taken their turns.) The person will be OK if someone—anyone—can express back to her what she was trying to say.

9. Rituals for developing shared meaning and belonging could include the indigenous ritual of passing a "talking stick" or feather to indicate who has the floor.

10. Do not acquire any group money, resources, or possessions, as they will change the nature of the group and you will then need a hierarchy of some kind.

11. Refrain from advice-giving unless it is specifically requested.

12. End on time.

Some will argue correctly that we need a lot more than just attention to have good mental health. Psychologist Abraham Maslow maintained that there was a hierarchical scale of psychological needs. According to Maslow, once basic physical needs (food, safety, shelter) are taken care of, other needs (a sense of belonging, meaning) come to the forefront. We agree, but see attention as the principal ingredient in the alchemical process of connecting to self, others, and the Divine.

Books

Eugene Gendlin, *Focusing* (Bantam Books, 1981). The classic description of focusing theory and technique.

Organizations

Focusing Institute
34 East Lane
Spring Valley, NY 10977
(914) 362–5222 or (800) 799–7418 (phone)
info@focusing.org (e-mail)
www.focusing.org (website)

This not-for-profit organization makes focusing available to the public and the international professional community through teaching, research, and written materials. The institute provides an international e-mail discussion list; information on the use of focusing in schools, religious congregations, medical, and other settings; an on-line focusing chat room; an international network of certified focusing teachers; a certification training program; and an annual international focusing conference.

2
Spiritual Encounters in Psychotherapy

The interface between spirituality and psychotherapy is not new. In fact, it has a distinguished history beginning at the turn of the twentieth century, when William James gave a series of lectures at the University of Edinburgh, which were later published as the now-classic *The Varieties of Religious Experience*. These addresses marked the first time a psychologist had explored the relationship of psychology and religion. James's interest in religious feeling was coupled with a wide-ranging knowledge of world religions and religious phenomena. He explored in these lectures subjects as diverse as the mental state of Quakerism's founder, George Fox; the nineteenth-century mind-cure movement; Sufism; "sick souls"; and mystical experiences, which he viewed as the "root and center" of personal spiritual experiences.

Whereas Freud saw religion as "the universal obsessional neurosis of humanity," James reached a much different conclusion. "We and God have business with each other," he said, "and in opening ourselves to his influence, our deepest destiny is fulfilled." Thus James declared that the religious impulse was not only a worthy area of psychological study but also a vital part of human life.

About the time James was delivering the famous Gifford lecture series that became *Varieties* in 1902, C. G. Jung was beginning his career at Burghölzli Mental Hospital in Switzerland. Fascinated with the workings of the psyche, Jung was drawn to Freud's work, particularly to his theories about dreams because of their role in reflecting unconscious processes. Despite the fact that Jung and Freud grew quite close, the two broke painfully in 1913, mainly about differences over Freud's sexual theory. According to David Rosen, a psychiatrist and the McMillan professor of analytical psychology at Texas A&M University, one of the reasons for the split was that Freud believed the ego was the primary force in people's lives. Jung, on the other hand, theorized that at the center of one's consciousness was a universal or archetypal consciousness, of which the ego was only a small part.

The practical implication of this theoretical difference, Rosen explains, was that Freud believed that people's frustrated sexual and aggressive instincts were at the root of all their symptoms and emotional problems. By contrast, Jung didn't think that all symptoms and emotional problems could be reduced to these factors. Furthermore, he theorized that people are affected by more than their own histories. Jung himself reports in his 1961 autobiography, *Dreams, Memories, Reflections*, that he had premonitory dreams and visions of the coming bloodbath of World War I. Thus he could maintain that individuals were also affected by the evolution of the human psyche, which encompassed dreams, myths, and a universal need for meaning and purpose, and by their connection with the larger universal consciousness.

For many years Jungian analysis was considered esoteric and remained fairly isolated from mainstream psychotherapy professions. Even today it is not embraced by academic psychology. In the entire United States, only at Texas A&M University's Department of Psychology can Ph.D. candidates in clinical psychology specialize in analytical psychology. However, Jungian analysis is studied and integrated by individual psychotherapists and widely used by church and synagogue study groups, mainly because the spiritual journey occupies such a central place in Jung's theories. Indeed, many translate the Self, Jung's core of consciousness, as God or the Divine. Jung also made it clear that he thought the second half of one's life involved a spiritual quest.

In recent years, Jungian psychology has generated tremendous grassroots interest. In 1992 the weekly newsmagazine *U.S. News & World Report* published a major feature article on Jung and his psychology. What was so astonishing about the article, "Spiritual Questing," was the fact that reporter Erica E. Goode made no snide asides or deprecating comments. She simply presented a balanced and straightforward account of the surging interest in Jung's psychology, which is occurring just over thirty years after his death. This kind of treatment is not often afforded such topics by the print and broadcast media. Dubbing this psychological school "a cultural touchstone, a lens for processing experience, and . . . almost a religion," Goode investigates Jung's personal and professional life and discusses his main theories, but most important, she places Jungian analysis in its contemporary context. After interviewing laypeople, scholars, critics, and Jungian analysts, she concludes that Jung's appeal "represents an effort to forge connections in an increasingly fragmented world, its myths and symbols creating what [University of Chicago professor Wendy] Doniger terms 'an invisible community.'"

In some ways, Jung's psychology was a precursor to humanistic psychology and the human-potential movement—a branch of psychology developed in the 1960s—because his central concept, individuation, focused on "self-realization."

Abraham Maslow, one of the founders of humanistic psychology, referred to this process as "self-actualization," an innate yearning to fully express the self through the development of latent capacities and potentials. Whereas Freud believed that we become sick when we don't get enough safety, security, and affection, Maslow claimed, in his 1963 book *Towards a Psychology of Being*, that Freud's view was only part of the story. Once the primary needs for safety, security, belongingness, affection, and respect have been satisfied, wrote Maslow, human beings need to grow and expand, to create ultimate meaning, and to seek optimum wellness and health. To validate this theory he studied people who had found self-fulfillment by functioning at the farthest reaches of their human potential. He labeled these people "peak experiencers" and concluded from his many interviews with them that the *only* thing people needed for the sake of their mental health was to strive toward fulfilling their potential.

Later in his career Maslow came to believe that the quest for self-actualization was only a preparation for meeting a higher need, that of experiencing "something bigger than we are, that we can be awed by and commit ourselves to." It was at this stage that his interests expanded beyond humanistic psychology to transpersonal psychology, a psychology that takes into account experiences "beyond the person" (i.e., having to do with the mystical, the religious, and the spiritual).

During the 1960s and 1970s, humanistic psychology explored new avenues of self-expression and attempts at self-mastery. Thousands of people went to "encounter" and "sensitivity training" groups. Growth centers modeled after the prototype Esalen Institute in Big Sur, California, sprouted up around the country. Like Esalen, these centers helped people achieve greater self-expression by overcoming social inhibitions against the open expression of feelings. At Esalen, for example, the emphasis was on actively experimenting with new ways of being and relating to others rather than passively attending dry lectures and seminars held around a conference table. Here the focus was on experiencing yourself in your body—your visceral, emotional, and sensual experience—rather than having just "head-level" experiences.

Other concepts such as authenticity, the expression of feelings, self-responsibility, and reaching one's higher potential figured prominently in what was dubbed "third force" psychology—the other two being psychoanalysis and behaviorism. Humanistic psychology generated an expansive, almost giddy ebullience about possibilities, and an emotional and sexual let-it-all-hang-out attitude colored Association for Humanistic Psychology gatherings.

At the same time, droves of mainstream men and women attended the three-day Erhard Seminar Training (est). Werner Erhard, a former car salesman, originated these events by synthesizing and packaging the many personal-growth techniques that were then being used all over the country. In fact Erhard, John Hanley, and Russell Bishop all worked together at Mind Dynamics (now defunct) in San Francisco and went on to found *est*, Lifespring, Inc., and Insight Seminars (with John-Roger), respectively.

The *est* philosophy declared that we must become aware of our basic attitudes about how life works and take responsibility for changing them if they aren't giving us the kind of life we want. In other words, he argued that "we create our own reality" with our attitudes. By "taking responsibility" for our experiences, he argued, we could become the masters of our fate.

These principles were taught in trainings consisting of two intensive weekend seminars. A Socratic-type dialogue between the trainer and a participant demonstrated—often to the great amusement of fellow participants—how much the participant in the dialogue was choosing the kind of life and interactions he or she was complaining about. *Est* had incredible penetration into the culture, "graduating" over a million people and even being parodied in the movie *Semi Tough* starring Burt Reynolds. One scene showed Reynolds taping a tube and canister to his leg and ankle to circumvent the infamous, controversial rule that you couldn't leave the room during sessions to go to the bathroom.

By 1985, as *est*'s crest of popularity was waning, Erhard had introduced an updated version called *The Forum*. In 1991, prior to the *60 Minutes* exposé of his alleged sexual and physical abuse of family and colleagues, he sold the corporation to employees, who renamed the company Landmark Education. It is still in operation today.

This all-out effort at self-mastery as exemplified in *est* seemed to symbolize the cresting of the human-potential movement. Over time, this preoccupation with self began to feel empty. Extreme self-consciousness became too limiting, and gradually aspects of the human-potential movement began to change. Ram Dass, then known as Richard Alpert, a Harvard University psychology professor, exemplifies this shift. Having gone from a traditional academic milieu to the cutting edge of psychedelic experimentation, his next step was to embrace a spiritual path. He emerged as a cultural icon and itinerant guru who gave lectures and workshops all over the country on unitive consciousness. His writings, especially *Be Here Now* (1970), described his leave-taking from Harvard, his trip to India, finding a guru, and replacing psychoactive drugs with meditation.

The mid-1970s also saw the publication of *A Course in Miracles* (ACIM), a three-volume 1,200-page "curriculum" for spiritual development, transcribed by the late psychologist Helen Shucman. Although Jewish, she believed she received "dictation" from Jesus. Shaken by the fact that she was receiving this information, she asked a colleague, fellow psychologist William Thetford, to assist her in transcribing the material, which came to her between 1965 and 1972.

ACIM's metaphysics blends New Age Christianity and Freudian psychology, borrowing traditional Christian concepts such as Jesus, the Holy Spirit, forgiveness, and miracles but recasting them in decidedly unconventional ways. Whereas the Bible teaches, for example, that God created the world in six days and rested on the seventh, ACIM states unequivocally that God did not create the world at all. Like Eastern philosophy and religions, ACIM views the world as a dream, a collective illusion.

And if the world is illusory, so are our problems. This is where psychology comes in, for ACIM sees the mind as the source of all illusions and views psychological dynamics as the key to changing people's perceptions about themselves and the world. Using such concepts as ego, projection, and denial, it delineates a step-by-step process of spiritual awakening. Transpersonal psychiatrist Roger Walsh, writing in the January/February 1989 issue of *Common Boundary*, explains that one unusual feature of ACIM is a perspective Ken Wilber termed the "always/already truth." By this, Wilber means that most world religions and spiritual paths can be divided into two types: paths of attainment and paths of recognition. In the former, there is a sense that human beings are deficient and must work to change themselves. In the latter, human beings are innately, divinely connected but are unaware of their spiritual core. Therefore the fundamental task of the latter path is not change and improvement but recognition and awareness.

Though ACIM has not been adopted by any mainline religious organizations, its nonaffiliation with a traditional religious group has not hindered the spreading of its message. More than 1,200 study groups meet nationwide. In addition, a number of centers based on ACIM principles, known as Attitudinal Healing Centers, have been established throughout the United States. The most famous center was founded in Tiburon, California, by Gerald Jampolsky, M.D. Many of the principles from ACIM have also been popularized by Jampolsky in his book, *Love Is Letting Go of Fear*, and by Marianne Williamson in her bestselling book *Return to Love*. To date, ACIM has sold over a million copies.

Another means of exploring one's inner world was the ingestion of mind-expanding psychoactive drugs. By chemically altering thoughts, perceptions, and sensations, they opened up a whole new reality filled with possibilities. For some, the drugs helped them recognize that there were states of consciousness (similar to the dream state) that were not bound by rational logic. An important figure in psychedelic research was Czech psychiatrist Stanislav Grof, who began his research on LSD in his homeland in 1960. Later he accepted an invitation to come to the United States to conduct research at Spring Grove State Hospital and at the Maryland Psychiatric Research Center. From 1967 to 1973, he studied the effects of LSD on people suffering from alcoholism, heroin addiction, and terminal cancer. Subjects ingested the drug in a series of sessions with a researcher who acted as a guide. Grof was able to describe several definite stages of consciousness induced by the psychoactive substance, some or all of which could occur in a single session or over several sessions. The earliest stage was called the "aesthetic phase," when people saw unusually bright lights and colors. In the next stage, they seemed to be exploring their unconscious, arriving at new psychological insights. In later stages, they had memories of events surrounding their birth and even prebirth experiences. They also encountered deeply religious and spiritual material. This research provided important validation for the existence of transpersonal states.

A sixteenth-century woodcut by an anonymous artisan aptly captures the psychedelic experience. It depicts a kneeling figure whose body is resting on the earth but whose head has popped outside the earth's atmospheric bubble. With surprise and awe, he beholds the wonders of the universe. This stepping outside of traditional, culturally sanctioned, and conventional thinking, coupled with a strong transcendent experience—a sense of oneness with all that is—brought a sense of possibilities, new values, and ways of living into the cultural dialogue. Phrases such as "mind-blowing" and "far out" reflected actual experiences with these psychoactive substances and carried a positive connotation, even though not everyone encountered unitive bliss on their "trips." (At a 1997 symposium on psychedelics sponsored by the Association of Transpersonal Psychology, there seemed to be a consensus among speakers that having had these experiences, they now no longer needed to use the drugs. The value of opening up new horizons had been accomplished, and in one case a panelist testified that his current work was bringing his youthful visions of possibilities into the real world of medicine.)

In 1978 came M. Scott Peck, M.D., a psychiatrist who authored *The Road Less Traveled: A New Psychology of Love, Traditional Values, and Spiritual Growth*. Writing in the tradition of William James, Peck gave his scientific imprimatur to the spiritual journey. Millions of readers were assured by a representative of the medical profession that it was not only acceptable but sometimes critical to their mental health to work on spiritual issues.

In fact, Peck chastised his psychotherapy colleagues for their tendency to "consider any passionate belief in God to be pathological." He argued that everyone had either an implicit or an explicit set of values and beliefs about the essential nature of the world (i.e., a religious worldview). Therefore, he reasoned, clients were not well served by therapists who did not address or who reacted negatively to spiritual beliefs and concerns. He urged therapists to become more sophisticated in their attitudes toward religion and to learn to distinguish between destructive understandings of God—what he termed "monster-god"—which were harmful to clients, and more mature god-concepts that provide succor and strength amid life's trials.

But perhaps the most notable thing about Peck's first book was his impassioned declaration that "we live our lives in the eye of God, not at the periphery but at the center of His vision, His concern." This statement, coupled with the famous opening line of the book, "Life is difficult," reflected his view that although God is central to our lives, human beings must still grapple with life's challenges and pains. Peck recommended facing our problems consciously, with self-discipline and courage and an acceptance of grace, which is a powerful force and a gift of God. Taking this path to deeper meaning is indeed difficult, he states, and for this reason it is "the road less traveled."

Clearly his book touched a cultural nerve because it made publishing history by remaining on the *New York Times* bestseller list for a record-breaking thirteen years. Though Peck carefully cultivated an audience for his book—in the six years between the book's publication in 1978 and its appearance on the *New York Times* bestseller list in 1984, he maintained an active lecture schedule—no one could have anticipated the intensity of its appeal and its astronomical sales. Interest in the book was so great that a group discussion workbook was published as well as two other books: *Further Along the Road Less Traveled* (1992) and *The Road Less Traveled and Beyond* (1997). In 1998, twenty years after the publication of the first *Road*, all three books are being republished by Simon & Schuster.

Another publishing and cultural phenomenon was embodied by the guru of the recovery movement, John Bradshaw. In the late 1980s and early 1990s, Bradshaw's public-television series and his string of bestsellers introduced the language of addiction to the popular culture. *Inner child, codependency, and toxic shame* became psychospiritual buzzwords (see page 41). With dramatic emphasis, Bradshaw estimated during his popular PBS series, *Bradshaw On: The Family*, that 96 percent of all families are to some degree dysfunctional (i.e., emotionally impaired) because of the poisonous dynamics and unhealthy rules for living that they inherited from previous generations. The most poisonous rule is that you never question the rules. This rule guarantees that all other rules will be passed on unchanged to the next generation. The object of the rules is to help the parents remain unaware of the shame they felt when they didn't get the emotional caring they needed from their own caretakers. Not feeling safe enough to protest, they blamed themselves for not being worthy of receiving care. This is the same shame that the parents' own parents felt when they were growing up. Thus the unconsciousness of the father is visited upon the sons, and the sons pass that same blindness on to their sons.

Other covert rules that Bradshaw identified as operating unconsciously in families include maintaining control of all interactions, feelings, and personal behavior, so that the parent avoids experiencing the original shameful vulnerability that came from being dependent on others; when control breaks down, retaining an illusion of control through blame; keeping the same fight going for years so that everyone can stay upset and confused and successfully avoid contact, which could lead to feeling vulnerable and needy again; and maintaining an illusion of self-sufficiency. And finally, if everyone acts either so aloof or so needy that it discourages contact, then no one will have to trust anyone to get their needs met.

While M. Scott Peck may have seemed somewhat stern in his advocacy of self-examination and self-discipline, Bradshaw went to the other extreme and—whether justifiably or not—was seen in the media as an advocate for the "feel good" movement. Unlike the leaders of the previous self-actualization, self-mastery craze of the 1970s, Bradshaw, a former Roman Catholic seminary student, offered a new form of salvation. He preached about one's recovery not only from the tentacles of addiction to alcohol and drugs but also from work, abusive relationships, and the quest for perfection. He even attempted to modify people's feelings of guilt by changing the biblical doctrine of original sin into a more self-esteem-friendly version known as "original pain," explaining that we didn't begin life permanently damaged but that the psychological pain of growing up distorted our original beauty. He offered hope that recovery from the pain of living was possible.

Bradshaw On: The Family

Addiction Bradshaw defines addiction as "a pathological relationship to any mood-altering experience that has life-damaging consequences." In addition to substance addictions such as alcohol or drugs, Bradshaw also identifies process addictions such as gambling or workaholism.

Toxic Shame This is the ever-present feeling that one is flawed and therefore will never be able to measure up. It differs from guilt, which says I've *done* something wrong or made a mistake. Shame, on the other hand, says there is something wrong with me; I *am* a mistake. Healthy shame, Bradshaw says, lets us know that we are finite and frail creatures who need feedback and human community. It lets us know we are human beings, not gods.

Codependency Noting that the term was first used to label the spouse of an alcoholic, Bradshaw extended the term to include the whole family. In dysfunctional families, he explains, there is a primary stressor. The stressor can be a parent's addiction, violence, or moral righteousness. As a survival strategy and to control the situation, all family members have to sacrifice their true self-identity and accept the role they believe is needed. For example, a child can become a parent to his or her parent, or take on other roles, such as the scapegoat, star, rebel, perfect one, and so on.

Inner Child In childhood, we are dependent on parents for a host of needs as basic as food, shelter, protection, affection, and security. If normal dependency needs go unmet, however, our bodies may mature into adulthood but we remain "adult children" emotionally. Bradshaw suggested paying attention to this wounded "inner child," so that one could nurture it and eventually integrate it into the adult personality.

Another bellwether was the late mythologist Joseph Campbell, who had toiled quietly in the academic vineyard for years but became an "overnight" sensation after Bill Moyers interviewed him for a six-part public-television series entitled *The Power of Myth*, which aired in 1988. By introducing viewers to ancient myths, archetypal art, and symbols, Campbell excited people's interest in the study of mythology—another aspect of the invisible world that affects our lives. By speaking outside the context of any one specific religion, Campbell addressed the universal aspects of people's spirituality. He proved to be immensely popular with the public for the same reasons that Jung's psychology has become so. Both men valued myths and archetypes and sought to find the universal wisdom in them. Campbell and Jung appealed to religious people whose souls were hungry for a way to bring vitality to their worship by seeing the universals that were a part of their current tradition. This awareness inspired them to find ways to make their worship rituals more relevant.

For the unchurched, Campbell offered an acceptable form of spiritual guidance. Toward the end of the series, he made the now-famous statement "Follow your bliss," which became the spiritual motto for millions of theologically uncertain people who felt that Campbell had legitimated their inclination to look inside their hearts and let their deepest desires direct them.

RETURN OF THE SOUL

In 1992, former monk and now psychotherapist Thomas Moore, through his bestselling book *Care of the Soul*, opened a floodgate by reintroducing the long-neglected theological term *soul* to the general public. In a simple, masterful stroke, the title of his book not only acknowledged the existence and reality of an inner life but gave permission to focus on that part of us that is connected to eternity. Indeed he urged that we tend to this part of ourselves. Moore identifies the great malady of the twentieth century as "loss of soul" at both the individual and collective levels. When the soul is neglected, it doesn't just go away; it appears symptomatically in addictions, violence, and depression, all of which are concerns in our society today.

Moore defines as "soulful" anything having to do with genuineness, relatedness, and depth, as in "good food, fulfilling work, satisfying conversation, genuine friends, and experiences that stay in the memory and touch the heart." While Bradshaw's writing contains an unspoken but clear salvational tone (if you could only be self-forgiving, your troubles would be over), Moore prefers to offer recipes for soulful living without striving for salvation.

Moore differs from the leaders of the human-potential and self-mastery movements insofar as he gives weight to the role of mystery and fate. Instead of backing the modern therapeutic view that a person is what he wills himself to be, Moore believes that we are directed by our destiny because "a piece of the sky and a chunk of the earth lie lodged in the heart of every human being" and that to understand ourselves "we will have to know the sky and the earth as well as human behavior." Included in this knowing the sky and earth is Moore's defense of astrology as a reasonable tool of self-reflection. Terming astrology "applied poetics," he explains that it is a system that can fuel the imagination with its stories and images, and as such nourishes the soul.

Astrology, we know, has been ridiculed by the media and other segments of society along with the human-potential, New Age, and consciousness movements. In fact, Washington political commentator Charles Krauthammer in a 1996 *Time* essay once lumped together homeopathy, false-memory syndrome, and alien abductions, concluding that Americans are escaping into such irrationality to avoid the harsh realities of contemporary life. Having such an opinion blasted through the bullhorn of a major U.S. magazine, it's no wonder that those of us who pay attention to feelings, dreams, and creative urges—in short, to our soul's promptings—might feel isolated and at odds with the culture at large.

Still, Moore's book and the public's response to it—it occupied a place on the *New York Times* bestseller list for two years—lent more weight and credence to the importance and necessity of paying attention to and tending the soul.

Moore's approach to deepening spirituality is different from the transpersonal psychology approach, which focuses on achieving transcendence through spiritual disciplines such as contemplation, chanting, meditation, tai chi, and yoga. Moore believes this course of action pulls us away from "the messy conditions of actual life." Moore's way of intensifying our quest for spirituality is to bring soul back into our daily lives, into our homes, relationships, and workplaces.

❀ In Conversation with Thomas Moore: ❀ The Soul's Mysteries

Though it is impossible to define precisely what soul is, we can work intuitively toward an understanding of soul by looking at the way the term is commonly used. For example, an ad in the newspaper says, "Take a cruise. It's good for your soul." Or, as I read in *Keyboard* magazine, "We want to get to the soul of music, not just to the technique." That kind of talk says a lot about soul. It says that while we can't define it, we know that it involves substance and an inwardness; it is the essence of a thing or person.

But soul is frightening because it makes life more complicated. It is iconoclastic; it brings new thoughts. It says, "The things that I believed in all my life may not be true. This relationship I've had for a long time may not exist anymore." Soul is always offering new life, new ideas, new imagination.

I like what Renaissance philosopher Nicholas of Cusa said: The person who wants to live soulfully has to cultivate ignorance. He has to say, "I really don't know the answers and I never will. I will never know the reasons why I did what I did. I can never fully explain what happened to me in childhood."

People come to me and say, "I think my uncle abused me as a child, but I'm not sure. If only I could find out the facts, then I'd know why I feel the way I do." But Cusa says that as human beings, we are not allowed to have that knowledge.

People travel all over the country trying to dig up relatives to ask, "Did this happen to me?" Imagine them giving up and saying. "You know, I can live my life without knowing that." That kind of attitude puts you in the mystery of who you are, and that's where soul is. Soul has no explanations. The words *explanation, interpretation, meaning* don't apply to soul at all. Words that do apply are *reflection, poetry, imagination,* and *experience.* The poet Keats says that the whole point of all life's pains is to *feel* existence. A lot of us try not to be affected by things, and I think this is a mistake. For example, often a person who has gone through a divorce will be counseled not to look back but to get on with life. Well, soul is always looking back. Soul says, you have to live with that experience and be affected by it, and by doing so you will be a more profound person—a person that other people can relate to—because of it.

In the Renaissance tradition, Saturn is the god of depression, and his metal is lead. (All gods and goddesses were associated with different metals—Venus's was copper, Mercury's was quicksilver, and so on.) In depression, you allow life to come into you in a saturnine way. It ages you, gives you weight and authority, so you're no longer a fluffy, light person bouncing all over the place. It can be very important to the soul to have that maturity and weight. Now that's not to say that you want to be depressed all your life, but you want to let that symptom ripen into what it wants to become.

This brings us to the difference between the Aristotelian and Platonic views of the soul. It's Aristotelian to think that we are who we are only because of what we've experienced; that all knowledge comes through the senses. The Platonic view is that we are who we are from eternity. For instance, in my daughter I can sense the presence of a soul that has been there eternally. Her personality was there from day one. That idea of an innate soul is part of the Platonic view.

The Renaissance Platonists believed that a man was born under a particular star that colored his character and influenced the course of his life. What a different perspective that is from our American notion of the self-made man creating his own destiny! That's why in this country it's a bit radical to suggest living soulfully. Living soulfully does not mean *making* yourself into somebody, but discovering who you are *eternally*. This is a very interesting way to think about life—with a sense of soul that goes on and on both before and after this life. I'm not talking about an afterlife or reincarnation but about a way of imagining ourselves so that we realize we are that mysterious.

This demand that we have to be perfect, that we have to get ourselves emotionally right, is such a burden. The more we try, the worse it gets! We try one type of therapy after another. But soul thrives in failure and imperfection. Jung said that soul moves at the weak point where the personality is thin, where things are not secure and stable. That's where soul has an entry. We need those vulnerable points. Even getting into serious trouble—with hallucinations and emotional breakdowns and so forth—can be seen as a soul movement.

I learned from the Florentine Neoplatonist philosopher Ficino that we can live our whole lives this way, giving a beautiful reflection to all our difficulties and moods. So if we're depressed we should wear a beautiful black coat or suit. Renaissance gardens would have a place devoted to Saturn, where one could go to be away from people, where one could feel the beauty of solitude and melancholy. Here we're made to feel guilty if we're away from people.

Even our jobs can be made sacred, not by slapping some kind of foreign spiritual practice onto them, but by recognizing the deeper dimensions in the work itself. For example, the Trade Building in Chicago has a statue of the goddess Ceres on it. That says that being associated with food and agriculture is a religious activity. To be a farmer or to be a broker in meat or wheat is a sacred occupation.

So often our spiritual practices themselves lack soul; they're set up to keep imagination under reins. To have a spirituality that nourishes, we need to go back to our religious traditions in a way that involves imagination. We need to read sacred literature as poetry, not as dogma; to immerse ourselves in the images, symbols, rituals—all in a poetic way.

How can we become more soulful? We could pay attention to our memories. We could tell the stories of our families and ancestors; we could keep our historical buildings standing instead of tearing them down.

People like the alchemists and like Ficino knew the importance of concealing insight as much as revealing it. When things become public, people want them to be clearly drawn, sensational, easy. But soul is not easy. Not easy at all.

Thomas Moore is a former monk, archetypal psychotherapist, philosopher, and bestselling author of the books *Care of the Soul* and *The ReEnchantment of Everyday Life*. His most recent book, published in 1998, is *The Soul of Sex: Cultivating Life as an Act of Love*.

This essay is adapted from an interview that appeared in *Common Boundary* magazine.

Moore's archetypal and imaginative approach to spirituality is balanced by the theories of transpersonal author Ken Wilber. After dropping out of graduate school in chemistry at the University of Nebraska, he taught himself by way of voluminous reading, extended periods of meditation, and therapy. With all the ferment in the psychospiritual field, Wilber then set out to create a model broad enough to integrate all these new concepts and theories. He introduced this model in a seminal series of books including *No Boundary*, *A Sociable God*, and *Up from Eden*. In 1986 he joined two clinical psychologists, Jack Engler and Daniel Brown, in editing a book, *Transformations of Consciousness: Conventional and Contemplative Perspectives on Development*, that demonstrated how the stages of psychological growth and the stages of spiritual development could be viewed as a "spectrum of consciousness" beginning in the prepersonal (i.e., pre-ego development) phase and moving through the personal (ego development) to the transpersonal (beyond ego development) phase as described in the psychology of Eastern religions.

With his spectrum model of the levels of consciousness, Wilber and his colleagues could identify the types of psychotherapy and spiritual practice that would be most beneficial to an individual at each stage of his or her development. What was revolutionary about the model was that it showed that there were stages of psychological development beyond what most conventional theories considered the developmental end point. Freud had pessimistically capped the upper limit of normal psychological development at the point where one suffers only "life's ordinary discontents and unhappiness." In his writings, Wilber discussed how growth (expanded through meditation and other forms of spiritual practice) continued beyond this traditional end mark of normality. Turning the tables on critics, Wilber argued that clinging to lower stages of development could be interpreted as a resistance to experiencing the higher states of development.

Archetypal psychologist and author James Hillman offers a counterpoint to the transcendent tendencies of the transpersonal field. His 1996 bestselling book, *The Soul's Code: In Search of Character and Calling*, takes a fresh look at the reasons why we are here on earth. Hillman believes that each of us is more than the product of our genetic heritage and our social environment. Indeed, he maintains that each of us has an in-dwelling core character that carries within it a uniqueness that asks to be lived, just as the acorn fulfills its destiny by becoming an oak tree. Hillman refers to this invisible inward presence as an "image in the heart," or the calling of the soul. Among the many famous people Hillman uses to illustrate his theory is Winston Churchill, who began stammering at age fourteen and was placed in a remedial reading class. Hillman argues that Churchill had these difficulties not because of family stresses or childhood wounds but because at his young age he could not contain his immense oratorical abilities in his small, undeveloped body.

It's interesting to note that Hillman is by background a Jungian analyst, trained in Zurich, where he held the position of director of studies for ten years. He invented the term *archetypal psychology* in 1970 to apply to—depending on your point of view—an extension, branch, wing, or faction of Jungian psychology. Although Hillman acknowledges Jung as the primary influence in archetypal psychology, he includes others such as French scholar, philosopher, and mystic Henri Corbin; Freud; American poet-philosopher Wallace Stevens; English poets William Blake and John Keats; as well as the arts, philosophy, literature, and ancient myth and religion. His longtime student Thomas Moore says that Hillman provides a way to think about psychology within the context of the humanities instead of the sciences. "Just his use of the word *soul* has placed psychology among the traditions that care for the soul," Moore explains.

But Hillman himself is not your typical soulful character. Indeed, he is more of an intellectual provocateur than a high priest. In a book he co-authored with Michael Ventura entitled *We've Had a Hundred Years of Psychotherapy and the World's Getting Worse* (the book consists of edited transcripts of conversations between them), the two men discuss the same premise as that of *The Soul's Code*—namely, that one's life is shaped not so much by historical events such as childhood trauma as it is by one's soul, which has within it a predetermined trajectory, or what one might call fate. Because of this distinction, Hillman and Ventura criticize writers like Swiss psychoanalyst Alice Miller and John Bradshaw for focusing on healing childhood wounds rather than seeing them as a part of what the soul has to go through to fulfill its destiny. While we think Hillman's perspective is an interesting one, there's a danger in jumping too quickly from psychological healing to philosophical speculation.

People abused in childhood *already* have a hard time directly expressing their anger. They believe they were abused because they were bad. It never occurs to them that their parents were behaving in an immature and inappropriate manner. In therapy one can learn to trust the safety of the present-day situation and start expressing anger about what happened in the past. We don't think it is helpful for a therapist to say, "Wait a minute, let's imagine the way this abuse has helped your soul achieve its unique destiny," or "Just think, the abuse you received as a child has probably enabled you to become the sensitive and empathic person you are today." If a therapist said this, a client might hear: "You still have no right to feel angry; it was done for your own good, or because it was God's will."

The archetypal-psychology notion that therapy is too self-absorbed and antipolitical makes it sound as if people who are in therapy stop doing anything else in the world. This is not our experience. Because Chuck's therapy practice is based in the Washington, D.C., area, he has a number of therapy clients who are active in the political and governmental arena. Never during the course of therapy have any clients lessened their community or political involvement, nor have they withdrawn their commitment or energy from serving the public good.

Indeed it seems to us that the more personal pain is reduced, the more effective one can become in carrying out communal responsibilities. Hillman and Ventura don't seem to believe this will happen. They seem to fear that once people encounter their wounded inner child, they will get stuck in childish blame for the rest of their lives.

In this respect Hillman and Ventura are not alone. Many people are afraid of contacting the hurt, vulnerable side of themselves; they fear it will take over and get them in deep trouble, which of course is why they banished these feelings from awareness in the first place. It is our belief, however, that once this child voice is heard, seen, and expressed, it will become once again a vital source of energy and creativity. We think an argument can be made that therapy and Twelve-Step alumni, because they were able to get angry about their caretakers' abuse, can now get angry—in an effective way—about the failings of the political system. Therapy didn't immobilize Vice-President Gore, who has talked openly about family therapy sessions he participated in following an accident involving his son. Why should it deter other therapy alumni?

Soul work involves both inner- and outer-directed work. Sometimes one must focus inwardly, sensing the direction one must take; other times, soul work is wholly other-oriented. It might involve caring for family members, taking up an environmental, social, or political cause, creating a business, or founding an organization. In the best of all worlds, one maintains a harmonious balance between inward and outer focus. But no matter what the orientation, the essence of soul is meaning and connection, depth and fullness. It's listening to Yo-Yo Ma play Bach's cello concertos on a rainy day, receiving an exquisitely misshapen object made by your enthusiastic child, walking beneath trees that wave to you as you pass, and listening to the gurgling monologue of an urban stream. It's sitting at the bedside of a loved one and posting flyers announcing a neighborhood meeting.

The wonder of soul is its ubiquity. Angeles Arrien, a cultural anthropologist, author, and teacher, has very simple soul work guidelines:

- Show up.
- Pay attention.
- Tell the truth.
- Don't be attached to results.

Her point, of course, is to see soul work not as something esoteric or special but as an attitude, a stance, a process of full engagement with life. And as distinctions of inner and outer fall away, what is left is a fullness of experience, an effortless transformation of the mundane into the sacred.

3

Spiritual Psychotherapy

Before launching into a discussion of contemporary spiritual psychotherapy, it is important to give some background about how each of the mental-health professions became involved in spirituality.

Twenty years ago, the kind of therapy you received depended in large measure upon which professional you chose. Four major professions offered psychotherapy: psychiatry, psychology, social work, and nursing. The field of psychiatry, a specialty within the medical establishment, was heavily influenced by Freudian psychoanalysis. Psychiatrists were trained in Freudian theory and practiced psychodynamic therapy with sessions scheduled on a once- or twice-a-week basis. Psychoanalysts, for the most part psychiatrists who had undergone additional in-depth psychoanalytic training and a personal analysis, saw clients four or five times a week. Their clients would lie on a couch with the analyst sitting behind them out of their view. Psychiatrists are the only mental-health professionals allowed to prescribe drugs; psychoanalysts rarely prescribe them during psychoanalysis.

Analytical psychology, or Jungian analysis, was founded by a former psychoanalyst, C. G. Jung, but his approach was not widely accepted in either psychiatry or psychology training programs. The first stirrings of an interest in religious matters within psychiatry came in 1961 when the Christian Medical and Dental Society formed a psychiatry section. It meets during the annual American Psychiatric Association (APA) convention (as does the National Guild for Catholic Psychiatrists). In recent years, presentations in transpersonal psychiatry have been included in the annual APA convention programs.

The field of clinical psychology comes out of an academic and scientific background, and in the early days many programs in psychology were part of philosophy departments. Clinical psychologists, while trained in a variety of techniques including behavior modification and humanistic-existential psychotherapy, also seemed to prefer the Freudian psychodynamic model. A large part of their practices, however, were devoted to administering and evaluating psychological and psychoneurological tests.

In 1956, a Christian Association for Psychological Studies was formed; twenty years later, members of the American Psychological Association formed the Division of the Psychology of Religion. These two groups have for the most part looked mainly at the relationship between social psychology and Christianity. In 1970 the Association for Transpersonal Psychology, an outgrowth of the humanistic psychology movement, was established, and its original emphasis was on the relationship between psychology and Eastern religious practices like meditation. In 1982 the California State Psychological Association authorized the organization of a task force on spirituality and psychotherapy. The task force, borrowing from Jung's writings, defined *spirituality* as "the courage to look within and to trust" and added, "what is seen and what is trusted appears to be a feeling of wholeness, belongingness, connectedness, and openness to the universe." The task force then undertook a research study of a sample of 1,440 licensed California clinical psychologists, assessing their preparation before and after licensure to deal with their own and their clients' problems of spiritual development. The findings indicated that there was almost no preparation for these issues before licensure.

There are more than fifty divisions representing professional interests under the umbrella of the American Psychological Association. As mentioned above, one such interest group is called the Psychology of Religion, or Division 36 (formerly known as Psychologists Interested in Religious Issues). The division recently created a national task force on the topic of religious issues in psychology and clinical training. The American Psychological Association also published a book called *Religion and the Clinical Practice of Psychology* (1996), edited by Edward Francis Shafranske, Ph.D. Publication of this book represents the first formal acknowledgement of the psychospiritual field by this organization. It is interesting to note that according to Ken Pargament, Ph.D., past president of Division 36, the book was one of the bestselling volumes at the 1996 annual convention.

The profession of social work came out of a different background than did the other mental-health professions. In the late 1800s, the social work profession was begun by those employed in settlement houses helping recent European immigrant families get settled into their new communities and those who worked in religious charitable organizations assisting the poor. The first professional degree-granting schools were founded in 1898: the New York School of Philanthropy (later to become the Columbia University School of Social Work) and the Simmons College School of Social Work.

Because of this early history of working with the poor and needy, the profession has a different focus than either psychiatry, which evolved as a specialty out of medicine, or psychology, which began as a field of academic study. Social work's understanding of the individual includes not just biological and psychological contexts, but social and cultural ones as well.

However, because of the increasing popularity of psychotherapy, social workers, like other mental-health professionals, have been increasingly drawn to clinical work. While many social workers continue to pursue careers in community organizing, public policy, public welfare (e.g., adoptions, welfare casework), and private religious charities, the largest group has entered into the private practice of psychotherapy as clinical social workers.

Not only is clinical social work the largest specialty within the social work profession, but clinical social workers have become one of the largest groups of practicing psychotherapists in the United States. Even more telling for the future are the numbers of graduates each year: 11,500 master of social work graduates compared with 1,300 Ph.D.s in clinical psychology and 1,300 psychiatric residents in 1993 alone. With stiff caps imposed by managed care on the cost of outpatient psychotherapy and the consequent increased burden of higher copayments on the insured, clients have begun shopping for lower-cost therapists; social workers are one of the professions leading the list.

Psychiatric nurses mainly worked in hospital settings. For reasons that are not clear, psychiatric nursing has been declining in numbers over the last ten years. Calling themselves psychiatric mental-health clinical nurse specialists, some choose to belong to the American Holistic Nurses Association, which was formed in 1981.

Lastly, a relative newcomer to the mental-health field is counseling, which has grown substantially in the last twenty years. It is the professional home of many of the addiction counselors. Because Alcoholics Anonymous (AA) has had so much success in helping alcoholics and other substance abusers recover from their addictive behaviors, many recovering addicts go on to become addiction counselors, and because AA is so grounded in spiritual principles, counseling has strong representation in the psychospiritual field.

Beginning in the late 1960s and 1970s, more and more mental-health professionals left the mental hospitals, public agencies, and clinics where they had practiced, in favor of setting up a private practice, where they felt freer to use whatever worked best with their clients. As a result, the distinctions between them became less a matter of the mental-health profession in which they were trained than the efficacy of the method they used (e.g., behavioral, cognitive, crisis intervention, Jungian, existential-humanistic, family systems). Yet despite the fact that so many psychotherapists practice an eclectic brand of therapy, the mental-health professions have institutionally responded quite differently to the spiritual awakening occurring in the United States. The following sections trace the history of spirituality within the various professions.

TRANSPERSONAL PSYCHOLOGY

The name *transpersonal psychology* is a bit confusing. Although it is called a psychology, it actually refers to a multidisciplinary field in which all the other mental-health fields plus business, education, and medicine participate.

The term *transpersonal* refers to a kind of psychological orientation that includes stages of development beyond the conventional stages of personality (or ego) development. For example, it includes the advanced psychological stages of spiritual development that come about as a result of ongoing spiritual practice such as contemplation and meditation.

This field originated from two main sources. The first was the field of humanistic psychology. Specifically, Abraham Maslow, one of the founders of humanistic psychology, studied the characteristics of people who had achieved high levels of self-actualization, a goal of humanistic psychology. On September 14, 1967 he gave an address at the First Unitarian Church in San Francisco in which he declared that psychology had much farther to go to explore the full range of human possibilities. Three days later, according to Miles Vich, executive director of the Association of Transpersonal Psychology, Maslow announced the founding of the *Journal of Transpersonal Psychology*. In 1970 the Association for Transpersonal Psychology was established and began holding annual conferences. Maslow had teamed up with colleague Anthony Sutich, also a psychologist, six years earlier to found another professional publication, the *Journal of Humanistic Psychology*. Both were very aware that the field of humanistic psychology did not pay sufficient attention to what lay beyond the self; namely, mystical, religious, and spiritual experiences. Maslow and Sutich joined with other kindred spirits such as psychiatrist Stanislav Grof to begin to define this new field.

Sutich and Grof represent the second source of transpersonal psychology. Sutich, for example, was interested in the psychological effects of the meditation practices of Eastern religions; Grof was interested in altered states of consciousness connected to his research with psychedelic drugs. In association with Maslow and Viennese psychiatrist Viktor Frankl, Grof is credited with suggesting the term *transpersonal* for this emerging field. The field received a major boost from the theoretical work of Ken Wilber, who in a series of books described the various stages of psychological and spiritual development. His later work with the clinical psychologists Jack Engler and Daniel Brown demonstrated how the stages of psychological growth and the stages of spiritual development could both be viewed as spectrums of consciousness. Their conceptualization proved useful to people seeking to understand the relationship between the different tasks involved in their spiritual and psychological development.

Books

Stanislav Grof, *The Adventure of Self Discovery* (State University of New York, 1988). This Czech psychiatrist and transpersonal psychology pioneer describes experiences beyond ordinary day-to-day awareness, including those states induced by psychedelics. He also attempts to chart a comprehensive map of the inner terrain.

Roger Walsh and Frances Vaughan, editors, *Paths Beyond Ego: The Transpersonal Vision* (Jeremy P. Tarcher, Perigee, 1993). An earlier version, entitled *Beyond Ego*, was published in 1980 and has been widely used as a textbook in academic and professional mental-health graduate programs as an introduction to the study of transpersonal psychology.

John Welwood, editor, *Awakening the Heart: East/West Approaches to Psychotherapy and the Healing Relationship* (Random House, 1983). This introduction to transpersonal approaches to counseling shows among other things how the therapist is affected by the client when matters of the heart are involved.

Ken Wilber, Jack Engler, and Daniel Brown, editors, *Transformation of Consciousness: Conventional and Contemplative Perspectives on Development* (Shambhala Publications, Inc., 1986). Wilber is the leading consciousness theoretician. His "spectrum of consciousness" model, which describes the states of awareness (from ego consciousness to beyond ego consciousness), shows which kinds of psychotherapy and spiritual practice are most beneficial at each stage of consciousness.

Organizations

American Psychological Association
Psychology of Religion (Division 36)
750 First Street, NE
Washington, DC 20002
(202) 336-5500
www.apa.org (website)

Founded in 1976 as a division of APA, Division 36 seeks to encourage research in the psychology of religion and to integrate these findings into current psychological theory and professional practice. The division has been predominantly focused on social psychology from a Judeo-Christian perspective, but the relationship between spirituality and religion and other topics are beginning to be addressed.

Association for Transpersonal Psychology (ATP)
P.O. Box 3049

Stanford, CA 94039
(415) 327-2066 (phone)
(415) 327-0535 (fax)

Founded in 1970 by Anthony Sutich and Abraham Maslow, ATP is a major voice of the transpersonal movement. It publishes a journal, directed by long-time editor Miles Vich, and holds an annual conference. It also publishes a national listing of professional members and educational programs in transpersonal psychology.

Periodicals

Journal of Transpersonal Psychology
P.O. Box 3049
Stanford, CA 94309
(415) 327-2066 (phone)
(415) 327-2114 (fax)
atp@igc.apc.org (e-mail)
www.igc.apc.org (website)
Semiannual; $29

Begun in 1969, this scholarly journal addresses the research, theory, and applications of altered states of consciousness, mystical states, and Eastern spiritual practices.

Psychotherapy Theory: Research and Practice
3900 East Camelback Road, Suite 200
Phoenix, AZ 85018
(602) 912-5329
Quarterly; $60 ($35 student)

This publication is part of the Division of Psychotherapy (Division 29) of the American Psychological Association. Occasionally there are articles that report research findings regarding some aspects of psychology and spirituality.

TRANSPERSONAL PSYCHIATRY

In 1970 the Association of Transpersonal Psychology (ATP) was founded to further understanding of the interface between Western psychotherapy and Eastern and Western spiritual disciplines, as well as other nonordinary states of consciousness. The language of psychology provided a common frame of reference for communicating about the inner world of spiritual and nonordinary experience. Because ATP was formed to include the study of psychospiritual growth and development, a variety of professionals, including psychiatrists, eagerly joined the fledgling organization.

More recently, however, psychiatry has taken steps to acknowledge the existence and significance of nonordinary states of consciousness and to advance clinical work that takes these states into account. In 1992, for example, the prestigious Menninger Clinic sponsored the first transpersonal psychiatry symposium. In 1994 the fourth edition of the *Diagnostic and Statistical Manual* (DSM-IV) published by the American Psychiatric Association included, for the first time, a separate category for religious and spiritual problems. Achieving a place in the DSM-IV was an important step because health insurance companies make reimbursements based on the diagnostic categories in this volume. Recent annual meetings of the American Psychiatric Association have also featured presentations on the interface between psychiatry and spirituality. In 1996 Basic Books published a *Textbook of Transpersonal Psychiatry and Psychology*, edited by Bruce W. Scotton, Allan B. Chinen, and John R. Battiston, which is a comprehensive collection of essays that offers chapters on the historical background of transpersonal psychiatry, its cross-cultural roots, the research done on altered states of consciousness, issues related to clinical practices, and more. It is a solid introduction to the field by the top theorists, practitioners, and researchers.

While there is still no formal association of transpersonal psychiatry, some of the more prolific and noteworthy psychiatrists writing in this field are Allen Chinen, who has written several books on the importance of fairy tales and storytelling; Mark Epstein, known for his writing on psychoanalysis and Buddhism; Charles Grob, a researcher on the cross-cultural dimensions of psychedelics; Stanislav Grof, one of the founders of ATP and a major transpersonal theorist and researcher; Ann Massion, a researcher concerned with the therapeutic applications of meditation; and Roger Walsh, author and professor at the University of California Medical School at Irvine.

Organizations

Albert Hofmann Foundation (AHF)
1278 Glenneyre Street, #173
Laguna Beach, CA 92651
(310) 281-8110

The AHF was established as a nonprofit organization in 1988, named in honor of the man who discovered LSD and the ritualistic use of psilocybe mushrooms by indigenous cultures. The purpose of the foundation is to establish and maintain a library and world information center dedicated to the scientific study of human consciousness.

American Psychiatric Association (APA)
1400 K Street, NW
Washington, DC 20005
(202) 682-6000 (phone)
(202) 682-6850 (fax)
Apa@psych.org (e-mail)
www.psych.org (website)

The APA is a national society whose over 38,000 physician and medical student members throughout North America and in numerous foreign countries specialize in the diagnosis and treatment of mental and emotional disorders. APA's roots extend back to October 1944, when thirteen eminent physicians who specialized in the treatment of mental illnesses gathered in Philadelphia to found the Association of Medical Superintendents of American Institutions for the Insane. The American Psychiatric Press publishes numerous books, journals, and reports, including the *Diagnostic and Statistical Manual* (DSM), the authoritative text on categories and definitions of mental illness.

Christian Medical and Dental Society
P.O. Box 5
Bristol, TN 37621-0005
(423) 844-1000 (phone)
(423) 844-1005 (fax)
75364.331.compuserv.com (e-mail)
www.cmds.org (website)

Founded in 1931, the purpose of this society is to encourage Christians who practice psychiatry to investigate and discuss the relation between their faith and their professional work and to incorporate such examined beliefs into their personal life and daily practice.

Heffter Research Institute
330 Garfield Street, Suite 301
Santa Fe, NM 87501-2676
(505) 820-6557

Arthur Heffter, Ph.D., for whom the institute is named, was the first scientist to systematically study the chemistry and psychopharmacology of a naturally occurring psychedelic. The institute was established to foster and promote legitimate, rigorous, and ethical research on psychedelics.

Multidisciplinary Association for Psychedelic Studies (MAPS)
2121 Commonwealth Avenue, Suite 220

Charlotte, NC 28205
(704) 334-1798 (phone)
(704) 334-1799 (fax)
info@maps.org (e-mail)
www.MAPS.org (website)

MAPS, a nonprofit organization founded in 1986 by Rick Doblin, is a membership-based organization that helps researchers around the world design, fund, conduct, and report on psychedelic research in humans. According to Stanislav Grof, Humphrey Osmond, an LSD research pioneer, coined the term *psychedelic*, which "literally means mind manifesting or revealing the psyche."

National Guild of Catholic Psychiatrists
c/o Dr. Robert McCallister
Taylor Manor Hospital
4100 College Avenue
Ellicott City, MD 2041-0396
(410) 465-3322 (phone)
(410) 461-7075 (fax)

The National Guild brings together psychiatrists and other mental-health professionals who share a belief in the spiritual dimension of human experience. It advocates the integration of psychiatry and religion through the exchange of clinical experience and knowledge by means of professional meetings and the publication of educational materials.

COUNSELING

In 1972 the Virginia State Board of Psychologist Examiners sued a professional counselor for conducting a private practice in career counseling (*Weldon* v. *Psychologist Examiners*), arguing that he was practicing psychology and that the formal training needed to do this effectively required at least a doctoral degree. The verdict: unprecedented recognition by the Virginia Supreme Court that counseling was a profession separate from psychology. Since this decision, the American Counseling Association (ACA) has continued to build on the Virginia ruling.

Since its inception in 1952, the ACA has been the professional home base for mental-health counselors, counselor educators, and human development specialists. It serves as an umbrella organization for diverse and specialized areas such as school guidance, rehabilitation, vocational, marriage and family, and substance abuse counseling. It also hopes to widen its scope by inviting similar-minded professions, such as the expressive art therapists, to join its ranks, provided they meet ACA's education guidelines.

There is a rift between the American Psychological Association and the American Counseling Association, but their differences seem to be as much political and economic as ideological. The APA tends to support a psychology based on the medical model of diagnosis and treatment of disease. The ACA, on the other hand, supports a holistic approach based on a wellness model that includes the diagnosis and treatment of mental and emotional disorders but places more emphasis on mental *health* than on *illness*.

Nevertheless, the future success of either profession will depend largely on the public's trust in the field's practitioners. The public may not be willing to pay higher fees for a psychologist who is highly trained in academic subjects and research but insensitive to the spiritual dimensions evoked in a client during therapy. According to a recently administered Gallup poll in which 1,000 persons (50 percent male and 50 percent female) were surveyed, 67 percent preferred a professional counselor who recognized the importance of spiritual values and beliefs, and 81 percent preferred to have their own values and beliefs integrated into the counseling process. Yet because state legislatures (indirectly) and insurance companies (directly) regulate which types of mental-health professionals receive reimbursement—and in light of APA's defensive reaction against counseling's continued growth—it is not difficult to predict that the struggle for legitimacy will continue to revolve around political and economic issues more than idealogy and therapeutic efficacy.

All professional counselors hold at least a master's degree, and most have a bachelor's level major in psychology, sociology, or anthropology. Professional counselors provide mental-health, rehabilitation, substance abuse, employment, educational, and other counseling services in a variety of settings, including community mental-health centers, hospitals, schools, universities, hospices, and government agencies. In 1988 more than two out of three counselors were working in educational settings, mostly in secondary schools. Trends are showing an increase in noneducation settings such as community-based organizations and city agencies.

The counseling specialties we are most interested in are substance abuse and marriage and family counseling because both have found doorways into the spiritual. The spiritual foundation of Alcoholics Anonymous's Twelve-Step Program and the fact that many substance abuse counselors are themselves recovering from one or more addictions creates a natural alliance between psychological and spiritual aspects.

Originally, marriage and family counseling was part and parcel of the clergy's pastoral duties. However, with the growth of family therapy as a distinct specialty, and since the state of California's certification of marriage and family counselors as bona fide mental-health professionals, this area has gradually pulled away from its initial religious setting. Spirituality is returning to the field through the work of Harville Hendrix and his wife, Helen Hunt (see page 101). Also in California, many alternative therapies are being practiced under the aegis of marriage and family certification. Graduates of counseling programs in alternative schools like the California Institute of Integral Studies, for example, may apply for marriage and family counseling certification but employ Jungian, bodywork, and other modalities in their practice.

Organizations

American Association for Marriage and Family Therapy (AAMFT)
1133 15th Street, NW, Suite 300
Washington, DC 20005
(202) 452-0109 (phone)
(202) 223-2329 (fax)
www.aamft.org (website)

AAMFT lobbies for the advancement of marriage and family therapy, holds conferences for its members, and offers a referral service and speakers bureau. With a membership of 21,000, it's smaller than the California Association of Marriage and Family Therapists (CAMFT), which represents marriage, family, and child counselors (MFCCs) only in the state of California. However, AAMFT's numbers are misleadingly small because other licensed therapists (such as clinical social workers, psychiatrists, and psychologists) may practice marriage and family therapy but not necessarily join AAMFT. In other words, it's not just family therapists who practice family therapy.

American Counseling Association (ACA)
5999 Stevenson Avenue
Alexandria, VA 22304
(703) 823-9800 (phone)
(703) 823-0252 (fax)
www.counseling.org (website)

Founded in 1952, the ACA is a nonprofit professional and educational organization dedicated to the growth and enhancement of the counseling profession. The ACA is the largest international counseling organization in existence, with a membership of more than 50,000 counselors and human development specialists. Within the Mental Health Counselors Division of the ACA, there is a religion and mental-health interest group.

California Association of Marriage and Family Therapists (CAMFT)
7901 Raytheon Road
San Diego, CA 92111-1606
(619) 293-2638 (phone)
(619) 292-2638 (fax)
www.camft.org (website)

CAMFT is an independent professional organization that lobbies for the advancement of the Marriage and Family Counselor (MFC) license in the state of California. With approximately 23,000 members, it is the largest representative of marriage and family counselors in the United States. CAMFT is independent of the ACA and the AAMFT.

	Professional Training	Professional Credentials	Unique Characteristics
Body Psychotherapy	No national standardized official requirements have yet been developed	Currently no standardized certification process. Specific therapies (such as massage therapy) have certification and licensing regulations	Trained to combine talking and nonverbal physical methods to address problems that need mind/body level intervention
Clinical Psychology	Ph.D. or Psy.D. in clinical psychology or related field plus one year of clinical internship	Most states require Ph.D. or Psy.D. in clinical psychology or a related field plus 2,000 to 4,000 hours of supervised post-doctoral experience	Training in scientific and research techniques for administering and evaluating psychological tests (e.g., intelligence, personality, and neuropsychological, etc.)
Clinical Social Work	Master's of social work (M.S.W.) from school of social work	For license most states require an M.S.W. and 2 years of supervised experience	Consider contextual factors such as family, neighborhood, ethnic and socioeconomic status, etc.
Creative Arts Therapy	Master's degree in specific areas such as art therapy, dance therapy, music therapy, etc.	Certification offered through the various professional associations	Can use the arts as a medium for diagnosis and treatment of psychological problems

Professional Spiritual Expression	Membership*	Fees**	Referral
Varies among different schools and approaches	Varies among different schools and approaches. Newly formed United States Association of Body Psychotherapy (USABP) has 200 members	Not available	USABP can provide information on the different forms of body psychotherapy but no referrals: (301)587-4011 (phone); Goodrich @ ix.netcom.com (e-mail)
American Psychological Association has a Division of the Psychology of Religion; its Division of Humanistic Psychology sponsors transpersonal psychology presentations at the annual convention	140,000 psychologists, of whom 70,000 are licensed clinical psychologists	$100**	APA, (800) 964-2000 (phone); www.apa.org (website)
Society for Spiritually Sensitive Social Work, founded in 1990, explores the relationship of social work and spirituality. It publishes a newsletter and bibliography on religion and social work and holds an annual conference	155,000 M.S.W.s. Of these 75,000 are licensed clinical social workers and 25 percent are in private practice	$80**	National Association of Social Workers (NASW), (800) 638-8799, ext. 291 http://www.socialworkers.org (website)
None	11,500 members of the National Coalition of Arts Therapies Associations (NCATA)	Not available	NCATA c/o American Dance Therapy Association, 2000 Century Plaza, Suite 100, Columbia, MD 21044, (410) 997-4040

*It has been estimated that there are 4,000 practicing psychotherapists in the United States.

**These figures were provided in 1997 by *Psychotherapy Finances*, a newsletter for psychotherapists. For more information call (800) 869-8450.

	Professional Training	Professional Credentials	Unique Characteristics
Marriage and Family Therapy	Only recently have professional schools offered Master's and Ph.D. degrees in this specialty	M.A., Ph.D., M.F.T. or allied field (plus additional course work and 2 years of supervised experience). Other psychotherapy professions practice the discipline under their own license	Trained to work conjointly with whole family or couple when desirable
Mental Health Counselor	Master of arts in mental-health counseling or a related field	Most state licenses require M.A. in mental-health counseling or a related degree	Focus on regaining health rather than uncovering source of illness. Seeing counselor can be less stigmatizing than seeing psychiatrist or psychologist
Pastoral Counseling	No official requirements. American Association of Pastoral Counselors (AAPC) is working on developing criteria	No commonly agreed-upon requirements. Only four states currently license pastoral counselors	Because of theological training, some are prepared to read scripture and pray with client during sessions
Psychiatry	M.D. degree from medical school in addition to 1 year of medical internship and 3 years of residency in psychiatry	State licenses require M.D.	Prescribe medication when needed

Professional Spiritual Expression	Membership*	Fees**	Referral
None	46,000 licensed marriage and family therapists (20,000 in California, the first state to grant an M.F.T. license	$80**	American Association of Marriage and Family Therapists, (800) AAM-FT99, does not make referrals. Check the Yellow Pages under marriage and family therapy
American Counseling Association has a Religion and Mental Health Interest group within its Mental Health Division	80,000 licensed mental-health counselors	$75**	American Counseling Association (703) 823-9800
Intrinsic to field	3,000 members of AAPC	Not available	For referral to a member of AAPC, (703) 385-6967 (phone); www.metanoia.org.aapc (website)
Some members of the American Psychiatric Association present on transpersonal psychiatry	22,000 members of the American Psychiatric Association (APA) in the United States	$110**	Call (202) 682-6000 for the number of your state's branch of the APA

*It has been estimated that there are 4,000 practicing psychotherapists in the United States.

**These figures were provided in 1997 by *Psychotherapy Finances*, a newsletter for psychotherapists. For more information call (800) 869-8450.

✸ Spiritually Sensitive Social Work ✸

By Beth Baker

Unlike the scientifically based practices of psychiatry and psychology, social work has roots in the Christian and Jewish charitable work movements. Early on, however, there was a push for professionalism and a gradual abandonment of social work ties to religion.

In her autobiography, social worker Bertha Reynolds writes of her early teaching experience in 1926: "I could not agree that subjects connected with religion should be banned from intelligent discussion as syphilis and sex had been a few years earlier. Could we not overcome our reluctance to use the religious resources which clients might choose in their communities for better mental health?"

The profession answered Reynolds's query with a resounding no. When it came to understanding human behavior, theology was out and science was in. Proselytizing to social service clients was regarded as unseemly. As social work became more entwined with government agencies, separation of church and state further shoved aside religion and spirituality.

"Many of the cautions were well founded, but the mistake was throwing out the baby of spirituality with the bathwater of sectarianism," says Edward R. Canda of the University of Kansas, who directs the Society for Spirituality and Social Work.

In recent years, there have been signs of another shift. Out of 114 masters of social work (M.S.W.) programs, a dozen are part of religious institutions, including Catholic University and Southern Baptist Theological Seminary, the only Christian seminary to have an accredited M.S.W. program.

"What the school attempts to do is be current with its presentation of technique and theory, but we also want to make sure students can deal with issues that religiously oriented people come to grips with," says Southern Baptist faculty member Lawrence Ressler, who also serves as president of the North American Association of Christians in Social Work (NAACSW).

NAACSW, which has 1,100 members, was created to explore the relationship between social work and the evangelical Christian church. "NASW [National Association of Social Work] has neglected spiritual matters historically," says Ressler. "There's been a reemergence of spiritual and religious matters [in the public eye], but for the most part the profession hasn't given much attention to that."

Psychotherapists need to be able to address the spiritual concerns of their clients, Ressler says. "How can one not speak about religious matters when such a high percentage of people are religiously oriented?" he asks. "Social work says you begin where the client is. If you have clients who have religious thought as their underpinning, how can the profession be sensitive if they neglect or minimize those things, which are extremely important?"

A similar motivation—teaching social workers how to speak in the language of a particular faith—led to the creation of a dual master's program in social work and Jewish studies at the University of Maryland and Baltimore Hebrew University. University of Maryland professor Paul Ephross says students not only gain a firm foundation in social work but also learn about Jewish history, philosophy, and sociology, which enables them to better serve Jewish social-service agencies.

"Why do people come to the Jewish family service? The fact that it's Jewish has a lot to do with it," says Ephross. "For some, it's in their neighborhood and their community, for some it means 'These people will understand me,' for some it has to do with the values that underlie the service. You don't learn that in a public university school of social work."

Beyond these links between organized religion and social work programs, many clinical social workers and their clients are bringing a spiritual dimension to the psychotherapy process. Kelsey Menehan, a licensed clinical social worker who works with cancer patients in Takoma Park, Maryland, finds herself constantly handling spiritual concerns. "My patients are dealing with many levels of meaning and what's important. That brings in questions about 'Why did God allow this to happen?' I was really surprised how very often spiritual issues come up," she says.

Most schools of social work have yet to incorporate spirituality into the curriculum. Edward Canda has been encouraging the Council on Social Work Education to address the spiritual dimension in its revised curriculum policy statement. A modest step in this direction was made recently when the council added "religious and spiritual" to the variety of client backgrounds—along with social, cultural, racial, and class—that social workers should be prepared to work with.

"Social work educators are usually about ten years behind what is happening in clinical practice," says clinical social worker Belleruth Naparstek. When she came to teach at Case Western Reserve University in 1985, she offered to conduct a workshop on the spiritual dimensions of psychotherapy. "Colleagues thought I was nuts," she says, but she was allowed to offer the workshop through the continuing-education program. "They were expecting fifteen to twenty people—a hundred and forty-three showed up."

More recently, social work students requested that Naparstek teach a course on the same subject. "My course was nixed at the curriculum committee level," she says, despite much interest among students. "There's a terror that a course on spirituality will be too fruitloopy. Social work schools are overly concerned about being legitimate and being as 'good' as psychiatry and psychology."

Beth Baker is a contributing editor to *Common Boundary* magazine and freelance writer in Takoma Park, Maryland.

SPIRITUAL PSYCHOTHERAPY

The first major form of psychotherapy to take root in this country was psychoanalysis. Before the advent of Freudian psychoanalysis after World War I, moral exhortation and physical restraint had been the most frequently used tools for bringing about change in people's behavior. Psychoanalysis provided a quantum leap with regard to clinical theory and practice. Freud's introduction of the concept of the unconscious helped people understand that there were hidden reasons that explained why they behaved the way they did. Reaching insight into their history or the dynamics of their personality was supposed to give people the ability to choose a different pattern of behavior. For example, if a client understood that she was always attracted to older, married men because she desired a father figure in her life, the assumption was that this knowledge would help her change her behavioral pattern. Dreams and free association were the primary psychoanalytic means of uncovering the sources of one's hidden motivations. These techniques revolutionized the way people went about trying to change their behavior and their feelings.

For the most part, until the 1960s the Freudian model had the psychotherapy stage to itself. But society was changing. People had to develop an inner self to find meaning in a culture that no longer provided clear-cut social roles and whose social institutions were losing credibility, thus contributing to the erosion of commonly accepted values and beliefs. As people began to develop individual identities, they realized that they were more complex than the external social roles they played. They sensed that there was something more to them but did not have a way to explore and describe it. They felt empty and their life at times seemed to be meaningless. These twenty years, from 1960 to 1980, can be seen as a transitional period when people felt inwardly empty because they could no longer find meaning within their social roles and routines but had nothing else meaningful with which to replace them. During this period, existential philosophers spoke of needing the courage to be, regardless of having no belief system or outer authority to hold on to. Out of this dilemma evolved the humanistic-existential psychotherapy represented by American psychologists Carl Rogers, Rollo May, and Abraham Maslow, who, like self psychology pioneer Heinz Kohut, all came from the Freudian psychoanalytic tradition.

Unlike humanistic or existential psychotherapy, self psychology has remained within the framework and traditions of Freudian psychoanalysis, with some major changes in theory and practice. Whereas psychoanalysis addressed the psychic components of superego, ego, and id, self psychology specifically addresses disorders related to identity, theorizing that repair of the self should be the first priority before attempting to deal with unconscious material. Self psychology offers a therapy for the disorders of the complex selves that people are developing, but it remains a pathology-based model, not one that explores the farthest reaches of human nature, such as humanistic psychology's vision of self-awareness, growth, and the actualization of human potential.

Humanistic and existential psychotherapies and relational therapy are also responses to the perceived limitations of the Freudian framework. None explicitly embrace the spiritual dimension of psychotherapy. However, humanistic psychology provided a conceptual launching pad for those who would eventually go on to develop a transpersonal framework for psychotherapy. Once we move beyond the psychoanalytic framework, we discover a range of openness to spirituality among the various modes of psychotherapy. For example, shamanic counseling derives from the most ancient form of spiritual practice and works entirely within a spiritual framework. Jungian analysis, which grew out of psychoanalysis, reflects Jung's search "for something that might confer meaning upon the banality of life."

Common Elements of Spiritual Psychotherapy

The cumulative impact of the historical developments in these mental-health professions has been the creation of a new kind of psychotherapy that integrates a spiritual dimension. This psychotherapy in its generic form goes by many names, including transpersonal, holistic, and psychospiritual therapy, and also includes a large number of therapists of all orientations. Following are some of the prominent features of this therapy and its implications for both the client and the therapist:

- People have within themselves the seeds of their own healing.
- The therapist's own state of mind is a critical aspect of healing.
- The therapist is reciprocally affected by the client.
- Clinical diagnoses, such as depression, can have spiritual implications.
- Mind, body, and spirit are interrelated.
- All approaches to healing contain implicit values.
- There is awareness of other levels of knowing.
- There is a place for intuition, Divine guidance, and grace.

SELF PSYCHOLOGY

While the name is somewhat awkward and misleading, self psychology is rapidly becoming one of the most popular new forms of psychoanalysis. This psychological treatment of the disorders of the self (or personal identity) was developed by Austrian psychoanalyst Heinz Kohut, who moved to the United States in the 1950s after attending medical school in Vienna. He subsequently wrote a number of very influential books about people's need for what we are calling psychological nourishment (such as recognition, empathy, and love) and the damaging effect on their positive sense of self (healthy narcissism) when they do not receive sufficient amounts of this nourishment. Self psychology is a branch, an advance, and a modification of psychoanalysis that addresses the unmet narcissistic needs of patients. Self psychology practitioners are both cognizant of and sensitive to patients' needs for empathy and understanding, unlike psychoanalysis, in which analysts refrain from offering any emotional gratification.

Basic Theory

In order for children to create a healthy sense of self-love, they need to be seen for who they are rather than who their parents wish them to be. They need to receive sufficient empathic responses from parents to validate their feelings ("I see that you are feeling sad"), and their basic self-worth needs to be acknowledged ("You certainly worked hard on that project"). These kinds of responses are essential not only in childhood but throughout one's life. In order to maintain a stable positive feeling about their identity, people need regular supplies of affection, empathy, and recognition. If these needs are not met, people's positive feeling about themselves will begin to erode. They will compensate by focusing attention on things they believe will make them feel better, such as other people's evaluation of them as important, capable, and powerful.

If people are only temporarily compensating for a momentary deprivation of psychological nourishment, they will return to a state of equilibrium when their needs are met. However, if they did not receive sufficient psychological nourishment while growing up, their capacity to absorb nourishment now may be so damaged that they cannot bounce back.

Organizations

Institute of Contemporary Psychotherapy (ICP)
6256 Clearwood Road
Bethesda, MD 10817
(800) 432-0508 (phone and fax)

ICP was founded by a multidisciplinary group of colleagues in the Washington, D.C., Maryland, and Virginia area. ICP offers a comprehensive program in self psychological theory and clinical training in exploratory psychotherapy.

Institute for the Psychoanalytic Study of Subjectivity
350 West 58th Street
New York, NY 10019
(212) 582-1566

This institute offers a training program for candidates whose interest in psychoanalysis extends beyond clinical practice to include psychoanalytic scholarship and the development of psychoanalytic theory and research with a central interest in self psychology and intersubjectivity theory.

Psychoanalytic Psychotherapy Study Center (PPSC)
31 West 11th Street, Suite 1B
New York, NY 10011
(212) 633-9162 (phone)
(212) 675-4386 (fax)
ppsc@worldnet.att.net (e-mail)
www.infoteam.com/nonprofit/ppsc (website)

PPSC fosters a community of students, graduates, faculty, and staff who operate from the premise that psychoanalytic training is enriched by exposure to all major theoretical orientations, including Contemporary Freudian, Modern Psychoanalytic, Object Relations, and Self Psychology.

Training and Research Institute for Self Psychology
Society for the Advancement of Self Psychology
15 West 96th Street
New York, NY 10025
(212) 663-3508 (phone)
www.selfpsychology.org (website)

The institute is dedicated to encouraging discussion and disseminating information about Kohut's psychoanalytic psychology of the self and contemporary developments in that area. It also sponsors an annual conference.

RELATIONAL THERAPY

Until twenty years ago the dominant theory of human development held that people's sense of well-being comes from feeling self-sufficient, independent, separate, and superior to the "rest of the pack." While this underlying philosophy is seldom articulated in such raw terms, it has nevertheless been the unstated assumption underlying most modern human development theories. Until, that is, a group of psychotherapists at Wellesley College's Stone Center, inspired by the women's development researcher Carol Gilligan and psychotherapist Jean Baker Miller, realized that this stance, constructed by men and for men, was harmful not only to women's development but to men's as well. In 1976 the leader of the group, psychiatrist Jean Baker Miller, published a groundbreaking book, *Toward a New Psychology of Women,* in which she claimed that separation and ascendancy over others violated the "feminine" ideals of sensitivity and concern for others as well as running counter to women's desire for joining and establishing a sense of commonality. Not surprisingly, her book provoked considerable controversy.

In response the group began publishing a series of papers on relational aspects of psychotherapy. In one of these papers, psychologist Judith V. Jordan argues that if both people in a relationship are trying to be separate and elevated above the other, then both will experience a mutually defeating exchange that is deadening and isolating. Being meaningfully engaged in a relationship, Jordan believes, cannot occur when two people are trying to impress each other by managing the presentation of their self-image to get approval and accolades. Jordan acknowledges that receiving praise and mirroring are part of some relationships, but they are not as meaningful and nourishing, she says, as being able to connect in a deep way with another.

To demonstrate this point, Jordan gives an example of a therapist who allows herself to be vulnerable enough to let her client see that his expression of grief has palpably touched her. In a therapy session the client, who has difficulty expressing emotions, is talking about his father's lingering illness. The pain he feels is evident, and the therapist is moved by his expression of filial love. Her eyes well up with tears. When the client sees this, he realizes that he has affected another person. The therapist is not only listening to him and understanding his pain but is also empathizing with him. A natural human connection is made. In this interaction the client is helped by knowing that he matters to someone, thus lessening his feeling of isolation. Similarly, the therapist feels empowered by knowing that her response matters to the client. Jordan believes that people long for this mutual feeling of meaningful connection and that most psychological problems are at some level compensations for the lack of connection.

Jordan acknowledges that this approach is a radical shift from the conventional psychoanalytic mode of neutrality and distancing in which the therapist is not supposed to be influenced or affected by the client. This traditional therapeutic stance, she contends, resonates with the preoccupation of boys and men not to be influenced by others and can only end in mutual frustration.

In a telephone interview, Jordan acknowledged that the longing to connect extends to a spiritual longing to be part of "something larger," beyond the individual human psyche. She added that this model suggests that people are not primarily motivated by self-interest but profoundly want to contribute to the well-being of others and to participate in the growth of others. This involves moving out of narrowly defined egocentricity and transcending a sense of isolation and separation.

Books

Judith V. Jordan et al., *Women's Growth in Connection* (The Guilford Press, 1991). This collection looks at the ways relationships are central in women's lives. The need for connection is viewed as the primary human need, and these essays explore the ways in which this need develops, especially for women. The importance of empathy and mutuality in relationships is explored.

Judith V. Jordan, editor, *Women's Growth in Diversity* (The Guilford Press, 1997). This volume continues the work of *Women's Growth in Connection* by looking at the ways in which differences among women inform their participation in relationships. In particular it addresses issues of race, ethnicity, and sexual orientation. The movement out of isolation and shame into connection through relational therapy is explored.

Jean Baker Miller, *Toward a New Psychology of Women* (Beacon Press, 1976, 1986). This groundbreaking book examines the societal forces that have shaped women's development. It highlights the considerable strengths that women bring to relationships.

Jean Baker Miller and Irene Pierce Stiver, *The Healing Connection* (Beacon Press, 1997). This work explores the essential importance of connection in people's lives and particularly points to the importance of establishing a good connection in therapy.

Organizations

Stone Center
Wellesley College Center for Research on Women
106 Central Street
Wellesley, MA 02181-8268
(781) 283-2500 (phone)
(781) 283-2504 (fax)
epalmer@wellesley.edu (e-mail)
www.wellesley.edu/WCW/sub.html (website)

The Stone Center was founded in 1981 to conduct research on psychological development and the prevention of psychological problems among people of all ages as well as to provide services and research to enhance the psychological development of college students. The center publishes *Works in Progress*, a series of papers and audiotapes devoted to a better understanding of relationships.

✖ Analytical Psychology or Jungian Analysis ✖
By David Rosen

As a young Swiss psychiatrist, Carl Gustav Jung (1875–1961) was fascinated by the concept of the unconscious that the more senior psychiatrist Sigmund Freud (1856–1939) wrote about in *The Interpretation of Dreams* (1900). The book supported Jung's research on complexes (neurotic conflicts) and the unconscious mechanism of repression. In 1906 he was welcomed by Freud, who brought him into his inner circle and eventually anointed him the "crown prince" of psychoanalysis. This strong father-son bond made their parting in 1913 all the more painful.

Fortunately, Jung committed what I term *egocide*; that is, he figuratively killed off his false self or Freudian dominant ego image and identity to allow for the birth of his repressed true self. This process facilitated his accessing the collective unconscious and a larger universal awareness as his source of direction in determining the life story he was to live. Knowing that the story he was living was part of a larger story gave him the sense of purpose and meaning that literally saved his life.

Jung went on to make what is now considered the most important large-scale formulation since William James about the central role that spirituality plays in people's lives. Just as Copernicus showed that the earth revolved around the sun rather than vice versa, Jung argued that one's ego awareness was not the center of one's experience. At the center was the Self, a universal consciousness, of which one's ego was only a small subsidiary part. Similar to Copernicus, Jung's radical beliefs were not appreciated by his Freudian colleagues, and the conventional Freudian psychoanalysts saw him as a heretic.

Jung believed that the Self was the central archetype around which all the other archetypes were organized. One's spiritual life task is to surrender one's ego awareness in order to create an empty space in which the deeper movements of one's soul and spirit (or true self) can emerge. It is this surrender of the ego awareness to the greater Self that allows our lives to become radically different.

One of the major ways Jung found to surrender to the Self was through a process he called active imagination. Whereas leaders in the human potential movement advocated beating on pillows and screaming as a way of releasing one's authentic self from the constrictions of the false self, Jung believed that this energy needed to be channeled into creative forms such as painting, singing, dancing, and writing. He set his adult ego aside and adopted the state of mind of a three- to five-year-old child at play. He did this in the belief that the material that was released could take the form of universal archetypal symbols and open the door to a discovery of our personal connection to the universal.

For example, if you used crayons to draw a black withered tree without leaves, it might symbolize profound depression. Using a process that Jung called *amplification*, you might make associations, personal and archetypal, that might lead you to realize you were in a winter phase. True, you may appear dead, but upon questioning it becomes clear that your depression will lift just as spring naturally follows winter. Active imagination, which uses creative methods such as painting, drawing, movement, journaling, and so on, allows us to discover our own life story or personal myth.

Archetypes, according to Jung, are related to *imago Dei*, the image of God in human beings. A well-known expression of archetypes can be found in fairy tales and myths. They can also find life in a personal myth, an individual's story that resonates with universal themes and carries meaning for the person. For example, the story of the English environmentalists who were taken to court by McDonald's parallels the battle between David and Goliath.

While Jungian psychology overlaps considerably with transpersonal psychology, it differs in terms of emphasis. Whereas transpersonal theorists emphasize the importance of spiritual disciplines because of their capacity for transcending one's personal ego identification (a function Jung refers to as the work of animus, or spirit), Jungian psychology gives equal attention to matters of the soul (which Jung refers to as anima). Jung was concerned that with too much focus on spirit, people might become stuck at the "beyond the personal level" and not be sufficiently involved on the earth. Those who identify too completely with a divine image or archetype can start to believe that they *are* the divine archetype. For example, some patients in mental hospitals in the West believe that they *are* Jesus Christ.

As I maintain in *The Tao of Jung: The Way of Integrity*, Jung was essentially a Taoist. Like Lao Tzu and Chuang Tzu, Jung maintained that at birth we emerge out of wholeness, out of the Self or Tao, and that we strive to balance yin/yang, feminine/masculine, dark/light, anima/animus, soul/spirit, earth/sky, mother/father throughout our lives. We strive to balance elements that are the opposite of each other. In the end through death we enter back into the Self or Tao. Jung termed this process toward wholeness *individuation*.

There is some confusion outside the Jungian community regarding terminology. Jung referred to the field as *analytical psychology*. The term *Jungian analysis*, which essentially describes the same thing, became popular only after Jung's death.

Jungian societies, which exist in most major cities, can supply a list of analysts who have attended one of the institutes certified by the International Association for Analytical Psychology in Zurich, Switzerland. Most Jungian analysts do not ask their clients to lie on a couch facing away from them, as is done in traditional Freudian analysis, but sit face-to-face. They see their clients only once or twice a week at most instead of the three to five days a week in traditional Freudian analysis. Jungian analysts also tend to rely less heavily on interpreting their clients' free associations and spend more time with active imagination and looking at both the personal and archetypal dimensions of their clients' dreams.

David Rosen, M.D., is the McMillan Professor of Analytical (Jungian) Psychology at Texas A&M University, where he is also Professor of Psychiatry and Behavioral Science and Professor of Humanities in Medicine. He is the author of two recent books: *Transforming Depression: Healing the Soul through Creativity* (1996) and *The Tao of Jung: The Way of Integrity* (1997). Dr. Rosen is a senior Jungian analyst.

Certified Jungian Training Institutes

C. G. Jung Institute
116 St. Botolph Street
Boston, MA 02115
(617) 267-5984

C. G. Jung Institute
1567 Maple Avenue
Evanston, IL 60201
(847) 475-4848 (phone)
(847) 475-4970 (fax)
jung@jungchicago.org (e-mail)
www.jungchicago.org (website)

C. G. Jung Institute
10349 West Pico Boulevard
Los Angeles, CA 90064
(310) 556-1193 (phone)
(310) 556-2290 (fax)
jungla@earthlink.net (e-mail)
www.home.earthlink.net/~junginla (website)

C. G. Jung Institute
28 East 39th Street

New York, NY 10016
(212) 986-5458 (phone)
(212) 867-0920 (fax)
cgjungnyc@worldnet.att.net (e-mail)
www.cgjung.com (website)

C. G. Jung Institute
2040 Gough Street
San Francisco, CA 94109
(415) 771-8055 (phone)
(415) 771-8926 (fax)
stephen@sfjung.com (e-mail)
www.sfjung.org (website)

C. G. Jung Institute
320 Garfield Street, Suite 100
Sante Fe, NM 87501
(505) 989-8595 (voice mail)
(505) 989-4313 (programs)
(505) 984-0101 (training)

Those regions not served by an institute can affiliate with the Inter-Regional Society of Jungian Analysts, 4890 Isabella, Montreal, Quebec, H3WW 1SS, Canada, (514) 737-2235. Contact the institute closest to you for the name of the Jungian society in your geographic area.

Books

Joan Chodorow, editor, *Jung on Active Imagination* (Princeton University Press, 1997). This collection of Jung's writings on active imagination, gathered together for the first time, includes a discussion of Jung's writings and ideas in Dr. Chodorow's excellent introduction.

Clarissa Pinkola Estés, *Women Who Run with Wolves* (Ballantine Books, 1992). A classic, brilliant, and timeless collection of folktales, myths, and stories with interpretive narratives.

Calvin S. Hall and Vernon Nordby, *A Primer of Jungian Psychology* (New American Library, 1973, 1996). Selections from the vast writings of Jung present the elementary terms and themes of analytical psychology, trace the scope and direction of Jung's thought, and provide an introduction to his collected works.

Robert Johnson, *Inner Work* (Harper & Row Publishers, 1986). A primer on how to use dreams and active imagination. Johnson also wrote *He*, on men's psychology, *She*, on women's psychology, and *We*, on relationships. In these books he interprets a myth in order to shed light on basic inner dynamics.

C. G. Jung, *Memories, Dreams, Reflections* (Vintage Books, 1963). Jung's superb autobiography was recorded and edited by Aniele Jaffe.

Verena Kast, *Joy, Inspiration and Hope* (Fromm International Publishing Corporation, 1990). An uplifting volume on essential but neglected emotions in psychology.

David Rosen, *The Tao of Jung: The Way of Integrity* (Viking Arcana, 1996). An introduction to Jung, his psychology, and Taoism.

Andrew Samuels, *Jung and the Post-Jungians* (Routledge & Kegan Paul, 1985). A survey of the various branches and schools of Jungian psychology and how they are similar and different.

June Singer, *Boundaries of the Soul*, (Anchor Books, 1973). The best introduction to Jung's psychology, by an outstanding clinical psychologist and Jungian analyst.

Murray Stein, *Transformation: Emergence of the Self* (Texas A & M University Press, 1998). This book clearly elucidates the complicated psychological process of transformation. Also of note are his *In Midlife* (1984) and *Practicing Wholeness* (1995).

Anthony Stevens, *The Two-Million-Year-Old-Self* (Fromm International Publishing Corporation, 1993). A comprehensive, scientific, and clinical treatise on Jung's analytical psychology. Other books by Stevens—*Archetypes: A Natural History of the Self*, *On Jung*, and *Private Myths: Dream and Dreaming*—are well worth reading.

Marion Woodman, *Addiction to Perfection* (Inner City, 1982). This book grapples with the negative internal voices behind eating disorders and other addictions. Other titles by Woodman include *The Pregnant Virgin*, *The Ravaged Bridegroom*, and *Leaving My Father's House*, a book she cowrote with three other women.

Polly Young-Eisendrath, *Gender and Desire: Uncursing Pandora* (Texas A & M University Press, 1997). An illuminating treatise on gender and Jung's psychology. See also her other outstanding books: *You're Not What I Expected* (1993) and *The Gifts of Suffering* (1996).

Organizations

Centerpoint
c/o The Educational Center
6357 Clayton Road
St. Louis, MO 63117

(314) 721-7604 or (800) 624-4644 (phone)
(314) 721-2388 (fax)
TheEdCentr@aol.com (e-mail)

Founded in 1972, Centerpoint offers nondegree correspondence courses in Jungian-related subjects, publishes the newsletter *In Touch*, and sponsors an annual autumn Jungian conference held in New Hampshire.

C. G. Jung Foundation
28 East 39th Street
New York, NY 10016
(212) 697-6430 (phone)
(212) 953-3989 (fax)

The foundation offers educational programs for the lay public and maintains the Archives for Research in Archetypal Symbolism (ARAS) library. It also publishes *Quadrant: The Journal of Contemporary Jungian Thought*.

C. G. Jung Institute of Zurich
Hornweg 28
8700 Kusnacht
Zurich, Switzerland
01-910-53-23

Training at the Zurich Institute is not required for becoming a Jungian analyst, although Carl Jung's direct affiliation with it makes the institute an understandably prestigious choice.

Dallas Institute of Humanities and Culture (DIHC)
2719 Routh Street
Dallas, TX 75201
(214) 871-2440 (phone)
(214) 981-8805 (fax)

Founded in 1980 to awaken a sense of the sacred in the world through studies in literature, art, spirituality, psychology, architecture, city planning, and economics, the institute offers courses, seminars, and public conferences.

Journey into Wholeness (JIW)
P.O. Box 169
Balsam Grove, NC 28708
(704) 877-3568 (phone)
(704) 877-3568 (fax)

JIW programs combine spirituality and the psychology of Carl Jung.

New York Center for Jungian Studies
121 Madison Avenue, Suite 31
New York, NY 10016
(212) 689-8238 (phone)
(212) 889-7634 (fax)

The center sponsors the annual Jung-on-the-Hudson summer programs in Rhinebeck, New York.

Periodicals

Harvest: Journal for Jungian Studies
Spring Publications
P.O. Box 583
Putnam, CT 06260
(860) 974-3428 (phone)
(860) 974-3195 (fax)
spring@neca.com (e-mail)
www.neca.com/~spring (website)

A journal with both clinical and nonclinical contributions.

Journal of Analytical Psychology
Routledge Subscriptions
Blackwell Publications, Journals Division
350 Main Street
Malden, MA 02148
(617) 388-8200 or (800) 835-6770 (phone)
(617) 388-8210 (fax)
Lhill@blackwellpublishers.co.uk (e-mail)
www.blackwellpublishers.co.uk (website)
Quarterly; $83

The major scholarly research journal for the field.

Library Journal
C. G. Jung Institute of San Francisco
2040 Gough Street
San Francisco, CA 94109
(415) 771-8055 (phone)
(415) 771-8926 (fax)
stephen@sfjung.com (e-mail)
www.sfjung.org (website)
Quarterly; $36

This journal is dedicated to reviewing books relevant to readers interested in a Jungian perspective.

Psychological Perspectives
C. G. Jung Institute of Los Angeles
10349 West Pico Boulevard
Los Angeles, CA 90064
(310) 556–1193 (phone)
(310) 556–2290 (fax)
junginLA@earthlink.net (e-mail)
home.earthlink.net/~junginLA (website)
Biannual; $20
    This journal seeks to integrate psyche, soul, and nature through its essays, articles, short fiction, poems, visual art, and reviews.

Round Table Review
P.O. Box 807
Port Washington, NY 11050–2319
(610) 647–4235 (editorial)
(516) 883–8620 (subscriptions)
RTReview@aol.com (e-mail)
5 issues; $21.50
    A comprehensive review of Jungian work and activities.

Quadrant: The Journal of Contemporary Jungian Thought
C. G. Jung Foundation
28 East 39th Street
New York, NY 10016
(212) 697–6430
Semiannual; $32 individual
    A journal with both clinical and theoretical papers.

Spring: A Journal of Archetype and Culture
P.O. Box 583
Putnam, CT 06260
(860) 974–3428 (phone)
(860) 974–3195 (fax)
spring@neca.com (e-mail)
www.neca.com/~spring (website)
Semiannual; $24

This journal focuses on publishing articles with an archetypal psychology perspective.

Websites

The Eranos Foundation
www.eranosfoundation.com
This website provides information about the Eranos Foundation, an organization formed around annual meetings with C. G. Jung in Ascona, Switzerland. Conference topics always relate to aspects of psychology, anthropology, religion, and the classics.

www.cgjung.com
This site was established to stimulate conversations among analysts, students, scholars, and friends of Jung. It has a list of Jungian publishers, a forum for discussion, editorial page, articles, and interviews.

Jung Net On-Line
www.Jungindex.net
This site includes editorials, book reviews, links, e-lists, etc.

❀ Working with the Mysterious Dream Maker: ❀
A Brief Summary of My Work in Analytical and Archetypal Psychology

By Clarissa Pinkola Estés

In the archetypal and analytical psychology of symbols, images, and myths, I find that the strengthening and refining of one's ability to realize the psyche's drive to consciousness and thereby to enact a creative and soulful life is what causes the gradual transformation of the psyche's leaden sleepiness into a golden awareness of the self and the greater Self. The process of striving toward transformation is known as *individuation*. The interpretation of dreams, images, and myths is understood as a way to illuminate this process. Carl Gustav Jung, the Swiss psychiatrist, held that a purposeful psychology centered on insights into the pragmatic journey of the soul and psyche toward knowing the greater Self. He compared this process to an alchemical transformation. In this metaphor, the base lead of the psyche can become, through one's striving toward consciousness, an extraordinary gold.

Over my nearly three decades of clinical practice, I have found that the kind of individual who derives great benefit from analytical, archetypal, and depth psychology is often one who is an artist, or who is gifted in other ways; one who is interested in images, who has the ability or the desire to understand layers of metaphor, the symbolic language of dreams and images. Scientific minds that are interested in mystery and rational understanding are also drawn to this work. Because psychoanalysts who are trained to be practitioners in this psychological discipline come from varied backgrounds, bringing their various personalities and typologies to the work, there are ample opportunities for persons of many different personality styles and points of view to find excellent analytic matches.

However, even the deepest forms of analysis, though likely to provide symbolic insights, will not, at this time, cure organic disorders. The latter are best treated in conjunction with other medical modalities. Once stabilized organically, a person can undertake analysis successfully. A sturdiness of ego formation greatly assists the efficacy of an analytic undertaking. By whichever name—analytical, archetypal, or depth psychology—the process is suitable for psychic, creative, and spiritual development for an extremely broad spectrum of individuals.

The Golden Self-Awareness of Individuation

One specific concept useful to understanding the individuation process is that of the *daimon*. *Daimon* is the name Socrates gave to the inner voice, a deep intuition that urges us to travel in one direction or another in life and, *for a purpose*—that of becoming wise, developing one's talents, meeting one's calling, and seizing one's destiny.

Listening to the inner intuitions of one's daimon enables one to gradually perceive and thence to unravel many insights necessary for unfolding the life of soul. The perception of a personal destiny is much deeper, much broader than the ego's goals alone. Because the ego too often responds to superficial external and internal pressures and appetites, it cannot be entirely relied upon to guide the journey of the psyche toward knowledge and soulfulness. Rather, the daimon, typified symbolically as "the great mind" or as the "still, small voice," can also, or instead, guide. This often occurs naturally when one has gathered enough years of knowing. It is this mysterious interior sensibility that helps to infuse the mundane psyche with the treasure of a creative self-awareness—one that flows inwardly, as well as outwardly, toward the world.

Striving toward the immense creativity of soul and psyche is a self-full, rather than a selfish, endeavor. One's work toward a useful and noble life, inquiry into the roles and uses of suffering, and experiencing the satisfaction of living a creative life—all these evolve by using one's imagination to perceive the mythic dimensions present in daily experiences with dreams, meaningful coincidences (synchronicity), and images and impulses that arise spontaneously in the psyche.

One advances through the individuation process by, consciously or not, separating from the collective and gradually becoming oneself in an undivided manner. By gathering one's night dreams and daydreams, by paying close attention to symbols and images that arise or capture the imagination, one taps into these deeper and more meaningful layers of the psyche. By using archetypal patterns to amplify the myriad meanings therein, one experiences more than one might in ordinary states of awareness alone.

For example, we spend most of our waking hours with our minds dominated by mundane experiences. We refer to our banal experiences as consensual reality, that is, a particular view of the world we all, more or less, agree upon. We share a broad consensus about what things mean—that is, a house is just a house and a tree is just a tree. However, when we move into a more mythic dimension and enter into a different way of observing and thinking, which are a combination of daytime rationality, imagination, and nighttime dreaming, then ordinary objects and events often take on extraordinary meanings—a house is an image that might call to mind a structure that has many rooms, perhaps like the psyche itself; a tree, in mythos, may be understood as a schema for living life, like the patterns explicated in the Hebrew kabbalah, which teaches about the Tree of Life.

Imagine that a man dreams of a great serpent. The dream penetrates his consciousness as a thorn pierces flesh. The image of the serpent does not quickly fade from his consciousness. Something within him resonates to this image, perhaps in fear or fascination, or both. When we apply rationality and imagination to amplify a symbol archetypally, we realize the serpent has meanings other than the ordinary. The symbol of the serpent carries layers of history from far back in time through to the present. The dreamer thus finds unique and formerly unknown resonances in this symbol; both symbol and now dreamer too are richer in meaning. It is almost as though dream images demand to be contemplated and puzzled through in order to release their hold on the dreamer, in order that the dream's meanings and potentials for elucidation stand fully revealed to the one who is seeking.

Once unfolded, the layers of meaning in the dream image are likely to be ingenious and startling, in both portent and effectiveness. Most often, unfolding the many layers of meaning inherent in an image prompts us to look beyond mundane understanding, to the work of the soul. Images can cause material or momentum to be moved from one place in the psyche to another, thereby igniting a transformative process, wherein a more conscious soul terrain is created; that is, a realization that one does not live in only one facet of existence alone, but on several, all at the same time—not in confoundedness or in a fantasy, but in a more and more orderly and creative wholeness.

The dream or symbol prompts one to think, to strive to understand in different and nonordinary ways, to realize that there are other layers of meaning in day-to-day experiences, that most events carry transformative sparks that differ from the ordinary surface-only meanings usually assigned to them. Though we may lose track of the individuation process off and on throughout life, we return again and again to the sense that we live at several levels all at once, and that weaving these strands together constitutes the sense of psychic wholeness we strive for in soul, spirit, mind, and body.

There also exist spiritual layers of the psyche that can be experienced through images. These states are extraordinary because in the dream state we find ourselves no longer situated solely in the ego—but also seated in the greater territory of that which is called the Self. In analytical, archetypal, and depth psychology, the Self is perceived as a force that is the center of the psyche, as well as larger than the psyche alone. Jung saw the Self as a numinous archetypal image of our fullest potential.

Dream States

Dream states carry us into the mysterious realms of our psyches. In *curanderismo*, it is said that there are waking trance states that allow us to experience life beyond the reaches of our rational thinking capacity, and in ways that fuel creative reason, sometimes in addition to and sometimes in contrast to a sequential logic. Experiencing these states urges us to transmit, through whichever form of artistic expression we might choose—song, paint, poetry, dance, and more—whatever it is that we have perceived.

The creative, symbol-making capacity of the psyche was put forth in Jung's empirical explorations of the psyche. Maintaining a pursuit of the symbolic life can often help when we are in distress. Symbolic expression urges us to fashion a creative act that will consciously inaugurate and gradually bring about an evolution of mind, body, and spirit. This helps greatly to move the psyche off ground zero.

The Self also appears to have vast compassionate resources. For instance, on television we see how a poor small family eating dinner in Sarajevo is hit by a mortar that kills the young daughter and hits the mother in the belly, decimating her flesh, so that even if she recovers, she will never again bear children. When we see egregious and heinous assaults on innocent human beings, we cannot help but feel not only grief, but also anguish and compassion.

Why do we cry out for someone we do not know, for a family on the other side of the world that we are unlikely ever to meet? I believe we cry out because the Self is filled with empathic and profound mystical love that transcends all known boundaries. The Self finds in others its own likeness and its most sensitive linkages with all other human beings. Whether it is oneself or a stranger that is being harmed, one feels one's own spirit being massacred. Taslima Nasrin, the fierce and brave Bangladeshi poet, whose work I know from being involved with writers in prison through PEN [an organization made up of poets, playwrights, essayists, editors, and novelists], writes: ". . . a woman is being stoned [by men in the marketplace]. I feel her pain in my head. Do you not feel it also?" When we enter the compassion of the Self, we may feel as though we have been touched by the wings of angels who are completely unafraid of the darkest hells—our own hells, and those of others.

Images, dreams, fantasies, and daydreams offer us flashes and tastes of creativity, strength, insight, and transformation evoked by closeness to the divine Self and given through us to others. In these cases it is as if our tears become for a moment diamonds, shining light on the mysterious ties humans have with each other. These understandings manifest physically: There may be sudden flashes of knowing, which like a great opening of the heart embrace what seems inconsolable in us and transform it in significant ways so as to make meaning. Also, this awakening to the Self often moves us to help mediate others' pains and agonies, whenever and wherever we might be able. This too is an outcome of a consciously pursued deep individuation, which brings us nearer to the life of the soul and also nearer to the world than ever before.

The symbol-making function of the psyche appears to react to our own suffering and to our realization of the suffering of others. The psyche gives off enormous numinosity; that is, evocative images and ideas that rouse and infuse us. These symbols reach far down into the wonder- and wholeness-seeking self. It is as if the symbols are leading us toward the greater Self that indicates, "I can see that you long for a place where there is yet left a definable and dependable ground of hope, creativity, and insight. Yes, come stand here with me."

Yet there is also a caveat. Even as I speak about this, it must be said too that the clearest experience of these matters is like hearing a pure prolonged tone when you are alone. Efforts to explain one's deepest experiences of a conscious individuation process to others often cause necessary stammers and clatterings. Even though we might manage to explain the *process*, we cannot even come close to explaining its *essence*. Words alone cannot describe the numinosity of the transformative function. It must be experienced.

When a conscious individuation is undertaken, some small communication about its effects can be made known. Certainly there will be changes in lifestyle, behavior, and deportment. The great artists of the world have, through art, writing, music, and poetry, made their best efforts to convey the ineffable. Experiences of the essence of dreams and what might be called "the mysterious dream maker" remain available to all, but the process is not explainable in mechanistic ways, rather and most often in artful ways. Nevertheless, the soul and spirit appear often to be extraordinary as well as ordinary, and most people are able to comprehend these psychic facts naturally and fully, and to feel their knowledge of the world in psyche greatly increased, their creativity and insights greatly enabled.

The Mythic Dimension

In addition to investigating expansive, deepening, and healing images from our dreams and daily lives, meaningful mythic patterns also seem to be lodged in the simple recall of prior events in one's family life—the joys, banalities, and traumas. Moreover, there appears to be an entire pattern at the core of every life event that, when unfolded and understood as narrative or story, spills out its own mythic elements.

Imagine that a woman has a psychological issue with her father. In analysis, she might consider the mundane facts, but also consider the issue in the context of the myth of Electra or Medea or the narrative of Cordelia or other personages whose lives commingle with archetypal patterns of the father. This dual manner of inquiry assists the person in measuring her issues in the context of both cognitive and imaginal worlds. This can help a woman begin to understand the many layers of her relationship with her father, often causing her to feel less divided, less one-sided, less bereft, and gradually more illumined.

In amplifying a person's life events, as in the case of a woman longing for an authentic relationship with her emotionally distant father, a modern synthesis can be applied as well. For instance, in William Styron's brilliant novel *Sophie's Choice*, the heroine longed to be with her father and found herself constantly trying to be "useful" to every man in her life, even when it went against her own basic needs, both ethical and emotional. This situation is ubiquitous. For most women, an overly dutiful attachment to the father is not composed of sexual feeling. Wanting to be with and to please only one parent, to the exclusion of the other parent as well as all others, points to a daughter who is wounded by her father's lack of a heartfelt relationship with her.

In such lives, the daughter often willingly sacrifices all of her own feelings and her own thoughts because they do not fit well with what her father feels and thinks. She becomes the blood sacrifice of the family: willing to figuratively cut off every arm, leg, finger, and toe that does not conform to the shapes her father has hollowed out for her. She does this so that she can feel "loved." She feels that to be lovable she must be what the father most desires, whether it makes sense to her or not.

Recognizing the mythic patterns of one's family life can expand one's viewpoint, free one from prescribed or rote behavior, and ultimately mend and expand the psyche, as well as one's relationships with others.

Taking Analysis Beyond the Individual Session

I have been deeply influenced by one of my most beloved elder teachers this past twenty years. Dr. Arwind Vasavada, a Jungian psychoanalyst, originally from Bombay, India, manages what he terms "a fee-less practice." Although much of my clinical training is in diagnostics, fifteen years ago I ceased supplicating for health insurance reimbursements. As a specific kind of healer, I felt it was best to be guided by the client's real life, not by often ill-fitting diagnostic codes required for remuneration by insurance companies. The health insurance industry at present does not have a diagnostic code for "angst for and of the soul." No. In order to create a comfort zone for my analysands, I lowered my fees, keeping them moderate, so as not to make anyone dependent on an industry that seems to forget that the word *psychology* is the study not of *logos* but of the *soul*.

About 30 percent of my work is near gratis for students and pensioners who are struggling financially. There is a long waiting list, but as a Latina from the underclass who was once a single mother raising children, I was encouraged by several souls while working hard for my education for many long years. To proceed in this way now seems right and proper. I do not see people as frequently as some might in other offshoots of analytical psychology. It takes time for matters to cook. The analysis is deep and the psyche is patient. One ought not to take the lid off the pot too often or too soon. Cooking too fast psychologically can leave the middle undone. Cooking slowly and consistently is best for most of those with whom I work.

I believe a weekly analysis with a diplomate Jungian psychoanalyst is a very desirable endeavor. I also diverge from some of the older psychoanalytic customs by encouraging people who have adequate knowledge and ability to form their own leaderful, or leaderless, groups for dream analysis. Images are accessible to everyone. Although an individual analysis is extremely powerful, not all persons, especially those of very little means and those who have dependent children, can easily afford it. Alternately, I recommend saving up for a one-on-one analytic session with a psychoanalyst from time to time to critically check and/or to reset the compass one is using on one's own inner voyage.

I encourage people who are single parents, working more than one full-time job, or those who for whatever reason cannot afford weekly analysis, to come together and choose a useful book, read it, and discuss it in order to study their inner lives together. They ought also to study and work with the symbols and images in everyone's dreams.

Dreams are so profoundly imaginative and informational that one could literally spend years analyzing the many layers of a single dream, its mundane, objective, subjective, imaginal, archetypal, and mythic meanings.

In a dream analysis group, one person ought to tell a dream. Then, each person can speak to that dream, with it and about it, as though it were his or her own dream. Each can say how they would feel about such a dream. No one's dream is separate from anyone else's life. This sharing of dream images does much to rouse the compassionate Self.

As Walt Whitman wrote:

The grass before me and the very soil of the earth
I am made up of those.
I am not separate from anything that has atoms.

Matters seldom go wrong in leaderless groups unless one person decides to manipulate, exploit, or criticize another in a way that hurts the heart instead of bringing respect to bear all around. Happily, with maturing individuals of good-will, regard for one another most often grows more and more stable with each gathering.

The Need for Community and a Daily Practice

I am not a joiner or a "true believer." But I have memberships in several communities by virtue of birth, vocation, mercy, and blessing. I am a practicing Catholic, and in addition to an intense lifetime consecration to *La Nuestra Señora Guadalupe* (Our Lady of Guadalupe), my family and I belong to a small faith community of several families that meet for Mass in the home of our seventy-five-year-old monsignor. Our celebrant has taught first-grade children all of his priestly life, and so has a heart as close to that of a child as anyone could imagine. He also has a deep devotion to She Who Is Clothed Like the Sun, Our Lady, in all her representations. We love him as family, and he, us.

I also belong to a worldwide community of distinguished and talented Jungian analysts, as well as to a worldwide community of dedicated souls who work for social justice, who speak up for those who cannot speak for themselves. I am part of a hardscrabble community of performance poets, and we raise heck whenever we can. I belong to several other groups that have in their midst the call to help, to heal, and to protect others.

As I traveled throughout the country after publishing *Women Who Run with the Wolves* and read the many heartfelt letters I received from readers, I saw clearly that many, many people did not have a group of people to belong to, did not have a practice to reorient to the Self day after day. To assist in creating this, I founded the Desert School, held at different locations throughout the nation. During the Desert School, participants learn how to enter into the ancient tradition of the Great Silence, a tradition that taught the passions of prayer, solitude, walking meditations, and self-examination.

I also began to encourage people to inaugurate their own circles. Group praying is different from solitary praying. I recommend reading about the monastic communities of Hildegard of Bingen and Mechtild of Magdeburg and modeling after them. I hope to remind people that a *sangha* or a monastery can be built anywhere—in the shattered-glass cities, in palaces, in the most hospitable and in the most inhospitable environs. It only takes two souls—one great soul, and one Greater.

> Clarissa Pinkola Estés, Ph.D., is an internationally recognized scholar, award-winning poet, certified senior Jungian psychoanalyst, and *cantadora*, a keeper of old stories in the Latina tradition. Translated into twenty-two foreign languages, her bestselling book *Women Who Run with the Wolves: Myths and Stories of the Wild Woman Archetype* has been hailed as the seminal work on the instinctual nature of women. Other books by Dr. Estés include *The Gift of Story: A Wise Tale About What Is Enough,* and *The Faithful Gardener: A Wise Tale About That Which Can Never Die.* Her next book, forthcoming from Alfred A. Knopf, is *The Dangerous Old Woman.*

HUMANISTIC PSYCHOLOGY

Humanistic psychology was another rebellion against Freudian determinism. Abraham Maslow studied creative people, such as Eleanor Roosevelt and others. He found that people not only need the basics that Freud talked about: food, warmth, sex, and other necessities, but they also have another type of need—for sunsets, for creative work, and for spirituality.

Maslow and others began to develop humanistic psychology in the 1950s. The field started small; for some years adherents met in one small room during the conventions of the American Psychological Association (APA). Through the years, however, humanistic—and existential—psychology have brought lasting changes to the psychotherapy field. The once dominant Freudians are now a small group, and most psychotherapists now work with an emphasis on the development of the person with empathy and care for what arises in clients from inside.

The core of the humanistic movement is the importance of trusting one's internal experience as opposed to an external belief system. What is most important in this view is inner experience, how one actually feels inside. This new focus on self-development and self-exploration ultimately opened up questions about the heights to which one's consciousness could grow. Instead of trying to adjust to the society around them, people began having aspirations higher than simply coping. Releasing one's potential became a possibility, and many techniques were developed for doing this. Thus a sizable and visible subgroup in the culture, known as the human potential movement, developed a new set of group rituals that permitted screaming loudly, beating pillows with tennis racquets, encountering one another in hot tubs, and touching and holding each other in twenty-four-hour marathon groups, as ways of releasing one's inhibitions and social constraints and finding one's authentic self.

Today existential and humanistic psychologies and the human potential movement are not as visible as they were when they were at the height of popularity. This is due in large measure to the development of transpersonal psychology, body psychotherapy, the arts therapies, and other therapeutic methods such as Eye Movement Desensitization Reprocessing (EMDR).

Organizations

Association for Humanistic Psychology (AHP)
45 Franklin Street, #315
San Francisco, CA 94102-6017
(415) 864-8850 (phone)
(415) 864-8853 (fax)
ahpoffice@aol.com (e-mail)
www.ahpweb.org (website)
    Founded in 1962, AHP is a worldwide network for the development and application of human sciences that recognize the distinctly human qualities and innate potentialities of each individual. AHP links, supports, and stimulates those who share this humanistic vision of the person.

Division of Humanistic Psychology (Division 32)
American Psychological Association
750 First Street, NW
Washington, DC 20002
(202) 336-5500
    or
c/o Dr. Christopher Aanstoos
Psychology Department
University of West Georgia
Carrollton, GA 30118
(710) 836-4578
    This division publishes the journal *The Humanistic Psychologist*.

Midwest Association for Humanistic Psychology
6826 Chrysler Street

Indianapolis, IN 46268
(317) 592-1875 (phone)
(317) 328-1475 (fax)
midwestahp@aol.com (e-mail)

The Midwest AHP conference, held every year in March at the Indianapolis Marriott, is a gathering of people from a variety of disciplines interested in the journey of self-discovery, acquiring new information for working with clients, and self-renewal.

Periodicals

The Humanistic Psychologist
Psychology Department
University of West Georgia
Carrollton, GA 30118
(770) 836-4578 (phone)
(770) 836-6791 (fax)
3 times a year; $15

This is the official publication of the Division of Humanistic Psychology (Division 32) of the American Psychological Association.

Journal of Humanistic Psychology
Sage Publications
2455 Teller Road
Thousand Oaks, CA 91320-2218
(805) 499-9774 (phone)
(805) 499-0871 (fax)
order@sagepub.com (e-mail)
www.sagepub.com (website)
Quarterly; $56 individual; $209 institution

This journal is the official publication of the Association of Humanistic Psychology, with Saybrook Institute providing editorial support. Topics of special interest are authenticity, identity, personal growth, self-actualization, I-Thou encounters, existential and humanistic politics, synergy, creativity, and holistic learning.

✿ Spirituality and the Recovery Movement's ✿ Twelve-Step Program

By John Davis

Participation in a Twelve-Step Program is a spiritual practice. When you introduce yourself at the beginning of a Twelve-Step meeting by saying, "My name is John and I'm an alcoholic" (or whatever substance you abuse), you are saying the very thing you have wanted to avoid. This acceptance of your addiction as a part of your identity is a transformative experience because now you are no longer hiding it as if it were a badge of shame. You are also transformed when you listen as other members tell their life stories in a way that is genuine and authentic. And finally, when others are telling their stories, you may go into an altered state or trance, which is similar to when you watch a gripping film or theater performance that transports you out of your ordinary ego state. As they are telling their stories, your unconscious may start to "digest" your own story in a new way, and you may find yourself telling yourself your own story in a different way while they are telling theirs.

One of the cardinal rules of the Twelve-Step Programs that make this work different from that of other groups (and even group therapy) is the rule of no cross-talk. This is an important rule because cross-talk, feedback, or group discussion may be contaminated by other's unconscious projections or judgments. This freedom from judgment is critical because when you are "confessing," the Twelve-Step Program is like a meditation practice. You sit and watch your statements pass by without you or anyone judging them. This kind of unconditional acceptance is hard to find elsewhere in our society.

Four Basic Tenets of the Twelve-Step Program

While there are twelve steps in all recovery programs, there are four basic tenets to the recovery movement:

1: Honesty. Members are expected to be completely honest in what they say. This has vast healing powers because there are few places that allow for this kind of authenticity. As members are honest with the group, they find they can be more honest with themselves.
2: Community. Feeling deep relationship and connection with others and their life stories reduces alienation, isolation, and loneliness. We may have used substances to substitute for relationships and connections that were missing in our lives, but the substances only momentarily relieved our loneliness, isolation, and lack of connection.
3: Relationship with a Higher Power. Many people abuse substances as a way of numbing their heartache and longing for connection with that which is larger

than we are. Without such an anchor, we do not feel whole and always sense that something essential is missing in our lives. Several of the Twelve Steps are used for evaluating our relationship with this Higher Power.

4:   Abstinence from substance abuse. This is both a goal and a basic necessity.

Why Twelve-Step Programs Favor Jung Over Freud

Sigmund Freud had a cocaine addiction and a nicotine addiction so strong that he continued to smoke even after he was treated for cancer of the jaw. In short, Freud did not understand the treatment of addiction, nor is his theory compatible with Twelve-Step Programs. Freud believed that psychological problems were the result of early traumatization and that we built up psychological defenses or resistance as a response to this trauma. Leaders of the recovery movement, however, do not focus on a person's past traumas but are more interested in what the person is becoming. The focus is on what will help people achieve wholeness rather than on tracking down the origins of their problems. Jung said that there was no recovery from alcoholism without a spiritual awakening. The founders of Alcoholics Anonymous were greatly influenced by Jung's writings concerning the need for putting spirituality at the center of one's life. This is also a critical difference from the Freudian approach.

The Impact of Codependency

In the early 1990s, the notion of codependency took hold—the idea that for every person who is dependent on substances, there is another person who is dependent on the other person's continuing abuse. The codependent therefore "enables" or makes it possible for the other person to continue his or her substance abuse. All over the country, large numbers of Co-Dependents Anonymous Twelve-Step Programs were started. The plight of the adult children of alcoholics (ACOA) was chronicled in a spate of popular books that listed the disabling symptoms of those who grew up in alcoholic (or as they were called, dysfunctional) families.

John Bradshaw's very popular PBS television series and his bestselling books on these topics stimulated more interest, accelerating the level of activity almost to a frenzy, and the original kernel of truth was blown out of proportion. Codependence became a justification and rationalization for being a victim. Today the number of Co-Dependents Anonymous and Adult Children of Alcoholics meetings have waned. In the Baltimore area, for example, meetings are down from 120 to 60 a week. Despite these declining numbers, the naive view that it is only the substance abuser in a family that suffers and needs help has been abolished for good.

John Davis, Ph.D., is the founder of The Resource Group in Baltimore, Maryland, and a therapist and innovator in the chemical dependency field.

Books

Alchoholics Anonymous, 3rd ed. (1976). AA's "Big Book" is the basic text that contains the principles of recovery as well as stories written by dozens of recovered alcoholics. It is available at most AA meetings.

William Alexander, *Cool Water: Alcoholism Mindfulness and Ordinary Recovery* (Shambhala Publications, Inc., 1997). AA suggests living "one day at a time." This guide describes how to live in the present moment by applying the mindfulness approach of Zen Buddhist meditation.

John Bradshaw, *Bradshaw On: The Family* (Health Communications, Inc., 1988). A good summary of family dynamics and family dysfunction with regard to addictive behaviors.

Gerald G. May, *Addiction and Grace* (HarperSanFrancisco, 1991). As a psychiatrist and a spiritual director, May argues that addiction is a sacred illness that requires us to recognize our need for grace.

Pia Mellody, *Facing Co-Dependence* (HarperSanFrancisco, 1989). The best, most useful treatment of recovery from codependence.

Janet Woititz, *Adult Children of Alcoholics* (Health Communications, Inc., 1983). The first and possibly the best description of this problem.

Organizations

AA National Office
P.O. Box 459
Grand Central Station
New York, NY 10163
(212) 870-3400 (phone)
(212) 870-3003 (fax)
www.aa.org (website)

Write for lists of books and publications. For local meetings, look in telephone directory under Alcoholics Anonymous.

Adult Children of Alcoholics (World Service Organization)
P.O. Box 3216
Torrance, CA 90510
(310) 534-1815 (phone)
aca.Lafn.org (e-mail)

Check your telephone directory for local meetings.

Al-Anon/Alateen Family Group Headquarters
1600 Corporate Landing Parkway
Virginia Beach, VA 23454-5617
(757) 563-1600 (phone)
(757) 563-1655 (fax)
www.al-anon.alateen.org (website)
    For local meetings, check your telephone directory.

Salvation Army
P.O. Box 269
Alexandria, VA 22313
(703) 684-5500 (phone)
www.salvationarmy.org (website)
    The Salvation Army developed the first treatment program for alcoholics in 1840 and is still the nation's largest treatment program.

Workaholics Anonymous
P.O. Box 289
Menlo Park, CA 94026–0289
(510) 273-9253 (phone)
wa2@juno.com (e-mail)
www.ai.mit.edu/people/wa (website)
    Founded in 1983, this organization aims to help those who suffer from compulsion to work.

Work-Anon
(914) 235-6026
    Founded by Barbara G., the spouse of the founder of Workaholics Anonymous, this group speaks to those in a relationship with a workaholic.

⚘ Shamanism, Shamanic Journeying, ⚘ and Shamanic Counseling

By Michael Harner and Sandra Ingerman

A shaman is a man or woman who makes journeys to spiritual realms in an altered state of consciousness to bring back information and healing for others. These are typically journeys to what are known cross-culturally as the Upper and Lower Worlds. Shamanism is not limited to such journeys, but they are perhaps the most distinctive aspect of shamanic practice.

    Shamanism, the earliest known spiritual practice, dating back 30,000 to

40,000 years, is known to have been practiced in most indigenous cultures, including those in Australia, Africa, North and South America, Siberia, and other parts of Asia and Europe, surviving into the twentieth century in Samiland (Lapland).

The shaman's change of consciousness for journeying to other realms is most typically facilitated by monotonous percussive sound, such as drumming, or, in a minority of cultures, by the ingestion of psychotropic plants.

The name *shaman* comes from the Tungus people of Siberia. It is used today to avoid terms such as *medicine man, wizard, magician,* and *witch doctor,* which have ambiguous meanings in our language and do not necessarily apply to someone who makes the distinctive journey of the shaman.

How Shamanism Works

Shamanism is system of methods rather than a religion. Shamans depend upon helping spirits such as power animals and spirit teachers to provide advice and healing. Power animals are personally acquired guardians, as opposed to totem animals, which are the ancestors of all members of a tribal clan.

Shamans are best known as healers and diviners, working to relieve suffering and to help obtain solutions to problems in their communities. By journeying to other worlds, the shaman is able to go beyond prayer to interact directly with divine powers.

Shamans can also be psychics, mediums, or channelers, but their work remains distinguished by the journeys into nonordinary reality. Shamans should also be distinguished from priests and similar ceremonial leaders whose ritual work does not involve the shamanic journey.

What Is Core Shamanism?

Core shamanism consists of basic universal or near-universal shamanic principles and practices found worldwide, separate from local or regional specialties and elaborations. By employing core shamanism, which is not derived from any one cultural tradition, Westerners do not imitate any specific culture but rather acquire a foundation of fundamental shamanic knowledge upon which they can build their own practice of shamanism.

Core shamanism is a spiritual system, not a psychotherapy, and is not intended to deal with neuroses or other mental or emotional problems. Core shamanic practitioners do basically the same kinds of things indigenous shamans have traditionally done, but within the context of contemporary Western culture. In other words, they apply core shamanic methods to healing and helping others spiritually, typically within a holistic approach to health. They also engage in divination to gain solutions to problems that their clients wish to have solved. Their general, basic purpose is to help alleviate suffering and spiritual ignorance.

What Do Shamanic Counselors Do?

Shamanic counselors may use a system that Michael developed in 1982—the Harner Method of Shamanic Counseling (HMSC)—to train clients to solve their own problems using the shamanic journey for divination. (The name *Harner* is employed to avoid confusion with the practices of others who may also call their work shamanic counseling.) Shamanic counseling is a method of personal spiritual empowerment. The counselor trains the client in the shamanic methodology for interpretation of divination journeys, reserving the interpretation itself to the client alone.

In HMSC work, the counselor teaches the client how to frame questions most productively, while preserving the client's autonomy with respect to their content. She also teaches the client how to travel to the Lower and Upper Worlds to encounter and get advice from spiritual helpers, especially spirit teachers (who inhabit those realms).

The client lies on a couch and through earphones hears recorded drumbeats (audiocassette or CD) in the range of 4 to 7 Hertz (in the same range as theta EEG waves), which alter the client's state of consciousness. The sound initiates a journey in which the client poses a specific question to a spirit teacher regarding some problem that personally concerns him or her; for example, about a relationship or difficulty at work. The client describes his or her experience, as it is happening, into a tape recorder while the counselor listens and takes notes. After approximately half an hour, the counselor and client listen to the tape together and the counselor asks open-ended questions to help the client understand how the journey answers the question posed to the spirit teacher. Typically, at least six sessions are required to gain the experience necessary to begin practicing independently.

It is important to note the difference between shamanic counselors and shamanic practitioners. A shamanic practitioner makes the journey *for* the client and asks the spirit beings for healing help or counsel for the client (which is what traditional shamans have done); the shamanic counselor coaches clients in the methodology for making the journey themselves. The practitioner uses many classic shamanic healing methods. For example, often a practitioner will heal a client by journeying to retrieve some portion of the client's soul that has lost its connection with the client as a result of trauma or to restore a lost power animal connection. Sometimes a client's family and friends will attend such a session to lend community spiritual support, a crucial aspect of shamanic practice in traditional indigenous cultures.

What Are Helping Spirits?

Helping spirits are guardians appearing most commonly in human or animal form during a shamanic journey, who protect you, teach you, look out for your safety, heal you, and give you power. They are similar in this respect to guardian angels, as well as to the gods and goddesses of many cultures.

Different spirits have different things to teach or heal. For example, some help with matters of health and others with advice. There is no way to predict what will happen, because every journey experience is unique.

The identity of one's spirit helpers and teachers is discovered through one's own journeys. They are not known ahead of time. Some clients when journeying discover that they have spirit teachers in the form of Buddha, Christ, or Mary; others have teachers that are not historically famous at all.

Are You Only Imagining What Happens?

In our culture, we are trained to believe that anything others cannot see exists only in our imagination. Shamanic students and clients are not asked to fight this belief. They simply experience what occurs, without prejudice, during the journey. Over time, however, as one continues the practice, one tends to receive remarkable, and often miraculous, results and soon realizes that much more is involved than individual imagination.

> Michael Harner, Ph.D., an internationally known anthropologist, was initiated into shamanism during his work with the Conibo tribe in the Upper Amazon in 1961. Since then he has pioneered the contemporary revival of shamanism and shamanic healing. He developed core shamanism in the 1970s in response to requests by Westerners who wished to be trained in shamanism and healing. Founder and President of the Foundation for Shamanic Studies, he has taught at Columbia, Yale, and the University of California at Berkeley and served as chair of the Graduate Faculty Anthropology Department of the New School for Social Research in New York. His books include *The Way of the Shaman*, *The Jívaro: People of the Sacred Waterfalls*, and *Hallucinogens and Shamanism*.

> Sandra Ingerman, M.A., M.F.T., is a licensed professional mental-health counselor and Educational Director of the Foundation for Shamanic Studies. She is the author of *Soul Retrieval: Mending the Fragmented Soul* and *Welcome Home: Following Your Soul's Journey Home*.

Books

Mircea Eliade, *Shamanism: Archaic Techniques of Ecstasy*. Translated by Willard R. Trask (Bollingen Foundation, 1964, 1972, 1974). This classic text provides a comprehensible discussion of shamanism from initiatory sickness and dreams to the acquisition of power. It also covers shamanic cosmology, rites, myths, symbols, and costumes.

Joan Halifax, editor, *Shamanic Voices: A Survey of Visionary Narratives* (E. P. Dutton, 1979). The author has collected personal accounts of shamans' visionary journeys.

Michael Harner, *The Way of the Shaman* (HarperSanFrancisco, 1980, 1990). This book, which has become a classic, is a guide to the ancient art of shamanic healing. It provides historical information as well as current resources.

Sandra Ingerman, *Soul Retrieval: Mending the Fragmented Soul* (HarperSanFrancisco, 1990). As a source of healing and an adjunct to therapy, Ingerman's book describes a shamanic way of looking at psychological issues.

Organizations

Foundation for Shamanic Studies
P.O. Box 1939
Mill Valley, CA 94942
(415) 380-8282 (phone)
(415) 380-8416 (fax)
www.shamanism.org (website)

The foundation offers introductory workshops throughout the United States and Canada, as well as overseas, and many advanced training courses, ranging from weekend workshops to three-year programs. The foundation also provides a listing of certified Harner Method Shamanic Counselors, all of whom are graduates of the foundation's certification program and practice independently of the foundation. The foundation does not certify persons as shamans or shamanic healers; it is the clients and communities that must make that judgment.

Periodicals

Shamanism Magazine
c/o Foundation for Shamanic Studies
P.O. Box 1939
Mill Valley, CA 94942
(415) 380-8282

A semiannual journal of the Foundation for Shamanic Studies.

Shaman's Drum: A Journal of Experimental Shamanism
290 North Main Street, Suite 5
Ashland, OR 97520
(541) 552-0839 (phone)
sdrm@mind.net (e-mail)
Quarterly; $18
This magazine is published by the Cross-Cultural Shamanism Network, a nonprofit educational organization. Its policy is to study how archaic shamanic practices can best be applied today and to document and support the survival of shamanic cultures across the world.

❀ Sacred in Imago Relationship Therapy* ❀
By Harville Hendrix and Helen Hunt

The emergence of marriage and family therapy in the 1930s made couples therapy a mental-health specialty. Before that time, marriage counseling had not been available outside a religious context, where it was offered mainly by clergy as part of their pastoral duties. Since then pastoral counseling has become an independent profession and a new mental-health resource, even though institutional clergy continue to offer marriage counseling. Though marriage has been considered a sacred institution by religion, neither the clergy nor the couseling profession has viewed marriage itself as a spiritual path. Through the training offered by the Institute for Imago Relationship Therapy, we hope to emphasize an awareness of the spiritual dimension, not only to marriage but to all forms of relationships.

The Theory of Imago Relationship Therapy

Imago is the Latin word for "image." The core theory of Imago Relationship Therapy is that each of us carries from childhood an unconscious image or picture in our minds that guides us in our selection of a marriage partner. When we meet someone who fits the image, we experience a powerful romantic attraction to them, which in turn becomes the basis of our mate selection.

This process of choosing a partner, however, is problematic because the internal image we use to select a mate is based on a composite picture in our unconscious of our total experience with both our mother and father, with all their pos-

---

*While there are many kinds of marriage and family therapies, most of them do not include a spiritual dimension. We present this model because its originators recognize the spiritual dimension of relationship therapy.

itive and negative characteristics. In childhood this image served our survival needs by helping us distinguish our parents from other adults and remain steadfastly connected to them. In adulthood the image serves the function of guiding us to a partner who is similar to our parents and with whom we remake the connection. Unfortunately, this is done in the unconscious hope of getting certain needs met by our partner that were not satisfied by our parents. Since we are selecting someone who is like our parents, however, the partner is likely to become the catalyst for the same issues that were unresolved within our childhood rather than the nurturing source for which we had unconsciously hoped.

The rupture of this illusion, which results in a power struggle, occurs rather quickly because, at the time of selection, neither partner can provide the other with the emotional or behavioral resources each unconsciously expected. Does this unconscious union of incompatible partners, each wanting from the other what neither can give, seem like a cruel cosmic joke? Or does it represent an opportunity for both partners to heal their childhood frustrations with their parents by working the same issues through to resolution with their mate? Not only do we believe it is the latter, but we believe that the construction by our unconscious of these dynamics in an intimate partnership is Nature's brilliant plan for healing our childhood wounds. To achieve this, Nature seems to engage in a bit of beneficent subterfuge. From our perspective, it created romantic love as an anesthesia to blind us to the reality of the person to whom we are attracted. When bonding has been secured, Nature then removes the anesthesia. After an initial honeymoon period, we are confronted with the reality of our mutual incompatibility and inevitable frustration. Yet this situation gives us the opportunity for profound healing if both change in specific ways relative to each other's needs. Childhood wounds can be healed best in a context similar to the one in which they were originally experienced. Thus the selection of a partner whose personality reactivates the emotional situation unresolved as a child paradoxically provides a second chance to finish childhood.

The Practice of Imago Relationship Therapy

As a couple, we have been through this experience of imago selection. For example, Helen's father was frequently preoccupied with business and her mother preoccupied with him; thus neither was very aware of Helen and her emotional needs. Harville's parents had both died by the time he was six years of age, and during that time they were preoccupied with health and financial issues. Both of us had parents who were, for the most part, emotionally and physically unavailable to us when we were children. Not surprisingly, given that we are an Imago match, both of us, because of our professional interests and commitments, tend to be preoccupied and self-absorbed, thus reactivating feelings in each other of emotional abandonment and loneliness. We have had to invoke what we call the *stretching principle* and learn the unique ways we can be available for each other. We call this mutually healing process a *conscious marriage*.

The active agent in healing is a dialogue process that creates a bridge to each partner's inner world. You and your partner may originally have felt connected because you both had the illusion that you felt the same way about things. In truth, you were only mutually dependent on each other. After a period of time, you came to the sad conclusion that you held very different points of view. This discovery (that you live with a real living, breathing person rather than the constructed person of your dreams) is the necessary beginning of the healing process. At the time of this realization, one or both of you may have felt betrayed, lonely, and misunderstood and may wonder what happened to the person with whom you fell in love. Instead of having your needs met, you relive the same tensions, frustrations, and ecstasies that you experienced with your parents. If your response is like most couples, you engage in a power struggle in which you use coercive rather than romantic means to get your partner to conform to your ideal image and meet your unmet childhood needs. The outcome of this struggle, which is really growth trying to happen, is either a hot conflictual marriage, a parallel marriage, or a divorce, the current solution for around 60 percent of married couples. Another alternative is to create a conscious marriage and begin a time of growth and healing.

Becoming the Parent Your Partner Needs

In Imago Relationship Therapy, we help couples begin their mutual healing by introducing them to the dialogue process. Through dialogue, each partner becomes aware of the other's childhood wound and the specific behaviors that are needed to provide what each did not get from their parents. We help them understand that they must consciously become a surrogate parent to each other, the parent neither had as a child. This is difficult because to become the parent your partner needed, you have to accept the fact that some of your character traits (like always being late, for example), which perhaps are dear to you, are similar to the negative aspects of your partner's parent. These traits have become such a part of you that you identify yourself with them. But those are the traits that have to be changed. This requires stretching into new behaviors and attitudes, which at first may be disorienting and scary; you may feel that you are no longer "yourself." However, what we have discovered is that the character traits and behaviors that cause your partner pain are, in fact, defenses you erected as a child to protect yourself. They are not "you" but coping mechanisms that you can and need to change into more effective behaviors. In an early act of self-protection, a part of you was split off and lost to consciousness. So when both you and your partner stretch to meet each other's needs, not only do you give each other what you should have had as a child (thereby healing the connection with each other and simultaneously healing the old unconscious rupture with both sets of parents), you also activate and grow new aspects of yourself that were stunted or repressed in childhood. Healing and the recovery of wholeness occur in the act of reciprocal giving.

Steps in the Dialogue Process

The dialogue process is the means of communication by which couples are able to contact each other more deeply. It creates safety and facilitates growth. Dialogue consists of three parts, each of which deepens contact until connection at the level of empathic attunement occurs. And that induces healing. The steps are as follows:

Step 1: Mirroring To mirror is to play back the gist of what you just heard until your partner feels her thoughts and feelings have been received accurately. The flatter the surface of the mirror, the more accurate the reflection; concave or convex mirrors distort the message. An accurate mirror might look like this. "If I am getting it right, you feel angry that I was late and did not call you. Did I get it right?" If the answer is yes, then the receiver asks: "Is there more?" and continues to mirror until there is no more. The mirroring process is then completed with a summary of all that has been said, which begins with this sentence stem: "Let me see if I got it all." The skill of accurate paraphrase can take a considerable amount of practice, but with patience and persistence, what feels at first mechanical and impersonal can eventually become an art form and a lifestyle.

Step 2: Validation Validation is seeing the truth of your partner's reality, seeing that it is logical and that it makes sense. It does not mean that you agree or have to surrender your point of view. It means that you must accept your partner's point of view as their reality, equal in validity to your own. After successfully mirroring, the receiving partner might respond with this sentence stem: "You make sense. I was late. I can see that when I am late and don't call, you feel I don't care about you." Mirroring is necessary for contact; validation is essential for making a bridge to your partner's inner world. It breaks the symbiotic fusion, enabling you to see your partner as truly an "other." This seeing through the veil of one's own construction transforms your partner into an "I" and you into a "Thou" to your partner.

Step 3: Empathy Empathy has two phases. The first is cognitive empathy, the experience of recognizing your partner's feelings and mirroring those feelings back with accuracy. At a deeper level, called affective empathy, you actually feel, not just cognitively recognize, your partner's feelings. After mirroring and validation, a sentence stem that can lead to an affective empathic response is "And I can imagine that you feel hurt by that." A statement indicating such empathy may look like this: "And right now I am experiencing how painful that is for you." When you achieve empathic attunement or a real connection with your partner, rather than your imaginary construction, a bond is created and healing occurs.

Step 4: Behavior Change Requests (optional) While dialogue (when carried to the level of empathic responding) always establishes a deep connection, it often clarifies some changes that both must make in order to heal specific memories. This can be effected by making a behavior change request (BCR). A BCR might go like this: "Now that I know that my being late hurts you and makes you feel I don't care about you, what specifically can I do that will help that not happen again?" Your partner then needs to state up to three specific behaviors that would make her feel you care. For instance, she may say: "My deepest desire is that you will never be late, but since I know that is unrealistic, when you know you are going to be late again, give me a call and tell me exactly when you will be home." Or, "The next time you are late, bring me a dozen red roses." Or, "When you are late next time, come home with plans to take me out to dinner."

Your response should be to choose one request, so that you can succeed and give it to your partner as a gift with no counter-requests (i.e., no strings attached). Usually our partners want from us what we are least capable of giving at that time. But when we stretch into those behaviors, we recover or develop nonfunctioning parts of ourselves and grow into the ability to give it naturally. In this example, the request may require a partner to grow as a person in areas that have not been developed, such as sensitivity to the feelings their behavior stirs in others, and this will contribute to the partner's evolution toward wholeness.

The imago therapist acts more like a coach than a therapist. She operates with the assumption that the primary aim of both partners is to be meaningfully connected and that their behaviors are a result of a rupture of that connection. She also sees all problems as resulting from early ruptures with parents, a relationship failure that has stunted the emotional growth of each partner and left them fixated at a particular developmental stage. Therefore she operates with the assumption that problems of this type cannot be solved, partners can only grow out of them. Instead of using analysis, interpretation, and other attempts to induce insight within either of the partners, she facilitates dialogue to focus on the space *between* partners. The goal is to create safety and restore connection. Using dialogue creates emotional safety, which enables the couple to cross the bridge to each other and overcome their isolation and aloneness. Then their problems tend to dissolve in the chemistry of emotional bonding. The safety of knowing your partner will listen and validate your feelings allows you and your partner to be more truthful, let down defenses, and become more intimate with each other.

Spiritual Implications

Helen was the first to point out that creating a conscious relationship in which couples satisfy their yearning for the restoration of connection (and in the process, achieve personal wholeness) is a spiritual process. To help us understand how it is possible for consciousness to exist within a relationship, as well as the miraculous power of reconnection, we have developed a set of assumptions about the nature of the universe and thus the nature of human nature.

We believe that we live in an evolving, conscious universe, which is itself in the process of self-completion, self-repair, and becoming self-aware through human self-reflection and healing. The "stuff" of the universe is Consciousness, which is organized as an interconnected field, which we call metaphorically the "tapestry of being." Consciousness itself mutates into energy and matter, thus giving rise to the universe as we know it, including ourselves.

Since humanity is a result of this mutation, each person is essentially a node or point of conscious energy in a larger field of conscious energy, connected to all other points and thus intricately to the whole of the universe. At birth, all of us are whole, connected to all parts of ourselves and to our social and ecological context and intuitively aware of our union with the cosmos. The original and essential condition of the human person is relaxed joyfulness. Thus human beings are conscious, and can create a conscious marriage, because they are made of consciousness. Because we are conscious, we can also become self-conscious and self-reflective, and when we do, we become the point in the universe where it is becoming conscious of itself. We yearn for this connection because we are one with everything. When relationship to our context is restored, we experience reconnection to all parts of ourselves, and thus we are healed and made whole again.

Wordsworth captures this point poetically in the lines:

> Our birth is but a sleep and a forgetting:
> The Soul that rises with us, our life's Star
> Hath had elsewhere its setting,
> And cometh from afar:
> Not in entire forgetfulness,
> And not in utter nakedness,
> But trailing clouds of glory do we come
> From God, who is our home:
> Heaven lies about us in our infancy!

The goal of couples therapy, therefore, is not to *find* our connection with each other, but to *become aware of it again*. In this sense the dialogue process, although beginning as a communication tool, becomes a spiritual practice. Unlike meditation, which focuses our concentrated attention inward, dialogue focuses it outward toward our partner. The partner as the focal point of attention becomes a sacred subject of our attention. In this process, partnering maintains our awareness of love as a sacred bond we have with each other and with the larger whole.

Harville Hendrix, Ph.D., and Helen Hunt, M.A., are cofounders of the Institute for Imago Relationship Therapy and intellectual partners in the creation of Imago Relationship Therapy. Harville is the author of the bestsellers *Getting the Love You Want: A Guide for Couples* and *Keeping the Love You Find: A Personal Guide*. He and Helen are also coauthors of the *Couples Companion* and *The Personal Companion* and are currently writing *Giving the Love They Need: A Guide for Parents*. A frequent guest on television and radio throughout the United States and Canada, one of Harville's eight appearances on *Oprah* won an Emmy Award for its socially redeeming value. The couple have six children and live on a ranch in northern New Mexico.

Books

John Gottman, *Why Marriages Succeed or Fail* (Fireside, 1994). Through self-administered tests, this book helps readers determine the type of marriage they have as well as its strengths and weaknesses. The author also provides valuable information on behavior that damages relationships, including criticism, defensiveness, and stonewalling.

Harville Hendrix, *Getting the Love You Want: A Guide for Couples* (Pocket Books, 1990). Written for the general audience, this book is the first published discussion of Imago theory and therapy.

Harville Hendrix, *Keeping the Love You Find: A Personal Guide* (Pocket Books, 1992). For single persons who want to prepare for intimate partnership.

Howard Markman, Scott Stanley, and Susan L. Blumberg, *Fighting for Your Marriage: Positive Steps for Preventing Divorce and Preserving Lasting Love* (Jossey Bass Publishers, 1994). Based on the view that intimacy involves working out difficult conflicts, this book provides exercises for couples looking to build a spiritual and meaningful life together.

Organizations

Coalition for Marriage, Family and Couples Education
5310 Belt Road, NW

Washington, DC 20015-1961
cmfce@smartmarriages.com (e-mail)
www.his.com/cmfce/ (website)
www.smartmarriages.com (website)

This organization is a new clearinghouse for marriage preparation and enrichment programs.

Institute for Imago Relationship Therapy
335 Knowles Avenue
Winter Park, FL 32789
(800) 729-1121 (phone)
Rick Imago@aol.com (e-mail)
imagothe@imagotherapy.com (website)

In addition to offering professional training internationally, the institute makes referrals to the approximately 1,100 mental health professionals who are certified to practice Imago Relationship Therapy and to the 300 workshops for couples and singles that are offered annually.

Marriage Savers Institute
9500 Michaels Court
Bethesda, MD 20817
(301) 469-5870 (phone)
www.mj_McManus@compuserv (e-mail)

Designed to help any church community minimize divorce rates by supporting couples in strong marriages and teaching them to assist other couples at key stages—engagement, midlife, partner illness, and stepfamily formation.

Practical Application of Intimate Relationship Skills (PAIRS)
1152 N. University Drive, Suite 202
Pembroke Pines, FL 33024
(800) 477-2477 (phone)
marjorie@pairs.org (e-mail)
www.pairs.com (website)

PAIRS is a 16-week course for couples.

Prevention and Relationship Enhancement Program (PREP)
P.O. Box 102530
Denver, CO 80250-2530
(800) 366-0166 or (303) 759-9931

PREP was created by the University of Denver Center for Marital and Family Therapy. It teaches communication and conflict resolution skills. A specifically Christian version is also taught.

Body

Once a week, whether the money is there
or not, I write a check for her lessons.
But today, as I wait in the car for her
to finish her chores, after she has wrapped
this one's delicate legs, brushed burrs
and caked mud from that one's tail,
I saw her stop and offer her body
to a horse's itchy head. One arm up,
she gave him the whole length of her side.
And he knew the gesture, understood
the gift, stepped in close on oiled hooves
and pressed his head into her ribcage.
From hip to armpit he raked her body until,
to keep from falling, she leaned into him
full weight, her foot braced
against a tack post for balance.
Before horses, it was snakes, coiled
around her arms like African bracelets.
And before that, stray dogs, cats
of every color, even the misfits,
the abandoned and abused.
It took me so long to learn how to love,
how to give myself up and over to another.
Now I see how she has always
loved them all, snails and spiders,
from the very beginning, without fear or shame,
saw even the least of them, ants,
gnats, heard and answered
even the slightest of their calls.

—DORIANNE LAUX, "FOR MY DAUGHTER
WHO LOVES ANIMALS"

4

The Healing Power of Art

In the mid-1980s, Chuck and I hired an organizational consultant to help us sort out Common Boundary's various functions and our respective roles. Up to that point, we had slowly and organically grown the organization ourselves. But having begun to hire staff, we needed to define what we were doing, where we were going, and who was responsible for what. We met the consultant for an all-day session in Little Washington, Virginia, in a space that was both a conference room and an art gallery. It was an agonizing meeting. Having operated amoeba-like for several years, it was time to differentiate, to create specific roles and structures, but the reassigning of responsibilities was difficult. We discovered how desperately one can cling to work and responsibilities, to old patterns and structures, simply because they are familiar and comfortable. Climbing out of the deep rut of habit— "But that's the way we've always done it," we whine—and envisioning a new form requires enormous effort, on the one hand, and the ability to surrender, on the other. Finally, after much discussion and pages of notes on large newsprint, we popped out of our organizational straitjacket. We realized that we naturally fell into two divisions: publishing (magazine) and education (conference), and it was very clear who had the greater affinity for each function. Anne, with her degree in magazine journalism and experience as a writer and editor, naturally gravitated toward publishing. Chuck, on the other hand, enjoyed networking and convening people; the conference division clearly was his love. With that recognition, specific duties and responsibilities fell into place. What seemed so obvious in hindsight was the result of flailing about in unknown waters. What had seemed like wild and possibly futile casting about had, under expert guidance, landed us safely on a new shore.

We went back to our B and B late that afternoon, exhausted and relieved. The next morning when we woke up, we lay in bed musing over our experience. Suddenly, we had an epiphany. The day before we had wrestled with chaos. By staying aware of our feelings, keeping our attention focused on the problem, and working with structured exercises to clarify tasks and responsibilities, we had discovered a new form. Our "Aha!" had to do with the realization that creativity is an inner process akin to psychotherapy and spirituality. Each provides a doorway into the inner world, the imagination, where one leaves behind the ordinary world and enters a numinous space resonant with meaning.

Since that weekend, we have been acutely aware of how integral creativity is to soul work. One need not write the great American novel or paint a masterpiece to hang in the Whitney or Guggenheim. Each day affords ample opportunities for flexing creative muscles. Existential-humanistic psychologist Rollo May, in his book *The Courage to Create*, describes the creative act as any encounter that engages us completely. In the creative process we overcome our dualistic stance of subject-object, of "us" and "it." Instead we give ourselves wholeheartedly to whatever endeavor we are involved in. We surrender and in that exchange make space for something new.

British psychoanalyst D. W. Winnicott connected creativity to the quality of one's life. Without it, we lose our sense that life is real and meaningful because we lose our connection to our world. "We find that either individuals live creatively and feel that life is worth living or else that they cannot live creatively and are doubtful about the value of life," he wrote. May expanded on this point when he wrote that "anxiety comes from not being able to know the world you're in, not being able to orient yourself in your own existence."

By allowing our imagination to create images, symbols, stories, and rituals, we organize meaning from the jumble of everyday experiences, feelings, and thoughts. The more we can bring the creative process into daily life, the greater our sense of well-being becomes. It is not complicated. Gardening, problem-solving, negotiating sibling truces, singing full-bellied in the car or shower, planning a wedding, a funeral, or a birthday party all provide opportunities to create and express meaning. As Abraham Maslow once declared, "A first-rate soup is more creative than a second-rate painting."

But unfortunately, as creative arts therapy pioneer Natalie Rogers points out, most of us think of the artist as someone else. "Time and time again I have listened to touching stories from clients, friends, and group participants who can pinpoint the exact moment they stopped using art, music, or dance as a form of pleasure and self-expression," writes Rogers in *The Creative Connection: Expressive Arts as Healing*. "A teacher gave them a poor grade, someone ridiculed them as they danced, or someone told them to mouth the words while others sang. . . . The self-image that remained was, 'I can't draw,' 'I'm not musical,' 'It's not fun anymore.'" The experience Rogers describes is a familiar one to many of us. As we go from childhood to adulthood, we tend to leave art-making to others, to those who pursue the training to make creativity their vocation. The "real" artists, we tell ourselves, are those who are paid for their music or painting or writing; the rest of us should know better than to think we could achieve such heights of self-expression.

Sierra Club President Adam Werbach confirmed this observation with a story. In the February 1997 issue of his organization's bulletin, he reported that researchers had gone to a preschool and asked children, "Who knows how to sing?" Everyone's hand shot up. "Who knows how to dance?" They all waved their hands enthusiastically. "Who knows how to draw?" Again all hands were raised. The next week the researchers posed the same questions to a class of college students. "Who knows how to sing?" A few hands went up. "Who knows how to dance?" Two hands were raised shyly. "Draw?" No response. Werbach concludes that between preschool and so-called higher education, "we lose track of our most vital and effective means of expressing ourselves."

Rogers and her colleagues argue that the joy of spontaneous artistic expression can and should be available to everyone—because using paint, movement, or language to express our emotions is an inherently renewing and healing act.

How does this renewal occur? Alice Walker, when asked how writing helps to transform pain, replied, "When you feel pain, one of the hardest things to do is to look at what is causing it and then express what is causing it. You think you can avoid it, but actually you can't. If you do, you just get sicker, or you feel more pain. But if you can speak it, if you can write it, if you can paint it, it is very healing."

This healing requires that the artist have faith in the process of art-making, even when—or some might say, especially when—it seems to be beyond the artist's conscious control. Poet and potter M. C. Richards writing about working with clay instructs: "We must be able to let the intensity—the Dionysian rapture and disorder and celebration of chaos, of potentiality, the experience of surrender—we must be able to let it live in our bodies, in our hands, through our hands, into the materials we work with." Audrey Flack described a similar process encountered in painting: "When you're in the studio painting, there are a lot of people in there with you. Your teachers, friends, painters from history, critics . . . and one by one, if you're really painting, they walk out. And if you're really painting, you walk out."

Richards's and Flack's descriptions have as much to do with the spiritual realm as they do with psychology. And indeed, art has always had some connection to the religious and even mystical impulses of human beings. For example, religious artists in the Middle Ages did not sign their works, so devoted were they to the belief that what they made came *through* rather than *from* them. Contemporary artist and teacher Meinrad Craighead—whose images of strong, earth-based female figures are haunting in their mystical intensity—reminds us that from the beginning of time, human beings have celebrated divine visitations by speaking, writing, singing, drawing, and dancing them. "We cannot *not* tell of God's presence in our souls," she says. "We create, we build, we choreograph, we play music, paint paintings, or write poetry to communicate this divine presence." Craighead believes that God, or Spirit, penetrates us in our creative soul. "The Creator Spirit seeks out our own creativity," she says. "Fire begets fire."

Still, one need not be directly involved in the creative act to reap rewards. One of the earliest statements about the healing power of art can be found in Aristotle's *Poetics,* in which the philosopher describes the psychological effect of drama on the audience. Tragedy, he writes, "achieves, through the representation of pitiable and fearful incidents, the catharsis of such pitiable and fearful incidents." Although scholars and analysts have interpreted Aristotle's statement many different ways, most of us know the experience of having been touched by a work of art. When we are deeply moved by a film, a book, a dance performance, or a painting, it's probably because we identify with the characters and the events portrayed. Through that identification, aspects of our own psyches are clarified and released; we feel purged, uplifted, and oftentimes subtly changed.

Jungian analyst Marion Woodman offers *Othello* as an example of how interacting with a work of art can alter our perceptions of ourselves. To Woodman, Othello's jealousy, which is blindly acted out, is transformed by Shakespeare's imagination into an activity in which the audience can participate. "The play in performance is the metaphor that allows a destructive intent to be raised to a level of moral and spiritual contemplation," she explains. "It allows us, without acting out, to recognize and even redeem the murderer in ourselves."

Such definitions of the healing power of art focus on the observer rather than the creator. From influential turn-of-the-century visual artist Marcel Duchamp to contemporary choreographer and dancer Liz Lerman, those who study creativity have long noticed that the audience engages in art-making when they actively witness what is being presented to them. A large part of Lerman's career has always involved making dance participation available to everyone—whether by teaching boys on the soccer field, office workers downtown at lunchtime, or senior citizens in a retirement home—and she insists that the moment when an audience feels the "click" of connection is, in a sense, a moment of art-making. "When an audience goes, 'Oh, I never thought of that before,'" Lerman says, "that's their moment of connecting and creating."

A young woman moves silently across the floor on her hands and knees, then rises and slowly begins to stretch toward the ceiling, seemingly reaching for the skylight. Seated on the floor near her, a social worker watches, observing the details of the woman's movement for later discussion. In another room, a psychologist encourages a middle-aged man to sing from the place in his body where he has chronic pain, to "give that pain a voice." Another counselor, working in group therapy, gives everyone in the group the same poem, which the group then acts out, finding movement, sounds, and words to elaborate on or embellish the poem's themes. At the close of the session, each group member writes his or her own lines of verse in response to what has been read.

All of these counselors have very different backgrounds and training. But they and many other contemporary therapists have one thing in common: a belief in the healing power of creativity and art. In fact, one of the fastest-growing areas in psychotherapy is the arts therapies, which are based on the idea that all human beings are endowed with the ability to unleash, examine, and transform their emotions through creative endeavor, be it painting, writing, dancing, or singing. The emphasis in such therapies is not on producing a finished work of art—although that can happen—but rather on the process of expressing feelings and increasing self-awareness. This process is, as British psychiatrist Anthony Storr points out in *The Dynamics of Creativity*, "that of the child at play." Many writers on the subject echo Storr. They insist that play is an integral element in creativity. One must be willing to try things one way, then another; to write two pages, then go back and excise one and a half. Stephen Nachmanovitch, who wrote a book on improvisation entitled *Free Play*, sees play as "the taproot from which original art springs. . . . Artists play with sound and silence. Eros plays with lives. Gods play with the universe. Children play with everything they can get their hands on."

But creativity also involves discipline, and like any muscle in the body, our creative muscles need regular exercising. The more we exercise the stronger we get. Just as keeping a dream journal to record our nocturnal imaginal creations over time encourages our remembering more dreams in greater detail and with greater specificity, so too if one sticks with a creative endeavor, progress is made—no matter whether we are cooking or writing, honing a craft or singing. The trick is simply to reconnect with the imagination, the ground of creativity, and "go with the flow."

Despite the ambivalence of Sigmund Freud—whose attitude toward the function of the artist seemed to contain a blend of envy, awe, and distrust—contemporary psychotherapists are probing more and more into the realm where the arts deliver healing messages. In fact, arts therapies are on the cutting edge of psychotherapy today. And the cutting edge of arts therapies is creative arts therapy, which combines art modalities. For example, dance therapists are incorporating painting into their sessions, poetry therapists have patients act out poems, and drama therapy now includes creating masks and other visual aides. One major consideration, however, has to do with choosing the right medium for the client.

Peggy Heller, a registered poetry therapist and founder of the Poetry Therapy

Training Institute in Potomac, Maryland, has found that people in crisis spontaneously begin to write. They write poetry, they start a journal. If clients know that their "words are welcome," they bring their writing into therapy. Other therapists have found that clients suffering from schizophrenia, which often leaves them unable to articulate their feelings verbally, respond well to dance therapy.

Making the symbolic language of the arts welcome in a therapeutic context gives both the therapist and the client opportunities for exploration not available in traditional talk therapy. Shaun McNiff, a pioneer in the field of creative arts therapy and currently provost of Endicott College in Beverly, Massachusetts, uses drumming, vocal work, and movement in addition to painting when working in his studio with clients. "I believe that imagination is an interplay of intelligences. . . . We encourage imaginative expression by painting from the body. I drum and play other percussion instruments and encourage people to paint as they are dancing. They use both hands and realize that their expression is kinesthetic and dramatic as well as visual." This blending of modalities, sometimes also called *expressive arts therapy* or *multimodal therapy*, recognizes that people are multidimensional and sometimes require a combination of various creative approaches. Making the symbolic language of the arts welcome in a therapeutic context may be innovative, but it also makes sense. In bringing the process of art-making into the therapy room, contemporary expressive arts therapists allow the psyche to express itself simply and directly; the hope is that after expression comes the release, and then the healing that Aristotle referred to so many centuries ago.

ART THERAPY

Art therapy uses painting, drawing, and clay modeling to help enhance creativity and self-expression. The essence of art therapy, according to art therapist Judith Rubin, is that it blends art-making and therapy in equal portions. One not only paints, draws, or sculpts, but the very process of creation serves therapeutic aims such as the healing of psychological and emotional conflict, increasing self-awareness, and encouraging personal growth. The entire gestalt—the art-making process, artwork, and subsequent discussion about or associations to the work—is seen as reflecting the person's inner state and experience. Thus unconscious material can be accessed and expressed in a less threatening manner than in verbal dialogue alone.

"Sometimes people can't find the words to express something," said art therapist Chris Wilkinson in a 1996 article in *Intuition* magazine, "or they don't understand the problem enough to put it in words, but it comes out in their work." Thus the goal of art therapy is to use the creative process to bring to light inner thoughts, feelings, and conflicts; insight is the primary product. According to art therapist and author Pat Allen, "Consciousness is the crucial element that art therapy added to the equation that is not always present in the practice of art-making by artists. By adding intention (the clear desire to know something through art) and attention (the honest consideration of meaning in the image), we experience art-making as creating or deepening consciousness."

According to a 1996 article in *Intuition* magazine, art therapy can be traced to nineteenth-century mental hospitals where psychiatrists noticed that patients were drawing on the floors, walls, and toilet paper. They carefully studied these artistic renderings in the hopes that they might shed light on the patients' state of mind. But the term *art therapy* was not coined until the early 1940s, when Adrian Hill used it to describe his work with patients in British sanitoriums. As a convalescing soldier during World War II, Hill had begun to paint to relieve his boredom. Other soldiers soon joined him, and he noticed that they were painting horrific battle scenes from the war. As they painted, the soldiers began to describe brutal events and the fears and other emotions accompanying them. This observation led Hill to believe that art in conjunction with talk therapy could be a more effective way to gain access to the subconscious than talk therapy alone. Thanks in large part to Hill, art therapy was recognized as a profession in Britain in 1940.

On this side of the Atlantic, four major art therapy pioneers emerged. Margaret Naumburg and Edith Kramer well deserve to be seen as the grandmothers of the field. While Naumburg, the first person in the United States to combine classical psychoanalysis with art, thought that *talking* about the art was important for healing, Kramer felt that the very act of *making* art was healing. In other words, Naumburg emphasized the therapeutic function of art therapy, while Kramer stressed the healing function of art-making itself. For Naumburg, the therapist's role was that of facilitator and guide, assisting patients in uncovering the meaning of their art and therefore aspects of themselves. Kramer, although trained in Freudian analysis, worked mainly with children and saw herself as more of an artist/educator.

Naumburg and Kramer's work took place in the 1930s and 1940s. Two other first-generation art therapists' careers began developing in the 1950s. The first, Elinor Ulman, during a ten-year stint at the District of Columbia General Hospital, formed a friendship with the chief psychologist there, Bernard I. Levy. Together, the two founded the art therapy program at George Washington University. She also started two art therapy journals. Her stance vis-à-vis Naumburg and Kramer was that at times she leaned more heavily toward art psychotherapy and at other times toward art as therapy.

Hanna Yaxa Kwiatkowska worked at both St. Elizabeth's Hospital in the

District of Columbia and the National Institute of Mental Health in Bethesda, Maryland. Influenced both by the dynamically oriented art therapy of Margaret Naumburg and the theories in the newly emerging field of family systems, she developed family art therapy. Later others came along with variations in the field such as Gestalt and archetypal art therapy, as well as art therapy with object relations, cognitive, and psychoanalytic approaches. Expressive arts therapy is one of the new directions the field is taking.

An art therapy session can be held as easily in a mental-health clinic or hospital setting as in an artist's studio. Traditionally trained art therapists usually ask a patient to focus on one specific issue and then to draw or paint the scene or the emotions involved. Some therapists analyze elements such as the images, colors chosen, pressure applied, or width of the brush stroke, seeing these interpretations as an essential step to discovering what a client's psyche is expressing. However, more and more art therapists are beginning to feel that it is important to let the painting or collage speak for itself. Shaun McNiff, for example, employs "dialoguing" with the art, a process by which patients speak from the artwork's point of view. At one level, this approach seems to help clients get outside of their ego, to express feelings or thoughts without an internal censor judging them; at another level, McNiff sees these creations as having a life and energy of their own and as containing "medicine."

Other art therapists such as Michell Cassou believe strongly in allowing spontaneity to rule the process. Regardless of the art therapy approach, crayons, paint, charcoal, and pastels are all keys that can open the doorway to consciousness and healing.

Books

Pat B. Allen, *Art Is a Way of Knowing* (Shambhala Publications, Inc., 1995). This guidebook assists readers in seeing and using the creative process as a tool for self-awareness and spiritual growth.

Michell Cassou and Stewart Cubley, *Life, Paint and Passion* (Jeremy P. Tarcher, 1995). Based on the authors' method of painting, entitled the Painting Experience, the book encourages spontaneity, exploration, and application of the artistic process to one's daily life.

Peter London, *No More Secondhand Art* (Shambhala Publications, Inc., 1989). Aimed not only at artists, art students, and art teachers but also at those of us who swear we can't draw, the book discusses ways to free our creative self and sees art-making as a transformational process.

Shaun McNiff, *Art as Medicine: Creating a Therapy of the Imagination* (Shambhala Publications, Inc., 1992). The author, one of the pioneers in creative arts therapy, takes an archetypal psychology approach to art-making, offering provocative ideas about artistic images and the healing power of art.

Shaun McNiff, *Trust the Process: An Artist's Guide to Letting Go* (Shambhala Publications, Inc., 1998). This is a useful book for people who want to bring more creativity into their lives. In a friendly, conversational tone, the author shares insights and experiences from both his personal and professional life. He also offers practical suggestions, such as how to set up a space and why warming up before painting is helpful, and observations about the source of creativity and the role of imagination and improvisation.

Judith Aron Rubin, editor, *Approaches to Art Therapy: Theory and Technique* (Brunner/Mazel Inc., 1987). This book is a collection of articles that explain a variety of art therapy approaches, including those based on object relations, Jungian analysis, Gestalt and humanistic psychology, and the behavioral, cognitive, and developmental approaches to this healing method.

Michael Samuels and Mary Rockwood Lane, *Creative Healing: How to Heal Yourself by Tapping Your Hidden Creativity* (HarperSanFrancisco, 1998). This book is about ways in which the arts—such as music and movement, poetry, drama, painting, sculpture, and dance—can bring about physical healing.

❂ Michell Cassou on Spontaneity ❂

Having a definite idea of what you want your creative project to look like when complete is not always a good idea. If you have a strong image, let it come, but also allow it to evolve, move, and flow without making a decision as to the outcome. Allow your inner spontaneity to guide you. Universal energy inspires creative movement. The point of any creative project is to get out of the way and let this energy move through you.

When you paint spontaneously, you have to use your intuition and allow what is inside you to surface without judgment. Intuition knows exactly what you need to paint and when you need to paint it. It comes from an inner place that longs to be whole. It is normal to be fearful of what your intuition may bring, because what it usually brings is completely outside the range of what you expect. Intuition forces you to face your feelings rather than your mental concepts. So it may take you awhile to accept what comes out when you paint spontaneously. I teach my students not to fight what comes out but to allow it to happen without judging it.

If you feel stuck and decide to do some spontaneous painting, you will find that as you paint, you move to a detached space, and at the end of the painting session you are able to look at your mental problems in a different way. This does not mean that your problems are resolved and that you have a definite answer, but you will have a new perspective.

I believe that the purpose of creativity is for each of us to open up to what we really are, to break the boundary of what we think we are. Breaking this boundary is healing because you liberate yourself from all the "shoulds" and "coulds" and allow yourself to be in the moment. When you paint spontaneously and intuitively, you have to be present and honest. What I love about painting spontaneously is that the process teaches you to listen to yourself.

Michell Cassou grew up in southern France and was inspired by watching children paint. She founded the Painting Experience Studio in San Francisco in 1976 and now teaches classes and workshops throughout the United States. She is the coauthor of the book *Life, Paint and Passion*.

Organizations

American Art Therapy Association (AATA)
1202 Allanson Road
Mundelein, IL 60060
(847) 949-6064 (phone)
(847) 566-4580 (fax)
estygariii@aol.com (e-mail)
www.arttherapy.org (website)
Founded in 1969, AATA, with a membership of approximately 4,750 professionals and students, is dedicated to educational research through conferences, symposiums, videos, and awards.

Center for Liturgy and the Arts
Rev. J. Bruce Stewart, Director
4327 Ravensworth Road, #210
Annandale, VA 22003
(703) 941-9422 (phone)
(703) 941-9422 *23 (fax)
The center provides teaching, performing, and consulting services in the application of the arts to worship—including drama, music, juggling, clowning, mime, storytelling, poetry, and the visual arts for all ages.

Erdahaus
2712 Campbell Road, NW
Albuquerque, NM 87104
(505) 344-7109
Erdahaus offers creative retreats for women led by artist and author Meinrad Craighead.

New England Art Therapy Institute
216 South Silver Lane
Sunderland, MA 01375
(413) 665-4880 (phone)
(413) 665-3041 (fax)
cccNEATI@javanet.com (e-mail)

Founded in 1981, the institute provides courses in art therapy and creativity for the general public and a certificate program for professionals in related fields. It is a division of the Center for Creative Consciousness, which is dedicated to research, development, and training in creativity as applied to social service, educational, and corporate environments.

Round Oaks Creative Center
3434 Ridge Road
Charlottesville, VA 22901
(804) 973-7543 (phone and fax)

The center offers programs in expressive arts and nondegree certificate programs, accredited sand-tray training, individual therapeutic assessments, and therapist consultations.

Periodicals

American Journal of Art Therapy
Vermont College of Norwich University
Montpelier, VT 05602
(802) 828-8540
Quarterly; $30 individual, $25 members of American Art Association

Art Therapy: Journal of the American Art Therapy Association
American Art Therapy Association
1202 Allanson Road
Mundelein, IL 60060
(847) 949-6064 (phone)
(847) 566-4580 (fax)
estygariii@aol.com (e-mail)
www.arttherapy.org (website)
Quarterly; free to members, $50 individual nonmember, $77 institution nonmember

Arts in Psychotherapy
Elsevier Science Ltd.
Pergamon Press Journals Division
P.O. Box 800 Kidlington
Oxford, England OX51DX
(44) 1865-84-3000 (phone)
(44) 1865-84-3010 (fax)
nlinfo-f@elsevier.nl (e-mail)
www.elsevier.nl (website)
5 times a year; $60

EXPRESSIVE ARTS THERAPY

Expressive arts therapy, sometimes called creative arts or multimodal therapy, is grounded in the belief that art therapies work best when used in conjunction with one another. Shaun McNiff, who started the first creative arts therapy graduate program in 1974 at Lesley College in Cambridge, Massachusetts, works with a number of different media even when the primary focus of a studio is painting. He may drum during studio time and encourage studio participants to dance while painting and to vocalize or improvise a movement as a response to their artwork to help them understand the painting better. He and other expressive arts therapists employ a mix of tools that can include dance, movement, art, and music as well as journaling, poetry, guided imagery, and improvisation.

Former Lesley College professor and creative arts therapist Paolo Knill likens multimodal therapy to filmmaking: A filmmaker has to understand light, color, sound, and the environment when creating, and so too does the expressive arts therapist. For example, a client may see a therapist about an emotional problem, and the therapist might decide to have the client paint his or her feelings while moving to specially chosen music.

Jack S. Weller, founding director of the Expressive Arts Therapy Program at the California Institute for Integral Studies, explains that unlike some art therapists, creative arts therapists avoid using art to diagnose and do not see clinical interpretation of artwork as useful. Rather, the therapist focuses on the healing aspects of the artistic process. McNiff agrees. "Art diagnosis," he explains, "takes the offsprings of imagination and fits them into ready-made classifications. The procedure is a mental operation: red means this, and black means that." The theory behind the use of interpretation is that information helps a person get better through insight and self-understanding. McNiff sees healing more holistically. Without completely dismissing insight as a valuable therapeutic tool, he tries to balance clinical precision with a commitment to the imagination. "In fact," he says, "the tension in this polarization can be a sign of creative vitality." McNiff firmly believes that the energies in the process of painting as well as in the painting itself are themselves transformative. That's why the product takes a backseat to the process of art-making.

Natalie Rogers, founder of the Person-Centered Expressive Therapy Institute, stresses that creative arts therapy "is not about creating a pretty picture. It is not a dance ready for the stage. It is not a poem written and rewritten to perfection." Instead of focusing on the aesthetics of the work of art, the style of writing, or a song's harmony, multimodal therapy uses the arts as vehicles "to let go, to express, and to release." Furthermore, she adds, the therapist's critical contribution in this process is "offering the client an opportunity, rather than insisting on a method."

Lawrice Dolan, a holistic health counselor and expressive arts therapist in Silver Spring, Maryland, begins each session by asking how the client is feeling. She believes that clients tell her where they need to go. Their words or movements offer clues to what would assist them in their process. For example, if the client uses a lot of movement terms, Dolan would recommend using the body in a more specific way. "I might suggest that they accentuate the movement or see if there is a sound under it. I want them to see, feel, hear, taste what is there and then go deeper. For the client who is speaking in colors, I always have my art book, colors, and clay handy. I might say, 'If what you are saying had a rhythm or color to it, what would it look like?'" Two other tools frequently used in expressive arts therapy are modeling clay and sand trays, two media that, says Dolan, "we used when we were young, usually without grown-ups judging us."

Just as art therapy was on the cutting edge in the 1960s, some see expressive arts therapy as the wave of the 1990s. Traditional art therapists are beginning to incorporate expressive art techniques because they see its advantage over traditional art therapy in its ability to allow clients to discover their own creative path.

Organizations

Atira
8307 Plateau Road, Box 427
Baileys Harbor, WI 54202
(920) 839-2530 (phone)
(920) 839-9714 (fax)
emcneil@maio.wscnet.net (e-mail)
www.Atira.org (website)

A creative artistic training and education center focusing on the incorporation of the expressive arts in spiritual transformation.

Institutes for the Arts in Psychotherapy
Chelsea Arts Building, Suite 309
526 West 26th Street
New York, NY 10001
(888) 225-2787 (toll-free number)
    The institutes offer programs in drama, dance/movement, and music therapies.

International Expressive Arts Therapy Association
P.O. Box 641246
San Francisco, CA 94164-1246
(415) 522-8979 (phone)
Lindabgold@aol.com (e-mail)
    IEATA is a professional organization created to support the expressive arts community in establishing recognition of the profession and to encourage the growth and evolution of an integrated arts approach to psychotherapy and education.

International Network of Creative Arts Therapy Associations
Friesstrasse 24
CH-8050 Zurich
Switzerland
    This organization includes an international network of ten independent training institutes in eight countries, including one in Israel and one in Canada. Emphasis is on multimodal expressive arts therapy, but each institute emphasizes a particular modality. Teachers, graduates, and others gather each spring for a symposium.

National Coalition of Arts Therapies Associations
c/o American Dance Therapy Association
2000 Century Plaza, Suite 108
Columbia, MD 21044
(410) 997-4040 (phone)
(410) 997-4048 (fax)
info@ADTA.org (e-mail)
www.adta.org (website)
    The coalition works to unify the field and lobbies for the inclusion of the creative and expressive arts in health-care legislation at the national and state levels.

Oasis Center
624 Davis Street
Evanston, IL 60201

(847) 475-7303 (phone)
(847) 475-7606 (fax)

The center sponsors adult education programs in the areas of personal growth, spirituality, expressive arts, bodywork, and energy work, among others.

Person-Centered Expressive Therapy Institute
P.O. Box 6518
Santa Rosa, CA 95406
(707) 584-5526 (phone)
exartspc@aol.com (e-mail)
www.members.aol.com/exartspc/mdex.htm (website)

The institute is dedicated to personal and planetary healing through training in person-centered expressive therapies.

Tamalpa Institute
P.O. Box 794
Kentfield, CA 94914
(415) 457-8555 (phone)
(415) 457-7960 (fax)
Tamalpa@igc.apc.org (e-mail)

Founded in 1978, Tamalpa is a nonprofit organization offering training and education in the movement-based expressive arts therapies.

Periodicals

International Journal of Arts Medicine
3526 Washington Avenue
St. Louis, MO 63103-1093
(314) 531-9635 (phone)
(314) 531-8384 (fax)
mmbmusic@mmbmusic.com (e-mail)
www.mmbmusic.com (website)
Semiannual; $20

This is the official journal of the International Arts Medicine Association and the International Society for Music in Medicine.

New Thought Journal: Reflections of the Creative Spirit
2520 Evelyn Drive
Kettering, OH 45409
(937) 293-9717 (phone and fax)

NTJMag@aol.com (e-mail)

Quarterly; $15

A magazine that links creativity and spirituality through poetry, essays, and articles by philosophers, authors, artists, and musicians.

❈ In Conversation with Julia Cameron: ❈
The Creative Contagion

For my whole life, I have been a creative artist—a writer, a painter, a film-maker, and a poet—and I have always experienced creative and spiritual energies as identical. Whenever you write or paint or dance, you align with and open your-self to spiritual guidance. Like a flow of electricity, this spiritual connection is always there. You don't need to beg, cajole, or plead with it. It's not an anthropo-morphic, gray-bearded God who decides whether to give you a good story idea. There is instead a sense of companionship between the Creator and creators forged by the latter's constant low-key listening. Carl Jung once said, "Seek daily the will of God." That's the kind of listening an artist does.

What I said about creativity and spirituality in *The Artist's Way* is not very dif-ferent from what other artists have said through the centuries. Many, many artists experience inspiration as a spiritual faculty that is inherent in the creative act. Giacomo Puccini attributed the ideas for Madame Butterfly to God; William Blake said, "not I but the Holy Spirit does the work"; and Gerard Manley Hopkins saw the world "charged with the grandeur of God." That is my experience as an artist.

Creativity *is* spirituality, just as creativity *is* healing. Art, by definition, is ther-apeutic. And even though healing may not be the primary reason you take up an artistic endeavor, it's an automatic byproduct. It's very difficult to be creatively unblocked and unhappy at the same time. We think of creative artists as unhappy but they are not. When people are immersed in their art-making they are quite happy and balanced. A lot of what we think of as neurosis is really blocked cre-ativity. I know that since *The Artist's Way* came out, many therapists are using it with clients who are suddenly "cured." But I don't think of these clients as being cured, because they were never neurotic, just blocked.

There are a few simple things that people can do to ensure that their creative flow is powerful and steady, strong and dependable. Two tools, in particular, if used regularly, will greatly enrich one's creative flow. The first is "morning pages": three pages of longhand writing about anything each and every morning. The second thing is a weekly hour of solitude during which you do something enjoyable. When people utilize these tools, they build a spiritual radio kit. With the morning pages, they send the message "This is what I want; this is what I don't want. This is what I like; this is what I don't like. Here's what I want to try; here's what I am scared to try." Then they switch over to a receptive state, opening themselves up to a flow of intuitive information that they might ordinarily have blocked.

Writing each morning teaches you to listen and to write without censorship because there's no wrong way to do it. Your censor can scream, "You sound so negative! You sound so whiny! You sound so petty!" But simply by continuing to write the pages, you are saying to your censor, "I'm sorry, but I'm going to keep right on writing." Because there's no wrong way to do this, your censor is made to understand that you mean business. It is to stand aside. This allows you to try any form of writing and to do it more freely. The exercise also puts all of your little gripes and worries and what I call "the inner movie" on the page, which then renders you far more present in your daily life. If you are more present in your daily life, you increase your image flow because you are tuned in, not tuned out. If you increase your image flow, you improve your image bank. And if you improve your image bank, when you go to draw on it, it's full. That makes the process much more playful because you are not fishing a fished-out pond; you are not panicking and yelling, "I need an image! Where is it?" You have an abundant supply of images.

There are another 120 tools in *The Artist's Way* but I always tell people that if you would just use these two tools, you would experience a huge sea change. These tools are a kind of spiritual chiropractic. Hyperactive people calm down and underactive people become more active. If you need to get sober, you get sober. If you are overweight, you end up exercising more. In a twelve-week workshop, people begin to look physically different only three or four weeks into morning pages. I have always said that people ought to do this just for vanity. Friends come up and say, "Have you fallen in love? Have you had a facelift? You look so different." That's what happens when people get in touch with their inner juice: their skin tone improves, their color changes, they rearrange the furniture in their home.

When I teach now, I should take a basket with me because so many people come up and say, "I used the tools and I made a CD." "I used the tools; here's my children's book." "I used the tools and made a videotape of our high school production of my first play; I want you to have a copy." I don't feel that we have even scratched the surface of where people are going with this. It's like we are in a quiet revolution. I call it a "creative contagion" because if one person looks happier, her friends ask, "What did you do? Are you having an affair? You seem so happy." Then they get involved in this process.

People are far more gifted than they know. When I teach a course, a person will say, "I don't know what I am doing here." Then she starts writing morning pages. On the third weekend, when we are doing something like a collage or a photo project, this person, who has sworn that she has no talent, will come in with amazing things. I look at them and think, "How did you get to be fifty-five years old without realizing you had this gift?" But people never received the proper mirroring. Until I started writing music at forty-five, I had no idea that I was musical. But I discovered that I have a huge gift for melody; I just didn't know it.

You might say that I am a good floor sample for *The Artist's Way* because in the last year alone I have done a wonderful poetry album, I've had my first musical produced, I've written three novellas, I'm finishing a book on writing, and I'm writing a book adapting *The Artist's Way* for the business world. I'm productive as a playwright—I have two plays going up this year—and as a poet and a novelist. I also teach full-time.

It's my experience that if someone is good at something, we discourage them from trying to do something else. As I was listening to a series of tapes about famous composers, I was struck by the fact that in the past, a composer often specialized in writing a particular form of music, say operas. Then he got bored and started writing sonatas. Soon he didn't like sonatas, so he started writing symphonies. Nobody said, "Bach, get a grip on yourself." Today we live in a culture where, when people are about to leap into a new arena, we discourage them; we tell them to be sensible. But we don't have any proof that being sensible works. In fact, it seems to have gotten a lot of us depressed. There's no reason that someone can't begin playing the piano in their mid-fifties. That's what Artist's Way groups are: people in their thirties, forties, and fifties who suddenly realize they can do a lot more than they thought.

> Julia Cameron is a multifaceted creative artist and the author of *The Artist's Way* and *The Vein of Gold*.

DANCE THERAPY

When we were children, most of us danced and moved spontaneously. As we grew older, however, we lost our ability to play and to move naturally. Dance therapy, which combines dance and psychotherapy, addresses the inhibitions we have accumulated over the years and seeks to restore our ease and freedom of movement. According to dance therapist Sharon Chaiklin, "By recognizing the language of movement, the dance therapist enables an individual to reach the source of emotional constriction and to explore new and more satisfying systems of behavior." Through dance therapy, people gain a visceral sense of their bodies, breathing patterns, and tension levels and are helped to develop, change, and function better physically, socially, mentally, and emotionally. Additionally, dance movements act as vehicles of self-expression that can bring unconscious material into awareness.

A full fifty years before the founding of the American Dance Therapy Association in 1966, C. G. Jung, in describing his technique of active imagination, pointed to the arts, including dance, as a nonverbal way of accessing unconscious material in the service of greater self-understanding and psychological and spiritual growth. It was not until World War II, however, that artistic media were married to therapeutic endeavors.

Marian Chace, who has been called the grande dame of dance therapy, is one of the earliest pioneers of the field. In the 1930s, she taught dance to groups of children with emotional problems. She noticed that as a result of taking part in these classes, the children's physical coordination improved, their self-confidence increased, and they were able to concentrate better, which then positively affected their school work. Working as a volunteer at St. Elizabeths Hospital in Washington, D.C., during the 1940s, she began to use her expertise and understanding of modern dance with the hospital's patients, primarily soldiers suffering from what was then called *battle fatigue*. Today we use the term *post-traumatic stress disorder*. Servicemen had been shipped stateside to mental hospitals, and the influx of these patients pressured clinicians into experimenting with various forms of group therapy, including dance.

Chace was hired in 1947 as the first dance therapist at St. Elizabeths, and over the next twenty years, she developed and refined both the techniques and theory of dance therapy. For example, she discovered how to establish a therapeutic relationship based on movement. Highly attuned to nonverbal communication, she mirrored the patients' body postures for the purpose of empathizing with them and communicating this empathy. In one instance, a female patient was making threatening advances toward the nurses. At the suggestion of a physician, Chace began to dance with her, mirroring her hostile movements. "The patient danced all manner of assaults . . . playing the role of a child in a tantrum, stamping her feet and pounding her fists in direct attack, seemingly bent on destroying her partner in the dance," Chace reported. However, patient and dance therapist never touched, and all movements were in rhythm with the music being played on the phonograph. Finally Chace "sank to the floor in simulated defeat," marking the end of the session. Later that day when Chace was about to begin a dance therapy group, the patient came to the door, asking to join the group and saying, "Now, I can dance with you instead of against you."

On the West Coast during this same period, Trudi Schoop was developing her own approach to using dance with patients in mental hospitals. Her unusual background in dance (her debut as a dancer at sixteen was very successful despite having had no formal training) and mime, as well as a well-honed sense of humor, all influenced her style of dance therapy and shaped the contributions she made to the field.

According to author, social worker, and dance therapist Fran T. Levy, Schoop believed very strongly in the healing power of humor, and although she never specifically wrote about this element in professional papers, it was extremely evident in her practice and teaching.

In addition to humor and mime, Schoop's work had other signature characteristics. For example, she used movement extremes, a technique, writes Levy, that is still well known and used by dance therapists today. Reminiscent of progressive relaxation exercises, it involves physical motion at two ends of a spectrum (e.g., tightening muscles and stiffening one's range of motion, then shifting to loose movements), with the goal of having the client arrive at an acceptance of conflicting emotions.

"From the tightest, I can then ask for less . . . less . . . still less . . . and finally, least," she wrote in her 1974 book, *Won't You Join This Dance?*, coauthored with her friend and fellow dance therapist Peggy Mitchell. "And from the loosest, more . . . more . . . still more . . . and finally, most. The body becomes more flexible as the patient practices the tension scale, and the patient can find one degree in which her body feels most comfortable. She discovers her functional, basic level of energy."

Other significant elements of Schoop's approach were her focus on posture, exploration of the fantasy life of patients, and the development of planned dance sequences based on spontaneous improvisational moves.

In the 1950s, another dance therapy pioneer, Mary S. Whitehouse, was the first to link dance and movement to depth psychology. Unlike Chace, who worked with hospitalized patients, Whitehouse worked with individuals interested in inner exploration. Whitehouse had both a dance background—Martha Graham was one of her teachers—and training in Jungian analysis. Thus it was natural that she link the two. Whitehouse distinguished between motions that were directed by the ego and motions that came directly from the unconscious. She instructed her students to listen deeply to inner sensations and to allow these impulses to take form in physical movements. Called Authentic Movement and Movement-in-Depth, her approach taught the person to shift consciously from moving the body intentionally to having the body be moved by the unconscious. "It is here that the most dramatic psychological connections are made available to consciousness," Whitehouse declared.

Joan Chodorow, registered dance therapist, past president of the American Dance Therapy Association, and Jungian analyst, was a student of Whitehouse beginning in 1962. "In the early months of my work," she writes, "I'd start to move, and she would say, 'No!' Then I'd wait, and start to move again, and she would say, 'No!' This happened so many times that I did more waiting than moving."

Gradually, writes Chodorow in her book, *Dance Therapy and Depth Psychology*, she realized that she could allow movement to happen. "I didn't have to form the movement consciously. It had its own form. I learned that I could listen to my body, and something would happen, then something else would happen."

Chodorow likens the process to working with dreams, where you focus attention on an image and as you observe it, it changes. In this way, the image—or in authentic movement, the movement—develops independently and spontaneously.

With Authentic Movement, there is usually a mover and a witness. The mover moves with eyes closed, allowing thoughts and images to surface in the mind while keeping the body in motion. The witness is there simply to provide a nonjudgmental presence.

One branch of Authentic Movement, which encompasses meditative, creative, and spiritual aspects, is the Contemplative Dance Program, cofacilitated by Alton Wasson, Mary Ramsay, and Daphne Lowell in Haydenville, Massachusetts. Although similar to other Authentic Movement programs, Contemplative Dance is not as formalized; the eyes do not have to be closed all the time; the facilitator can be more involved; and psychological narrative, drawing, and play are also utilized.

Like Whitehouse, Blanche Evan, a dancer, choreographer, and performer, also worked with adults outside institutional care, those she termed "normal functioning neurotics." Wedding her background in creative dance with the psychological theories of Alfred Adler, Otto Rank, Freud, and others, she created a psychotherapeutic approach that she eventually named Dance/Movement/Word Therapy. This approach balanced verbal interaction with dance and movement.

Other notable dance therapy pioneers include Alma Hawkins, who taught at UCLA, and Liljan Esperak, a Norwegian-born dancer who integrated Adlerian and Bioenergetic theories in her dance therapy work with mentally retarded individuals.

Following the groundwork laid by these women, other influences began to work on dance therapy in America. According to Sharon Chaiklin, who was among those instrumental in organizing the American Dance Therapy Association, the movement analysis theories of Rudolf Laban, including the Effort-Shape system of observation furthered by Irmgard Bartenieff, and Marion North's work with personality assessment based on movement all helped to describe and define what dance therapists were seeing when their clients moved.

As for today, Chaiklin sees dance therapy completing a cycle by returning to its roots; that is, the recognition that "what matters is movement." Dance therapists have integrated the verbal and psychological in their practices and can return to the basic structure of movement and dance, Chaiklin explains—the wellspring of dance therapy.

At present dance therapy is used with a broad range of client populations, including the mentally ill, the elderly, cancer patients, children on oncology wards, and those suffering from chronic pain, muscular dystrophy, and body image distortions such as those caused by breast cancer and eating disorders.

Books

Janet Adler, *Arching Backwards: The Mystical Initiation of a Contemporary Woman* (Inner Traditions, 1995). The author chronicles visionary experiences that came about as a result of her involvement in Authentic Movement.

Joan Chodorow, *Dance Therapy and Depth Psychology* (Routledge, 1991). Registered dance therapist and Jungian analyst Joan Chodorow explores and explains the relationship of depth psychology and dance therapy by discussing her personal journey, including the work of teachers Mary Whitehouse and Trudi Schoop and concepts such as active imagination, the unconscious, and shadow.

Fran J. Levy, *Dance/Movement Therapy: A Healing Art* (American Alliance for Health, Physical Education, Recreation, and Dance, 1988). This book takes a look at many of the dance therapy pioneers as well as the field's theories and applications to specific patient groups.

Fran J. Levy, editor, with Judith Pines Fried and Fern Leventhal, *Dance and Other Expressive Art Therapies* (Routledge, 1995). A collection of articles by therapists working with a wide range of problems from anxiety and addiction to multiple personality disorder. The book also contains sections on working with adults and with children.

Patrizia Pallaro, editor, *Authentic Movement* (Jessica Kingsley Publishers, 1996). A collection of essays by Mary Whitehouse, Janet Adler, and Joan Chodorow.

Susan Sandel, Sharon Chaiklin, and Ann Lohn, *Foundations of Dance/Movement Therapy: The Life and Work of Marian Chace* (The Marian Chace Memorial Fund, American Dance Therapy Association, 1993). A collection of essays by dance therapists covering aspects of Chace's personal and professional history and her contributions to the dance therapy field along with a selection of her papers.

Organizations

American Dance Therapy Association (ADTA)
2000 Century Plaza, Suite 108
Columbia, MD 21044
(410) 997-4040 (phone)
(410) 997-4048 (fax)

info@ADTA.org (e-mail)
www.adta.org (website)
   A membership and advocacy group for dance therapy.

Authentic Movement Institute
P.O. Box 11410
Oakland, CA 94611-0410
(510) 237-7297
   The institute develops new training approaches and opportunities for inves-
tigative study using an approach to authentic movement that is informed by
developmental psychology, somatic epistemology, Jungian thinking, dance ethol-
ogy, and mystical studies.

Periodicals

American Journal of Dance Therapy
Plenum Publishing
233 Spring Street
New York, NY 10013-1578
(212) 620-8000 (phone)
(212) 807-1047 (fax)
books@Plenum.com (e-mail)
www.plenum.com (website)
Semiannual; $36 individual, $150 institution
   This publication presents the latest findings in dance therapy theory, research,
and clinical practice by presenting original contributions, case materials, reviews,
and studies by leading practitioners and educators in the field.

Contact Quarterly: A Vehicle for Moving Ideas
P.O. Box 603
Northampton, MA 01061
(413) 586-1181 (phone and fax)
Semiannual; $14
   Supported in part by a grant from the New York State Council on the Arts
and the Massachusetts Cultural Council, this publication focuses on dance,
improvisation, and emerging movement-based bodywork modalities.

A Moving Journal
168 Fourth Street
Providence, RI 02906

(401) 274-2765 (phone)
(401) 781-2887 (fax)
3 times a year; $15 individual, $30 institution

The journal provides a forum for exploring Authentic Movement as a psychological and physical form of healing, a creative wellspring, a spiritual practice, and a means of community-building.

DRAMA THERAPY

Drama as a form of therapy began to be explored in the 1960s. The field that developed subsequently uses traditional performing arts techniques—reenactment of stories and real-life events, improvisation, role-playing, pantomime, mask work, and puppetry—to promote psychological healing and emotional growth. According to the National Association of Drama Therapy, this approach "helps the client tell his or her story to solve a problem, achieve a catharsis, extend the depth and breadth of inner experience, understand the meaning of [personal] images, and strengthen the ability to observe personal roles while increasing flexibility between roles."

One of the field's pioneers, Marian Lindkvist, began working with drama and movement in the 1960s and eventually developed a distinct form of drama therapy known as the Sesame Approach. Sesame's central focus is to create a safe space in which participants enter into a process of exploration and reflection in order to discover new possibilities within themselves. It aims to unify the physical, emotional, and mental aspects of the client by bringing these elements into harmony through imaginative drama. Jenny Pearson, in *Discovering the Self Through Drama and Movement: The Sesame Approach*, describes a typical session: "People move or dance to the sound of music—sometimes from a cassette player, sometimes played on simple musical instruments; a circle is formed and a story told; people take on parts, enact the story, become absorbed in a scene; they improvise like actors in rehearsal, using their voices; they sing, chant, call out words; they try on hats and use them as a starting point for role-play." After these dramatic enactments, people return to their "everyday selves." The work done in the session is not analyzed or interpreted.

Although many drama therapists have clients reenact events from their lives, they do not dwell exclusively on real-life occurrences. What is deemed most important is for clients to step outside themselves and participate in theater activities beyond their own life experiences. A drama therapy group might, for example, choose to act out a contemporary play or to improvise a real-life situation. But the group does not concentrate on a specific person and attempt to act out his or her life issues.

By contrast, psychodrama, founded by Jacob Moreno, M.D., more than seventy years ago, exclusively uses reenactment of a client's real-life experiences. In psychodrama, the client may play the roles of other people who have been significant in his or her life, but all role-playing involves real-life events and characters. Psychodrama uses groups of people, but the group focuses on one person's life events at a time.

Psychodrama's roots can be found in Moreno's involvement in Spontaneity Theatre, an improvisational group of actors who would work from suggestions offered by the audience. But he also became aware as early as 1925 of personal therapeutic benefits to such role-playing. The husband of one of the popular actresses who brilliantly played ingenue roles complained that she was in fact "a bedeviled creature when she is alone with me." Moreno began to give her saltier, more vulgar, and violent roles with the result that she became less angry at home and the relationship with her husband improved.

Psychodrama involves five "instruments"—the stage, actor (patient or client), director (counselor or analyst), auxiliary egos, and audience. What happens psychologically in the drama is that the actor/protagonist/patient reowns energies that he has projected onto others in his life. According to Moreno, "He takes his father, mother, sweethearts, delusions and hallucinations unto himself and the energies which he has invested in them, they return by actually living through the role of his father or his employer, his friends or his enemies; by reversing roles with them he is already learning many things about them which life does not provide him. . . . His own self has an opportunity to find and reorganize itself, to put the elements together which may have been kept apart by insidious forces, to integrate them and to attain a sense of power and of relief. . . ."

Drama therapy is used for many different problems—for example, learning disabilities, substance abuse, emotional conflict, disorders associated with aging—in a wide variety of settings including psychiatric hospitals, mental-health facilities, community programs, schools, businesses, and prisons. The benefits too are many: reducing a sense of isolation, developing social skills and coping mechanisms, broadening one's range of emotional expression, and developing relationships.

One unique program that does all of that and attempts to effect community-wide healing as well is City at Peace. Established in 1994 in Washington, D.C., the program annually brings together nearly a hundred students between the ages of thirteen and twenty from more than two dozen schools. Chosen not so much for their talent as for their commitment to participate with their peers in efforts to transform community violence and divisiveness into cooperation and collaboration, the teenagers meet for seven or eight hours every Saturday for a year. Because they represent socially and economically diverse neighborhoods, they begin by exploring issues related to their differences in order to build relationships across these social divides. Once trust is built, the youngsters begin to share the stories of their lives and to explore problems and themes such as substance abuse, sexuality, racial tension, and societal and familial dysfunction.

From their stories and discussions, a script is developed, songs are written, and dances choreographed. Midway through the year, the young people stage a musical drama—a moving and energetic production—in a major theatrical venue, and then go on to tour the schools and other community sites.

The program has become so popular that a second group of youngsters has been organized, so that beginning in 1998, performances will be presented both in the fall and spring.

City at Peace aims to develop self-awareness, increase self-esteem, encourage relationships, and motivate students to become responsible and productive members of the community. What the program and the teenagers give to the city is a powerful look at what adolescents are feeling and thinking, caring and worrying about. The program is an opportunity for opening up communication at several different levels: interpersonally, intergenerationally, interscholastically, and between different socioeconomic classes and community groups.

Organizations

Beyond Mask
336 Randolph Place, NE
Washington, DC 20002
(202) 526-2008

Beyond Mask was founded by Sirkku Sky Hiltunen, Ph.D., and Margaret "Muggy Do" Dickinson, Ph.D., to provide training in the transpersonal expressive arts and in preventive behavior management. Special training is also offered for professionals working with persons with mental retardation and multiple disabilities.

City at Peace
3305 8th Street, NE, Studio A
Washington, DC 20017
(202) 529-2828 (phone)
(202) 529-1654 (fax)
Citypeace@aol.com (e-mail)

National Association for Drama Therapy (NADT)
15245 Shady Grove Road, Suite 130
Rockville, MD 20850

(301) 258-9210 (phone)
(301) 990-9771 (fax)
nadt@mgmtsol.com (e-mail)

Established in 1979, NADT is a membership and advocacy group for drama therapists.

Psychodrama Training Institute
19 West 34th Street, Penthouse
New York, NY 10001
(212) 947-7111 (phone)
(212) 239-0948 (fax)

The institute, founded in 1968, provides professional training in psychodrama as well as information on local psychodrama practitioners.

Creativity Books to Charge Your Muse

Books that help jump-start the creative process are everywhere today, often making the task of choosing one seem overwhelming. Several, however, stand out.

Writing workbooks are the most abundant. Although new ones appear every year, each writing workbook owes a debt to Brenda Ueland's *If You Want to Write*. Published in 1938, Ueland's book is not a workbook per se, but it contains all the wisdom, advice, and support a writer could want. She starts from the premise that "Everybody is talented, original, and has something important to say." In her estimation, only our inhibitions and social conditioning hold us back. Ueland was one of the first to advocate keeping a journal in which all thoughts are written down uncensored.

Another classic is Dorothea Brande's 1934 book, *Becoming a Writer,* an excellent resource for training the mind to see and think in a writer's way. A more up-to-date version is Natalie Goldberg's *Writing Down the Bones* (1986). In it, Goldberg explains the importance of selecting different places in which to write and demonstrates how daily life always offers material to write about. In 1990, Goldberg followed up *Bones* with *Wild Mind: Living the Writer's Life.* The book is a collection of brief personal essays about life and writing, many followed by exercises, some of which reinforce one's identity as a writer, while others provide topics on which to write. Another useful book is Deena Metzger's *Writing for Your Life*, which discusses writing as a spiritual practice. Speaking in terms of archetypes and myths, Metzger argues that everyone can learn to find an inner guide for support in writing. "Creativity is . . . a path, [and] writing is one of its practices," she explains, "and the muse with her sweet breath or fiery torch stands in the dark place and lights our way."

Other books that are less how-to manuals and more autobiographical reflections of the writers' lives include Eudora Welty's *One Writer's Beginnings* (1983), an all-too-brief memoir based on a Harvard University lecture series; Annie Dillard's *The Writing Life* (1989), an invitation to peek into her writing process; and *Bird by Bird* (1994) by Anne Lamott, lessons on writing taught through stories and anecdotes. Whereas Welty's voice is richly Southern and mellifluous and Dillard's is lean and piercing, Lamott's quirky humor has us turning the pages with a smile and knowing nod.

There are also a multitude of workbooks designed for painters, actors, writers, and other artists. One of the best, *The Artist's Way* by Julia Cameron, is a guide to discovering your creative potential. The book is set up in a twelve-week format, the core of which revolves around writing three "morning pages" every day and going on a weekly "artist's date" with yourself. Cameron's book provides concrete steps to remove blocks to creativity. One of her major points is that we can unlock our creative ability one step at a time: "Take a small step in the direction of a dream and watch the synchronous doors flying open." She also warns that we sometimes wish for events to occur to further our creative dreams, but after they do we turn away from them out of fear. The book helps readers work with this fear. Cameron's second book, *Vein of Gold* (1996), again describes her basic tools, adding "creative clusters" (creativity support groups) and daily walks to morning pages and artist dates. She then goes on to offer exercises aimed at enhancing self-knowledge ("The road to authentic art is through the self"), self-esteem, and perceptual abilities such as seeing and hearing. In both her books, Cameron links creativity to spirituality and likens the creative process to a spiritual path. Thus *Vein of Gold* also offers exercises to clarify one's image of God, hone intuition or inner guidance, and see accepting help as a spiritual practice. Whereas *The Artist's Way* uses an addiction recovery model, *Vein of Gold* wraps itself in a more imaginative context.

Eric Maisel's *Fearless Creating* is another useful workbook for all types of artists. From finding your creative ideas to fine-tuning and actualizing them, this book covers it all. Maisel knows the excuses we employ to keep us from completing our creative ventures, and he offers a multitude of solutions, from stopping and analyzing the moment to surrendering to the work and not listening to the voices that say it can't be done. The book also includes a section of anxiety management exercises.

Barbara Sher's *Wishcraft: How to Get What You Really Want* is an excellent resource for helping you get unstuck. Sher believes that to be creative and happy, you have to discover what it is you truly enjoy doing. In *Wishcraft* she asks the reader to identify past events that have caused mental blocks, then explores the type of environment that fosters creativity and growth. The book provides practical exercises for discovering what your goal is and plotting it out. Sher has also written two other books—*I Could Do Anything If Only I Knew What It Was* and *Live the Life You Love*—and produced several audiotapes, available from the Barbara Sher Tapes Company (800-548-3027), that may be helpful in harnessing your creative potential.

There are many more good workbooks out there. Go to your local bookstore, browse through the creativity and arts sections, and take time to read some of the exercises to see if they suit you. Choose a workbook as if you are choosing a friend. The rewards can be just as lasting.

POETRY THERAPY

Although references to the healing power of language go back to ancient Greece, the field of poetry therapy is relatively new: 1998 marks the eighteenth anniversary of the National Association of Poetry Therapy (NAPT), which establishes standards and requirements for professional poetry therapists.

Practitioners cite Jack Leedy as a key figure in the development of the field. Leedy was a psychiatrist who in the late 1950s began to use poems or sections of poems to help group therapy clients evoke and explore feelings and to focus discussion. Though therapists had been writing on the uses of bibliotherapy—therapy involving the assignment of particular reading matter to the client—since the 1930s, Leedy was the first to publish extensively on the uses of poetry in therapy, beginning with the seminal *Poetry Therapy* in 1969. Kenneth Gorelick, a psychiatrist, registered poetry therapist, and former NAPT president, says that Leedy's books helped therapists who had been using poetry with clients to give a name to what they were doing. "Suddenly, they could identify each other and share ideas," Gorelick says. In 1969 Leedy and his associates formed the Association for Poetry Therapy, which was a precursor to the NAPT.

There are now training sites for poetry therapy all over the country, but the program at St. Elizabeths Hospital in Washington, D.C., is often cited as a model for the others. The oldest continuous training program for poetry therapists in the United States, it was begun in 1975 by Arleen Hynes, the hospital librarian. Although Hynes left in 1980 to become a Benedictine nun, Gorelick and codirector Ruth Monser carry on the program.

Peggy Heller, a graduate of the St. Elizabeths program who went on to found the Poetry Therapy Training Institute as an alternative to graduate work in poetry therapy, believes that poetry can play a unique role in psychological healing. Although Heller often uses what she describes as the "traditional" method of poetry therapy—group therapy in which everyone reads and responds to the same poem—she and her colleagues often branch out in other directions, such as having the group act out specific passages in a poem or write their own poems in response to material they've read.

John Fox, author of *Finding What You Didn't Lose: Expressing Your Truth and Creativity Through Image-Making* and a certified poetry therapist, writes that "making poetry part of your life can give you a kind of peripheral vision, a new way to see your life and the path you are on." For Fox, the field's potential is infinite. "Name any issue," Fox says, "and poetry can address it."

❁ Sister Arleen McCarty Hynes on Poetry as Prayer ❁

As the deer longs for the running waters, so my soul longs for you,
O God.

—Psalm 42

It is no accident that the Bible so often turns to poetry, for this form of expression touches heart, mind, and soul. A good poem is concise and dynamic, with metaphor and imagery incorporating feelings and experiences that extend and enrich literal meaning. Because of this, a poem need not contain overtly religious elements to lead to prayer, to a true communication with the Divine.

In "poetry as prayer" sessions, the focus is specifically on participants' spiritual welfare. The leader is a spiritual director who facilitates dialogue about a work of literature to help the group members attune themselves to the presence of the Greater Power as they search for the spiritual in the ordinary.

In practical terms, "poetry as prayer" sessions open with the facilitator leading the group in a brief prayer, introducing a poem or text, and then inviting dialogue. The facilitator's role is neither to preach nor to interpret but to help participants sort out and share their reactions, and to explore and clarify the spiritual implications of responses to the work and to one another's perceptions. In the fifteen or so minutes of this discussion, even a very short text will prove itself a rich resource. Think, for example, of all that might emerge about one's spiritual life or one's ability to pray from an image of doors opening and closing, or from a metaphor about stopping on a snowy evening.

After the dialogue, the group again prays individually, and members meditate on what they have learned or understood from the text and discussion. At times the reflection will be a form of silent prayer; at other times, members may write a poem or make an entry in a journal. The session usually concludes with the members again asking the Spirit to guide them as they share with one another their intuitions.

Whereas modern Jewish philosopher Martin Buber asked, "How may I understand my experience of God?," I ask, "How am I able to experience God?" Both

Gregory the Great in the Christian Middle Ages and Rumi, a Sufi of the thirteenth-century Arab world, might have responded that personal wisdom and sanctity are rooted in what we learn from others. This is what the dialogue in "poetry as prayer" sessions provides.

Both poetry and prayer are of the mind, heart, and soul. In the abiding love of God, they can lead us to the longed-for running waters.

Sister Arleen Hynes, a registered poetry therapist and a nun at St. Benedict's Monastery in St. Joseph, Minnesota, started the first poetry therapy training program, at St. Elizabeths Hospital in Washington, D.C., in 1974.

Books

John Fox, *Poetic Medicine* (Jeremy P. Tarcher, 1997). Starting from the thesis that "poetry is natural medicine," the author, through commentary, poems, and exercises, shows how readers can access the healing power of poems.

Clark Strand, *Seeds from a Birch Tree: Writing Haiku and the Spiritual Journey* (Hyperion, 1997). This book explains how to use haiku as a meditative practice and a tool for self-awareness.

Organizations

National Association for Poetry Therapy (NAPT)
P.O. Box 551
Port Washington, NY 11050
(516) 944-9791 (phone)
(914) 944-5818 (fax)
aseeger@mcimail.com (e-mail)
www.poetrytherapy.org (website)

This membership and advocacy organization provides a list of NAPT-approved mentors and supervisors and publishes a newsletter, *Museletter*, and *The Journal of Poetry Therapy*.

Poetry Therapy Training Institute
7715 White Run
Potomac, MD 20854
(301) 983-3392 (phone)
(301) 299-8330 (fax)
PegOheller@aol.com (e-mail)

The institute offers a two-year training program in the uses of literature and poetry in psychotherapy and personal growth.

Pudding House Writers Resource Center
60 N. Main Street
Johnstown, OH 43031
(740) 967-6060 (phone)
www.puddinghouse.com (website)

Directed by poet Jennifer Bosveld, Pudding House provides workshops, seminars, and individual opportunities to explore poetry therapy both personally and professionally.

Wordsworth Center for Growth and Healing
2625 Woodley Place, NW
Washington, DC 20008
(202) 232-4338 (phone)
Kengorel@erols.com (e-mail)

The center offers programs in the use of story, myth, folk and fairytale and other genres of poetic language for restoring the authority of the self.

Periodicals

Journal of Poetry Therapy
Human Sciences Press
P.O. Box 735, Canal Street Station
New York, NY 10013-1578
(212) 620-8000
Quarterly; $32, free to NAPT members

Official journal of the National Association for Poetry Therapy.

MUSIC THERAPY

Music therapy is the marriage of ancient healing methods that employed sound, percussion, rhythms, and melodies with contemporary Western medical protocols. The first creative arts therapy to organize itself professionally (in 1958), the field reflects a remarkably broad range of therapeutic interventions. From innovative uses of music for patient populations such as victims of Alzheimer's and Parkinson's disease, cancer, and stroke, to the use of music to stimulate imagery and further psychological exploration, to pioneering investigations of the power of sound to heal, music therapy in its various forms is used to restore, maintain, and enhance mental, physical, emotional, and spiritual health. The means of accomplishing this include musical instruments—from piano and guitar to kazoos and whistles—songs, and audiotapes. A music therapy session can consist of anything from singing a popular song with an Alzheimer's patient to an expectant mother listening to soothing music in the delivery room, to performing voice exercises that open up the body to toning (i.e., projecting certain sounds inward in order to release emotions, relax, or maintain an energetic balance in the body).

Although music therapy has officially been practiced in the United States for about forty years, the use of music as therapy is as old as human beings. Medicine men and shamans utilized chant, drumming, vocalizations, and the music of instruments such as bells, rattles, and whistles to effect healing. Later Pythagoras, often called the father of Western music therapy, used melody to promote physical healing. He believed that melody and rhythm originated in cosmic laws and were infallible in restoring harmony to the human soul and psyche.

In medieval times, medical practitioners employed melody to assist in surgery and midwifery and recommended it at mealtimes to promote good digestion. Also during the Middle Ages, Gregorian chant became popular in monasteries throughout Europe. This type of chant, named after Pope Gregory I, is a form of plainsong, simple liturgical music sung without instrumental accompaniment in unison and with no harmony. According to Katherine Le Mée in her book *Chant*, these songs, which are derived from psalms, hymns, and antiphons, are generally sung during the Roman Catholic Mass or during the daily canonical hours or "office," periodic devotional services held through the monastic day.

Although the aim is to bring both singers and listeners into a closer relationship with God, the chants also have a calming and harmonizing effect both on individuals and on the community as a whole, and serve as an anchor to the contemplative monastic life. This fact was dramatically highlighted by an incident described by Dr. Alfred Tomatis in a 1978 interview conducted by Tim Wilson. In the late 1960s, Tomatis was invited to visit a Benedictine monastery in France. Following reforms instituted as a result of Vatican II, the monks had begun to experience lethargy, fatigue, and mild depression. Tomatis diagnosed the problem as the elimination of chanting from their daily routine. He theorized that the chanting had rejuvenated the monks. Without it, they became tired. Six months after following Tomatis's recommendation to restore the daily chanting, the monks were once again lively and energetic.

Gregorian chant exploded on the American scene in 1994 with the release of the compact disk *Chant*. Recorded by Spanish Benedictine monks, who sang the chants in Latin, the recording rose to the number one spot on *Billboard* magazine's classical chart and to the number three slot on its pop chart. Today more than four million copies have been sold in more than forty-two countries. The *Chant* phenomenon attests to the fact that people all over the world respond to music that soothes the spirit and calms the mind.

The eighteenth-century German mystical poet Novalis took this idea one step further when he wrote, "Every sickness is a musical problem. The healing, therefore, is a musical resolution." Today music therapy is used to address physical, psychological, and spiritual conditions.

Healing the Body

Although music has been used throughout history to prevent as well as treat illness, the medical community has been reluctant to bestow its blessing. As late as 1996, the *Journal of the American Medical Association* noted that because music therapists tended to report benefits in individual case studies and in small groups of patients, research on the benefits of music therapy did not make "much of an impression in clinical medicine." While the article conceded that the situation may be changing, it also cautioned that acceptance by the medical community still depended upon "hard evidence from controlled studies."

Perhaps this is why the American Music Therapy Association, the field's professional organization, seems to stress research to a greater extent than any of the other creative arts professional organizations. Studies such as those conducted by researchers at Colorado State University at Fort Collins on the effects of rhythmic stimulation in patients with Parkinson's disease are seen as critical to providing evidence of the physical benefits of music. Research conducted as part of a dissertation by Melinda Maxfield supported the theory that drumming by indigenous cultures had specific neurophysical effects. After having study participants listen to three different drumming tapes, each with a different rhythmic pattern or beat, she asked them to write a brief account of their experience and then interviewed them. What she found was that they experienced enhanced imagery, which she theorized is connected to increased theta activity (a brain wave pattern that generally occurs just before awaking or falling asleep and is associated with dreamlike imagery). "Percussion in general and rhythmic drumming in particular has the ability to elicit temporary changes in brain wave activity and thereby facilitate imagery and possible entry into an altered state of consciousness," she concluded.

While the medical community awaits further tangible evidence and research results, ample anecdotes abound that attribute physical benefits to singing songs or listening to and playing music. For example, British-born neurologist and bestselling author Oliver W. Sacks, at a hearing before the Senate Special Committee on Aging, declared: "The power of music is very remarkable. . . . One sees Parkinsonian patients unable to walk, but able to dance perfectly well or patients almost unable to talk, who are able to sing perfectly well. . . . I think that music therapy and music therapists are crucial and indispensable in institutions for elderly people and among neurologically disabled patients."

Along these lines, a 1994 *Washington Post* article on the benefits of music therapy poignantly reported that a man with Alzheimer's disease, upon hearing ballroom music, took his wife into his arms, looked into her eyes, and danced with her. Afterward, the wife broke down and tearfully told the music therapist, "Do you realize what you have done? That was the first time my husband has held me in three and a half years. I've missed him so." Family members who have had to contend with the loss of a spouse, parent, or sibling to Alzheimer's also know the incalculable emotional value of even the briefest glint of recognition from or connection with them.

Other physical conditions and ailments for which music therapists offer relief include stroke, heart disease, traumatic head injuries, migraine headaches, chronic illness, stress, cancer, and recuperation after surgery.

Music as Midwife

More and more, music is being utilized at both ends of life: at birth and at death. In Austin, Texas, for example, two music therapists set up a service to provide musical programs for women in labor. Working with the pregnant mother and her birthing partner, taped music is selected that corresponds to the various stages of labor. For example, early in the birth process the music would be "slow, relaxing and calming," but in later stages it would progress to a steadier and faster beat. Following delivery, a particularly meaningful piece is usually included. In addition to providing relaxation and support, the music stimulates the release of endorphins, thereby decreasing the need for pain relief medication.

In other hospitals, soothing instrumental or vocal music has been piped in to premature babies, who responded by gaining weight faster, using oxygen more efficiently, and leaving the intensive care unit more quickly.

At the other end of life, hospices have found the value of music in assisting the dying process. One of the pioneers in this area is Therese Schroeder-Sheker, founder of both the field of music thanatology and the Chalice of Repose Project at St. Patrick's Hospital in Missoula, Montana. Schroeder-Sheker did not specifically set out to found music thanatology. As an undergraduate music major, she worked as a nurse's aide in a geriatric home. One day the staff was told that a particular emphysema patient was close to death. One of the home's oldest residents, he was a hardened man who regularly pushed people away and could be abusive to the nurses and staff. When Schroeder-Sheker saw him on his deathbed, he was thrashing about and struggling. She went to him and took his hand. This time he did not push her away but held on to her. Taking this as an assent, she got into bed behind him, and began singing and gently rocking him.

"He had been so frightened that he was thrashing around, and his arms and legs were flailing. The minute the rocking and singing began he stopped flailing," Schroeder-Sheker explained in a 1990 *Common Boundary* interview. "He breathed the longest sigh I ever heard and he died in my arms." Realizing that she had been given a "precious" experience, she made an internal resolve to be there for the dying.

A harpist who is also a composer, scholar, and concert performer specializing in the music of the late Middle Ages eventually found what she now terms "monastic medicine." Her research turned up an eleventh-century repertoire of music played in the abbey at Cluny, France. The monks who worked in the infirmary had a great devotion to music and were dedicated to helping their fellow monks have a peaceful and blessed death. To that end, working in teams of two they played chants, hymns, and songs to their dying brethren to ease them in the transition while reassuring them that they were not alone.

Schroeder-Sheker has revived that tradition with the delivery of "prescriptive music" to the bedsides of the dying. The process begins when the Project is referred a patient. She or one of the musician-clinicians she has trained takes the vital signs of the dying person and then begins to play in a manner that synchronizes with the patient's breathing. Because they see a direct relationship between the melodic content of music and the patient's neurology, between music's harmonies and the respiratory and circulatory systems, and between rhythm and metabolism, each patient is given a unique musical blend specifically geared to where they are. In a 1997 Sounds True videotape, Schroeder-Sheker stressed that playing at the bedside of a dying person is "never a bedside concert," but rather a means to "help unbind people from what binds them stubbornly to the body when it is time in fact for them to go."

Schroeder-Sheker's Chalice of Repose project not only offers musical palliative care but training for professionals as well.

Exploring the Psyche

In the early 1970s, music therapist and musician Helen Bonny, one of a few pioneers researching the effects of music, imagery, and consciousness at that time, developed what is known as Guided Imagery and Music (GIM). According to Bonny, the purpose of her method was to access altered states of consciousness for the express purpose of gaining insight, increasing creativity, and catalyzing spiritual experiences. Whereas she originally thought of the method as a technique, she later realized that it was more of a process of deepening consciousness and self-understanding. A typical GIM session begins with the client (traveler) lying on a sofa or floor with his or her eyes closed. The GIM therapist or "guide" then creates a "musical space" with specially chosen tapes of classical music. This musical space serves as an auditory "mirror," reflecting the client's inner tensions and stimulating specific imagery experiences associated with those tensions. The music both evokes and contains the therapeutic process. While listening to the music, the client will report any images, feelings, or sensations that arise. Contrary to what one might think, Bonny believes that this verbal feedback engages the client more immediately and therefore deepens the imagery as well as the bond with the guide. "A feeling of co-adventure, a sense of security and support, allow the traveler the freedom to let go of usual defenses and explore realms . . . usually hidden from conscious view," she wrote. To end the GIM session, the guide brings the traveler back to a present-day, here-and-now consciousness, then discusses any issues that may have arisen during the musical portion of treatment. GIM has been effectively used to treat depression, anxiety, eating disorders, post-traumatic stress disorder, and other problems.

Bridging the physical, psychological, and spiritual realms is the Tomatis Method, used in over two hundred centers worldwide. It utilizes electronically filtered music to heal and retrain the inner ear. This therapy was originally created by Alfred Tomatis, a French ear, nose, and throat specialist, to help opera singers improve their voices. After discovering that the ears guide one's singing—because one can only reproduce the sounds that one can hear—Tomatis had patients listen to certain frequencies of music, a technique that he found to be effective with stutterers, the hearing-impaired, and children with autism and learning disabilities.

The Tomatis Method involves listening to tapes of Gregorian chant and Mozart, which Tomatis believes have a healing power that other compositions do not possess. (Children also listen to tapes of their mothers' voices recorded in such a way as to re-create the sounds heard in the womb.) Gradually the music is "filtered" to eliminate all but the higher frequencies. The resulting sound, which has been described as "listening to an old phonograph played down the street," is aimed at exercising the ear muscles. Slowly, through repeated sessions with the filtered sound tape, two tiny ear muscles are reconditioned to respond to a wider frequency of external sounds. In other words, hearing is improved. According to Pat Dixon, director of the Spectrum Center in Bethesda, Maryland, "When we're hearing perfectly, it's almost like being at a higher level of consciousness. We are integrated with nature and with the world; we are touching a level of being and sense a connectedness with a higher level of consciousness." Thus the Tomatis Method has potential not only for healing physical and emotional problems but also for enhancing spiritual development.

Sounding for the Soul

In the 1960s the phrase "far out" carried a positive connotation. Among the hip and hippies, it roughly translated into "Wow!" or "That's great!" Today it can either mean very advanced in the sense of avante garde or nonconformingly "out there." With regard to sound therapy from the medical standpoint, the latter translation applies. But for those immersed in subtle energy and energy medicine, sound healing is the cutting edge of music therapy.

The basis for sound healing is the theory that vibrations and tones of sound can have direct curative effects. In a 1996 issue of *Music Therapy Perspectives*, an AMTA publication, Barbara Crowe, a professor of music at Arizona State University at Tempe, and Mary Scovel, a music therapist in private practice in Tahlequah, Oklahoma, describe various sound healing techniques. These include sounds that are self-generated, sounds that are projected into the body, ways to "sound the body," listening techniques, healing compositions, and sound environments.

Several principles are inherent in the sound healing field. For example, seeing the body as a vibrational system in which energy or a "web of energy" interpenetrates the dense matter of the body and extends beyond it is a basic tenet of many approaches.

One sound healing approach is toning, a technique in which the client produces sounds, projecting them into his or her body-energy system for the express purpose of "release and relief of emotional and physical stress."

In the category of healing compositions is rhythm drumming. Citing Grateful Dead drummer Mickey Hart, indigenous drummer Babatundje Olatunje, and European-based drummer Reinhard Flatischer, Crowe and Scovel see the value of rhythmic input based on the theory that "all organisms, including humans, are intrinsically programmed for rhythm." They point to the rhythmicity of bodily processes, rhythms in nature, and rhythms in the brain as evidence that regular recurrence of beats and tones is inherent in human organisms. In a 1994 *Washington Post* article, Anne Lipe, a Montgomery County music therapist, confirmed this observation, stating that rhythm is "a very primitive, innate response and experience." According to Lipe, who works with the elderly, long after cognitive and verbal skills have disappeared, rhythm skills can be accessed. "Even people who are clearly very very cognitively impaired can do most of the rhythm tasks," she said.

In concluding their article, Crowe and Scovel wondered what place sound healing might be afforded in the music therapy association. One might extend that query and ask what role sound healing might find in the larger healing and medical communities.

Books

Joachim-Ernst Berendt, *The World Is Sound: Nada Brahma* (Destiny Books, 1987). Europe's foremost jazz producer tours the globe via sound as it is apprehended through the lenses of cybernetics, literature, tantra, the new physics, and mysticism and then introduces techniques for awakening the ear's capacities for spiritual perception.

Meribeth Bunch, *Dynamics of the Singing Voice* (Springer-Verlag/Wein, 1982). Designed as a reference text for teachers of singing, singers, choral directors, speech and voice therapists, and other health professionals and psychologists, this book explores the physiological, psychological, musical, and emotional aspects of the voice, especially as they relate to singing. There are strong sections on the emotional and psychological aspects of voice and its connection to our life energy.

Don Campbell, *The Mozart Effect* (Avon Books, 1997). A comprehensive and persuasive state-of-the-art summary of the methods for applying music to strengthen the mind, unlock the creative spirit, and heal the body. It includes numerous exercises and anecdotal accounts of treatment and cure, organized by symptom and disorder.

Kay Gardner, *Sounding the Inner Landscape* (Element Books, 1990). This book summarizes the author's explorations of the esoteric, scientific, philosophical, and medical approaches to music and sound gleaned from her own experience as a teacher, conductor, and composer. It also guides other musicians in performing for the well-being of self and others and includes a discussion of each instrument or instrument family's special strength or niche in healing.

Jonathan Goldman, *Healing Sounds: The Power of Harmonics* (Element Books, 1992). The author, who is the director of the Sound Healers Association, instructs the reader in the singular power of harmonics to heal and transform physically, emotionally, mentally, and spiritually.

Kristin Linklater, *Freeing the Natural Voice* (Drama Book Publishers, 1976). Linklater describes the natural voice as revealing inner impulses of emotion and thought, directly and spontaneously. She believes that to free the voice is to free the person. This volume is a densely packed distillation of her approach to working with actors and others motivated to give up the familiar for the challenge of exploring the "wide range of pitch, intricate harmonics and kaleidoscopic textual qualities of the natural voice."

Paul Newham, *The Singing Cure: An Introduction to Voice Movement Therapy* (Shambhala Publications, Inc., 1994). Newham details the history, theory, and application of a new expressive arts therapy that treats the voice as a bridge between mind, body-soul, and spirit and, as such, is the vehicle and the indicator of healing.

Organizations

American Music Therapy Association (AMTA)
8455 Colesville Road, Suite 1000
Silver Spring, MD 20910
(301) 589-3300 (phone)
(301) 589-5175 (fax)
info@musictherapy.org (e-mail)
www.musictherapy.org (website)

In January 1998, two professional music therapy associations—the American Association for Music Therapy and the National Association for Music Therapy—united to form the AMTA. In addition to professional activities for its members, AMTA sponsors public education programs, maintains a database of music therapists by geographic location, publishes a membership listing broken down by county and state, and offers technical assistance to those interested in music therapy.

Bonny Foundation: An Institute for Music-Centered Therapies
2020 Simmons Street
Salina, KS 67401
(913) 827-1497 (phone)
(785) 827-5706 (fax)
hbonny@ibm.net (website)

The Bonny Foundation, founded by Helen Bonny in 1988, is a nonprofit organization that provides resources and training in the therapeutic use of the arts for professional therapists.

Chalice of Repose Project
St. Patrick's Hospital
Missoula, MT 59802
(406) 329-5616

The Chalice of Repose is a center for training in and provision of prescriptive music for attending the dying at bedside in hospital, geriatric home, hospice, and personal home settings with the intention of helping both patients in pain and families in grief.

International Society for Music in Medicine
Contemporary Arts Building
3526 Washington Avenue
St. Louis, MO 63103-1093
(314) 531-9635 or (800) 543-3771 (phone)
(314) 531-8384 (fax)

mmbmusic@mmbmusic.com (e-mail)
www.mmbmusic.com (website)

    The society is an advocacy group for the use of music in the practice of medi-
cine. It holds a conference approximately every three years.

Mozart Effect Resource Center
3526 Washington Avenue
St. Louis, MO 63103
(800) 721-2177 (phone)
www.mozarteffect.com (website)

    The center is a clearinghouse for information found in the book *The Mozart
Effect,* by Don Campbell. It also coordinates Campbell's workshops, which are
held across the country.

Sound Healers Association
2510 West 47th Street, Suite 212
Boulder, CO 80301
(303) 443-8181 (phone)
(303) 443-6023 (fax)
soundheals@aol.com (e-mail)

    An organization dedicated to providing research on and expanding awareness
of the uses of sound and music as therapeutic and transformation modalities.

Sound Listening and Learning Center
2701 E. Camelback, Suite 205
Phoenix, AZ 85016
(602) 381-0086 (phone)
(602) 957-6741 (fax)
bthompson@soundlistening.com (e-mail)
www.soundlistening.com (website)

    This is the principal Tomatis center in the United States. It provides onsite
and outreach Tomatis Method programs on listening, language, and learning for
all ages and adult-level programs designed to develop communication, relationships, the musical ear, and creativity.

Tomatis International Headquarters
144 Avenue des Champs Élysées
Paris 75008, France
01 53 53 42 40

    International headquarters of the Tomatis Method and training.

Periodicals

International Journal of Arts Medicine
International Society for Music in Medicine
Contemporary Arts Building
3526 Washington Avenue
St. Louis, MO 63103-1093
(314) 531-9635 (phone)
(314) 531-8384 (fax)
mmbmusic@mmbmusic.com (e-mail)
www.mmbmusic.com (website)
Semiannual; $20

This journal explores healing through the creative arts and includes peer-reviewed theoretical, clinical, and philosophical articles along with networking activities, conferences, interviews, research, resources, discussions of performance-related disorders, and arts medicine.

Journal of Music Therapy
American Music Therapy Association
8455 Colesville Road, Suite 930
Silver Spring, MD 20910
(301) 589-3300 (phone)
(301) 589-5175 (fax)
info@musictherapy.org (e-mail)
www.musictherapy.org (website)
Quarterly; $85

This publication is a research journal published by AMTA.

Open Ear Journal
6717 NE Marshall Road
Bainbridge Island, WA 98110
(206) 842–5560 (phone)
(206) 842–1968 (fax)
pat@openearjournal (e-mail)
www.openearjournal (website)

This publication is dedicated to exploring, reporting, and advocating the uses of sound and music in health and education.

Healing Music

11,000 Virgins: Chants for the Feast of St. Ursula, written by Hildegard of Bingen and sung by the Anonymous 4, Harmonia Mundi USA, 1997.

Chant, by the Benedictine monks of Santo Domingo de Silos, Angel Records, 1994.

Music for the Mozart Effect, by Don Campbell, Spring Hill Music, 1998.

Rivers of One, traditional Sufi healing music, by Orus Guvenc and Tumata, Interworld, 1998.

Shaman, Jhankri & Nele: Music Healers of Indigenous Cultures, by Pat Moffitt-Cook, Ellipsis Arts, 1997. This CD is a collection of authentic healing songs from indigenous peoples around the world.

Sound Body, Sound Music, brainwave music with information by Andrew Weil, Upaya, 1998.

Women in Chant: Gregorian Chants for the Festal Celebrations of the Virgin Martyrs and Our Lady of Sorrows, by the choir of Benedictine nuns at the Abbey of Regina Laudis, Sounds True, 1997.

5
Reclaiming the Body

We have inherited a long-standing tradition in the West that values all that is rational and intellectual and devalues that which is intuitive, sensual, and soulful. Author and lecturer Morris Berman traces the roots of this tradition, which splits body from mind and alienates human beings from nature, to the sixth century B.C. Before that time, human beings lived at one with themselves and with their surroundings in a way that seems incomprehensible today. Berman tells us that at that time there was no distinction between mind and body, between inner and outer self. The *Iliad*, for example, contains no words for internal states. The word *psyche*, he says, would have been translated as "blood." But by the time of the *Odyssey*, a hundred or so years later, the word *psyche* clearly referred to "soul." With this distinction came the beginning of a cleft between body and soul, body and intellect.

This same cleaving occurred between human beings and the natural world. At one point in our collective history, human daily life was intimately intertwined with the cycles of the earth and its other creatures. By performing dances honoring the spirits of animals and plants or by telling stories of their ancestors' origins out of storm and soil and seas, human beings made bridges between themselves and the vast untamed cosmos. And even though it was unpredictable and often harsh, the natural world provided a source of identity and continuity.

"The pre-Homeric Greek, the medieval Englishman (to a lesser extent, of course), and the present-day African tribesman," writes Berman, "know a thing precisely in the act of identification, and this identification is as much sensual as it is intellectual." Intimate physical rapport with the surroundings was a natural state of being, one that not only enhanced chances of survival but also seamlessly wove individuals into the fabric of life. There was no need to search for meaning or purpose; one had a place in the scheme of things: in the tribe, in the environment, in the cosmos.

Laurens van der Post captured this sense of connectedness when describing the Kung! (the name given by outsiders to the Jul'hoansi people) tribesmen of the Kalahari Desert. Atuned to their natural surroundings and organized tribally, the

Jul'hoansi "were rich in the sense that they belonged," said van der Post. "They had great joy and happiness. They had great physical hardships but in the sum of things, they were deeply content and full of the sense of meaning and joy." Meaning came, he explained, because "they lived in this great desert world, and that great world which contained them was in turn truly in every detail contained within them. For instance there was a constant traffic of meaning between the stars and starlight, and themselves and their spirit; they participated deeply of one another's being."

The Jul'hoansi maintained a respectful relationship with other creatures. They never killed an eland, an animal that held deep meaning for them, without holding an elaborate dance in its honor and thanking it for giving its life to them. Contrast that attitude with that of T. H. Huxley, the nineteenth-century author of *Haodurche's Science Gossip,* who in defining zoological physiology stated that it "regards animal bodies as machines impelled by various forces and performing a certain amount of work."

What ignited this process of differentiation and why did it drive a wedge between body and soul? Between body and mind? Berman points an accusing finger at Socrates and Plato who, he argues, disdained and sought to destroy a kind of participation mystique wherein members of their society easily surrendered their individual identities in gatherings such as Greek theater. Empathic resonance was their way of learning about the world. Plato's ideal, however, was a psyche organized around a center (ego) with a will that controlled instincts. "Reason thus becomes the essence of personality," explains Berman, and the major force in distancing ourselves from all that surrounds us.

Still, it wasn't until the seventeenth century, when rationalism dismantled the medieval world view, that the gap separating body and mind, body and soul widened into a chasm. The Scientific Revolution shattered our mutuality with other beings and with the planet. By emphasizing domination and control rather than cooperation and reciprocity, we created a fissure between human beings and nature, between men and women, between intellect and body. In the Middle Ages, the universe was seen as organic and alive. But the Scientific Revolution sundered our relationship to nature, to God, to each other, and to ourselves by introducing the worldview in which human beings—indeed all of creation—were seen as machines. Instead of being in a reciprocal and equal relationship with nature, man worked to measure, analyze, control, rise above, and hold dominion over it.

Don Hanlon Johnson, who directs the Somatics Program at the California Institute of Integral Studies in San Francisco, shared a fascinating etymological discovery in his book *Body: Recovering Our Sensual Wisdom* that reflects this historical fracturing. The word *body* comes from the German *bottich,* "a cask, a brewing tub, or a vat." In the last two hundred years, a new word, *corpus*, inveigled its way into scientific and intellectual circles. This word, he says, is defined only in contrast to *soul* and *spirit*. Indeed if one looks up the definition of *corporeal* in *Webster's New World Dictionary*, it is "of, for, or having the nature of the body . . . not spiritual." *Spiritual* is defined as "not corporeal." But the most astonishing and revealing sense carried by the word is in the first definition of *corpus*: "a human or animal body, especially a dead one." Johnson contrasts the notion of deadness (corpse) with the images evoked by *body*, that of "a pot brimming over with hearty mead or of oaken casks in which Armagnac is aging. It's an appropriate word for the ruddy bodies in a Breughel painting of a country fair, delighting in food, ready for love."

Too many of us today are aligned with corpus, living almost exclusively in our heads, prisoners of our intellects; our bodies, encased in layers of tension, merely provide the means of transportation for our brains. We are effectively severed from our bodies, and feel cut off from our natural surroundings as well. We no longer feel that we occupy a purposeful place in a tribe, in a place, in creation. Those cut-offs have profound effects on the soul because, as Wallace Stevens has written, "The soul is composed of the external world."

How so? The soul of each individual is part and parcel of the *anima mundi*, or world soul, along with everything in existence. The soul's essence is therefore connectedness; it thrives on relationship. Indigenous people know this instinctively. Their survival depends upon their relationship with their environment. They must know the terrain where they live, the plant and animal life around them, the weather patterns. They need to know where shelter, food, and water can be found. But they do not know these things as objective facts separate from themselves; they know them intimately as themselves. Calvin Luther Martin, former biologist turned historian, calls this connection between human beings and plant and animal beings a "palpable kinship." Based on his experience and discussions with his biologist friends, he has come to the conclusion that natural systems are deeply interdependent. "Predator and prey are stamped with one another's psychic personality, or nature," he writes. "The one mirrors the other in a vital, vibrant way." Martin goes on to say that human beings that rely on hunting and gathering see "out-there"— the external world—as self. And not only are they resonant with each other, but what they kill to eat becomes a part of them. The act is transformative. Perhaps this is why native, or *nature-based*—a term coined by author and ecopsychologist Chelles Glendinning—peoples see the sacred in all things, and why they are so respectful. They understand viscerally the profoundly deep exchange inherent in all of life. Laurens van der Post, who was raised on a South African farm close to the natural world and to indigenous tribal people, spoke to this point when he admitted to not being "tempted to commit the metropolitan error of assuming that the sun rises and sets, the day burns out and the night falls, in a world outside oneself. These are great and reciprocal events, which occur also in ourselves."

Thus the soul's rhythms are the rhythms of natural cycles: seeding, birthing, growing, and dying; the sun's magnificent entrance at dawn, the building of its light and heat, its fading into dusk, and graceful exit, leaving the sky darkened for the stars and planets to dance with the ever-changing moon. Without attunement to these rhythms, we suffer. Our souls are exiled and isolated; we feel depressed, directionless, anxious, and adrift. We no longer know who we are. We end up carrying the burden of shaping our identities and finding our own purpose. But the current weltanschauung makes that an extremely difficult task. Like the poet William B. Yeats, we feel, "Things fall apart; the centre cannot hold." The only way to keep things from falling apart is to come back to ourselves, back to our bodies as the center of our experience. We desperately need to reconnect to our physicality, our instincts, and a slice of wildness untrammeled by analysis, rationalism, overintellectualization, and self-consciousness.

The field of psychotherapy—a field involved in healing or making whole—has not been immune to this split. Until recently only the traditional talk therapies received a modicum of professional and public approval and trust. Efforts by members of the human potential movement to encourage awareness of somatic experience have been lampooned by mainstream culture as "touchy-feely." However, the value of the body is making its way into people's ideas about healing and therapy. Therapists and their clients are learning that bodies are the natural repositories of experiences. Emotional traumas that the mind forgot or that cannot be resolved are stored in the body. Some, like Wilhelm Reich, say they reside in the body's musculature; others, like research scientist Candace Pert, locate them in neuropeptides, which are distributed throughout the body. Wherever memories are stored, it is a fact that beginning in childhood, we learn to ignore, dismiss, or avoid signals from our bodies in order to cut ourselves off from painful experiences. But as embodied creatures, we cannot escape the psychic, emotional, and spiritual events of our lives, which are literally impressed upon us and dynamically reflected in our comportment in the world. Only by reawakening our capacity to receive and understand the signals and sensations of our bodies can we come to full awareness of our experiences.

As we look back historically, the differentiation between inner and outer self, between self and other, was a necessary step in the evolution of consciousness. The early Greeks lived in a unitive state literally without self-consciousness. That is neither a desirable nor a completely achievable state for contemporary humankind. Today's challenge rests in striving to become fully differentiated and equally connected to all that is around us—other human beings, other creatures, and indeed the planet itself.

Bodywork, movement, conscious breathing, touch, and massage in their many forms all bring an awareness of the body's wisdom to spiritual practice, to psychological development, and to daily life. By sensing the meaning, purpose, and vision carried in and conveyed through the body, we may fine-tune our awareness of its messages, live more comfortably as integrated persons, and joyfully celebrate our embodiment.

Our bodies contain a great deal of natural wisdom. They have their own rhythms, signals, and urges to move, rest, and act. Too often we ignore our bodies because the messages interfere with the conduct of our daily lives. Anne is a list-maker. Every day she creates her list of things to do: calls, correspondence, and manuscripts on workdays; errands and groceries on the weekends. In the office, the pad of lists is like the crack of a whip, driving her on to check off yet another task. Anne's body has very little to say except to demand bathroom and lunch breaks.

The situation changes somewhat on writing and editing days at home. While there are long stretches at the desk, there's more attunement with regard to stretching, taking a break by walking to a nearby grocery store and deli, or spying on the feathered or furry visitors at the bird feeder, bird bath, and fountain. Her body is more of an active participant in finding the right words and ideas because she searches not just her mind, but her feelings and gut to come up with the right phrase or concept. She uses her ears to listen for the proper cadence and word choice.

Of course, embodiment is much more than taking an occasional good long stretch. It's living in your body and having it inform your actions. As a species we seem to be evolving away from physical work. More and more people are in service professions rather than manual labor. Sitting at a desk eight, nine, even ten hours a day or being on your feet for the same amount of time squeezes the body into a postmodern box. Although sailing, gardening, even roller-blading can enliven, invigorate, and renew our bodies, we need to come back to our physicality in such a way as to allow it to lead us. It's not easy to let go of the mind, to allow the body to direct our actions, moving us *where* we need to go, *when* we need to go there.

As people who are shaken into consciousness five days a week by an alarm clock—most of the year in the dark—we find nothing so refreshing as waking up naturally to first light. We emerge from the sleepy darkness along with the rest of the world. For a brief moment, we are in sync with the world around us. Before the mind makes its lists; before we step into our day's scheduled activities and responsibilities; before we push our bodies to type one more letter, dial one more number, read one more spreadsheet, there's a window, a space to breathe, a time to relish the start of a new cycle, a time to simply be with what is. Light softly filters through clouds or slowly inflames a vibrantly blue sky; the sound of birds or wind or early morning traffic, the creaks of the house, your partner's steady breathing—the gentle prelude to the symphony of the day.

BODYWORK

Richard S. Heckler, cofounder of the Lomi School and an aikido instructor, once suggested that bodywork could be classified into three categories: those methods that work *on* the body, those that work *with* the body, and those that work *through* the body. Because most methods, techniques, and approaches presented in *Soul Work* are either interdisciplinary or holistic, lines cannot be drawn with absolute rigidity. Opening up blocks lodged in the body, for example, has emotional, psychological, and even spiritual ramifications. Something as simple as receiving a massage at the end of a tense and hectic day can transform a person from a short-tempered, grouchy, and harried shrew into a relaxed, mellow, gracious human being. Still, categorical distinctions help to organize material and thinking. Heckler's system is useful because it divides bodywork approaches according to the role of the body in healing encounters.

For instance, in this chapter we will look at methods, techniques, and approaches that work *on* the body through a variety of manipulations of muscle, tissue, limbs, and skin. For the most part, the body is the recipient of touch and remedial action. In the following chapter we will describe body psychotherapy, which starts from a psychological perspective and works *with* the body to release tension, muscular armoring, and energetic blocks that hold and maintain self-destructive and dysfunctional patterns as well as psychological and emotional discomfort, even anguish. In this category, the client is more actively engaged in the healing process.

The last bodywork category, which is discussed in chapter 7, is somatic reeducation, a field that works *through* the body. Somatics is the most difficult to describe because it requires a radical shift of viewpoint. Instead of seeing the body as an object to be manipulated, opened up, or relaxed, or as a vehicle to a fuller enjoyment of pleasure and deeper experience of love and connection, somatics views the body as the context and ground of knowing, which if unobstructed naturally moves in ways that open up new and creative possibilities for feeling, perceiving, and living. Instead of an I-it relationship, somatics asks us to make the body, with its bubbling, burbling, pulsing sensations, the primary point of reference in the healing. It is a perspective that asks us to return to the concept of embodiment that Berman's pre-Homeric Greek experienced but with consciousness. It is a paradigm in which materialism drops its negative connotations and becomes the currency of knowledge. To truly know a thing is to meet it viscerally in an encounter not mediated or directed by intellect. And yet mind and awareness are not rebuffed or set aside. Not in the least. Somatics stresses awareness and consciousness but in the sense that the body leads the mind and not vice versa.

Before we get too far ahead of ourselves, let's return to some general principles. Bodywork, as the name suggests, tends to emphasize the physical over the mental, emotional, or spiritual. Deane Juhan, author and professional bodyworker, who practiced at the Esalen Institute for many years, beautifully described the benefits of bodywork in this way: "I have seen stoops straighten, gnarled deformities become more comfortable and functional, and injuries heal more quickly and completely. I have seen dozens of imminent surgeries averted, medications reduced or eliminated, eyeglasses upgraded or even occasionally discarded, chronic pain diminish or disappear, various degenerative conditions slow to a halt or even reverse." Additionally, he says, many personal changes that came about as a result of bodywork ended up positively affecting clients' relationships with spouses, partners, children, and colleagues. Juhan understands that everything, as Ida Rolf once wrote, is connected to everything else. Thus focusing on one area leads to changes elsewhere. In bodywork, that focus begins with physical structures: bones, tissue, muscle, fascia.

A 1991 *Massage Therapy Journal* article divides bodywork into three "fundamental, mutually inclusive, and interrelated" categories based on intention or goal: namely, relaxation, remediation, and holistic health. The first consists of massage techniques and touch that are "noninvasive, relaxing, pleasurable, sensual but not sexual, and stress-reducing." These are massages that one might encounter in health clubs. Ten years ago we might have also included health spas, but recently many, though far from all, have become quite sophisticated vis-à-vis holistic methods and have added Eastern techniques such as acupressure and shiatsu and Western methods such as Reflexology and Trager to their basic Swedish massage repertoire.

The second category involves "hands-on" healing methods that specifically address physical discomfort and pain. This group for the most part quite literally digs deeper into the body. For example, deep tissue work specifically addresses deeper layers of muscles and muscle groups and Reflexology works on specific areas of the feet.

The third category has to do with improving clients' quality of life and includes preventive care as well as transformational growth work. The approaches in this group see healing as an interplay of body, mind, and spirit. According to the journal article, "curing disease is not the primary purpose of approaches in this category, rather it is supporting growth toward a 'higher order of functioning.'" Ralph Golan, M.D., in his book *Optimal Wellness*, offers a good example of how bodywork led him to deeper and more enriching explorations. After his hectic medical practice left him with neck strain from holding too much tension, he began getting a weekly massage. "The massage treatments helped me see clearly that I'd simply been performing beyond my limits, trying to be everything to everybody," he writes. "In so doing, I was sacrificing my main interests and talents. Over the course of several months, I began to practice yoga and take other self-care measures that minimized my need to see a massage therapist regularly and helped me to function at my best. From the simple goal of reducing my neck pain, I grew to realize the depth of healing and self-knowledge inherent in bodywork."

In this chapter, you will find ways to relax, open, stretch, heal, and invigorate the body. The therapies in this chapter come from around the globe, from massage that originated in Sweden and Amsterdam to Breema bodywork, which hails from a small village in the Near East. Massage is the most familiar kind of bodywork, enjoying considerable attention and respect from both the research community and the public. As with many alternative remedies, massage has been practiced for centuries in different cultures. Although Western medicine until recently tended to overlook it, its therapeutic effects are easily recognized, and it has long been considered a legitimate, beneficial therapy.

In recent years, massage has been used increasingly in medical settings. The National Institutes of Health (NIH) Office of Alternative Medicine (OAM) has funded several projects to learn if massage therapy is effective in treating a wide range of illnesses. One project at the University of Miami studied infants who had been exposed to HIV and concluded that as a result of massage, the young subjects experienced increased weight gain and improved performance on the Brazelton Newborn Scale. Another, conducted at Dartmouth-Hitchcock Medical Center in Lebanon, New Hampshire, found that bone-marrow transplant patients had significantly lower levels of anxiety, distress, nausea, diastolic blood pressure, and fatigue following a massage, although these positive effects were not long-lasting. Other less serious conditions can also be relieved by massage, which is known to increase flexibility, improve posture and circulation, reduce pain, and ease muscle strain and tension. It can also help improve muscle tone and widen range of motion.

Just as different bodywork approaches emphasize different parts of the body—the spine, bones, joints, muscles, soft tissues, connective tissues (fascia), and various points in the hands or feet that correlate with other parts of the body—so too there is great variety in how each manipulates and works on these parts of the body. Some therapies are rigorous, even painful, during the treatment session, while others are gentle and subtle. Sometimes whether a technique is applied more rigorously or more gently is less dependent upon the method than upon the practitioner using the method. Anne was reminded not too long ago of a Reflexologist whose aggressive style was extremely painful but very effective. In this case, it was the practitioner's style, not the method, that determined the amount of pressure applied. In fact, in speaking with a variety of practitioners and therapists engaged in both bodywork and body psychotherapy, one theme that sounded again and again was how in the last twenty years, body-oriented methods have become gentler, more refined, and more subtle. In the 1960s and 1970s, the enthusiasm for experimentation and opening up blocks sometimes resulted in unnecessarily aggressive assaults on the body. Today some body therapists use hard pressure on discrete areas, others use gentle strokes, firm molding and kneading, or rhythmic "leans," as in Breema bodywork. Some bodywork methods are soothing, others more invigorating, but all serve the same end of easing tension, reducing stress, alleviating pain and discomfort, and making us more aware of our bodies.

"Awakening your body and becoming aware of its insights as well as its sensory delights can be a doorway into a spacious room," writes massage therapist Mirka Knaster in *Discovering the Body's Wisdom*. "It can reintroduce you to the areas you deadened in self-defense. It is also a means to slow down even in the midst of frenetic living, by physically experiencing each moment now instead of speeding along mentally. The body anchors you in the present, the place where time seems full and expanded, rather than short and limited. In that calm you rest, you learn, you change, you heal."

Books

Thomas Claire, *Bodywork* (William Morrow, 1995). This handbook is a combination of personal experiences with and descriptions of sixteen body therapies, including Swedish massage, Rolfing, Therapeutic Touch, and Holotropic Breathwork.

Deane Juhan, *Job's Body* (Station Hill Press, 1997). This is a densely packed reference about the workings of the human body intended for health practitioners, massage therapists, exercise instructors, and motivated seekers. But the fire of emotion in Juhan's nontechnical opening and closing chapters makes the book inspirational for any owner of a conscious body.

Mirka Knaster, *Discovering the Body's Wisdom* (Bantam Books, 1996). A comprehensive guide to over fifty body-mind practices that not only relieve physical stress and tension but also foster health and spiritual growth.

Elaine Stillerman, *The Encyclopedia of Bodywork: From Acupressure to Zone Therapy* (Facts on File, 1996). A comprehensive collection of bodywork techniques, terms, approaches, and therapies with concise and clear definitions and histories.

Audiotapes

Body Wisdom, Sounds True, 1994. These audiotapes from sessions at the 14th Annual Common Boundary Conference include 2½-hour workshops and 5-hour institutes given by Joan Borysenko, Rosalyn Bruyere, Marion Rosen, Bonnie Bainbridge-Cohen, Ilana Rubenfeld, Stanley Keleman, Jon Kabat-Zinn, and many others in the bodywork and somatics fields.

ACUPRESSURE AND SHIATSU

Acupressure, an ancient Asian healing art developed more than five thousand years ago, includes many specific methods such as Jin Shin Do®, a system developed by Iona Marsaa Teeguarden that combines Japanese-style pressure points with Jungian and Reichian theories, Taoist philosophy, and breathing techniques; shiatsu (Zen and barefoot), a Japanese finger pressure therapy that integrates Western anatomical and physiological principles with traditional Oriental massage (Amma) and other Eastern influences; Do-In, a self-massage technique introduced in the United States by macrobiotic advocate Michio Kushi among others. Each method is an amalgam of different influences, has distinctive characteristics, and incorporates various ways of using pressure on specific points on the body.

A traditional acupressurist works with the same points used in acupuncture but stimulates them with finger pressure rather than by inserting fine needles. Although considered older than acupuncture, acupressure tended to be overlooked when the Chinese developed more "technological" methods for stimulating points with needles and electricity. However, using the power and sensitivity of the hands, acupressure is effective in the relief of tension-related ailments, in self-treatment, and in preventive health care. Acupressure can also be combined with other massage techniques to increase circulation, reduce pain, and develop all-around health. Practitioners use acupressure as both a primary and an adjunct technique.

Organizations

Acupressure Institute
1533 Shattuck Avenue
Berkeley, CA 94709
(510) 845-1059 (phone)
(510) 845-1496 (fax)
www.healthy.net/acupressure (website)

Founded in 1976, the Acupressure Institute offers both basic and advanced acupressure training in traditional Oriental bodywork and massage. The institute can also help you find a training program located near you.

American Oriental Bodywork Therapy Association (AOBTA)
Glendale Executive Park
1000 White Horse Road, Suite 510
Vorhees, NJ 08043
(609) 782-1616 (phone)
(609) 782-1653 (fax)
aobta@prodigy.net (e-mail)
www.healthy.net/aobta (website)

AOBTA is an information and advocacy group that acknowledges and respects all traditions of bodywork but specializes in those based in the tradition of Oriental medicine. It sponsors continuing-education programs, a national conference, and a quarterly bulletin, *Pulse*.

International School of Shiatsu (ISS)
10 South Clinton Street, #300
Doylestown, PA 18901
(215) 340-9918 (phone and fax)
fayebo@juno.com (e-mail)

Founded in 1978, ISS offers a training program and a one-year apprenticeship.

BREEMA®

Breema originated in a remote mountain village in the Near East and for centuries was used by villagers as part of their daily routine. Breema was practiced by everyone—young and old—as a method of health improvement, exercise, movement meditation, and a means to harmonize relationships with themselves and others. Specific movements were done at various times of the day—there's an Evening Posture, for example—or as an aid to physical processes such as digestion. Some movements resemble everyday activities and are so named, such as Opening the Gate or Grinding the Wheat.

Breema, which means "flow of life," was introduced in the United States by Malichek Mooshan, whose great-grandfather had received Breema teachings and passed them along to him. The principal aim of Breema is to allow clients and practitioners to reestablish a connection to their spiritual nature and their natural vitality.

Breema sees the person as consisting of body, mind, awareness (spiritual essence), and emotions. Because an imbalance among these components is seen as the cause of illness, Breema's goal is to restore a harmonious balance, consisting of clarity of mind, emotional vitality, and physical flexibility. It does this by guiding the body to a natural, comfortable state ("body comfortable") and by supporting the body's natural healing power and homeostatic forces. Breema does not seek specific outcomes with clients; it does not force or direct energy to specific parts of the body. Rather the Breema practitioner's quality of touch and movement reassures clients that they are vital, vibrant, and naturally dynamic.

Breema is practiced with the client wearing loose clothing and usually lying on a carpeted floor or a soft mat. The Breema practitioner moves the client's body using the palms of the hands, the feet, arms, and knees. There is no muscular force or painful pressure applied in Breema; rather the practitioner uses rhythmic leanings, brushes, bends, and stretches.

Writing in *Yoga Journal*, Breema practitioner Cybele Tomlinson describes a typical treatment as beginning with work on the feet in order to ground the recipient; that is, to distribute energy throughout the body so that the mind is not using most of our life force. Then comes a series of "leans." Using the palms of the hands or the soles of the feet—sometimes the elbows, wrists, or ankles—the practitioner transfers weight from his or her body to the client. The lean consists of shifting weight onto the client, holding, and gradually shifting it back. Leans can be done rhythmically and are reportedly quite soothing.

After a series of lean motions, continues Tomlinson, the practitioner might change the client's position and begin another lean series. Other Breema motions include rocking, cradling, stretching, and brushing.

In addition to Breema sessions, Breema includes a body-centered meditation and exercises that can be done on one's own (Self-Breema).

Books

Jon Schreiber, *Breema: Essence of Harmonious Life* (California Health Publications, 1998). This book aims to familiarize readers with the basic principles of Breema through photographs and text.

Organizations

Breema Center
6076 Claremont Avenue
Oakland, CA 94618
(510) 428-0937 (phone)
(510) 428-2705 (fax)

center@breema.com (e-mail)

www.breema.com (website)

The center functions as a school, teaching Breema through workshops and classes.

Breema Health and Wellness Center
6201 Florio Street
Oakland, CA 94618
(510) 428-1234

The center offers Breema bodywork sessions.

CRANIOSACRAL THERAPY

CranioSacral Therapy, a gentle and noninvasive method for assessing and improving the craniosacral system to enhance health, originated from the scientific discoveries of two osteopaths, William G. Sutherland and John E. Upledger. Sutherland, working in the early 1900s, came to the conclusion that skull bone sutures (joints between the skull bones) were not fused as anatomists believed but definitely though minutely shifted in response to the movement of cerebrospinal fluid. Sutherland incorporated his findings into a system he termed Cranial Osteopathy, but it did not gain much attention or appreciation from his colleagues. In the early 1970s, Upledger discovered the same movement of the craniosacral system during surgery. After studying Sutherland's system and conducting research while a professor at Michigan State University, he developed Cranio-Sacral Therapy.

Upledger's therapy focuses on the craniosacral system, which is made up of membranes and cerebrospinal fluid, the environment in which the brain and spinal cord develop and function. The term *craniosacral* is used because the system extends from the bones of the skull, face, and mouth, known as the cranium, to the lower end of the spine, or tailbone, known as the sacrum. In his book *Your Inner Physician and You*, Upledger explains that the system, which consists of membranes called the meninges, the cerebrospinal fluid encased in the meninges, and the structures of the membrane system that control fluid input and output, is a kind of "semi-closed hydraulic system" that uses the dura mater membrane (outermost layer of the meninges) as the container for cerebrospinal fluid (the hydraulic component of the system). The movement of this system creates a rhythm that can be felt as clearly as the rhythms of the cardiovascular and respiratory systems. Upledger's studies have shown that the skull bones must be in a continual minute motion to accommodate the fluid pressure fluctuations. When the skull bones lose their ability to respond, the system is negatively affected and physical symptoms occur. For example, Upledger explained in a March-April 1998 article in *Common Boundary* magazine that dyslexia and other reading problems can often be traced to a restriction caused by the right temporal bone impinging on motor nerves of the eye. "I've seen kids advance two or three years in reading ability over a month to six weeks" as a result of CranioSacral Therapy, Upledger stated. He also indicated that CranioSacral Therapy has been helpful to some children suffering from attention deficit disorder (ADD). Pressure inside the skull essentially makes children with ADD unable to focus. "The central nervous system is under pressure all the time, and they jump from one thing to another."

CranioSacral Therapy consists of both evaluating and treating the craniosacral system using a gentle form of palpation. According to Upledger, the practitioner can monitor craniosacral rhythms with her hands on any part of the body. When restrictions are found, practitioners can gently adjust skull bones and stretch membranes to allow the cerebrospinal fluid to resume flowing freely again. When the restricting obstacle is freed, the system is then said to be able to complete its "self-correction."

In addition to the problems cited above, the Upledger Institute says that CranioSacral Therapy has been effective in treating a wide range of physical and emotional problems, including temporomandibular joint (TMJ) syndrome, depression, migraine headaches, chronic neck and back pain, chronic fatigue, scoliosis, traumatic brain and spinal cord injuries, the aftereffects of minor strokes, post-traumatic stress disorder, and orthopedic problems, among others.

CranioSacral Therapy is used as a primary approach as well as a complementary technique by a variety of health-care providers, including chiropractors, osteopaths, massage therapists, bodyworkers, nurses, physical therapists, dentists, acupuncturists, and physicians.

Organizations

Upledger Institute
11211 Prosperity Farms Road
Palm Beach Gardens, FL 33410
(561) 622-4334 (phone)
(561) 622-4771 (fax)
upledger@upledger.com (e-mail)
www.upledger.com (website)

Founded in 1985 by John Upledger, D.O., the institute is an educational and clinical research center that integrates naturopathic techniques with conventional and alternative health-care methods. Programs include the CranioSacral

Therapy workshop series, as well as training in Visceral Manipulation, Zero Balancing, Fascial Mobilization, the application of acupuncture principles to bodywork, and Process Acupressure, among other methods.

ECSTATIC BODY POSTURES

Ecstatic Body Postures are not easily assigned a place because no one manipulates a part of the body to relieve a physical symptom. However, we placed this approach in this chapter because the body is used as the vehicle for entering an alternate reality. One manipulates the body in the sense that one holds a position or posture for fifteen minutes and thereby gains access to an altered state of consciousness.

Anthropologist Felicitas Goodman's fieldwork in the late 1960s on religious trance led her to believe that certain ancient works of art were not simply aesthetic objects but ritual instructions on how to enter trance states and thereby travel in what Wallace Black Elk, an Oglala Sioux, called "the real world behind this world." Goodman found that many sculptures from the Olmec, Aztec, Cycladean, Mayan, and Native American cultures, among others, displayed body postures that, when combined with percussive rhythm such as the beat of a drum or the sound of a rattle, induced altered states of consciousness and visionary experiences; in other words, ecstasy. According to Jungian author and analyst Robert Johnson, *ecstatic* means "to stand outside oneself." The ecstatic experience, he explains, "involves escaping from the 'I-ness,'" which requires that we "break the boundaries of our separateness to experience a greater realm." Through this "travel," we achieve a respite from the sometimes grinding details of daily existence. We dip into the timeless and return refreshed—ecstatic. This is the very goal and function of the body postures.

Through research and observation, Goodman made the connection between various body postures and the specific altered state induced by holding those positions. For example, the Bear Spirit pose (named after a recurring image of a bear positioned behind a shaman who is standing with feet slightly apart, fists lightly pressing his torso, and head bent upward and slightly back) induces healing. Other postures are doorways to spirit journeys, divination tools, and ways to celebrate or offer thanksgiving.

Goodman views the experiences that people encounter while holding these postures as real trips to other worlds. People directly contact other realities, she told a *Common Boundary* interviewer; they have visions, not visualizations. "A visualized image is your own creation," she explained. "A vision comes about when you see what is 'out there.'" Goodman also believes that the designs on shamans' drums, clothing, and other sacred accoutrements are not simply symbols or design elements but signposts directing the way to these other realities.

In essence, ecstatic trance through body postures is available to everyone. However, some people can more easily access these states. To help facilitate the journey, one can prepare by fasting, practicing the body positions, and honing concentration skills.

In addition to a feeling of well-being, Goodman believes the body postures might be useful in treating addiction. Addiction, she says, is rooted in "ecstasy deprivation." The trances provide the connection with the sacred that can fill a person's need to connect to spirit rather than imbibe spirits.

Doorway to Ecstasy

The first step to inducing an ecstatic trance is to create a space that is quiet and protected from unnecessary distractions or intrusions. It is beneficial to make an effort to designate this space "sacred" either by smudging it or by bringing in sacred objects such as icons and images or natural objects such as rocks, feathers, grasses, and flowers. They not only enhance the beauty of the space but set an intention to protect the work and journey.

Next Goodman recommends making an offering such as blue cornmeal to the spirits of the drum, rattles, or other instruments that will be used for the ritual. After rattling or drumming four times to each of the six directions (north, south, east, west, up and down) and greeting and inviting spirits to join in the ceremony, one begins with simple breathing and concentration exercises. While in a comfortable sitting position, slowly breathe in and out fifty times, focusing on the breath as it comes into your body and as it leaves your body. As you do this, set aside any thoughts about what has to be done. Be as present as you can be.

Next assume the body posture and have a person begin to drum or rattle in a rhythm of 200 to 210 beats per minute. (Tapes can be used, but Goodman points out that they are not as effective as live music because of the difference in resonance.) The percussive rhythm should go on for fifteen minutes. Two strong beats signal the end. Gently come out of the position, slowly stretching and sitting quietly for a few minutes.

While the trance state poses no danger, Goodman urges beginners always to have a companion because occasionally one can encounter some difficulty coming out of trance. If that happens, she recommends having them slowly shift their bodies out of the specific posture, calling their name, and giving them some water. Trance states should not be accessed more than twice a day.

Books

Felicitas Goodman, *Where the Spirits Ride the Wind: Trance Journeys and Other Ecstatic Experiences* (Indiana University Press, 1990). Dr. Goodman and her coworkers investigate thirty ritual trance postures based on artifacts and images from all over the world. Through these positions, they experience re-creations of the sacred world of the hunter-gatherers. Divination, healing, shapeshifting, travel between worlds, and the embodied experience of certain mythical beasts are all accessed through conscientious replication of these postures. A practical guide is included for the reader who would experiment.

Belinda Gore, *Ecstatic Body Postures* (Bear and Co., 1995). This is a clearly illustrated and highly instructive guidebook for those who would undertake an investigation of body postures and their applications in meditation, yoga, shamanic practice, and bodywork.

Organizations

Cuyamungue Institute
Route 5, Box 358A
Santa Fe, NM 87501
(505) 455-2749

Founded in 1979 by Felicitas Goodman, Ph.D., the institute provides educational and training opportunities during the summer months that link anthropology, psychotherapy, ecology, and the arts. The institute employs ecstatic trance in its training methods.

POLARITY THERAPY

Founded at the turn of the century by osteopath, naturopath, and chiropractor Randolph Stone (1890–1981), Polarity Therapy is a natural health-care system that consists of subtle energy methods based on the philosophy and principles of Eastern healing systems such as *qigong*; Ayurvedic medicine with its five elements: ether, air, fire, water, and earth; and Chinese medicine's energy meridians. Based on what he knew about electrical currents, Stone posited that body energy (life force) must also have positive and negative poles. In Polarity Therapy there are five currents of energy that relate to the five elements as well as to particular energy centers (chakras), organs, and physiological functions such as digestion. These currents are positively charged on the right side and top portion of the body and negatively charged on the left side and bottom part of the body. There is a neutral zone in the middle. Polarity Therapy maintains that an open, free flow of energy between positive and negative poles enhances the electrical charge (i.e., one's vitality) and keeps the system balanced. Once the practitioner evaluates the energetic state of the client, he gently places his hands or fingers on two areas, one negatively and the other positively charged, in effect creating a circuit.

Polarity Therapy's approach differs from acupressure and Myofascial Trigger-Point Therapy in that Polarity therapists do not use pressure to stimulate specific points. Rather they simply make contact to increase energy flow. Polarity Therapy is multifaceted insofar as it integrates bodywork (its primary focus) with counseling, nutrition, and an exercise program called Polarity Yoga or PolarEnergetics.

Technically, Polarity Therapy could be classified as a subtle energy approach, but we've included it in this chapter because massage practitioners frequently include one or more of the energy-balancing techniques as part of their overall massage repertoire. In fact, there are two certification levels: Associate Practitioner of Polarity, which allows professionals in other fields to use Polarity as a complementary technique; and Registered Practitioner of Polarity, a more advanced form of certification enabling practitioners to use Polarity Therapy as a primary technique. Most Polarity therapists are licensed or certified in some other discipline; they can be found working in private practice and counseling centers and with physicians and chiropractors.

After Stone's death in 1981, a second generation of Polarity therapists created a proliferation of modifications and extensions of his work, such as Synergy, an energy-based dance system developed by Charmaine Lee.

Youth Posture

One of the most popular and widely used Polarity Yoga exercises we've encountered is the Youth Posture, which can calm you if you are emotionally upset and revive you if you feel fatigued or are not sleeping well. It can also strengthen the back and spine.

The first step is to get into a squatting position with your feet about six inches apart and slightly splayed, right foot toward the right and left foot toward the left. Place your arms inside your knees and your thumbs on either side of your nose near your eyebrows. Then press your arms gently against your knees and press your thumbs into the bridge of your nose. Breathe deeply and relax into this position for several minutes.

Organizations

American Polarity Therapy Association (APTA)
2888 Bluff Street, Suite 149

Boulder, CO 80301
(800) 359-5620 or (303) 545-2080 (phone)
(303) 545-2161 (fax)
satvahq@aol.com (e-mail)
www.polarity.com (website)

Founded in 1984, APTA is the professional association for Polarity therapists and instructors. The organization holds conferences, publishes a quarterly newsletter, *Energy*, and provides a list of accredited Polarity Therapy training programs in the United States.

REFLEXOLOGY

Reflexology is an outgrowth and extension of Zone therapy, which was first developed by William H. Fitzgerald, a physician at the turn of the century. Fitzgerald, at one time chief of the Nose and Throat Department at St. Francis Hospital in Hartford, Connecticut, was interested in the idea of referred pain, the phenomenon where pain occurring in one area of the body reflects disease, damage, or pain in another part. While working in London, he explored therapies that utilized this concept.

Fitzgerald brought the idea to the United States, developed it, and published a book, *Zone Therapy, or Relieving Pain at Home*. Physical therapist Eunice Ingham became fascinated by it and using Zone therapy principles began to focus intensely on the feet. She painstakingly noted the correspondence between points she worked on and her clients' symptoms and subsequent relief. In time, she mapped the entire foot, identifying specific points and their corresponding limbs, organs, glands, and body parts. For example, the big toes correspond to the head, the arches to the spinal column, and the line across the center of the arch to the waist. In 1938 she published *Stories the Feet Can Tell: Stepping to Better Health*.

In a typical session, clients sit in a reclining chair fully clothed except for their feet. Using no lubricant, the Reflexologist begins to apply a steady and even pressure using a "walking" movement with the thumb over the reflex area. In some cases, they try to break up crystallized calcium, uric acid, or other mineral deposits by going over that same area slowly again and again. Occasionally they will press a specific reflex point, but the walking motion is the standard operating procedure.

Although Reflexology maps the body into ten zones, it concentrates primarily on foot massage. It is especially useful in inducing relaxation, stimulating circulation, and reducing stress-related disorders. One magazine writer told of her first encounter with the technique after having returned home from a long plane ride, exhausted by jetlag and bothered by a painfully sore shoulder. A one-hour session, she cheerfully reported, not only made her feel "energized but calm" but also reduced the pain in her shoulder and improved the range of motion in her arm.

Reflexology is one of those methods that one can encounter either by going to a certified Reflexologist, who works only on the feet (sometimes on hands or ears if the feet are too sore, swollen, or painful), or by going to a massage therapist who has been certified in Reflexology and who incorporates its techniques when working on the feet as part of the standard massage.

Books

Dwight C. Byers, *Better Health with Foot Reflexology* (Ingham Publishing, 1983). Authored by the nephew of the founder of Reflexology, this book was written to provide the most complete reference manual on the subject. In addition to offering a history and definition of the method, it addresses the body's various systems (e.g., lymphatic, cardiovascular, skeletal, respiratory) and Reflexology's potential impact on them.

Beryl Crane, *Reflexology: The Definitive Practitioner's Manual* (Element Books, 1997). This tome includes everything you ever wanted to know about Reflexology, including technical information about feet and hands (which also have reflex points that can be worked on) and discussions of professional issues such as ethical considerations and the nuts and bolts of setting up a practice.

Eunice Ingham, *Stories the Feet Can Tell* (Ingham Publishing, 1938) and *Stories the Feet Have Told Through Reflexology* (1984). Purists might enjoy owning and reading Ingham's original works, both of which have been combined in this single volume.

Organizations

International Institute of Reflexology (IIR)
5650 First Avenue North
P.O. Box 12642
St. Petersburg, FL 33733-2642
(813) 343-4811 (phone)
(813) 381-2807 (fax)
ftreflex@concentric.net (e-mail)

Founded in 1974 by Eunice Ingham's nephew, Dwight Byers, the institute offers two-day seminars and a certification program. It also has a worldwide referral service.

Reflexology Association of America
4012 South Rainbow Boulevard, Box K585
Las Vegas, NV 89103-2059
(702) 871-9522

This organization, established in 1995, serves as a clearinghouse for Reflex-ology.

REIKI

Reiki, a Japanese word derived from *ray* ("divine wisdom") and *ke* ("life-force energy"), is a healing technique that enhances the energy field that surrounds and penetrates the physical body. The healing system incorporates both self-treatment and the treatment of others even without direct contact and at great distances.

According to the Reiki philosophy, the life force is the primary source of nourishment for the cells and organs of the body. Disturbances in this field of energy, also called the aura, are thought to be the cause of illness. Reiki practitioners act as mediums by channeling life-force energy through their hands at various positions on the body or within the general aura of a client, tapping into the client's core sense of well-being, or innate wisdom, to know exactly where to place their hands. By releasing energy blocks, Reiki helps reestablish the natural flow of life force and thus helps restore a person to physical, psychological, and spiritual health.

Reiki was developed in the late nineteenth century after Mikao Usui, a Christian minister and teacher living in Japan, deciphered parts of the Buddhist sutras related to healing methods taught by the Buddha. His discoveries laid the foundation for modern Reiki, which was brought to the United States by Mrs. Hawayo Takata in 1935. The ability to channel Reiki is not taught in the usual sense but is simply transferred to the student by a Reiki master. Mrs. Takata transmitted the technique to twenty-two Reiki masters between 1970 and 1980, many of whom are still teaching today. There are approximately 2,000 Reiki masters and 150,000 practitioners worldwide.

This healing method is based on subtle energy work but is included here because some massage practitioners incorporate Reiki in their practice.

Organizations

International Center for Reiki Training
29209 Northwestern Highway, Suite 592
Southfield, MI 48034

(248) 948-8112 (phone)
(248) 948-9534 (fax)
center@reiki.org (e-mail)
www.reiki.org (website)

The center establishes and maintains standards for teaching Reiki (based on Mikao Usui's system), certifies students and teachers, and acts as an educational link to the public.

Reiki Alliance
P.O. Box 41
Cataldo, ID 83810
(208) 682-3535 (phone)
(208) 682-4848 (fax)
reikialliance@compuserve.com (e-mail)

The alliance is a membership organization that sets professional standards for teachers in the Mikao Usui system of Reiki.

THERAPEUTIC MASSAGE

Touch as a means of alleviating pain or of calming and soothing body and psyche is as old as human beings. When we bang our leg against a piece of furniture, strain our arm by pitching in an after-work softball game, or jam our neck after too many hours on the phone or in front of the computer, we instinctively seek relief by rubbing the painful, tired, sore, or tense area. And who has not reached out to stroke a sick child's head to comfort them. Touch encourages relaxation, restores vitality, and gives comfort. The body has enormous powers of regeneration and self-repair, and one way to stimulate these healing processes is through therapeutic massage.

Massage, which comes from the Arabic meaning "I stroke" and the French *amassar* or *masser* meaning "to knead," is the science of skillfully manipulating the body to improve health. It may take the form of kneading, stretching, stroking, or stimulating certain points or applying pressure to muscles, ligaments, and connective tissues.

Massage has been used from earliest times. It is found in Chinese literature as far back as 3000 B.C. Carved in a bas-relief on the tomb of an Egyptian priest circa 2200 B.C. is a man receiving a foot massage. Hippocrates, the Greek physician, father of Western medicine, and an advocate of massage, wrote: "The physician must be experienced in many things, but assuredly in rubbing." Although massage virtually disappeared during the Middle Ages, it was revived again at the beginning of the nineteenth century by Johan Mezger of Amsterdam and Pehr Henrik

Ling, a Swedish fencing master. Ling systematized the various methods used in Germany, Russia, the Orient, and the Scandinavian countries into a treatment known as Swedish massage, which was introduced to the United States over a hundred years ago.

Some of the more common massage techniques are *effleurage*, a stroking of the muscle; *petrissage*, the kneading and pinching of a muscle and other tissue; *tapotement*, the rapid striking of blows on the body; *vibration*, a shaking of the limbs; and *friction*, a deep, firm circular motion over small or large surfaces of the body.

Eastern influences are seen in shiatsu, or finger pressure massage, a method of stimulating specific points with the thumbs, fingers, or palm of the hand for short periods. Shiatsu is often used to stimulate acupuncture points, producing a sensation somewhere between pleasure and pain.

Based on a survey of its members, the American Massage Therapy Association (AMTA) reports that the most frequently used massage techniques are Swedish massage (77 percent), deep tissue work (54 percent), Myofascial Trigger-Point Therapy (44 percent), sports massage (38 percent), and acupressure/shiatsu (35 percent). Deep tissue massage is a generic technique that works on a deeper level of tissue and muscle than Swedish massage. During a deep tissue session, the massage therapist might focus on just one muscle or muscle group. Sports massage is devoted to conditions related to sports activities, both professional and amateur. It is used to prevent injuries, enhance performance, and work on spasms, cramps, and injuries. Sports massage pioneer and physical therapist Jack Meagher has written that athletic performance can be improved up to 20 percent with regular massage. (See the Acupressure and Shiatsu and Myofascial Trigger-Point Therapy sections for further information on those techniques.)

Another currently popular approach that many massage therapists are incorporating into their work is Neuromuscular Massage. Developed by Paul St. John, this approach, which has been effective in pain control, focuses on the nervous and musculoskeletal systems. Soft tissue and trigger point manipulation, as well as attention to nerve compression, postural distortion, and dysfunctional biomechanics, are all part of this approach.

No matter which technique you choose, the benefits derived from massage are numerous. The skin, muscles, fascia, blood vessels, lymphatics, nerves, and even the internal organs are positively influenced by massage. Massage can help reduce pain, cramping, swelling, and strains. It helps remove waste accumulations that can build up around cells and can break up calcium and mineral deposits in the tissue and help restore muscle tone. Massage also increases blood and lymph circulation. The skin becomes softer, more supple, more flexible and elastic. The nervous system may also be stimulated, soothed, or toned depending upon the type of massage, resulting in a more positive psychological state. Additionally, studies conducted at the Touch Reseach Institute (TRI), the world's first center devoted solely to studying the effects of touch on health, have concluded that massage therapy encourages weight gain in premature babies, positively affects the immune system, alleviates symptoms of depression, and reduces stress hormones.

Another interesting benefit of massage seems to confirm the old saying "It is better to give than to receive." TRI, while conducting research on infant massage, particularly babies that had been born prematurely or had been exposed to drugs or abuse, was looking for ways to deliver massage to babies of parents living in shelters. They created a "volunteer grandparent" program of senior citizens who would come in to feed, play with, and massage the children. Researchers found that not only did gentle daily massages allow the infants to sleep better and produce better temperaments, but the "grandparents" reported positive benefits as well. In a questionnaire, the volunteers said that their feelings of anxiety and depression diminished and they found themselves drinking less coffee, making fewer visits to their physicians, and increasing social contact. Additionally they felt better about themselves.

The institute then ran a study comparing elderly persons giving massage with those receiving massage and found that the positive effects on the former were much more pronounced. Tiffany Field, TRI director, told Bill O'Sullivan, reporting in *Common Boundary,* that the data seem to suggest that for the general population providing massage could be as beneficial as receiving it.

This may account in part for the tremendous increase in the number of massage therapists in the last sixteen years. According to Elliot Greene, past AMTA president, in 1982 the association had 1,200 members. Less than ten years later, when he took office in 1990, there were 8,500 members. In the four short years he served as president, membership ballooned to 22,500. Today it stands at around 30,000 members.

What caused the huge growth in both the number of professional massage therapists and the public's demand for their services? Greene cites a host of factors, including public awareness and a focus on health that began in the 1960s and grew throughout the 1970s, 1980s, and 1990s. Not only did people watch their diets, eating less red meat and fat and more vegetables, fruit, and chicken, but exercise and fitness regimes—"go for the burn"—became widely popular. These new lifestyle essentials naturally extended to massage, a healthy reward for tired or sore muscles.

Additionally, says Greene, the profession has over the years taken steps to upgrade certification procedures, licensing, and standards within the field. This has increased the credibility of massage with the public.

Lastly, Greene points to an increase in research. Studies funded by the NIH OAM and those conducted by TRI have enhanced medical and health professionals' opinions and attitudes toward massage and helped to make it one of the mainstream treatment options.

Katie Armitage of Associated Bodywork and Massage Professionals, another professional membership organization in the field, adds that people are also now more accepting of alternative medicine in general and have come to see massage not only as a means to relieve stress and tension but as both a preventive and curative tool. Even the notoriously tight-fisted and conventional preferred provider organizations and health maintenance organizations are beginning to recognize massage as a bona fide form of health care.

Books

Mark Beck, *Milady's Theory and Practice of Therapeutic Massage* (Milady's Publishing Co., 1994). A comprehensive and highly recommended textbook used in massage schools that offers practical information about physiology, massage techniques, equipment, and other basics of massage practice.

Lucinda Lidell et al., *The Book of Massage: The Complete Step-by-Step Guide to Eastern and Western Techniques* (Fireside, 1984). A comprehensive introduction to therapeutic massage techniques, which could be especially useful for those beginning to explore massage and bodywork.

Clare Maxwell-Hudson, *The Complete Book of Massage* (Random House, 1998). This lushly illustrated manual covers specific techniques such as shiatsu and Reflexology as well as specific client populations such as infants and pregnant women.

Frances M. Tappan and Patricia J. Benjamin, *Healing Massage Techniques: Classic, Holistic, and Emerging* (Appleton and Lange, 1988). One of the top three textbooks used in massage schools, this book provides a clear and detailed introduction to massage, including information on Swedish massage, shiatsu, Polarity Therapy, Reflexology, and others.

Organizations

American Massage Therapy Association (AMTA)
820 Davis Street, Suite 100
Evanston, IL 60201-4444
(847) 864-0123 (phone)
(847) 864-1178 (fax)
www.amtamassage.org (website)

A professional membership and advocacy organization, AMTA publishes a directory of approved training programs and the *Massage Therapy Journal*.

Associated Bodywork and Massage Professionals (ABMP)
28677 Buffalo Park Road
Evergreen, CO 80439-7347
(800) 458-2267 or (303) 674-8478 (phone)
(303) 674-0859 (fax)
expectmore@abmp.com (e-mail)
www.abmp.com (website)

An international professional membership organization founded to provide massage and bodywork practitioners with services and information. ABMP provides a touch training directory, which includes massage and bodywork schools and organizations worldwide.

Care Through Touch Institute (CTI)
2401 LeConte Avenue
Berkeley, CA 94709
(510) 548-0418

CTI draws upon the sacramental dimensions of massage and is known for pioneering an embodied approach to Christian spirituality. It also has a certificate program in massage and bodywork with sacramental and pastoral applications.

International Association of Infant Massage
2350 Bowen Road
P.O. Box 438
Elma, NY 14059-0438
(800) 248-5432 or (716) 652-9789

This association encourages the use of massage by parents of infants and promotes the benefits of such massage to the medical and governmental communities.

St. John Neuromuscular Pain Relief Institute
11211 Prosperity Farms Road
Palm Beach Gardens, FL 33410-3487
(800) 232-4668

This is the program registration office for the institute, which runs training courses all over the United States.

Swedish Institute of Massage and Acupuncture
26 West 26th Street, 5th Floor
New York, NY 10001
(212) 924-5900 (phone)
(212) 924-7600 (fax)

Founded in 1916, the Swedish Institute is the oldest massage school in North America. It offers courses in both massage and acupuncture.

Touch Research Institute (TRI)
Department of Pediatrics
University of Miami School of Medicine
P.O. Box 016820 (Dept. 820)
1601 NW 12th Avenue
Miami, FL 33101
(305) 243-6781 (phone)
(305) 243-6488 (fax)
tfield@mednet.med.miami.edu (e-mail)
www.miami.edu/touch-research (website)

TRI is the first center in the world for basic and applied research on touch. Its primary aim is to demonstrate scientifically the benefits of touch on health and thus establish its credibility with the medical community. There are currently three institutes. The original TRI based at the University of Miami was established in 1992. A second institute was established in 1997 at Nova Southeastern University in Fort Lauderdale and focuses on wellness issues for parents and children. The third center is being established in the Philippines by neonatologists researching the effects of massage on premature infants' weight gain.

Periodicals

Massage and Bodywork Quarterly
Associated Bodywork and Massage Professionals
28677 Buffalo Park Road
Evergreen, CO 80439-7347
(303) 674-8578 or (800) 458-2267 (phone)
www.abmp.com (website)
Quarterly; $17

The official ABMP publication, this magazine describes and covers various bodywork approaches and issues.

Massage Magazine
1315 West Mallon Avenue
Spokane, WA 99201
(800) 533-4263 (for subscriptions only)
(509) 324-8117 (phone)
Bimonthly; $24

This publication carries articles on body therapies, massage laws, the nature of massage practices abroad, and a host of related topics and issues.

Massage Therapy Journal
820 Davis Street, Suite 100
Evanston, IL 60201-4444
(847) 864-0123
Quarterly; $25
The official journal of the American Massage Therapy Association.

MYOFASCIAL TRIGGER-POINT THERAPY

Myofascial therapy evolved in the late 1970s from Trigger-Point Injection Therapy, which was developed by Janet Travell, M.D., a professor of pharmacology at George Washington University Medical School and the first female White House physician. (She treated President John F. Kennedy's back pain.) As a non-invasive, hands-on therapeutic program for the relief and control of myofascial pain (*myo* meaning "muscle"; *fascial* meaning "muscle covering"), Myofascial Trigger-Point Therapy has since been established as an effective independent therapy.

A trigger point is a hyperirritable area within the muscle or the fascia, the connective tissue that wraps muscles. Trigger points are identified by a taut muscle band that when compressed refers pain in predictable patterns. To correct this condition, Myofascial therapy identifies factors that perpetuate this condition, such as vitamin deficiencies, improper alignment, or anatomical problems, and attempts to correct them. It employs passive stretch techniques and direct pressure on trigger points and teaches corrective stretching exercises to clients.

There is an implicit connection between techniques used in Myofascial Trigger-Point Therapy and Eastern therapeutic traditions such as acupressure and shiatsu. They differ, however, in that Myofascial therapy is based on the Western medical model. It investigates factors predisposing to illness as part of its treatment program and always recommends a corrective stretch program. For this reason, it is best suited for rehabilitation and injury patients.

Myofascial therapists are knowledgeable in the areas of musculoskeletal anatomy, kinesiology, and corrective stretch exercise. However, because they are not medical diagnosticians, Myofascial therapists must rely on medical referrals given by a state-licensed physician, chiropractor, or dentist before beginning a treatment plan. They work in a range of settings, including hospitals and pain clinics, and with private practice physicians.

Organizations

Academy for Myofascial Trigger-Point Therapy
1312 East Carson Street
Pittsburgh, PA 15203-1510
(412) 481-2553 (phone)
(412) 381-6922 (fax)

The academy offers training in Myofascial Trigger-Point Therapy. Students learn to resolve myofascial pain syndromes by dealing with perpetuating factors, treating the appropriate soft tissues, and designing reeducation programs for the muscles involved.

Bonnie Pruden School for Physical Fitness and Myotherapy
7800 East Speedway
Tucson, AZ 85710
(800) 221-4634 (phone)
(520) 722-6311 (fax)
paineras@aol.com (e-mail)
www.bpmyo.com (website)

The school provides training in specific techniques of Bonnie Pruden Myotherapy and Exercise Therapy, as well as educational weekends, self-help seminars, and individual treatments.

National Association of Myofascial Trigger-Point Therapists (NAMTPT)
P.O. Box 68
Yarmouthport, MA 02675
(508) 896-4484 or (800) 845-3454 (phone)
painrel@frontiernet.net (e-mail)
www.frontier.net/~painref. (website)

NAMTPT promotes Myofascial therapy through its referral service, conference, directory of training programs, and a quarterly journal.

6
Body Psychotherapy

Body psychotherapy is a psychotherapeutic specialty area that sees a functional unity between mind, body, and emotions. Although it has a long—at least seventy-year—history, an accumulated store of literature, both popular and professional, and a body of knowledge based on theories and experience, body psychotherapy is just now gaining a foothold in the mainstream health-care marketplace.

A major part of the field is rooted in the work of Wilhelm Reich, a controversial and brilliant figure who ventured into uncharted territory with his theories, experiments, and methods of working with the body in psychoanalysis. While a young medical student, he became associated with Sigmund Freud and began to investigate resistance, the unconscious undermining of the psychoanalytic process. In his classic book *Character Analysis,* first published in 1933, Reich points out that Freud initially believed that by becoming aware of repressed unconscious material, patients would understand the origins of their symptoms and that this understanding would alleviate the symptoms, thus effecting a cure. Freud had to modify this stance because empirically he came to the conclusion that insight only *sometimes* changed behavior. In wrestling with this quandary—the patient's resistance to change—Reich theorized that what made patients able to change was their ability to experience adequate sexual gratification (i.e., reach orgasm) and that what made such gratification possible was a flexible and open body structure. (Freud had theorized that sex and aggression were the basic instinctual drives that motivated behavior.)

In a professional paper, Reich wrote: "The essence and goal of psychoanalytic therapy is to render unconscious material conscious by overcoming the emotional resistance to the awareness of the unconscious. The essence and goal of character-analytic vegetatotherapy [the original name of Reich's therapy] is to restore the biophysical equilibrium by releasing orgastic potency; that is, not only render unconscious material conscious, but to release vegetative energies."

When Reich spoke of orgastic potency, he was not specifically referring to sexual orgasms. Rather he saw the body as an organism that when freed of tension could experience waves of undulating rhythmic energy (an "orgasm reflex"). Reich realized that although many people reached orgasm during intercourse, they did not achieve a full and deep energetic release or a satisfaction that was felt throughout the body. Reich theorized that this limitation reinforced neurosis and led to impulsive sexual behavior, rigidity in the personality, and even violence. The problem stemmed from the fact that energy was bound up in chronic muscular tension. Because people experienced conflict between their natural impulse to express emotion and sexuality and their fear and acceptance of parental and societal constraints, they tightened muscles to hold back their feelings. "It is as if the affective personality put on an armor, a rigid shell on which the knocks from the outer world as well as the inner demands rebound," wrote Reich. "This armor makes the individual less sensitive to unpleasure but it also reduces his libidinal and aggressive motility, and with that his capacity for pleasure and achievement."

Reich attempted to figure out ways in which people could break through and eliminate this armor to free the pent-up emotions and thereby regain their ability to enjoy the natural flow of energy and engage in life instinctively, responsively, and deeply. He began to experiment with ways to do that. He used deep touch, pressing hard into the muscles to release them; devised exercises to open up the body; and observed the role of breathing with regard to emotional expression. He also formulated theories about the function of muscular defenses and how they affected the client's psychology.

Over the years, however, Reich's interests shifted from character analysis to scientific experiments with "orgone," the energy that he first identified as streaming in and around the body and that he came to see as a universal energy present in all things. He became convinced that this energy was capable of curing cancer as well as controlling weather patterns. He invented an orgone box, the function of which was to accumulate and store this energy. People would sit in the box—also called an orgone energy accumulator—absorbing the energy for therapeutic purposes. This line of experimentation eventually led him into conflict with the Food and Drug Administration (FDA), which would not give him permission to sell or use his invention. In 1954 the FDA issued an injunction against the distribution of orgone energy accumulators on the basis that the claims made about them were fraudulent. Reich, believing that his right to pursue scientific inquiry was being challenged, refused to abide by the injunction and was charged with contempt of court and sentenced to two years in prison, where he died from heart failure.

The tragic and disreputable end to Reich's life undermined and perhaps stunted the effect of his work. For many years, colleagues and former students distanced themselves from him. Initially some simply did not like the direction Reich was taking; later the fear of governmental interference or harassment drove supporters underground. It is remarkable therefore that in spite of this history,

Reich left a rich legacy. He coined the terms *sexual revolution* and *body armor*, developed the first body-centered psychotherapy (today called medical orgonomy), described orgone energy, which today would be termed a *subtle energy*, and suggested that the body, like a sponge, holds emotional content. Furthermore, much of what has come to be recognized as the field of body-centered psychotherapy can be traced to Reich's prolific writing. He also trained numerous therapists in his methods, with many—Alexander Lowen, John Pierrakos, and Chuck Kelley—going on to not only extend his theories but also establish other body-oriented therapeutic and educational approaches. There is both irony and poignancy in the fact that medical orgonomy remained a well-credentialed but small and rather esoteric method, while many of the better known body psychotherapy approaches trace their roots to Reich.

Reich, however, is not the sole ancestor in the body psychotherapy lineage. Just as Reich developed his work out of psychoanalysis, other body psychotherapies sprang up out of other traditions. Dance, for instance, was the source of Al Pesso and Diane Boyden's creation of Psychomotor Therapy, and the fusion of Gestalt therapy, the Alexander Technique, and Feldenkrais work were brought together by Ilana Rubenfeld in Rubenfeld Synergy.

Initially these new body psychotherapies evolved independently, although they are now beginning to cross-pollinate and to borrow liberally from one another. The field of body psychotherapy is a fertile one, says Barbara Goodrich-Dunn, an organismic body psychotherapist in Silver Spring, Maryland. "Each therapy is really different; it's not just repackaging. They're unique ways of dealing with the body-mind interface." Through various techniques incorporating everything from movement and touch to physical manipulation and role-playing, body psychotherapy can reach people at a deeper level than verbal therapy. Additionally, the field seems about to enjoy its day in the sun as acceptance of the concepts on which the field is based grows. PBS commentator Bill Moyers, for example, put together a series for public television that was aired in 1993, entitled *Healing and the Mind*. In an interview just before its debut, Moyers told *USA Weekend* that part of his involvement in the project stemmed from his father's death. Moyers revealed that his father had suffered for nearly twenty-five years from inexplicable headaches that the best medical facilities in the country could not diagnose. "I believe now that the headaches were a consequence of grief," Moyers declared. "My brother died suddenly in 1966 at the age of thirty-nine, [and] my father never got over it." Moyers went on to say that he believes that if his father had been able to "accept the emotional roots of illness and healing"—if he had been able to share his grief—he would have been a happier man. Thus Moyers concludes that "expressing emotions (negative or positive), talking, meditating, even touching, can make a tremendous difference in our physical, as well as emotional, well-being."

After several decades of branching out in many directions, practitioners in the body psychotherapy field are now joining forces and making an effort to find commonalities in order to strengthen the field. In June 1996, the U.S. Association for Body Psychotherapy was launched, twelve years after a similar association was established in Europe.

Books

Christine Caldwell, editor, *Getting In Touch: The Guide to New Body-Centered Therapies* (Quest Books, 1997). A collection of essays by body psychotherapists and many founders of body-oriented psychotherapies.

Wilhelm Reich, *Character Analysis* (Noonday Press, 1949, 1961). This is a much enlarged and appended edition of Reich's 1933 classic, which represented his first step away from psychoanalysis and toward the physiologically and energetically based aspects of emotional behavior.

Myron Sharaf, *Fury on Earth* (Ingram Books, 1983, 1994). A fascinating and definitive biography of the brilliant pioneer Wilhelm Reich by his student and colleague.

Organizations

Body Therapy Special Interest Network
c/o Erica Goodstone, Ph.D.
Murray Hill Station
P.O. Box 1931
New York, NY 10156
(212) 496-3050 (phone)
DrEricaG@aol.com (e-mail)

This network, founded in 1992, is affiliated with the American Mental Health Counseling Association, a division of the American Counseling Association. Members include counselors who use some form of bodywork or massage in their practice.

National Association of Bodyworkers in Religious Service (NABRS)
5 Big Stone Court
Baltimore, MD 21228-1018
(410) 455-0277 (phone)
nabrs@aol.com (e-mail)

NABRS is a nonprofit educational interfaith organization whose membership consists of ordained clergy, vowed religious, and laypersons who are also bodyworkers. They utilize a variety of modalities such as therapeutic massage, *qigong*, tai chi, and shiatsu. The group supports the concept that spirituality needs to be embodied and that intentional touch can be both healing and spiritual.

United States Association for Body Psychotherapy
c/o Barbara Goodrich-Dunn
8830 Cameron Court, Suite 206
Silver Spring, MD 20910
(301) 588-9341

    This association, established in 1996, is aimed at organizing and shaping the profession, clarifying the connections and differences among body psychotherapy, traditional verbal psychotherapy, and somatic practices. Additional goals include publishing a journal, setting up an ethics committee, promoting public education, and investigating liability issues.

Periodicals

Energy and Character: The Journal of Biosynthesis
Abbotsbury Publications
Chesil, London WC1N 3XX
England
Semiannual; $32

    This publication is a highly recommended neo-Reichian journal.

REICHIAN-ORIENTED THERAPIES

Reich's biographer Myron Sharaf once used the image of a mansion with myriad rooms, multiple stories, and wings to describe to a colleague the legacy of the grandfather of body psychotherapy. "Some rooms were at the ends of corridors, others could be close to the ground floor, or lost in the attic," he told Reichian scholar David Boadella. "But each room contained something unique and important." Boadella, who between 1981 and 1986 traveled extensively working as a trainer in most of the Reichian-oriented therapeutic traditions, says he found many commonalities as well as sharp areas of disagreement, even conflicts, among the various schools and approaches. But, he wrote, there was much "inspiration, fresh insights, and new ways of looking creatively at old problems."

    The following descriptions of American Reichian-oriented approaches attempt to show both the historical thread tying the approach to Reich as well as the innovations introduced that extended his knowledge and application possibilities.

Bioenergetic Analysis

Bioenergetic Analysis began as a collaboration between Alexander Lowen and John Pierrakos, both physicians who became enamored with Reich's ideas as young men. Lowen studied with Reich for about a dozen years, worked with him in therapy for three years, and in 1945 began seeing clients as a Reichian therapist (he charged $2 an hour) even before he had his medical degree. (This practice was not as unusual as it may seem, inasmuch as Reich had worked as a psychoanalyst under Freud while still in medical school.) Pierrakos had seen a copy of one of Reich's books when he was a teenager in Greece. When he came to America seven years later, he became a patient of Reich.

In 1947 Lowen left for medical school in Switzerland. When he returned to the United States, he found to his disappointment and chagrin that the Reichian community had changed dramatically. Reich had left New York for Rangeley, Maine, where he was conducting experiments with orgone. He had renamed his therapeutic approach "orgone therapy," reflecting his new commitment to orgone physics, which had replaced character analysis in his explorations.

Lowen and Pierrakos decided to cast their lots together and opened an office in Greenwich Village where they began to develop Bioenergetic Analysis. For three years they worked together—Lowen as the patient, Pierrakos as the therapist—experimenting with various exercises, techniques, and positions that would help open up the body to allow for deeper experiences of pleasure and also describing in great detail various character structures. What they discovered experientially extends Reich's concepts in three major ways. First, Bioenergetic Analysis organized character types by structure so that the therapist could read the "language of the body" (i.e., a person's posture, way of moving and expressing herself) and the emotional history that was embedded in the musculature and then bring this knowledge into the therapeutic work. These physical body patterns—and the unconscious material and emotional problems that they held—were seen as limiting a person's capacity for aliveness and fulfillment in life. By helping clients understand the nature and source of their inner conflicts and by helping them release their muscular armoring, Bioenergetic Analysis helps to relieve symptoms and change behavioral patterns.

Bioenergetics also introduced the concept of "grounding." Patients in Reich's vegetatotherapy worked lying prone on a couch. To the horizontal work, Lowen and Pierrakos added exercises and techniques that were done with the patient standing. They felt that this additional orientation would help clients deal with real world issues more effectively. Physically speaking, the goal was to have the patient feel connected to the ground; metaphorically, it meant being "grounded in reality." One typical exercise is called the Bow. With feet spread slightly apart, knees bent, and fists against the small of one's back, one would slightly lean back. This position would not only open up breathing and energy flow but help ground a person as well.

Lastly, Bioenergetics expanded on the role of breathing vis-à-vis a healthy, energetic organism. Observing that shallow breathing cuts off feelings as well as the flow of energy, techniques were developed to work with breath. Several techniques involve the use of a "breathing stool," the prototype of which was a two-foot stool onto which was strapped a tightly rolled-up blanket. (It subsequently evolved into a padded leather stool with handholds on either side.) Patients recline with their back over the stool, which stimulates breathing by opening up the chest muscles. Breath was viewed as the fuel that feeds the energetic fire of the organism, thus allowing for a deep experience of pleasure and joy.

Bioenergetic Analysis is also known for making the practice of Reichian therapy less medically oriented and more accessible. A medical orgonomist (the current name for a practitioner of the body therapy directly descended from Reich's work) must be a physician, whereas a Bioenergetic therapist may be a psychologist, social worker, or any licensed psychotherapist.

Today Bioenergetic Analysis has moved beyond the stereotypical image of a person standing in the Bow position or pounding a tennis racket on a bed (an exercise used to express anger). The work has evolved and become more subtle and refined. In addition to focusing on the basic emotions—fear, anger, sorrow, longing, and love—attention is paid to early preverbal issues and the connection and relationship between therapist and client. Psychoanalytic issues such as transference and countertransference remain central.

Books

Alexander Lowen, *Bioenergetics* (Coward, McCann & Geoghegan, Inc., 1975). A basic introduction to Bioenergetics Analysis, including concepts, therapeutic approach, and applications.

Alexander Lowen, *Joy: The Surrender to the Body and to Life* (Penguin USA, 1995). Using his nearly five decades of experience as a therapist, Lowen describes the therapeutic method he developed and how it can help individuals recover their full potential and enjoy vital, joyful lives.

Alexander Lowen, *Language of the Body* (Macmillan, 1971, 1977). A textbook primer on character structure.

Organizations

International Institute for Bioenergetic Analysis
144 East 36th Street
New York, NY 10016

(212) 532-7742 (phone)
(212) 532-5331 (fax)
IIBAnet@aol.com (e-mail)
www.bioenergetic-therapy.com (website)

Founded in 1956, the institute is a professional organization dedicated to the advancement of body psychotherapy as practiced in Bioenergetic Analysis. It is an international training institute with fifty-four affiliated training societies or institutes throughout the world. Local societies are composed of trainers, certified Bioenergetic therapists, trainees, and associate members; each society provides ongoing educational opportunities for its members as well as a bridge to the community and the psychotherapy field.

Core Energetics

In an interview with Barbara Dunn, a body psychotherapist and the treasurer of the U.S. Association for Body Psychotherapy, John Pierrakos recalled that ever since his childhood in Greece he had been aware of his body and enjoyed it, whether swimming, playing soccer, or being in the company of women. As a teenager he came across one of Reich's books, which utterly fascinated him. So much so that at the age of twenty-one, when he came to the United States, he became a patient of Reich. Later he collaborated with Alexander Lowen developing Bioenergetic Analysis. Their association lasted until the 1970s when he left to establish Core Energetics. About the same time, his interest in spirituality led him to attend "lectures" channeled while in trance by Eva Broch. These discourses on various aspects of psychological, emotional, and spiritual transformation, which Broch attributed to an entity called "the Guide," eventually numbered 258 and formed the foundation for a spiritual community called Pathwork. When Pierrakos and Broch married, their perspectives mutually informed their work.

Core Energetics, a body psychotherapy that combines Pierrakos's background in Reichian bodywork with the spiritual philosophy articulated in the Guide lectures, specifically places love and pleasure at the core of life and sees its task as helping individuals remove obstacles to opening the heart and living fully. Rather than simply dealing with physical energy, however, Core Energetics also works with the human energy field that interpenetrates the physical body and extends out around it. Even when working with Bioenergetics, Pierrakos was observing these energetic movements of the body, eventually coming to the conclusion that this energy is inextricably entwined with consciousness, love, and pleasure. Perhaps the most significant difference between Bioenergetic Analysis and Core Energetics is the latter's full embrace of spirituality as a part of therapeutic healing work.

The principal concept of Core Energetics is the belief that at the center of our being is a spiritual and energetic essence called the higher self. If unblocked and fully flowing, it pulsates love, pleasure, generosity, compassion, and joy. This core energy can be distorted by a layer of dense energy called the lower self. When emotions such as anger and fear generated by the flight-or-fight response are repressed, they feed into the lower self, creating defensiveness as well as other negative emotions. Jacqueline Carleton, Ph.D., editor-in-chief of *Energy and Consciousness*, the Core Energetics journal, explains that "these defensive emotions we refer to as the 'lower self' [are so called] because we judge them to be unworthy of us and yet we know we have them." They stand in contrast to the openness and love of the higher self. When individuals do not express emotional pain or these dark feelings, defenses are constructed, eventually becoming muscular armoring. On top of all this, individuals then create a social mask, yet another layer that deadens energetic vitality and spontaneity and moves them farther from their core. The mask is a facade that hides lower-self feelings that are deemed unacceptable to ourselves and others. Carleton explained the interplay of these aspects in a 1996 editorial: "My mask of serenity may cover my jealousy and greed. If I can find and express the jealousy and greed of my 'lower self,' I will be led back to the pain, fear, and deprivation that surely underlie them. If I can express these primary pains, the organism's self-regenerating system will be activated and my true generosity, a quality of my core, will emerge and help to heal the original deprivation as I give to others in my life."

Core Energetic sessions are similar to Bioenergetic sessions, which is not surprising given the collaboration between Pierrakos and Lowen. The therapist and client both wear comfortable clothing that allows freedom of movement. The client may do physical movements aimed at cathartic release, grounding, or energetic recharge or discharge. However, the use of meditation and the acceptance of work with the energy field and energy centers called chakras distinguish Core Energetics from Bioenergetic Analysis. Core Energetic therapist Karyne B. Wilner points to other differences, including the use of special breathing techniques to open the heart, replacement of the psychoanalytic model of personality with a spiritual model, and in some cases substitution of a roller for the breathing stool. The roller opens the diaphragm and chest muscles, as does the stool, but because it is closer to the ground it is considered safer—the client can't fall off of it, and it can be used at home by the client.

A Core Energetics session, according to Carleton, begins with a brief moment of meditation, deep breathing, or eye contact while holding hands to align energies. The client might then state his or her intention for the session or simply broach a topic or theme or describe an incident. The session would then move into energetic work by introducing a stress position, grounding exercises, breathing instructions, or hands-on work with either hard or soft touch (see Carleton's description below).

Core Energetic training is conducted in New York City, Mendocino, California, and Georgia. There are also training programs in Switzerland, Germany, Italy, Mexico, Brazil, and Canada.

Books

John C. Pierrakos, *Core Energetics: Developing the Capacity to Love and Heal* (Life Rhythm Press, 1987). This book tackles the subject of health and disease/dysfunction by explaining the pulsation frequencies and colors of the energy fields (auras) in human beings, animals, plants, and minerals.

John C. Pierrakos, *Eros, Love, and Sexuality: The Forces that Unify Man and Woman* (Life Rhythm Press, 1997). According to Pierrakos, energy and consciousness manifest themselves as eros, love, and sexuality. In this book, he discusses the interplay of these omnipresent forces, the ways they become blocked in the personality and body, and ways they can be freed. The book also contains an edited transcript of a six-day intensive Core Energetics workshop on the subject.

Organizations

Institute of Core Energetics East
115 East 23rd Street
New York, NY 10010
(212) 982-9637 (phone)
(914) 245-9449 (fax)
jagroom11@aol.com (e-mail)
www.core-energetics.org (website)

Founded over twenty years ago by John Pierrakos, M.D., the institute is an international organization that offers an array of professional training programs, seminars, workshops, and lectures.

✸ A Core Energetics Session ✸

By Jacqueline A. Carleton

Susan, a high-ranking communications executive, came to me for help with her difficulties getting along with some of her subordinates at work. In her second session, we began to gently stretch and move about the room in preparation for some emotional work. She began to cry softly, then harder as I asked her to massage her neck and shoulder.

She told me that she was remembering how trapped she felt as a child by her father's baffling and brutal punishments. If he loved her, which he clearly did, how could he strike her with such violence in response to minor infractions? I suggested she try to express her frustration physically by hitting the pile of pillows I keep in my office with a soft bat or with her fists.

As she began to strike the pillows, her sobs deepened. She began to cough and choke. This continued until she found her voice and began to say, "No! No! No!" as she hit. Her rage built as she pummeled the pillows and then, as she grew tired, her sobbing softened into a gentle weeping. As she shed a last few tears, her face shone with a realization: "I never knew until now how his blows hurt me inside."

From this realization, we were able to go on to discover how trapped she felt at work by subordinates who seemed to her so like the unruly younger siblings for whom she had always been responsible and for whose misbehavior her parents always held her accountable. Thus her work environment paralleled her childhood situation where she was accountable to her superiors for her subordinates and unconsciously feared similarly arbitrary punishments from them.

Her body held the key to the relationship between her difficulties at work and her early family situation. Although she had discussed it many times in previous therapies and groups, she had never before made a visceral, emotional connection to her father's sudden and seemingly arbitrary punishments. Not until she was able to fight back and say no could her body/mind allow her to feel different at work. Not until she could feel how her inner being had been damaged and how she herself continued her hitherto unconscious self-punishment could she begin to heal the inner wound, take control of that aspect of her life, and forgive both her father and herself.

It should be noted that her professional work also mirrored core qualities that had been developed in her family. Growing up as a caretaker of her siblings, she learned to care for people and to stay organized, which made her an excellent administrator. Holding core qualities in mind while working with clients is one of the characteristics of Core Energetics.

Jacqueline A. Carleton, Ph.D., has been a psychotherapist for twenty years. She is a senior faculty member at the Institute of Core Energetics in New York City and Core Energetic institutes in Germany, Switzerland, and Mexico. She is also on the faculty of the Center for Character Analytic Studies.

Medical Orgonomy

Whereas Freud and his followers focused on the meaning behind verbal content, Reich began moving away from the classical psychoanalytic theories of the 1920s by examining how individuals express, manifest, or suggest latent emotions through patterns in the body's musculature, posture, and movement. From these theories, Reich developed his own brand of therapy, which he initially called character analytic vegetatotherapy, and its corresponding methodology, character analysis, which observes and works with the interplay of body movements, breathing patterns, freedom to express emotions, and ability to reach orgastic potency. The latter involves the ability to achieve an "orgasm reflex," which does not mean ejaculation or climax. It refers to an involuntary full-bodied energetic response characterized by a rhythmic pulsation and undulating movements that can be induced in a therapy session. Alexander Lowen explained in his book *Bioenergetics* that theoretically a patient who was free enough to exhibit this reflex in therapy would be capable of experiencing full orgasm during intercourse. Later, Reich refocused his attention from character analysis to orgone, which he saw as universal cosmic energy. Although Reich himself used the word *cosmic* to describe orgone, he did not intend to imply a spiritual connotation, merely a deeply biophysical one. As Reich himself explained in a 1952 interview: "Psychoanalysis is a psychology of ideas while orgonomy is a science of physical energy." Thus what had been called vegetatotherapy evolved into orgonomy. Medical orgonomy, as it is now called, refers to the fact that practitioners who use it must possess a medical degree that includes a psychiatric specialization.

Organizations

American College of Orgonomy
P.O. Box 490
Princeton, NJ 08542
(732) 821-1144 (phone)
(732) 821-0174 (fax)
www.acoreich.org (website)

The late Elsworth Baker, psychiatrist, psychoanalyst, and author of *Man in the Trap*, founded the college in 1968 with the goal of preserving and extending Reich's work with orgonomy. The college offers educational programs such as conferences, trainings, lectures, and courses for professionals and laypersons and also supports research.

Center for Reichian Therapy
310 West 86th Street
New York, NY 10024
(212) 580-1750

The center offers a three-year training program in Reichian Energetic Therapy that includes readings, lectures, practical demonstrations, an ongoing process group, case study presentations, individual psychotherapy, and supervision.

Friends of the Reich Museum
P.O. Box 687
Rangeley, ME 04970
(207) 864-3443 (phone and fax)
wreich@rangeley.org (e-mail)
www.rangeley.org/~wreich/ (website)

Founded in 1959, the Friends of the Reich Museum offers educational programs on Reich's life and work, as well as an exhibit of the laboratory where he tested his theory of orgone and experimented with various inventions such as the orgone accumulator. It also provides a bookstore of Reich's published work and makes his unpublished writing available to the public.

Organismic Body Psychotherapy

Developed by clinical psychologist Malcolm Brown and body therapist Katherine Ennis Brown, this body psychotherapy weaves together American and European Reichian traditions. In addition to being influenced by Kurt Goldstein's writing on Gestalt psychology, Carl Jung's analytical psychology, the neo-Reichian therapy of Norway's Ola Raknes, and London-based Gerda Boyesen's Biodynamic psychology, Malcolm Brown studied Abraham Maslow's self-actualization theories, did a brief stint with Alexander Lowen, and studied Carl Rogers's client-centered therapy. The fact that both Browns have lived for extended periods of time in the United States and Europe has also affected the blending of American and European therapies in organismic psychotherapy.

For example, Lowen and Pierrakos developed the Bioenergetic Analysis notion of grounding. Based on ideas of Neo-Reichian body psychotherapist David Smith and others, the Browns distinguished between vertical and horizontal grounding. Whereas vertical grounding refers to standing firmly with "one's feet on the ground" (i.e., in reality), horizontal grounding, which is an integral part of organismic body psychotherapy, involves full awareness and presence but in a more diffuse and undirected state of feeling while lying prone. Whereas vertical grounding might be a helpful attitude vis-à-vis the world, horizontal grounding reflects more intuitive and creative processes.

After Brown met, began working with, and married Katherine Ennis, the two started to experiment with different kinds of touch, evolving two primary types: nurturing and catalytic. Influenced by the European Reichian forms of touch, which were much softer than either Reich's or Bioenergetic Analysis's early approach, the Browns developed nurturing touch, which involves very little movement. "The therapist makes gentle and safe contact, and through that contact helps the deeply buried energy in the core of the self 'melt' the armoring from the inside out," explains organismic body psychotherapist Barbara Dunn. Catalytic touch is a harder, more penetrating form of contact intended to physically work out and release muscular tension.

Dunn points out that observing client responses to touch, the Browns realized that it was not neutral. It produced, depending on whether the therapist was a man or women, dramatically different effects. Another important discovery the Browns made was that the dramatic catharsis of feelings, which was the goal of so many body psychotherapies and bodywork approaches in the 1960s and 1970s, was not necessarily responsible for hastening the healing process. Although the strong emotional releases were instrumental in loosening the mental and physical armor, it was the quiet and peace that followed such catharsis that allowed the core of the body and soul to expand and that allowed for deep change to take place.

Organismic body psychotherapy sees three steps in the therapeutic process; namely, loosening the muscular armor, successfully resolving conflicts that arise as a result of that loosening, and stimulating ongoing creative growth and self-expression. Initially the organismic therapist directs the session, although over time the process gradually becomes more client directed.

Books

Malcolm Brown, *The Healing Touch* (Life Rhythm Press, 1990). This book traces the author's journey from traditional psychotherapy to body-oriented psychotherapy and includes his own perspective on aspects of working with "embodied soul."

Organizations

U.S. Organismic Training Institute
2489 Lauderdale
Atlanta, GA 30345
(770) 938-5043
The institute runs training programs in organismic body psychotherapy.
Washington Institute for Body Psychotherapy
8830 Cameron Court, Suite 206
Silver Spring, MD 20910
(301) 588-9341

Contact the institute for information on organismic body psychotherapy training programs in the United States.

Radix®

Radix is a neo-Reichian educational process developed by Charles Kelley in collaboration with his wife, Erica, in the 1960s. Radix means "primary cause" or "source." The Kelleys use it to refer to the life force. The term is similar to but not identical with Reich's concept of orgone and Alexander Lowen's bioenergy. Radix employs a direct, largely nonverbal approach to loosening muscular armor and increasing body awareness so as to uncover "the natural flow and creative energy that are blocked by rigidity and stagnation."

Although heavily influenced by Kelley's teacher Wilhelm Reich, Radix differs from the Reichian model primarily in that it holds that muscular armoring can play a valuable role for people. Just as important as our need to access and express our feelings is our need to control impulses, delay gratification, and make and execute decisions. In Kelley's view, armor does not simply repress emotion, it also supports ego functions such as will, discipline, and self-control that, he says, are essential to leading a responsible life.

Given this orientation, all Radix programs begin by working from the top down and from the outside in. Eyes, hands, and feet are worked with to establish contact with reality: seeing things clearly, handling situations, and feeling one's feet firmly on the ground. Work with muscular armoring helps to reeducate the body to respond appropriately to emotional impulses. Although much of a Radix student's personal work is nonverbal, deep emotion often cannot be expressed quietly, so sound is an important element of this work.

More than in other neo-Reichian approaches, the eyes play an important part in Radix, mainly because Kelley became acutely aware of the role they play psychologically when he dramatically improved his own nearsightedness using the Bates Method. Subsequently trained as a Bates teacher, Kelley wrote his doctoral dissertation on "Psychological Factors in Myopia" and incorporated work with the eyes into Radix. Research and experience convinced him that visual problems are linked to muscular tension that needs to be released for emotional work to be fully integrated and for the person to be able to see clearly "what was past, what is before them right now, and what lies ahead."

Technically, Radix is not a body psychotherapy but an educational process aimed at self-discovery. The formal program devised by Kelley is called Radix Education in Feeling and Purpose. Kelley explained in an interview published in the U.S. Association for Body Psychotherapy newsletter that Radix Education was never intended to heal childhood wounds. "I was trying to help people develop beyond where they were, not trying to repair damage that had been done to them by their parents when they were young, but to help them grow beyond their present stage. . . . " Indeed materials on Radix emphasize that Radix students are not considered "sick" and therefore do not need to be "cured." Kelley's program involves a two-step process: dealing with feelings, then dealing with one's purpose and the relationship between the two. Over time, however, Kelley discovered that people were drawn much more to the former than to the latter. "The people who needed work on purpose in their lives were scared of it," he reported. "It felt better to them by far to yield to their spontaneous feelings . . . than to sit in a group and face difficult problems in their lives, face knowing themselves better, face developing the capacity to live for a long-range goal, to make the hard decisions that would make their lives work over time."

Kelley founded the Radix Institute in 1974 in Southern California. In 1986, after his retirement as director of the Institute, a rift occurred between him and the new administration. As a consequence there are now two separate organizations offering Radix training, each of which can legally train and certify teachers under the name originally procured by Kelley for the Radix Institute.

Organizations

Kelley/Radix Center
K/R Publications
13715 SE 36th Street
Steamboat Landing
Vancouver, WA 98683-7770
(360) 896-4004 (phone and fax)
kelley6@ix.netcom.com (e-mail)

Through the center, Chuck and Erica Kelley offer Radix sessions by appointment. Additionally Chuck offers training and supervision for professionals. Certification can be earned as an adjunct Radix teacher (one-year program) using Radix work in connection with an existing professional practice, or as a regular Radix teacher (two-year program), practicing Radix only.

Radix Institute, Inc.
6609 Fourth Street, NW, Suite J–125
Albuquerque, NM 87107
(888) 777-2349 (toll-free phone)
www.radix.org (website)

The Radix Institute offers a fifteen-month adjunct or twenty-six-month full training program that includes on-site workshops of four to twelve days, monthly tapes and articles, and phone or in-person supervision of trainees working with their clients. The second year requires on-site supervision.

❀ A Radix Case ❀
By Erica Kelley

The young woman lying on the mat looks vulnerable. She is on her back, knees up, with feet flat on the floor. Her brown eyes sometimes look frightened; sometimes angry. Her mouth is shaking. Her breathing is rapid but moving toward regaining its rhythm and depth. She is trying to say something. I ask her to get up onto her feet. At first she is shaky and needs support, but gradually she "feels" her legs, feels supported by them. She takes a deep breath, looks me in the eye and says, softly at first, "My opinion matters." But as she is encouraged to deepen her breathing and repeat the words, they gain intensity. A glitter comes into her eyes, she starts clenching her teeth and her fists. We switch to her saying, "My anger matters," then "My anger is important."

"Lisa" is shorter than I am but as her intensity builds, her voice gets louder, her eyes challenge mine, and she appears to grow several inches taller. As her excitement builds with the words and with the body language, her tone changes subtly. The challenge becomes a statement, then progresses into a quiet assertion. And there it is. There is nothing more either of us need to do except celebrate quietly, connected only through the eyes. Her opinions matter and her anger is important.

Lisa has lain on the mat on the floor many times in the last months in order to reclaim parts of herself. Often there have been no words at all, but sometimes there were sentences such as "Listen to me," "Please see me," "Notice me," "Please give me some attention." When words were not expressed, there were sounds— cries, screams, sobs—or there was total silence.

Since running away from home at age fifteen, Lisa had supported and defended herself in the world. Pretty, intelligent, and proud, she set out to prove that she could make it even if her parents had negated her every action and opinion. She had done it but at a cost. Her body reflected her struggle. Her neck and shoulders were so tense that they moved almost as one piece. Her jaw was stubborn and she was grinding her teeth most nights. Her little-girl defiance was reflected in her locked knees and arched back, and yet her eyes were appealing, soft, nearsighted. Her voice would develop a resigned quality and her breathing would almost cease. She didn't need to say the words, "What's the use?" Her body said it for her.

When Lisa increased her breathing, mobilized muscles in the rib cage, made her shoulders raise and lower, and permitted her heart feelings to show in her eyes, she experienced her resignation as something alive, something she could do something about. Her voice gave it a sound, and it developed into the racking sobs of deep hopelessness. Lisa's deep surrendering to and acceptance of the hopelessness brought up convulsive sobs that further loosened her armoring. Her diaphragm swung freely, allowing the pulsation to deepen into the belly. The work progressed from this point to allowing the mourning that she had never done. Over the next few months she grieved in her sessions for what was and what had not been; she grieved for herself and the way she had deadened herself and not experienced life fully. Throughout this process her muscle armor was loosening and her radix was flowing more freely. When the mourning ended and she gave up her expectations of the past, the pulsation was turned around. Energy flowed from her center to her body's periphery; it came out her eyes and hands and grounded her feet. The rage could then pour out. The anger was experienced and owned as *her* anger. The final step occurred when the content of her expression no longer needed to be that of anger, but transformed spontaneously to a sense of power—quiet strength and soft empowerment. Her opinions mattered; her anger was important.

The work with Lisa was done over a two-year period. Since then, she has become able to commit herself fully to a relationship, marry, and have children. She functions well as a professional and has progressively developed her career. She is an integrated, effective person. Her life is not without problems, but she has the confidence in herself that enables her to handle whatever comes along.

Erica Kelley has assisted her husband, Charles, with the development of Radix Education in Feeling and Purpose since the late 1960s and continues to practice part-time while enjoying the beauties of the Pacific Northwest.

Bodynamic Analysis

Founded in Denmark by Lisbeth Marcher and her colleagues, Bodynamic Analysis is a carefully researched and constructed body-oriented psychology. In twenty-five years of studying physical therapy and psychology, Marcher discovered that not only are emotions held in the body's musculature but there is a sequence to muscle development; that is, muscles become activated at certain ages to allow for physical activities. With this knowledge she created a developmental map for each age that included the implications of tense, collapsed, or healthy muscles. She also correlated specific muscles with their psychological functions (e.g., triceps are used in the motion of pushing away and therefore in the setting of boundaries). Ultimately, Marcher identified seven developmental stages and devised a Bodymap that begins with intrauterine life and progresses through adolescence.

Using this map, Bodynamic Analysts are able to find where blocks are located and are then able to work on developing the resources that were given up or held back when growing up. The Bodymap is a major tool of Bodynamic Analysis. It is probably the reason why Reichian scholar David Boadella reportedly called Marcher "the Scandinavian legacy of Wilhelm Reich" and pronounced Bodynamic Analysis "one of the most advanced character structure models" to emerge from the new generation of European body therapies.

The heart of Bodynamic theory and practice, however, is its emphasis on interconnectedness. Marcher sees breaks in what she calls "mutual-connection" as the cause of developmental arrest; therefore the core of her healing process is the restoration of "mutual-connection."

Marcher sees herself less as a Reichian than as one who operates in the field that Reich defined. She makes this distinction because she fundamentally disagrees with Reich's sexual theories. "I always felt Reich was wrong to make the sexual experience the core of his idea of relationship," she told an interviewer. "He, like Freud, took sexual energy to be the primary drive inside us." She believes humans' basic drive is toward being connected to other people. Thus Bodynamic Analysis helps individuals achieve fulfillment in their relationships. "It is through body awareness that we sense ourselves in *relation* to the other," she says. "The more body awareness we can attain—which includes an awareness of sensation, energy, and emotion—the more we are able to establish deep connections to others." Given Marcher's orientation, it is not surprising that the dominant presenting problem in Bodynamic Analysis has to do with relationships: with one's children, with one's spouse or partner, and with coworkers.

Marcher intentionally locates Bodynamic Analysis in the body psychotherapy field, stressing both elements equally. Therapy without body awareness lacks a vital element, she says, while body awareness work that is not grounded in solid therapy will not produce lasting change. She also makes a clear distinction between emotionally cathartic but unintegrated experiences and the slow, long-term therapeutic process.

Bodynamic Analysis begins with an initial meeting in which a personal history detailing relationships and traumas is taken. Then early on in the therapeutic process, a Bodymap is done. In a four-hour session, the tonicity of over two hundred muscles in the body is tested to see if they are either hypo- or hypertense. The Bodynamics Analyst then interprets the findings for the client. The next step is for analyst and client to make a contract that stipulates specifically what the client wishes to work on. The client could choose a specific issue, which would require only a short-term intervention, or a full Bodynamics Analysis in which he or she would work through all character structure and shock trauma issues.

According the Barbara Renshaw, a registered nurse, marriage and family therapist, and Bodynamics Analyst and trainer, the underdeveloped or collapsed muscles would generally be worked on first because by strengthening them, one supports the psychological resources associated with them. It is important, she says, not to break down or take away defenses. By building strengths and resources, defensive patterns that often kept the client safe—and in some cases alive—can be safely given up.

Clients can be of any age. In fact, Renshaw described a videotape that showed Marcher working with an infant who had had a particularly difficult and traumatic birth. As a result, the child was rejecting the breast and turning away from the mother. Marcher talked with the kicking baby. Then she placed her hands against its feet, creating a resistance much like the pushing action during birth. Next she instructed the mother to do the same, telling her to talk with her son, encouraging him and praising his efforts. This activity seemed to re-create the birthing process, but this time mother and son were working together. As a result of this work, the baby began to nurse and bond with the mother.

A typical Bodynamics session is two hours long and includes experiential work that combines physical movements (contracting or stretching muscles) with hands-on work (a gentle contact with muscles that energizes them and often allows the psychological material from the developmental age of the muscle—unconscious material that has been either blocked or forgotten—to be accessed as an image, sensation, memory, or emotion). The client and analyst then work with this information to integrate and reclaim early abilities and resources.

Ultimately, the goal of Bodynamic Analysis is to be able to make choices and experience healthy relationships. "I believe that we have the greatest choices, the deepest choices when we are in touch with our bodies and our emotions and our thoughts and our spirituality, and when we don't confuse them," explains Marcher. "Reality is very deep for me. I really want people to be in their reality because it is the only place from which you can make a clear choice."

While Bodynamics is typically a long-term primary therapy, it is also suitable as a short-term therapy and as an adjunctive technique. The developmental emphasis of Bodynamics makes it particularly suitable for work with infants and children. Group therapy is also available.

Organizations

Bodynamics Institute/USA
P.O. Box 6008
Albany, CA 94706
(510) 524-8090 (phone)
(510) 524-5884 (fax)
biusa@sirus.com (e-mail)

The institute, headquartered in Berkeley, California, is an international organization that conducts research and offers workshops and trainings. Three levels of training are offered by the institute. Level I is Foundation Training, which is open to anyone interested in their own personal growth. The second level is primarily for professionals such as massage therapists, physical therapists, nurses, and physicians. The Advanced Bodynamic Analyst training, Level III, is for mental health professionals who are licensed in their state or country to practice psychotherapy. Bodynamic Analysis centers are also located in Los Angeles, Boulder, Reno, and Kona, Hawaii.

EYE MOVEMENT DESENSITIZATION REPROCESSING®

Eye Movement Desensitization Reprocessing (EMDR) is a new approach that stands on its own. It does not focus on muscular armoring nor does it use exercises to open up breathing. What it does is use eye movements—or alternatively taps, lights, or auditory cues—to stimulate a process by which the effects of trauma are successfully eliminated. It is included here because it is most decidedly a psychotherapy that uses the body (the eyes) as the doorway into a healing process.

Developed by psychologist Francine Shapiro, Ph.D., over the last eleven years, EMDR has evolved from a simple treatment technique to a psychotherapeutic approach that assists victims of trauma in healing themselves. Though EMDR is best known for its eye movements—clients following the therapist's finger move their eyes back and forth from left to right and back again for several twenty- to thirty-second sets—Shapiro points out that other procedures such as establishing a solid therapeutic relationship, taking a full client history, addressing client vulnerability, and therapeutic timing and protocols are equally important to the client's successful EMDR experience.

Treatment begins with the therapist taking a history and getting a sense of the problem. Then the level of the disturbing emotion is rated: the client is asked to think of the incident and gauge how anxious, shamed, sad, or rageful—on a scale of 0 to 10—she feels. Next the therapist conducts a series of eye-movement sets—short periods of eye movement interspersed with feedback from the client (When you picture the scene, what do you feel? Where do you feel it in your body?). Periodically throughout the session, the intensity of the feeling is monitored (Thinking about the original scene, how disturbed do you feel now?). The emotions can decrease or escalate before stabilizing. Because there is a risk of retraumatizing the client (i.e., actually increasing the anxiety), Shapiro stresses the importance of working with a trained clinician.

Shapiro has reported studies showing that 84 to 90 percent of people who were treated with EMDR—victims of rape, natural disaster, catastrophic illness, and other traumas—recovered in only three sessions. Obviously more sessions may be needed depending upon the individual and the severity of the trauma.

Although Shapiro admits that she's not precisely sure why the stimulation component of EMDR works, she hypothesizes that human beings have a natural capacity to process disturbing life situations neurologically. If something upsetting happens, we think about it, talk it over with our friends or spouse, and dream about it until we've extracted the useful information from the situation and can face it with appropriate feelings—what she calls arriving at an "adaptive resolution." However, if a person is severely traumatized, an imbalance in the nervous system can disrupt this "information processing system." Information in the form of feelings, images, and body sensations experienced at the time of the trauma can become stuck and resist processing, resulting in nightmares, flashbacks, intrusive thoughts, amnesia, or the blocking of memories. The eye movements and EMDR procedures seem to trigger physiological mechanisms that jump-start the natural processing system, thus leading to a resolution.

In her book *EMDR: The Breakthrough Therapy for Overcoming Anxiety, Stress, and Trauma*, Shapiro describes one patient who came to her to overcome a phobia about leaving the country. When they began the session, the client had an image of herself arriving at an airport. Along with the image came feelings of desolation and abandonment. As they worked with the eye movements, a new and upsetting image appeared: the client at age six waving good-bye to her parents at a train station. Shapiro worked with the client until her disturbing feelings were defused and her thoughts about traveling abroad shifted from a negative "I can't do it" to a more positive "I can travel comfortably." One month later a follow-up revealed that the woman was planning a trip to Greece.

"More traditional psychotherapies certainly could have helped this woman," Shapiro writes. "However psychoanalysis might have taken years to unearth that pivotal childhood memory with no effect on her behavior; cognitive therapy might have changed her negative belief about herself but had no effect on her emotions; and behavioral therapy might have lessened her level of emotional distress but not enhanced her self-respect. The rapid change in her emotions (no more anxiety) and her behavior (traveling abroad), along with the recognition of the reasons for her distress and a radical change in how she viewed herself and her abilities, are results typical of EMDR."

EMDR has been used to treat phobias, panic disorders, excessive unresolved grief, chemical dependency, and post-traumatic stress disorder resulting from combat, sexual assault, natural disasters, and sexual abuse and molestation. It is also useful for any psychological complaint that has an experiential contributor.

Books

Laurel Parnell, *Transforming Trauma: EMDR* (W. W. Norton, 1998). The author, a clinical psychologist and senior EMDR Institute trainer, describes to readers how traumas are frozen in the psyches of her clients and then released through this new approach.

Francine Shapiro, *Eye Movement Desensitization and Reprocessing: Basic Principles, Protocols, and Procedures* (The Guilford Press, 1995). Reminiscent of Eugene Gendlin's method of Focusing, Francine Shapiro's EMDR approach has clients concentrate on physical sensations and emotions while performing directed eye movements. Thus it uses the body to reach and heal the mind. This text leads the practitioner through the eight-phase treatment of trauma victims, provides a conceptual framework for the approach, and evaluates the research conducted to date.

Francine Shapiro and Margot Silk Forrest, *EMDR: The Breakthrough Therapy* (Basic Books, 1997). This book, a follow-up to Dr. Shapiro's first book, is a basic overview of EMDR's clinical applications. It also includes the story of Shapiro's chance discovery of the effects of eye movements and her subsequent development of the method that reactivates traumatic memory and then desensitizes it. The book contains case studies of people who have been helped by the technique as well as topics and goals for research.

Organizations

EMDR Institute
P.O. Box 51010
Pacific Grove, CA 93950-6010
(408) 372-3900 (phone)
(408) 647-9881 (fax)
inst@emdr.com (e-mail)

The institute sponsors training workshops that take place throughout the United States. It also maintains an international directory for client referrals.

HAKOMI AND HAKOMI INTEGRATIVE SOMATICS

Hakomi is a Hopi word that means "How do you stand in relation to these many realms?" or more simply "Who are you?" Ron Kurtz developed this approach by experiencing a host of different therapies including Gestalt therapy, Rolfing, and Bioenergetics and working with several teachers including John Pierrakos, Al Pesso, and Moshe Feldenkrais.

Having immersed himself in the human potential movement with its confrontational encounter group tactics and active, almost aggressive style of bodywork with forceful pressure exerted on muscles to get them to release, Kurtz found that his natural therapeutic style was less provocative and more evocative. Attracted to Taoism, Kurtz began to evolve a method of working with people that embodied many of the principles of that ancient Chinese philosophy. In 1991 he and his colleague Greg Johanson wrote a book entitled *Grace Unfolding: Psychotherapy and the Tao-te-Ching* in which they explore the Taoist tenet that the nature of life is change and that the most beneficial way of doing therapy is to become aware of the natural movements that are already occurring and adjust creatively to them. One of the book's major points is the principle of nonaction, which is not passivity but a state of conscious preparedness in which the appropriate action occurs effortlessly.

This unique blending of Western therapeutic principles and techniques and Eastern spiritual values has made Hakomi both a body psychotherapy and a spiritual practice. The core of the method has always been mindfulness. Although it shares certain qualities with the Buddhist definition of the word, mindfulness in Hakomi means that the client is relaxed with a gentle and sustained focus of attention inward, attempting to be sensitive to changes in feelings, sensations, thoughts, or the appearance of memories and images. Kurtz describes mindfulness as a "relaxed, open, undefended, quiet state" that involves surrendering to and accepting what is happening in the moment. With mindfulness as its foundation, the work emphasizes the healing relationship between client and therapist and the practice of nonviolence.

In Kurtz's mind, healing can only occur with the cooperation of the client's unconscious, which requires "a deep person-to-person connection." In other words, Kurtz came to the same conclusion as the Stone Center research: the quality of the therapeutic relationship affects healing. For Kurtz this meant that Hakomi practitioners needed to be authentically "trustworthy, nonjudgmental, and compassionate" as well as "present, attentive, and understanding"—in short, nonegocentric. Thus the spiritual side of the therapist was called to the forefront. The practice consists of keeping focused on the core of goodness in the client, "the seed of Buddha"; maintaining the utmost respect and compassion; maintaining a state of mindfulness; and eliminating distracting mind-chatter.

With mindfulness and compassion established, the Hakomi practitioner can use several techniques to further the therapy: probes, taking over, and experiments. A *probe* is simply approaching a client with a question, a statement, or a touch and then observing the client's reaction. *Taking over* refers to supporting a defense or area of tension so that the client doesn't have to. If a client's stomach is tight, for instance, the therapist can exert pressure on the abdominal region in such a way that the person doesn't have to hold it in. Or the client's shoulders may be turned in such a way as to restrict any impulse to strike out or to reach out. If the therapist restrains the shoulders, the client can shift his or her point of view from creating the prison to feeling like the prisoner.

Experiments include probes and taking over but also cover situations such as those detailed in Kurtz's book *Body-Centered Psychotherapy: The Hakomi Method.* There he describes working with a female client who couldn't make eye contact with him. They experimented by having her look at him while his eyes were shut; look at him very briefly; slowly bring her eyes into contact with his eyes while staying aware of the feelings that came up; and other ways of approaching the problem in order to generate more information about the emotional content of that simple act. Kurtz stresses that all these techniques are used in a nonviolent fashion; that is, with deepest respect for the client's process. He realizes that force and pushing are not useful or effective because they create resistance. Therefore the Hakomi practitioner is supportive of the client's pace.

Today Kurtz teaches and leads workshops in what he calls Higher Ground Training, a method that has built upon his original Hakomi principles and techniques. The training consists of three six-month segments: Living Presence, which sees therapy as a spiritual practice; Emotional Skills, which works with the ideas presented in Daniel Goleman's book *Emotional Intelligence*; and Bonding and Service, which explores using skills acquired in the previous two segments in professional settings and community service.

Pat Ogden, who apprenticed with Kurtz and was a founding member of the Hakomi Institute, has extended his methodology and founded a branch of Hakomi entitled Hakomi Integrative Somatics (HIS). Her background includes massage therapy and social work as well as studies in Rolfing with Emmett Hutchins, Continuum with Emilie Conrad-Da'oud, and Somatic Experiencing with Peter Levine, who specializes in working with victims of trauma. More recently she has worked intensively with Bert Shaw from the Pathwork Community.

In the original Hakomi work, the psychotherapy components were emphasized more heavily than bodywork; in HIS, the body is the primary arena for healing wounds. HIS sees two sources of problems: developmental wounds and trauma. The former occur as a result of family dysfunction and appear as self-defeating or self-destructive behavior, relationship problems, and physical symptoms such as chronic and painful muscular contractions. On the other hand, trauma is the result of an event or events that seem to threaten one's survival. The situation is overwhelming, leaving one feeling helpless or out of control. The symptoms associated with unresolved trauma include migraines, headaches, insomnia, nightmares, anxiety, and hyperarousal. Training in work with victims of trauma—assisting with reassociation, the formation of boundaries, and embodiment—has become a large part of HIS.

Books

Ron Kurtz, *Body-Centered Psychotherapy: The Hakomi Method* (Life Rhythm Press, 1990). This book covers the guiding principles, patterns, and techniques of the Hakomi Method as developed by the author.

Ron Kurtz and Greg Johanson, *Grace Unfolding: Psychotherapy and the Tao Te Ching* (Bell Tower, 1991). This book explores the application of Taoist principles to the practice of psychotherapy.

Organizations

Hakomi Institute
P.O. Box 1873
Boulder, CO 80306
(303) 499-6699 or (888) 421-6699 (phone)
institute@hakomi.com (e-mail)
www.hakomi.com (website)

This nonprofit educational organization is dedicated to the evolution of body-centered therapy and the dissemination of information on the Hakomi Method.

Hakomi Integrative Somatics (HIS)
P.O. Box 19438
Boulder, CO 80308
(303) 447-3290 (phone)
(303) 402-0862 (fax)
lehrman@azstarnet.com (e-mail)
www.azstarnet.com/~lehrman/his/htm (website)

HIS is a branch of the Hakomi Institute that builds upon and extends the original Hakomi Method through workshops and trainings.

Ron Kurtz Trainings
P.O. Box 961
Ashland, OR 97520
(541) 482-6776 (phone and fax)
hakomione@aol.com (e-mail)
www.azstarnet.com/~lehrman/rk1.htm (website)

This organization offers training and workshops for professionals and the general public. The focus is on both therapeutic method and spiritual growth.

PESSO-BOYDEN SYSTEM/PSYCHOMOTOR

Pesso-Boyden System/Psychomotor—sometimes referred to as Psychomotor Therapy—is a group-based body psychotherapy developed collaboratively by Albert and Diane Pesso beginning in the early 1960s. Both Pessos have extensive dance backgrounds, and their therapeutic method, a combination of role-play, movement, and improvisational interaction, is grounded in body-centered kinesthetic awareness.

In various essays and interviews, Al Pesso has stated that though past painful events or deficiencies cannot be changed, a person's image of them can be molded. Memories, he says, are not absolute facts but subjective impressions and constructions that can be reshaped. "The past," he writes, "is embedded deeply in the experience of the present and woven into the anticipation of the future." Thus clients can access the past in the present and through symbolic enactment create a new kinesthetic, sensorimotor, and cognitive experience, which becomes a touchstone for acting in new ways.

The principal Psychomotor technique, called a *structure*, is a client-directed, organized role-playing activity in which a person gets in touch with and reexperiences painful feelings and the situation that gave rise to them. Then another group member, called an accommodator because her function is not to improvise but to reflect the needs and wishes of the client working in the structure, helps to create a scene in which conflicts are resolved, unmet needs satisfied, or old wounds healed. For example, if the client was the victim of physical abuse, an accommodator might represent a mother figure that protects the child.

Pesso-Boyden System/Psychomotor has a laundry list of terms related to their work—*true scene, witness, voices, shape/countershape, healing scene, center of truth*—but the essence remains the creation of an experience laden with symbolic meaning for the client that in effect replaces negative memories with satisfying, newly embodied alternatives.

Al Pesso's interest in the body began as a young child in Brooklyn in the 1940s when he took up muscle building. Then, through the girlfriend of the owner of the gym where he worked out, he was introduced to dance. When he visited the studio where she took lessons, the two women who ran it saw in him an ideal candidate for dance training, and he studied there before going on to Martha Graham's school and eventually earning a scholarship to Bennington College, where he met his future wife, Diane. After they married, they moved to Boston, where they taught and started a dance company. At that time, Pesso says, they were trying to discover how movement originates, finally arriving at three distinct types: voluntary, reflexive, and emotional. "We focused on the emotional movement, trying to see how action evolved from it," he says.

In an interview in the U.S. Association for Body Psychotherapy newsletter, Pesso explained that traditional psychotherapy relies on insight as the primary change agent. In contrast, Pesso feels that "patterns created by deficit remain until new patterns of satisfaction are experienced." Although one can't go back in time and change what one experienced, one can, Pesso believes, "create, while in touch with the memory of self as a child, a sensory motor, kinesthetic, tactile, verbal, auditory experience from which he/she can reconstruct, out of this symbolic moment, a new piece of memory."

Psychiatrists, psychologists, counselors, and social workers have incorporated Psychomotor Therapy into their primary practice, and the therapy has been used to treat anxiety, depression, substance abuse, incest, combative families, and chronic pain. Although the therapy was founded in the United States, it has achieved considerable recognition in Europe with the establishment of training centers in Belgium, Denmark, the Netherlands, Norway, Switzerland, and Germany.

Organizations

Pesso-Boyden System/Psychomotor Institute
Strolling Woods
Lake Shore Drive
Franklin, NH 03235
(603) 934-9809 or (603) 934-5548 (phone)
(603) 934-0077 (fax)
PBSP1@aol.com (e-mail)
www.pbsp.com (website)

The institute is a nonprofit corporation dedicated to furthering the development of Pesso-Boyden System/Psychomotor.

RUBENFELD SYNERGY®

The Rubenfeld Synergy method of body-oriented psychotherapy emphasizes the simultaneous use of gentle touch, verbal expression, and movement. It combines techniques used in Gestalt therapy, the Alexander Technique, the Feldenkrais Method, and Ericksonian hypnotherapy. Like other therapies, Rubenfeld Synergy helps open gateways to contacting, expressing, and understanding past memories and current feelings.

Ilana Rubenfeld's introduction to bodywork came through music. When teaching children how to sing and play instruments, she would have them moving, jumping, and playing different characters. In 1957 she entered the Juilliard School of Music to study conducting and developed a debilitating back spasm. Someone suggested that she try the Alexander Technique to alleviate her back pain. The Alexander Technique lessons not only allowed her to perform without pain but also evoked deeply embedded feelings in her. The Alexander teacher felt ill-equipped to deal with her emotional responses, so she suggested a psychotherapist, and for the next three years, Rubenfeld says, she shuttled between the two. She had a psychotherapist who talked but would not touch and an Alexander teacher who touched but would not talk. Although she eventually became an Alexander Technique teacher, she understood through personal experience the need to combine body and psyche in therapeutic work. "The unconscious desires and yearnings that we have, the preverbal memories—long before words—and how people look at us and treat us are all encoded in our bodies," she says. "It is very fitting to be able to journey and discover the story of the heart, the mind, the spirit, and the body all at the same time."

In 1966, while at Esalen, she met Fritz Perls, who became her mentor. In workshops, the master of Gestalt therapy would place her next to participants in the "hot seat"—an empty chair in the middle of the room from which participants worked with Perls—so that she could touch them while he worked with them verbally. She could "hear" the participant's story with her "listening" hands. Then in 1971, a small group of bodyworkers that included Rubenfeld brought Moshe Feldenkrais to Esalen for a six-week intensive training, and Feldenkrais exercises and movements were combined with Gestalt therapy techniques as part of her widening therapeutic repertoire.

The name for her approach came from R. Buckminster Fuller, the philosopher, engineer, and inventor of the geodesic dome, after he saw a Rubenfeld demonstration session. Having written a book titled *Synergetics*, he recommended the use of the word *synergy* because her work combined various methods and produced results that were greater than the sum of the individual parts. The concept is appropriate for Rubenfeld's work inasmuch as she learned much from several therapy and bodywork pioneers but integrated what they taught in a totally original way, adding a generous dollop of New York humor to the mix.

During a Rubenfeld Synergy session, the client generally lies on a massage table fully clothed but can also sit or move around if that feels appropriate. As Rubenfeld talks with the client, asks questions, and directs them to speak to various people who may have angered, abandoned, or hurt them, she moves around the body—holding the head, supporting the back, or gently touching the chest. In this way verbal dialogue is integrated with emotional and physical techniques. The goal is to become conscious of, express, and deal with emotions that are being held in the body. This resolution affords greater self-awareness and supports change and better decision-making abilities as individuals are able to be more in the present, not locked in the past of their body/mind.

Organizations

National Association of Rubenfeld Synergists
1000 River Road, Suite 8H
Belmar, NJ 07719
(800) 484-3250, code 8516

The association is dedicated to supporting the professional growth of its members, educating the public about the Rubenfeld Synergy method, maintaining high standards of professional ethics, and protecting the right of Rubenfeld Synergy practitioners to practice.

Rubenfeld Synergy Center
115 Waverly Place
New York, NY 10011
(800) 747-6897 or (212) 254-5100 (phone)
(212) 254-1174 (fax)
rubenfeld@aol.com (e-mail)
www.members.aol.com/rubenfeld/synergy/index.html (website)

The center runs Rubenfeld Synergy training programs and serves as a resource and referral center.

Touchy Subjects in Body Psychotherapy

Respect for boundaries and appropriate touch are important and much-debated issues in all the helping and healing professions. However, because touch is inherent in body psychotherapy and somatic therapies, these concerns are central to these fields.

The first concern is to prevent conflicting dual relationships, such as the roles of client and friend. Unconsciously a client might hold back material so as not to upset the status of a friendship or might be hesitant to express anger or criticism toward a therapist who is also a friend. Therapeutic process must be protected by firm boundaries so that a full range of responses, images, and material can be presented and shared without fear of hurting feelings or damaging a relationship.

Unfortunately, psychotherapy's early history does not present a good model in terms of contemporary professional ethics and what we know about the potentially destructive impact of dual relationships. While psychoanalysts kept their patients at a physical distance, sitting behind them as they lay on a couch during a session, dual relationships were far from uncommon among early psychoanalysts. Freud analyzed his daughter Anna, and Jung had affairs with two former analysands, Sabrina Spielrein and Toni Wolff. Jung's relationship with Toni Wolff was rather more complex than a simple affair because not only had she been an analysand but Jung demanded that she play an intimate role in his life as muse and colleague. "Jung's affair with Toni might have been less troublesome," writes Paul J. Stern in his book *The Haunted Prophet,* "if he had not insisted on drawing his mistress into his family life and on having her as a regular guest for Sunday dinner."

San Francisco psychiatrist Peter Rutter has done excellent work with regard to defining boundary violations. In his book *Sex in the Forbidden Zone,* he argues that it is up to the therapist to maintain appropriate sexual boundaries. The task is difficult, he writes, but absolutely necessary. The ultimate protection against abuse is the therapist's understanding of the harm he can inflict and his empathy with the client. Of course, a sexual relationship initiated by either therapist or client is strictly forbidden. Breaches of this boundary are serious and can result in professional censure, loss of license, and criminal and civil charges.

Another issue for body-oriented psychotherapy is the multiple roles a practitioner might play. For example, psychotherapists may incorporate into their practice some form of touch. Similarly, bodyworkers may incorporate therapeutic dialogue into their practice. But so long as bodywork remains the primary mode for the bodyworker and psychotherapy for the psychotherapist, clarity is maintained.

When an individual is seeing a therapist who does both psychotherapy and bodywork, it might be useful to establish and maintain a primary relationship before establishing a secondary and subordinate one. As we've seen, many body psychotherapy approaches emphasize bodywork and psychotherapy equally, in which case there is no conflict. However, some psychotherapists use bodywork and some bodyworkers use psychotherapy to augment their preexisting practice. In these cases, it is helpful to be clear about the work's boundaries. For example, one could be in therapy with a psychologist who suggests EMDR sessions, but those sessions are given in the context of ongoing psychotherapy. If one approached a psychologist for EMDR sessions, however, any therapy beyond the limits of EMDR should be discussed and mutually agreed upon.

It is important to recognize that some people in the helping and healing professions are debating whether boundaries are necessary—aside from issues of sexual misconduct. They contend that the creation of rigid boundaries is not only

unnecessary and artificial but even damaging and a hindrance to the optimal healing of both practitioner and client. While acknowledging that sexual abuse in
therapeutic relationships is very real and dangerous and must not be tolerated,
these scholars and practitioners claim that therapists must be careful not to eliminate empathy, intimacy, friendship, vulnerability, and other aspects of mutually
healing human relationships from their practice in the interest of maintaining
boundaries. Christine Caldwell, in the book *Getting in Touch*, offers a kind of base-
line: Touch violates a client's boundaries when it is "unwarranted, unwelcome,
and has the potential to cause physical or psychological harm. . . . In psychotherapy, any sexual touch is rightly considered unwarranted and is strictly censured,
even if it is invited by the client."

✸ In Conversation with Marion Woodman: ✸ A Full-Bodied Voice

Too often the psychological voice and the physical voice are separate though
they yearn to come together. When people say that they don't have a voice, they
may mean that they don't have a voice that comes with full-throated resonance.
Or they may mean that they aren't sure that they have anything to say. Even when
space is left open for them, they may be so frightened or have such low self-esteem
that they cannot speak. They have not articulated in their heads what they want
to say and therefore what comes off their tongues comes out muddled. They are
not used to talking to someone who cares enough to say, "I don't understand what
you're thinking" or "What you're saying is very confusing. Would you clarify?"

People who have been silenced as children are quite ashamed to speak.
They'll often say, "This sounds naive," "I know this sounds childish," or "I don't
know how to say this but . . . ." Probably one of their parents said to them, "That's
not what you really think," or "That's not what you feel," or "Aren't you ashamed
of yourself for talking like that." All of these "shut-up" words and phrases actually
lodge in the muscles of the body and not only silence the psychological voice but
silence the physical voice as well.

In people who are working on releasing complexes locked in their muscles,
dreams make it quite clear who put the silver cage on their mouth. The location
of the blocks in the body can also reveal which parent enforced the silence. The
mother complex, for example, often binds the chest. The lungs fundamentally
take in breath. Deep, rich patterns of breathing occur if there is no fear of what
may come in. Many people are terrified of crying, releasing anger, even laughing
because they fear that if they let go and allow their genuine emotions out of prison
they will go wild; therefore they breathe very shallowly. What a tragic waste of
life! You see the pattern beginning to form in a baby lying on its mother's chest. If

the baby feels absolutely comfortable, it splays itself on her, totally open. A fearful child holds its chest back from full contact with its mother's body. That holding back restricts the body, especially the lungs. The father complex is usually found deeper in the body, around the third chakra, the power center, the solar plexus. All of this is related to voice because not only are muscles like the diaphragm tightened, but so is the psyche because it is afraid to speak its own reality.

Individuals who work hard with their journals as adolescents learn how to express themselves even if they were quiet when they were young. As they mature, they can speak from their own center because they have never been imprisoned, although they often prefer writing to speaking.

People who have not used their voice physically tend to speak from the top of the throat so that the resonators in the head and body, especially the back, are not used. Most people are unaware of the lung capacity in their back or the air passages in their face and head. If you want an authentic, resonant voice that comes from your whole being, you must open and exercise those resonators.

A person who is speaking with a thin, little voice from the throat doesn't carry the weight of truth that a person with a deep resonating voice does. Now, of course, that's not always true. A trained actor may have a magnificent voice but have nothing to say. I'm not talking about that. I am talking about ordinary people in ordinary life. A voice that is coming from a body that is resonating with feeling is a voice that is in tune with the present moment. Whatever is in the body and psyche is manifesting in the voice. If the body is closed and/or the psyche is frightened, the voice is immature. On television, for example, you hear people strangling their feelings; they have very tight throats. You certainly hear that in politicians who are being very cautious about what they say or how much truth they reveal.

As a culture we are cut off from our feelings. One small example: If I say to a workshop participant, "Can you let those muscles in your buttocks relax?" they probably have no idea that their muscles are locked. On the other hand, if you look at a little child who is angry, its butt is up but, as the anger is expressed, the muscles relax and it goes down. People who wonder why they have such terrible back pain need to ask themselves what they never dare express.

Feeling needs to flow through the body. Only by experiencing the emotion that is moving through your body do you gain the wisdom of that experience. It's one thing to know in your head that you are going to die one day. It's quite another to be told that you have a year to live. That message comes into your body in a totally different way. It's not only the shiver that goes through you physically but the knowing in your heart that it is true. People who feel gain the wisdom that comes from their experience. And the wisdom of life experience can be heard in the voice. If you know something in yourself, you don't have to shout it; you don't have to whisper. People who are confident speak firmly and quietly. You sense their truth, their authenticity. They use their physical voice very differently from people who are trying to prove something they aren't sure of.

A woman who says to a man, "This is my truth," and brings it out from the top of her throat doesn't carry any authority. Whereas if she can relax, open up her voice channel, and say, "This is my truth," he might hesitate to question her. Authority and authenticity come from the same root, and the voice communicates both. The deeper you are grounded in your body, the more your voice rings true.

In workshops, I work with the breath because the breath is the breath of life. We try to allow the breath to drop as deeply as possible into the body, allowing the muscles to relax at the same time so that the body experiences itself as an instrument. The body *is* an instrument. It's a harp, a piano, a cello. If we are working with one of these metaphors, we sound into the body, working on the harmonic that brings the body into wholeness. We might have a dream that would give us a sound to work on. Jung said that the symbol heals. So we try to work with that mystery to find out in what way a particular metaphor ringing in our particular body can guide us to wholeness.

The metaphor is an image of a particular energy. A cello is a different energy from a flute. People who get mired in the old lizard down in the mud of the unconscious might need to work with flute energy. People who love to fly in the sky might need to work with a double bass. The dream imagery restores the balance if we bring it to consciousness.

It's also important to realize that the sound coming out of our body is creating resonances in the bodies of the people we speak to. Or it isn't. When we go to hear a great singer whose resonances are natural, our body begins to resonate to the sound that's coming into it. If that sound is false and we have worked on our own tuning, our bodies will pick up the fraudulence immediately.

A person sometimes dreams of going into a concert hall to play in an orchestra that is still tuning up. Everything is out of harmony. Often that is as far as the first dream on this theme goes. Then may come a whole series of dreams in which the first violinist, maybe the dreamer, is trying to bring the orchestra into harmony. Eventually, the conductor may appear and the musicians may actually start to play together. Then the dream moves into transcendent space. The energy systems of the body and psyche are in unrestricted harmony.

That brings us to the healing possibilities of sound. My sense is that few of us have any experience of the power of sound for healing because we don't yet believe in the metaphorical or energy body. We are still thinking only in terms of the physical body. But there is another body and it is very responsive to finely tuned harmony, as the Catholic Church certainly knows with Gregorian chant and as the Buddhist monks know with their overtone chanting.

Emily Dickinson understood this harmony[*]:

Better—than Music! For I who heard it—
I was used—to the Birds—before—
This—was different—Twas Translation—
of all the tunes I knew—and more—

Marion Woodman is a Jungian analyst based in Toronto and the author of many books, including *The Pregnant Virgin*, *The Ravaged Bridegroom*, and *Dancing in the Flames*, with coauthor Elinor Dickson. Her most recent book, with coauthor Robert Bly, is *The Maiden King*.

---

[*]Poem #503 from *The Complete Poems of Emily Dickinson*, edited by Thomas H. Johnson (Boston: Little, Brown, 1960).

7
Soma and Soul

A midwestern professor always begins his course in Human Movement Theory with the question "Where is your mind?" Inevitably students point to or tap their heads. Only once several years ago did a person respond differently—he put his hand over his heart. This student did not grow up in America but in Nigeria.

This anecdote not only underscores how pervasive and unconscious is our dualistic thinking, which locates intellect only in the brain, but opens the door to a vision in which knowing is no longer restricted to the head but seen as residing elsewhere in the organism. If mind can call the heart home, why not the gut? Or the skin? The feet, tissue, and bones? As Professor Yuasa once wrote: "True knowledge cannot be attained simply by means of theoretical thinking but only through . . . the utilization of one's total mind and body. Simply stated, this is to 'learn with the body,' not the brain."

Like body psychotherapists, somatic educators believe that our past lives on in our bodies. But whereas body psychotherapists focus predominantly on coaxing the muscles to release emotions, somatic educators hone in on not only muscle, tissue, and fascia but bones, organs, even cells in order to sense, to intently listen, and to intimately feel their condition, and what it says about where the organism is, holistically speaking. Some somatic educators go so far as to state unequivocally that this simple attentiveness can bring about change; all somatic educators look to the body for instruction on how to proceed in the healing.

Somatics is a difficult and demanding mistress because she requires a paradigm shift in our understanding of the relationship of body, mind, and spirit. While other holistic methods may take these into account, they can very well retain and disguise residual dualistic thinking. For example, bodyworkers from any approach can assume the mantle of healer, believing that it is their knowledge, expertise, sensitivity, or intuitiveness that is responsible for effecting change. No matter what language they use, it is clear that they believe their actions or verbal ministrations are the vital healing component. But somatics requires that practitioners tune into their own felt experience and simply teach or guide clients in connecting with the physical sensations related to inhibitions or obstructions, which deny them a full and vital experience of health and of life. Awareness of these sensations brings the mind and body together, and in somatics, the mind yields to the body in determining the direction of action or perhaps nonaction. The locus of healing lies in the client's body. The tissue, bones, muscles, and cartilage in collaboration with consciousness bring healing.

Historically somatics can be traced back to the nineteenth and early part of the twentieth centuries, to individuals who scrupulously observed their bodies in order to heal themselves. One somatic pioneer, F. Matthias Alexander, an Australian actor whose specialty was recitals of Shakespearean passages and other verse, wanted only to rid himself of a recurring, potentially profession-damaging case of laryngitis. When the only remedy physicians could offer was to rest his vocal chords (i.e., not perform), Alexander took it upon himself to find a cure. By watching how he held himself when conversing and comparing that with his posture when performing, he became aware of how he changed the position of his head and how that change not only affected his voice but created tension patterns in his body. Through self-observation and analysis, Alexander broke his deleterious habit and he went on to earn a certain amount of acclaim as an actor. The story might well have ended there but for the remarkable quality of his voice. That characteristic opened the door to inquiries from other actors and even members of his audiences regarding consultations. And so Alexander became one of the first somatic educators, teaching his method of attaining awareness of physical movements, inhibiting inefficient patterns, and replacing them with new ways of moving.

Some twenty years later, in 1910, halfway around the world in Berlin, a young physical educator, Elsa Gindler, was fighting tuberculosis. Without sufficient financial means to pay for proper treatment at a sanitorium and with her physician telling her she would never regain the use of one lobe of her lungs, she devised a daily regimen. Believing that her lungs needed rest in order to heal, she focused for hours on other organs and structures related to breathing, such as the throat, diaphragm, stomach, and rib cage. Her concentration was so focused that she not only regained her health but essentially created a body-centered form of meditation in which practitioners pay careful attention to the movements that make up simple daily activities such as eating, walking, standing, and sitting. Gindler had a great influence on the field of bodywork, influencing Wilhelm Reich and Gestalt therapist Laura Perls, among others. In this country, her work is known through the Sensory Awareness method taught by her student Charlotte Selver.

According to Don Hanlon Johnson, director of the graduate program in somatics at the California Institute of Integral Studies and author of several books on bodywork and somatics, the somatics field also has roots in the nineteenth-century Gymnastik movement. Going beyond physical exercises and work with apparatus such as parallel bars, rings, and balance beam, Gymnastik proponents rejected the separation of the human spirit from a mechanistically conceived body. They envisioned a unity among movement, body structure, health, intelligence, and spiritual consciousness and emphasized a respect for lived experience and the wisdom that can be found through attending to rather than conquering or controlling life processes. The practitioners of various branches of Gymnastik did sophisticated healing work using expressive movement, sensory awareness, sound, music, and touch. Instead of imposing a narrow standard of correct form on all bodies, the new practitioners encouraged individual expressiveness and a return to a more "natural" body, thus allowing unique forms of movement to emerge from within.

Fast-forward to the 1960s and the Esalen Institute, a growth center located on a wild and beautiful stretch of Pacific coast in California. The center was a hotbed of countercultural and human potential experimentation. It also hosted an abundant smorgasbord of bodywork adventures. A new generation of somatic innovators including Moshe Feldenkrais, Ida Rolf, and Milton Trager gathered in Big Sur to teach the healing capacities inherent in the cultivation of direct contact with bodily experience. Although these leaders had been toiling in the field for years before coming to Esalen, each attracted a following and gained visibility in that creative California cauldron. In effect, Esalen launched many into national prominence in the body therapy and somatics fields.

The term *somatics*, however, was not coined until the mid–1970s. Thomas Hanna, a philosopher and Feldenkrais practitioner, first named the field, defining it as the study of phenomena related to "the human being as experienced by himself from the inside." Rather than approaching the body from a "third-person perception," Hanna argued for "first-person perception." What he meant was that rather than maintaining an objective clinical distance from physiological and psychoemotional experiences, a person would attend to minute physiological realities involved in body functions and movements and thereby learn the language of posture and pulsations. Mind would not direct but come into an equal partnership, bringing attentiveness and consciousness with it.

Despite the differences in method and style among the thousands of practitioners who are the heirs of these innovators, today's somatics practitioners share a vision about the nature of reality. Rolfers, Rosen Method, and Feldenkrais practitioners may differ about many things but they all make the assumption that sensing, feeling, breathing, and moving are crucial factors in the human search for meaning. Whether you are being probed by a Rolfer's elbow, touched by a Rosen practitioner with a "relaxed full hand," or experimenting with one of the Feldenkrais Awareness Through Movement exercises, you are constantly reminded of cellular-level realities.

Furthermore, as Johnson points out, the fact that somatic approaches provide a link between aching muscles and frayed nerves at the one extreme and love and cosmic intuition at the other makes the soul of somatics a modern Western version of the ancient psychophysical disciplines of Taoism, Sufism, Buddhism, and Greek Orthodox hesychasm (a fourteenth-century physical method of achieving interior quietness), whose goal was and is attainment of unmediated contact with reality beyond dualistic illusions.

Somatic approaches share several common elements. First, the practitioner is less a therapist working with patients than a teacher working with students. Feldenkrais explained this reasoning when he declared: "Many of one's failings, physical and mental, need not be considered as diseases to be cured, nor an unfortunate trait of character for they are neither. They are an acquired result of a learned faulty mode of doing." Therefore the emphasis in Feldenkrais work and other somatic approaches is reeducation. But before one can reeducate oneself, one has to grasp the problem, which leads us to the second common element of somatic approaches: awareness. Somatic approaches begin with paying attention. Whether in Sensory Awareness or Body-Mind Centering, the first step is focusing inward, not in order to do something but simply to witness and observe the minute and subtle movements of various organs, muscles, and bones. "Only by means of concentration," wrote Elsa Gindler, "can we attain the full functioning of the physical apparatus in relation to mental and spiritual life." The beauty of such awareness lies in its directness. Pat Ogden, in a 1997 article in the journal *Somatics*, gave an example of a client who carried tension in her right arm. The client believed that it represented repressed anger. Yet when she focused her attention on that sensation, she spontaneously envisioned herself wanting to reach out and hug her father. The tension in her arm was restricting not her desire to hit but her desire to reach out.

This is a wonderful example of the woefully inaccurate ideas the mind can spin, which then control and direct our lives. Using the mind to become aware of the story the body wants to tell is a much more effective process than conjuring up somewhat randomly what might be going on with and within ourselves. As Don Hanlon Johnson has written, somatics requires a "radical sometimes uncomfortable shift of viewpoint" in order to find meaning and healing in the depths of our flesh. "Yet it is precisely this radical shift that constitutes the heart of the various somatics methods: entering a long, quiet, and demanding journey to contact one's breathing, moving, sensing, pulsing, and feeling."

And that is the final point about the somatic perspective: that the body in all its variety is the sun; the mind, the moon. We need to allow our physical elements to lead the way in offering us the information we need to heal ourselves and to live life in a way that is resonant with our deepest being.

In today's hurly-burly whirlwind of activity, something that Elsa Gindler once wrote stands out. She pointed out that we have gotten into the habit of rushing about so much so that "we do everything in order to be finished with it, and then the next thing comes along." And the next thing. And the next. We are like pinballs ricocheting between family obligations and work pressures, between social commitments and the daily demands of living—grocery shopping, laundry, exercise, car repairs. We live our lives breathlessly. Gindler suggests a simple antidote: observe how we breathe while doing simple tasks: driving a car, eating breakfast, talking on the telephone, writing a report. "Simply noticing the constriction already brings help, and the oftener we notice it, and the more we accustom ourselves to investigating whether it is not perhaps an interference with breathing, the more easily and naturally it will be relieved." Once we can literally breathe deeply—using all *four* phases of breathing: inhalation, pause, exhalation, pause—we will move more economically. And instead of becoming frazzled and fatigued, our actions will actually refresh and energize us. We will "begin to understand that the demands made upon us by life are not so overwhelmingly difficult, that they can be carried out with greater economy of strength, without our usual maximum effort and turmoil."

Don Hanlon Johnson has pointed out that people outside the somatics field often comment on the seemingly excessive number of different types of somatic approaches. While there are certainly some disadvantages in the extent of this differentiation, he believes that the number of approaches offers a healthy alternative to the "homogenization of the body" that conventional medicine and the physical therapy and fitness fields perpetrate. "In somatics one finds a high regard for the individuality of both teacher and student, and their particular movement style, breathing pattern, and idiosyncratic posture," he writes. "Somatics does not cut and paste people to fit into a single-sized Procrustean bed. Rather it recognizes that the individual manner of expression and body structure can itself be radically healing."

Books

Don Hanlon Johnson, editor, *Bone, Breath, and Gesture: Practices of Embodiment* (North Atlantic Books, 1995). A diverse collection of essays, interviews, and articles by and about somatic pioneers and their work, including Marion Rosen, F. M. Alexander, Moshe Feldenkrais, and others.

Don Hanlon Johnson, editor, *Groundworks: Narratives of Embodiment* (North Atlantic Books, 1997). This book contains case studies by Emilie Conrad-Da'oud, Bonnie Bainbridge-Cohen, Robert Hall, and others.

Don Hanlon Johnson and Ian J. Grand, editors, *The Body in Psychtherapy: Inquiries in Somatic Psychology* (North Atlantic Books, 1998). A collection of essays that explore the life of the body as a basis for psychological understanding.

Stanley Keleman, *Your Body Speaks Its Mind* (Center Press, 1975). With the emphatic statement "We do not have bodies, we *are* our bodies," the author places himself squarely in the somatics camp, describing the concepts, principles, and processes associated with somatic therapy.

Organizations

Association of Humanistic Psychology (AHP)
45 Franklin Street, #315
San Francisco, CA 94102-6017
(415) 864-8850 (phone)
(415) 864-8853 (fax)
ahpoffice@aol.com (e-mail)
ahpweb.org (website)

Among AHP's many activities and services is an interest group called the Somatics Community.

Center for Energetic Studies
2045 Francisco Street
Berkeley, CA 94709
(510) 845-8373 (phone)
(510) 841-3884 (fax)
www.centerpress.com (website)

The center, the home base of Stanley Keleman, a long-time body psychotherapy and somatic therapy proponent, offers personal and professional education in somatic therapy. Focus is on the body and its connection to the emotional and imaginative aspects of the human experience.

International Somatic Movement Education and Therapy Association (ISMEATA)
148 West 23rd Street, Suite 1-H
New York, NY 10011
(212) 229-7666 (phone)
(212) 242-1129 (fax)

The association is a nonprofit educational registry and advocacy organization dedicated to promoting the benefits of somatic movement therapy and education, ensuring a high quality of practice among educators and therapists, and fostering communication among practitioners.

Novato Institute for Somatic Research and Training

1516 Grant Avenue, Suite 212
Novato, CA 94947
(415) 897-0336 (phone)
(415) 892-4388 (fax)

The institute, founded by Thomas Hanna and currently directed by Eleanor Criswell Hanna, offers training in Hanna Somatic Education, a procedure for teaching voluntary conscious control of the neuromuscular system to persons suffering from muscular disorders.

Somatic Institute
8600 West Barkhurst Drive
Pittsburgh, PA 15237
(412) 366-5580 (phone)
(412) 367-1026 (fax)

The institute provides training in CoreSomatics, a psychophysical-psychospiritual healing modality created by founding director Kay Miller. This approach combines the neuromuscular reeducation approaches of the Alexander Technique with the expressive arts, Jungian depth psychology, and Gestalt therapy.

Somatics Society
1516 Grant Avenue, Suite 212
Novato, CA 94947
(415) 892-617 (phone)
(415) 892-388 (fax)

Founded by the late somatics pioneer Thomas Hanna in 1975, the society is a membership organization that links educators and bodyworkers from all somatic fields. It publishes the semiannual magazine *Somatics* and a semiannual newsletter.

ALEXANDER TECHNIQUE

In some ways the Alexander Technique is the granddaddy of somatic therapy. Developed by Australian Frederick Matthias Alexander, who was born in 1869, this somatic reeducation process had its beginnings in an entirely different cultural time and context. Alexander was an actor who mainly performed theatrical recitations. Thus he was particularly distressed when he began to lose his voice during performances. Physicians recommended rest, which helped to restore his voice, but once he started performing again, the problem returned.

At his wit's end, he decided to take matters into his own hands. He began to observe himself in mirrors, watching how he held himself when reciting. He discovered that when performing, he pulled his head back and slightly downward. By consciously changing that habit, he was able to overcome his problem. In fact, as Michael J. Gelb reports in his book *Body Learning,* Alexander not only managed to achieve a certain amount of fame and success as an actor but also became known for the quality of his voice. When word got out about his discovery and self-cure, fellow actors and even members of his audiences came to him for help.

As Alexander worked with himself—the entire initial process took almost nine years—he realized that it was not just his head and neck that were affected but that restricting his head movements caused other areas, especially in his torso, to tense and shorten. Therefore Alexander focused on two things, which became the foundation for his educational techniques: *awareness* of how one is moving and *inhibition* of habitual dysfunctional movements in order to bring about change. Frank Jones, a university professor and Alexander Technique practitioner, describes the method this way: The Alexander Technique "teaches you how to bring more practical intelligence into what you are already doing; how to eliminate stereotyped responses; how to deal with habit and change. It leaves you free to choose your own goal but gives you a better use of yourself while you work at it."

The Alexander Technique creates a kind of biofeedback system in which the teacher, using very light, gentle touch and minimal verbal instructions, directs the student in simple motions like sitting or standing in such a way as to make her aware of what she's currently doing, how she's doing it, and how she can do it more efficiently. The latter is crucial because it provides a kinesthetic marker so that the student arrives at a choice point: either continue to move in a way that feels familiar but is inefficient and detrimental or move in a way that may initially feel awkward but that affords greater ease in the long run.

Because Alexander's personal work started with attention to head and neck, the Alexander Technique also begins there. The concept of Primary Control sees a direct relationship between the position of the head and neck in relation to the torso as well as between the position of the head and the entire attitude of the organism. According to Gelb, if clients develop an understanding of the subtleties of balancing their heads, then they have the ability to respond spontaneously in graceful and efficient ways. They are freed from habitual, fixed responses. "In other words," he writes, "as we learn consciously to contact our balanced testing state, we increase the possibility that our actions will be fresh responses to the moment rather than predetermined by the unnoticed remnants of our past."

Gelb describes a typical lesson: Generally the Alexander practitioner will get to know the student and the reason for taking the lessons. After explaining the basic principles, a teacher might then begin to demonstrate the principles involved in simple movements such as walking, standing, or sitting. Others might work with students lying on the floor or on a short massage table. If the presenting problem has to do with repetitive motions—say how one types at a computer or talks on the phone at work—or specific activities such as singing, playing an instrument, or a sport—a teacher may start with these. The focus is always on proper alignment and efficiency of movement.

During the lesson, the practitioner works with the student, conveying what an efficient movement looks and feels like. The real task begins once the student returns to the daily activities and environment where the habitual movements occur. Thus it is critical to this reeducation process that the student, in the words of Alexander himself, "not focus on goal or 'end' [but] keep his attention entirely in the 'means whereby' this end can be secured."

Books

Michael J. Gelb, *Body Learning* (Henry Holt, 1981, 1987, 1994). The author, an Alexander Technique teacher, provides a basic introduction to the principles and techniques of this approach.

Edward Maisel, editor, *The Resurrection of the Body: The Writings of F. Matthias Alexander* (Dell, 1969). This book is a collection of writings by F. Matthias Alexander, who developed the Alexander Technique. The introduction by the editor contextualizes the method through Alexander's biography and discussion of his philosophy.

Daniel McGowan, editor, *Alexander Technique: Original Writings of F. M. Alexander, Constructive Conscious Control* (Larson Publications, 1923, 1951, 1997). Alexander wrote four books over the course of his career, including *Constructive Conscious Control* (1923), of which this book is an abridged and edited version.

Organizations

Alexander Technique International (ATI)
1692 Massachusetts Avenue, 3rd Floor
Cambridge, MA 02138
(617) 497-2242 or (888) 321-0856 (phone)
(617) 497-2615 (fax)
ATI@ATI-net.com (e-mail)
www.ati-net.com (website)

ATI, a membership organization of both teachers of and those interested in the Alexander Technique, provides information on issues about and teachers of this method. It also networks internationally.

North American Society of Teachers of the Alexander Technique (NASTAT)
3010 Hennepin Avenue, South, Suite 10
Minneapolis, MN 55408
(800) 473-0620

A nonprofit educational organization that establishes and maintains standards for the certification of teachers and teacher training courses. Contact the society for a current list of approved programs and certified teachers.

Periodicals

Alexander Journal
Society of Teachers of the Alexander Technique
20 London House, 266 Fulham Road
London SW10 9EL
England

ASTON PATTERNING®

Developed by Judith Aston in 1977, Aston Patterning is an integrated system of movement education, bodywork, fitness training, and environmental evaluation (ergonomics). Through specifically designed sessions, the teacher and client work together to reveal and define an individual's posture and movement patterns while training the body to reclaim the natural, unstressed structure that lies beneath the layers of unnecessarily held tension. Sessions can include any one or a combination of the following: movement education, which teaches alternatives to stressful habits; massagelike bodywork, which relieves chronic physical and mental stress; and environmental consultation, which modifies the individual's surroundings to suit the body's needs.

Aston had been a movement educator who worked with performing artists and athletes in a college setting. After being involved in two car accidents, she sought out Ida Rolf because of injuries she sustained in the crashes. Her physical improvement was so immediate and remarkable that she began to collaborate professionally with the Rolfing founder, helping those involved in the Structural Integration process to use their bodies with greater efficiency and fluidity. Over time, however, Aston came to believe that the alignment that Rolfing aimed for was neither achievable nor desirable, and she left the Rolf Institute to work on her own.

The movement education part of Aston Patterning, called Neurokinetics, is a system of principles and activities whereby one can relearn simple activities such as reaching and sitting. Aston has also developed other dimensions of her work, including Aston Massage and Aston Fitness, an exercise program aimed at improving cardiovascular conditioning, muscle tone, and joint resiliency.

Many Aston Patterners maintain private practices in which they assist a variety of clients, including athletes, dancers, the elderly, the disabled, and healthy individuals seeking structural and movement enhancement. Practitioners also work in physical therapy, pain management, sports medicine, biofeedback, chiropractic, psychological, and holistic health-care clinics. Sessions last one to two hours.

Organizations

Aston Patterning Training Center
P.O. Box 3568
Incline Village, NY 89450-3568
(702) 831-8228 (phone)
(702) 831-8955 (fax)

The center offers basic courses in movement education, soft-tissue work, environmental modification, and fitness training for professionals wishing to apply specific Aston concepts in their primary practice.

BODY-MIND CENTERING®

Body-Mind Centering (BMC) is a deep and finely tuned somatic exploration. According to its founder, Bonnie Bainbridge-Cohen, "It is an on-going, experiential journey into the alive and changing territory of the body." The method, a combination of movement reeducation and hands-on repatterning, brings us inside muscles, bones, ligaments, organs, and skin to hone awareness of unconscious inhibitions so that they can be removed and the body regain efficient functioning.

As its name implies, BMC focuses on body-mind relationships. Bainbridge-Cohen sees the mind as a powerful shaper of the body. "The mind is like the wind," she writes, "the body like the sand; if you want to know how the wind is blowing, you can look at the sand." Given this orientation, BMC uses attention (mind) coupled with touch and movement to effect healing and change. A BMC session is generally an hour long and involves a blend of remedial touch (repatterning), movement, sound and voice, and concentrative awareness.

The hands-on repatterning component of BMC involves touching rhythmically, attending to specific layers of the body, following existing lines of force and gently suggesting new lines, and/or changing the pressure and quality of touch. Through these actions, the BMC practitioner seeks to set up a resonance between herself and the client at the bone-to-bone and muscle-to-muscle level. In other words, the practitioner first contacts the same structures within herself that she is about to contact in the client. If a broken femur is to be worked on, the practitioner first connects with her own femur. This sets up a resonance and initiates a nonverbal dialogue and connection. Then the attention is focused on the quality of tissue. If there is tissue damage or trauma, the practitioner and client explore how surrounding supporting tissue might take over so the former can recover.

Bonnie Bainbridge-Cohen had an unusual childhood, growing up as she did in the Ringling Brothers, Barnum and Bailey Circus. She has described her early years as awe-filled as she regularly saw people performing amazing physical feats such as balancing themselves on one finger on a ball. She also spent great amounts of time with the many circus animals.

The year after the Big Top closed and went indoors, Bainbridge-Cohen began to study anatomy and to explore dance and music with children afflicted with cerebral palsy. She became an occupational therapist and dance instructor, studying over the years with dance pioneer Marion Chace, choreographer Erik Hawkins, and Irmgard Bartenieff, the founder of EffortShape. She also acquired a crazy quilt of experience in yoga, aikido, voice, neuromuscular reeducation, and CranioSacral Therapy, among other approaches. Throughout her career, however, the connecting thread has been her focus on working with children with neurological dysfunctions.

In the early 1980s, with a group of colleagues, she began a journey of minute explorations of various parts of the body, beginning with the bones. Their investigations consisted of focusing inward on what these structures felt like when the body was in motion or at rest. In 1994 she told an audience at the Common Boundary Conference entitled "Body Wisdom" that investigating the feet alone took six months, working five days a week. Their sensory awareness work was so finely tuned and comprehensive that they could conceivably answer the question, "Who am I in my fourth toe on my left foot?"

Practitioners use Body-Mind Centering independently or in conjunction with other fields, including medicine, chiropractic, psychotherapy, acupuncture, the arts, bodywork and massage, yoga, meditation, and movement, dance, and speech therapies, among others.

Books

Bonnie Bainbridge-Cohen, *Sensing, Feeling, and Action* (Contact Editions, 1994). This is a collection of essays on the method she developed.

Linda Hartley, *The Wisdom of the Body Moving* (North Atlantic Books, 1989, 1995). This book, a comprehensive introduction to Body-Mind Centering, includes anatomical analyses, developmental movement theory, and an explanation of this method's principles and applications. Illustrations, photographs, and exercises abound.

Organizations

Body-Mind Centering Association (BMCA)
16 Center Street, Suite 530
Northampton, MA 01060
(413) 582-3617
 Founded in 1985, BMCA is a nonprofit association of certified teachers, practitioners, students, and others interested in Body-Mind Centering. The association sponsors an annual conference, workshops, research, and other events that foster the work. Contact the association for a list of teachers.

School for Body-Mind Centering
189 Pondview Drive
Amherst, MA 01002-3230
(413) 256-8615 (phone)
(413) 256-8239 (fax)
 The school offers ongoing training and certification in BMC under the direction of Bonnie Bainbridge-Cohen.

FELDENKRAIS METHOD

The Feldenkrais Method is a two-pronged sensorimotor educational system that employs movement, touch, and verbal instruction to help people increase their capacity to move, think, and feel more freely, efficiently, vibrantly, and comfortably. Like other somatic approaches, the Feldenkrais Method had its origins in self-healing. Moshe Feldenkrais (1904–1984), a Russian-born Israeli, severely injured his knee in his twenties while playing soccer. Twenty or more years later, he reinjured it in an accident. Physicians strongly advised surgery but could not guarantee that the operation would help. Feldenkrais could not face the prospect of hobbling through life and so began to study anatomy, physiology, neurophysiology, exercise, movement therapy, yoga, hypnosis, and acupuncture, searching for a way to return his knee to full functioning. Remarkably, Feldenkrais not only regained his ability to walk but also resumed his practice of judo (the first European to earn a Black Belt in judo, he organized the first Judo Club in France, where he was working at the time, and wrote two books on the subject).
 A colleague, aware of Feldenkrais's successful recovery, asked if Feldenkrais

could help alleviate his severe back pain. Thus Functional Integration, one of the two branches of the Feldenkrais Method, was born. Feldenkrais's reputation as a healer was solidified after he was able to help David Ben-Gurion, Israel's first Prime Minister, who had a history of chronic back pain, breathing difficulties, and other problems.

Feldenkrais was adamant about the educational nature of his work. Unlike Reich, he did not believe that emotions were trapped or held in the body's musculature. Instead he saw a variety of ways individuals became habituated to ineffective, inefficient behavioral patterns. Some people, for example, simply never learned how to express certain feelings, so they got stuck in self-destructive or inappropriate emotional patterns. In other cases, childhood experiences impaired posture, self-image, coordination, and the ability to move and feel. Believing in the maxim "Use it or lose it," Feldenkrais also pointed out that people sometimes just stopped learning, in which case areas of their bodies, even their brain cells, fell into disuse.

Feldenkrais reasoned that because the nervous system was so intimately connected to movement and because certain cells in the brain's motor cortex activated specific muscles, physical limitations and restricted movements would also limit cortical activity. Fixed physical patterns were reflected in fixed brain patterns. If, however, new movement was introduced and gently repeated over and over, this new activity would stimulate and enhance brain activity. Steven Sharafman, in his book *Awareness Heals: The Feldenkrais Method for Dynamic Health*, cites a Columbia University research project that studied electrical cortical activity in adult monkeys. What these scientists did was, in effect, to take a snapshot of the area of the cortex related to the monkey's fingers. They then trained the monkeys to perform specific movements involving only certain fingers. After three months, the area related to the active fingers grew larger, while the area related to the fingers that were not used decreased.

But Feldenkrais went even a step further, writing that "Owing to the close proximity to the motor cortex of the brain structures dealing with thought and feeling and the tendency of processes in the brain tissue to diffuse and spread to neighboring tissue, a diagnostic change in the motor cortex will have parallel effects in thinking and feeling." That's probably why Sharafman reported that Feldenkrais "hated" to have his work described as limited to the body and berated those who called it a means only for relieving pain and improving movement. "We're interested in flexible minds, not just flexible bodies," Feldenkrais said repeatedly.

The second branch of the Feldenkrais Method, called Awareness Through Movement, consists of group exercises, simple actions that encourage and support the exploration of new ways of moving. In both branches, the Feldenkrais teacher through movement and touch attempts to communicate an easier and more efficient way of moving. In Functional Integration sessions, the student may be lying on a short massage table either face up, face down, or on either side. The teacher, through subtle manipulations, then seeks to open a doorway for the student to sense an entirely new way of experiencing various parts of the body. The experience registers neurologically and the change is programmed at that level.

This process is perhaps best exemplified by a curious pattern in the Awareness Through Movement exercises. Many years ago, as part of a body psychotherapy course, a Feldenkrais teacher came in to lead us through a set of exercises. But unlike other exercise regimes, he would sometimes work on only one side of the body. After completing a series of movements, getting up and walking around was a very unusual sensation. Half of the body felt longer, taller, and more internally spacious than the other half. Only later did we learn the purpose of working on only one side: to make the brain work harder. If left incomplete, the body and brain will adjust toward the more open, spacious, and comfortable state. But to do this, the brain is challenged and has to become more active and more engaged. The result is longer-lasting change.

The Feldenkrais Method can be used for pain relief in situations involving chronic back pain or spasms; for enhanced functioning for those with severe and debilitating physical ailments such as cerebral palsy, stroke, and multiple sclerosis; for improved athletic or artistic performance; and as a means to increase self-awareness and self-knowledge.

Books

Moshe Feldenkrais, *Awareness Through Movement* (HarperCollins, 1972, 1977, 1990). An explanation of the thinking behind the Feldenkrais Method along with exercises.

Steven Sharafman, *Awareness Heals: The Feldenkrais Method for Dynamic Health* (Addison-Wesley, 1997). A simple, experiential introduction to the Feldenkrais Method, which includes a brief history, explanation of the method, and description of six basic lessons that can be tried on one's own.

Organizations

Feldenkrais Guild
P.O. Box 489
706 Ellsworth Street
Albany, OR 97321-0143
(800) 775-2118 or (503) 926-0981
Contact the Feldenkrais Guild for a list of accredited training programs.

HELLERWORK

Developed by Joseph Heller, an aerospace engineer who researched the effects of gravity on rockets, Hellerwork consists of deep massage, movement exercises, and verbal expression. While chiropractic focuses on manipulating the vertebrae and other bones, and Swedish massage on manipulating muscles, Hellerwork focuses on the body's connective tissue, the link between the muscle and the bone. The similarities with Rolfing—work with the connective tissue called fascia and the eleven-session bodywork series—come because Heller not only studied with Ida Rolf but worked as a Rolfer for six years, serving as the Rolf Institute's first president for part of that time. But he recognized that Rolfing's restructuring of posture and alignment did not always produce permanent change. Therefore, when developing his own method, he included movement exercises similar to Judith Aston's (she was also associated with Rolfing for a time) and verbal interaction between practitioner and client. The movement exercises teach clients how to move efficiently and gracefully when standing, sitting, and walking so that movements are consistent with their newly aligned structures. In addition to working with biophysical elements, this approach also recognizes the body's relationship with the psyche. If, for example, work on a particular area yields an emotional response, the client is encouraged to talk about the feeling.

The eleven Hellerwork sessions follow a specific progression that parallels human development, both physically and psychologically, from infancy through childhood and adolescence to adulthood. For example, the first three sessions are related to early childhood breathing, standing, and reaching functions; sessions four through seven focus on adolescent concerns about identity, sexuality, and autonomy; the last four sessions have to do with integrating work from previous sessions, as well as the relationship of maturity and balance, and masculine and feminine energies.

Organizations

Hellerwork, Inc.
406 Berry Street
Mount Shasta, CA 96067
(916) 926-2500 (phone)
(916) 926-6839 (fax)
www.hellerwork.com (website)
    This organization offers professional training in the Hellerwork approach.

MOVEMENT

Movement as a somatic tool is a very broad and diverse area that encompasses, on the one hand, movement therapies and, on the other hand, unique methods developed by dancers and choreographers such as Emilie Conrad-Da'oud, the founder of Continuum, and Anna Halprin, originator of the Halprin Life/Art Process. It is distinct from dance therapy, which is a discrete field with its own history, definition, purpose, associations, and certification process (see chapter 4).

Movement therapy generally involves the use of hands-on repatterning, gentle touch, and verbal instruction to help students and clients recognize and improve psychological, physical, cognitive, and motor patterns. The movement referred to is not generally large, sweeping gestures but minute and fine micromovements, touch, and gentle limb adjustments, as found in Body-Mind Centering, Aston Patterning, the Feldenkrais Method, Rubenfeld Synergy, and others.

Continuum, another healing method that incorporates movement, was developed by somatics pioneer Emilie Conrad-Da'oud, who also seeks awareness and expression of deep natural movements. "I had been teaching 'my body' to dance," writes the former dancer and choreographer, "but deep inside there was already a dance going on, if I would perceive it—a dance of myriad movement forms beyond anything I could think of."

Continuum takes an evolutionary approach to movement. Conrad-Da'oud began her professional career as a dancer and choreographer specializing in primitive dance. On her return from Haiti in 1967, she experienced a kind of culture shock, which made her realize that culture not only shapes who we are but also how we move. It restrains natural impulses and therefore restricts movement. Believing that collectively and individually we have limited ourselves through conventional movements, she initiated a quest to recover deep, basic, spontaneous, biologically based motion.

Conrad-Da'oud stresses that all life comes from water, pointing not only to our individual amniotic beginnings but also to our communal emergence from the "primordial soup." Because she sees human beings as going back "to the first microbes wriggling in the water" and because she sees the wave motion as an intrinsic biomorphic action, she stresses fluidity. "What we call 'the body,'" she explains, "is basically an asymmetrical, nonlinear creative flux, a river that has slowed down and looks solid." She designs exercises that involve breath, sound, and extremely subtle, small movements, along with focused attention on internal responses to these exercises. By freeing these deep, spontaneous movements, Continuum supports each individual's unique creative expression in their life, relationships, and work.

The Halprin Life/Art Process developed by dance pioneer Anna Halprin is the result of an amalgam of influences including dance educator Margaret D'Houbler, architect and Bauhaus founder Walter Gropius, somatic pioneer

Moshe Feldenkrais, and Gestalt therapy master Fritz Perls. Based on the belief that imagination and creativity are pathways to growth, the Process provides a safe space for applying creative resources to aspects of life: to communication, interpersonal relationships, and the interplay of physical, emotional, mental, and spiritual dimensions. Daughter Daria Halprin Khalighi, who had a background in both the performing arts and psychology, began to develop ways of using this work as a therapeutic process aimed at personal growth. The holistic nature of the Halprin Life/Art Process makes it both a movement-based educational and an expressive arts or creative arts approach.

Organizations

Continuum
1629 18th Street, #7
Santa Monica, CA 90404
(310) 453-4402 (phone)
(310) 453-8775 (fax)
continuummove@earthlink.net (e-mail)
home.earthlink.net/~continuummove (website)

Continuum offers teacher training, residential retreats, studio classes, and special intensives designed to provide movement education that is also a visionary inquiry into human beings' capacity to innovate and participate, through movement and sound, with the creative and biological life processes.

Laban/Bartenieff Institute of Movement Studies
11 East 4th Street
New York, NY 10003
(212) 477-4299

Based on the work of Rudolf Laban (1879–1958) and Irmgard Bartenieff (1900–1981), this institute was founded in 1978. According to the institute, Laban Movement Analysis (LMA) is a theoretical framework and language for describing any movement, from a conversational hand gesture to a complex action. LMA allows one to look at aspects of the body, space, and dynamics and describe, record, and analyze the movement. The therapist then observes recurring patterns, notes preferences, and suggests new possibilities. Bartenieff Fundamentals is a system of body reeducation based in basic movement principles that uses exercises to facilitate greater efficiency of movement. Certified movement analysts observe, analyze, interpret, and prescribe movement experiences that value individual movement patterns, assess physical and dysfunctional blocks, and guide clients through healthy expressive and functional changes.

Tamalpa Institute
P.O. Box 794
Kentfield, CA 94914
(415) 457-8555 (phone)
(415) 457-7960 (fax)
tamalpa@igc.org (e-mail)
     The Tamalpa Institute, cofounded in 1978 by Anna Halprin and Daria Halprin Khalighi, is a movement-based expressive-arts center offering training programs, workshops, and classes in Halprin/Life Art Process, an integrative approach to movement, the expressive arts, and therapeutic models supporting transformation at the personal and collective levels.

ROLFING

Rolfing, initially called Structural Integration, was developed by Ida Rolf, who, according to Don Hanlon Johnson, "felt that physical therapists, chiropractors, and osteopaths failed to appreciate the revolutionary consequences for human consciousness inherent in a balanced body." Rolf saw the key to life experience in movement. Because movement is largely determined by the joints, and their condition is related to myofascial flexibility, she evolved a method of applying deep hands-on pressure to loosen the fascia (the connective tissue surrounding and penetrating the muscles).

     With a background in yoga, osteopathy, and homeopathy and with some additional study of the Alexander Technique, Rolf understood that bones, which gave the body its structure, were held in place by myofascia. Osteopaths and chiropractors could adjust the skeleton and spine, but if the soft tissue or muscles were tight or foreshortened, they would eventually pull the bones out of alignment again. Therefore she worked on the fascial level, which she saw as providing the web of the body, "connecting everything with everything else."

     Rolf envisioned the upright body as consisting of segments that were affected by gravity's constant pull. Cognizant that stable structures require balance, Rolf sought a way to align ear, shoulder joint, knee, and ankle, with the idea that balancing the body in this way would lead to more efficient movement.

     Rolfers use fingers, fists, hands, and elbows to stretch and lengthen myofascial tissue and muscles. This can be particularly useful after surgery or a serious car accident, when scarred tissue has shrunken and grown thick, exerting a pull on other muscles, tendons, and bones throughout the body. Rolfing lengthens the tissue, minimizing the physical compensations that may result from such injuries. Rolfing has also been beneficial for those suffering from repetitive stress injuries, scoliosis, cerebral palsy, and chronic neck and back pain.

But one need not be ill or recuperating from an accident to derive benefit from Rolfing. Professional dancers and athletes as well as weekend sports enthusiasts— tennis, basketball, and softball players, cyclists, even in-line skaters—often discover that Rolfing increases their kinesthetic awareness, efficiency of motion, and physical responsiveness. Research conducted at the University of California at Los Angeles and the University of Maryland also offers evidence that Rolfing leads to a more efficient use of muscles, thereby allowing the body to conserve energy and reduce chronic stress and positively altering the body structure.

Rolfing also recognizes the emotional and mental implications of structural realignment. "If we can change our position so it is more in line and more in harmony with gravitational energy," writes Rolfer Will Johnson in *Balance of Body, Balance of Mind*, "then our tendency to randomness, disorder, and deterioration will decrease. Put more simply, the quality of energy that is available to a human being depends on his ability to come to balance." What this means is that Rolfing has a positive impact on one's psychological, emotional, and even spiritual state.

Rolf studied and taught for many years, but it wasn't until her long-term relationship with the Esalen Institute in the 1960s that her work gained greater visibility and more adherents. She established the Guild for Structural Integration (now the Rolf Institute of Structural Integration) in 1971 with forty practitioners. In 1979 when she died, there were two hundred Rolfers in the United States; by 1997, more than nine hundred Rolfers were practicing in twenty-six countries.

The majority of practitioners work in private practice; however, a few work with other health-care providers in hospitals and rehabilitation centers. Treatments are generally given in ten one-hour sessions.

Books

Will Johnson, *Balance of Body, Balance of Mind: A Rolfer's Vision of Buddhist Practice in the West* (Humanics Ltd., 1993). This book explores how Buddhist principles and meditative methods can inform the somatic practice of Rolfing.

Ida Rolf, *Rolfing* (Healing Arts Press, 1977, 1989). The original classic text on Rolfing written by its founder.

Organizations

Rolf Institute of Structural Integration
205 Canyon Boulevard
Boulder, CO 80302
(303) 449-5903 or (800) 530-8875 (phone)
(303) 449-5978 (fax)

RolfInst@aol.com (e-mail)
www.rolf.org (website)

The Rolf Institute provides Rolfing training and continuing-education workshops. It also acts as a membership and advocacy organization.

ROSEN METHOD

The Rosen Method℠, developed by long-time physical therapist Marion Rosen, uses gentle, nonintrusive touch to evoke relaxation and change. The technique consists of touching tense muscles with a relaxed full hand while following and attending to the client's natural breathing pattern. As muscles relax and breath deepens, feelings, attitudes, and memories held in the body begin to surface. Together, the practitioner and client verbally note these changes and whatever images or feelings might arise (see Sandra Wooten's description below).

Marion Rosen began her training in the 1930s in Munich, Germany, where she studied with Lucy Heyer, a student of the respected somatics pioneer Elsa Gindler and the wife of a Jungian-oriented psychoanalyst. Clients would see the Heyers, who were part of a circle of professionals who combined massage, movement, and breath work with traditional talk therapy—Dr. Heyer for analysis and his wife for bodywork.

With Hitler's increasing anti-Semitic activities, Rosen, who was Jewish, moved to Stockholm, where she became licensed as a physical therapist. She eventually moved to Berkeley, California, and received a second physical therapy license, this one from the Mayo Clinic.

Over the years, Rosen developed her physical therapy work with little thought to creating a name-brand method, and as late as 1978 she had not specifically named her approach. That came in 1983 when an institute was founded.

Although this method may seem like a body-centered psychotherapy, it is considered by its founder to be more a form of bodywork. While the approach can be valuable to people who have suffered physical and emotional abuse and to those in recovery from addiction, many Rosen Method clients come simply because of physical discomfort or pain or to learn more about themselves.

Organizations

Rosen Method Center Southwest
P.O. Box 344
Santa Fe, NM 87504
(505) 982-7149 (phone)
www.mcn.org/b/rosen/swrc.html (website)

The center offers week-long trainings for personal growth or professional certification.

Rosen Method Professional Association
(800) 893-2622

By calling the association's toll-free number, one can get a directory of Rosen professionals and interns.

❀ A Rosen Method Session ❀

By Sandra Wooten

The Rosen Method looks like massage in that the client lies on a massage table and is touched by another person. However, no oil is used and pillows can sometimes be used to increase comfort. Clients are partially clothed, always wearing underpants, or if preferred, whatever clothing they feel comfortable with. The client is then covered with a light blanket for comfort and warmth. The session, which lasts fifty minutes, usually begins with clients lying on their stomachs; later they will be asked to turn over.

When I give a Rosen session, I put my relaxed full hand on top of the cover to start. Then as the client begins to relax and become more comfortable, I fold the cover down and work directly on the body, generally beginning on the upper back, but taking time to notice and feel where tension is held. One hand contacts the tension, while the other hand rests and "listens."

Some indications of tension are a reduced movement of the solar plexus or a raised area caused by a contracted muscle. Body temperature, color, and texture also reflect internal tension, constricted movement, and its effects on circulation. Sometimes the tension is not obvious at first. Everything may look just fine on the outside, but gentle exploration uncovers a layer of tension below the surface. The client's position on the table may also indicate that the body is not relaxed. For example, the client's chest may not be resting comfortably on the table, implying tension in the upper chest as well as across the shoulders. One hip may appear higher then the other or legs may be held tightly together. I often share with the client what I'm noticing, sometimes talking about how a particular area of the body would rest or move if the tension wasn't there.

When I am working with a client, I notice the shape and posture of her body. It tells me a great deal about her life experiences and how she presents herself in the world. I watch, feel, and listen to the client while at the same time drawing on my own experience, internal awareness, and knowledge in order to assist in the unfolding of the client's process. The questions that are always in my mind are What hurts? What does the shape and posture of this body tell me? What is the potential for movement and expression if this muscle relaxes? My attitude is one of not knowing, nonjudgment, and curiosity.

I will often verbally respond to the changes happening in the body in order to increase awareness for the client. I might say, "This muscle under my hand just softened," or "Your shoulder just let go (or tightened). What happened?" I use words sparingly to enhance awareness, not to interpret. If I feel a muscle change, I may simply say "Yes" in a soft voice. This acknowledges that a change has occurred but without interrupting the inner process. The yes is a suggestion that the client notice what else is happening (e.g., a thought, image, emotion, or familiar or unfamiliar sensation). Sometimes a memory or deep insight emerges. Often the client will talk about what she is experiencing at that moment. I listen carefully to what the client is saying while watching and feeling the body's responses to what is being said. At this point, more may be said to continue the unfolding of the inner experience. Often it is clear to me by observing the change in the body or the facial expression that the client has made a connection, something has been remembered, and nothing more needs to be said.

As clients embody the work, they learn about themselves. Often there is an accumulation of tiny changes and the client will simply notice at some point that she is feeling better and that living her life doesn't take as much effort as before.

The Rosen Method is a process that is gently self-revealing for clients, allowing reflection of their true being, recognition of their integrity and aliveness as well as the barriers that restrict these qualities. This in turn allows for awareness and choice. The work provides an environment of self-discovery and profound insight and makes it possible for the client to reestablish a conscious and personal sense of her inner process and a deep connection with self-trust and knowing.

Sandra Wooten has been involved with the Rosen Method for twenty years. She incorporated the Rosen Institute in 1983 and was the founding president of its board of directors. In 1990 she established the Rosen Method Center Southwest. Today she teaches in Santa Fe and is in private practice in Orinda, California. This essay was adapted from her book *Touching the Body, Reaching the Soul* (1995), available from the Rosen Method Center Southwest.

TRAGER® PSYCHOPHYSICAL INTEGRATION

Developed by Milton Trager, M.D., Psychophysical Integration (popularly called Trager work) is a form of somatic education aimed at providing an experience of "functionally integrated body/mind." Trager based his work on the belief that physical problems are inextricably related to mental attitudes and beliefs. In fact, he once wrote, "I am convinced that for every physical non-yielding condition, there is a psychic counterpart in the unconscious mind, corresponding exactly to the degree of the physical manifestation." Thus Trager work focuses less on the effect of manipulations on the quality of tissue and more on communicating a sense of lightness, freedom, spaciousness, and pleasure so that the experience can register neurologically and kinesthetically. In this way the client can feel that constricted physical and psychological habits that are leading to pain can be replaced by a more open and relaxed state.

Trager discovered quite unexpectedly at age eighteen that he had "healing hands." One day when his boxing trainer seemed weary, the young man offered to give him a rubdown. The trainer was amazed by his trainee's natural skills and told him so. Trager was so elated that he rushed home to help ease his father's sciatic pain. That accomplished, he went around looking for people to work on. One such "volunteer," a paralyzed sixteen-year-old polio victim, was helped to walk again. Trager pursued this calling, working toward a Doctorate of Physical Medicine from the Los Angeles College of Drugless Physicians and later a medical degree.

Perhaps as a result of Trager's involvement with Transcendental Meditation, Psychophysical Integration has a spiritual center represented by the concept of a *hook-up*, or meditative state. From this inner place of deep calm, the practitioner can move with ease, connecting deeply with clients.

Trager sessions last between one and one-and-a-half hours. The client wears underwear or swimming trunks and lies on a padded massage table. Without oil or lotion, the practitioner gently rocks, shakes, vibrates, and pulls various limbs and parts of the body, not so much to rearrange tissue or structure but to create a pleasurable sensation for the client that encourages a state of relaxation, openness, and fluidity.

To help them regain that sense of effortless movement without the aid of a practitioner, clients are taught a series of dancelike movements called Mentastics—a blend of mental and gymnastics—following each session.

Trager work can be done to help a variety of medical conditions including multiple sclerosis and muscular dystrophy, as well as less serious physical problems. People in fields as disparate as massage and bodywork, sports, education, and the performing arts learn and practice Trager.

Books

Jack Liskin, *Moving Medicine: The Life and Work of Milton Trager, M.D.* (Station Hill Press, 1996). The author discusses Milton Trager's life experiences that led to the development and growth of his somatic reeducation method.

Milton Trager with Cathy Hammond, Ph.D., *Movement as a Way to Agelessness:*

A Guide to Trager Mentastics (Station Hill Press, 1987, 1995). In a free-verse format, this book outlines the basics of Trager Psychophysical Integration, including it philosophy, principles, applications, and exercise movements.

Organizations

Trager Institute
21 Locust Avenue
Mill Valley, CA 94941
(415) 388-2688 (phone)
(415) 388-2710 (fax)
admin@trager.com (e-mail)

The Trager Institute, founded in 1980, provides training and information about Trager Psychophysical Integration and Mentastics movement education.

❀ A Mentastic Movement ❀
By Milton Trager with Cathy Hammond

Stand or sit in a comfortable position and just let your arms hang freely at your sides. Now slowly and without tension raise one hand in front of you as though you are about to strum a guitar. Gently play the guitar and feel the weight of your thumb as it bounces freely. You will feel the weight of the thumb about halfway up to the wrist. Now ask yourself, "What can be lighter? What can be softer?" Let these questions direct the movement and notice how they affect the feeling in your hand. Allow your hand to become even lighter. Notice how your movement becomes refined as it responds to the message from your mind.

Now continue this same strumming movement, and let your arm hang down from your shoulder, keeping it close to your leg or chair. Feel the weight of your thumb and the shimmering of the tissues in your arm. Do not try to make the tissues shimmer. It will happen if you do not make an effort. If you feel stiffness or rigidity in the movement, slow down and resume asking, "What can be lighter? What can be freer?" And ask these questions in a way that does not demand an answer—only suggests a sensation.

Now pause a moment. Feel the difference between your two hands, arms, and shoulders. Notice what impact a little bit of softness can have on the body/mind. The tingling sensations and gentle pulsations are signs of your own aliveness! The deeper you feel and play with the weights of your body, the quieter your mind will become.

This essay was reprinted from *Movement as a Way to Agelessness: A Guide to Trager Mentastics*, with permission from the Trager Institute.

Soul and Spirit

As swimmers dare
to lie face to the sky
and water bears them,
as hawks rest upon air
and air sustains them,
so would I learn to attain
freefall, and float
in Creator Spirit's deep embrace,
knowing no effort earns
that all-surrounding grace

—Denise Levertov, "The Avowal"

8
Spiritual Practice: Invoking the Sacred

Many people in our society, hungry for meaning, are drawn to spirituality because it stands for what is missing in their lives. But in the last twenty years, the word itself has taken on specific connotations in our cultural lexicon, leaving many to wonder what it really means. For example, reasonably intelligent people wonder if it is appropriate for them to get involved in it. They wonder if it is weird, flaky, or connected to strange cultish practices. They wonder if it is the fad du jour, the latest quick fix for baby boomer angst. They wonder if it is good for their mental health, or if it involves already familiar religious practices such as prayer, hymn singing, or worship services. In short, while people are strongly drawn to and intrigued by the spiritual, they are also wary of it.

Help with this ambivalence has come from a surprising quarter: psychotherapy. Today people turn to therapy for myriad reasons: to wrestle with depression, to deal with losses encountered through death or divorce, to work on issues arising in blended families or couple relationships, and to change self-defeating behaviors. Therapy sessions, along with pop psychology and self-help books, have embedded the language of the psyche in our culture, lending credibility to the inner world. Therapy has reinforced the notion that the inner world contains feelings, symbols, and intuitions that are invaluable aids to decision-making, problem-solving, and improving the quality, depth, and texture of life. And as we have shown in earlier chapters, many psychological schools and approaches not only understand the value of spirituality but promote it. This new role for psychology—to validate rather than debunk the spiritual—is partially responsible for fueling the current spiritual awakening.

But just what is spirituality? The dictionary defines it as that which is related to soul or spirit as distinguished from corporeal matters. Although spirituality encompasses the spirit, that inner wind that takes flight and draws us out of ourselves to connect with that which is larger than we are, it also involves soul. Spirit is often confused with soul because we encounter both in our inner psychic makeup and because the origins of the words are similar, both being etymologically connected to breath. We see the distinction in this way: spirit soars upward, beyond ourselves, and seeks union with the Other, while the soul remains behind as the eternal inner representative of the larger whole within us. As described by Kahlil Gibran: "The Great God separated a soul from His own essence and fashioned beauty within her."

Whereas soul needs the vitality of spirit to keep it connected to a transcendent source, spirit needs to be grounded in soul. This dynamic interplay perfectly mirrors the relational qualities of spirituality. For us, spirituality is a vital inner urge to connect with something that we care deeply about, something that is larger than ourselves, something that is completely apart from the mundane and therefore sacred and holy. One of the ways we relate to this invisible power is to give it a name—God, the Divine, Allah, Ultimate Reality, Shiva, Yahweh. Once we have named it, we begin to develop a relationship. It is the nature of building and expressing this relationship that shapes our spirituality.

Surprising as it may seem, the expression of spirituality (i.e., our relationship with the Divine) resembles sexual dynamics. Both sexuality and spirituality, for example, involve feeling incomplete without an "other." Because of social conventions, it is easier for us to see sexuality in terms of attraction, burning desire, and passion. Nevertheless, many spiritual teachers as well as poets and sacred texts have recognized that spirituality is based on a deep physical and emotional longing that draws us beyond ourselves, that propels us toward union with that which is sacred. Ben Zion Bokser, in his book *The Jewish Mystical Tradition*, puts it this way: "For the mystic, the visible is only a vessel which houses an invisible, inner reality. Love on a mortal plane is an intimation of a higher love between God and man."

One of the world's poets whose prodigious body of work embodies this blazing desire is Jelaluddin Rumi, a thirteenth-century Sufi mystic. This wealthy, well-respected, and extremely popular *shaykh*—religious scholar, teacher, and spiritual guide—had his life change abruptly when he met a mendicant dervish, Shams of Tabriz. The two fell into an intense mystical friendship. So close did the two become that Rumi neglected his worldly duties as well as his family and disciples. This generated much anger and jealousy, and Shams was first driven off, then later killed.

The emotions in Rumi's poetry run the gamut from ecstasy ("Now that you live here in my chest,/anywhere we sit is a mountaintop") to tender longing ("When I am with you, we stay up all night./When you're not here, I can't sleep") to a spacious acceptance of the searing pain caused by a lover's absence ("Whoever finds love/beneath hurt and grief/disappears into emptiness/with a thousand new disguises").

But this yearning is not a one-way street of humans seeking God. Some mystics, like Mechtild of Magdeburg, a thirteenth-century German abbess, see God not only as the object of intense love but as an active partner in it. In one of her poems, God addresses the soul and declares: "I desire you before the world began / I desire you now; as you desire me." The verse goes on with the soul calling out to God as "lover." God responds, "It is my nature that makes me love you often, / For I am love itself."

Dominican nun Carla Streeter explains in a 1997 article in the monastic journal *Review for Religious* that to imagine or grasp the nature of intimacy with the Divine, we must have an experience of loving and being loved. We must recall the felt sense of someone's presence when he or she was "really there for us" and when we were "really there" for someone else. This experience of intimacy, she writes, is what gives us an experience of the holy, which would otherwise be beyond our human capacity to apprehend. It is our memory of loving human contact that helps us imagine what the experience of the Divine presence is like.

Because of this emphasis on relationship to God, many contrast spirituality with religion in terms of private versus public context. Spirituality, they say, is a private affair, an individual's search for a relationship with God, whereas religion is the formal collective expression of beliefs and rituals that people have developed over time to maintain a relationship with the sacred. We feel, however, that spirituality too is deeply communal, not solely a private or individual experience. This fact was brought home to us in the early 1990s on a trip to Kraków, Poland, when we were amazed and moved to encounter a deep devotion and vibrant spirituality in many Catholic churches there. Prayers and songs carried desires, petitions, praise, and thanksgiving in a way we had never experienced in the United States. Spirituality seemed to exist quite robustly within the Catholic religious forms.

In contrast, many U.S. churches seem dulled by rote rituals. For example, not long after our return, we were invited to a christening at a Catholic church in Rhode Island. The church structure and the ceremony resounded with emptiness. Songs were sung and prayers prayed, but there was no living sense of a Divine presence. The elderly priest seemed distracted at some points and inappropriately jocular at others. Family members were most intent on capturing the moment in film. But what moment? The religious significance of welcoming the newborn into the fellowship of the church was lost. Except for the religious trappings—the flowers, baptismal font, statues, banners, stained glass, candles, and holy oil—we could have been sitting in a recreation hall for all the religious feeling the service engendered. Therefore, for us, the difference between spirituality and religion is that the former connotes a vital, ongoing process of forging a relationship with the Divine. The latter refers to the formal institution of beliefs and rituals whereby people come together to worship, which may or may not involve an encounter or relationship with God.

The root of the word *religion, religare,* means "to bind together again." Thus religion at its core is a way of binding ourselves to God. But it can also serve to bind us to others. We have noticed that in small prayer and meditation groups, the very act of praying and meditating creates a strong bond. It's as if in the course of dipping into the eternal we can view fellow seekers nonjudgmentally and relate to their deeper or higher selves. Over time we hear about their struggles spiritually and in the world. This witnessing and being witnessed not only offers support for the spiritual journey but builds community. Rabbi Zalman Schacter-Shalomi, founder of the Jewish Renewal movement, an organized effort to promote and support a vital Jewish spiritual life, put it this way: "Spirituality is something that requires reflection, meditation, inner working on oneself, and working with a group of other people so that all of us can share the process. . . . When people pray, meditate, and share their inner process together, it creates a shift. Instead of thinking 'I, I' you're thinking of 'us, we' and then the 'us and we' gets large enough to think globally."

Spirituality can lead people to recognize that others—family, friends, neighbors, and fellow human beings—mediate our relationship with God. The Gospel according to Matthew captures the essence of this when Jesus says, "I tell you this: Anything you did for one of my brothers here, however humble, you did for me."

The Varieties of Spiritual Paths

Generally speaking, the purpose of prayer in all major religions is to be intentionally and attentively open to the Divine presence. As a way of distinguishing the different forms of prayer, it can be helpful to look at them through the lens of the four different spiritual paths that seem to be present in the major religious traditions of the world.

Path of Devotion

This is the path of love, personal partnership, and friendship where individuals value their relationships with others and view their relationship with the Divine in much the same way. The love that you feel for others and for the Divine opens your heart to the point where prayer becomes an ongoing conversation. Its most emotional and fervent forms can be seen in Pentecostal revivals and in the speaking-in-tongues of charismatic Christians. In Hinduism, the path of love is called *bhakti yoga.* In Judaism, it is expressed in family rituals in the home.

Because this path involves intense feelings, however, it can slip over into an exaggerated emotionalism. In that case, it can be balanced with the path of analytic knowledge.

Path of Analytic Knowledge

Deep curiosity and a strong desire to know the truth lead to this path, where the pursuit of knowledge is a way of pursuing the Divine. In Hinduism, this path is known as *jnana yoga*. Judaism has a deeply rooted tradition of scholarship that includes not only careful study of the Hebrew scriptures but ongoing dialogue and debate. Tibetan Buddhist monastic training too includes rigorous study and debate. In worship services that favor this path, the preference is often for scriptural readings, group recitation of prescribed prayers, and formal rituals and liturgy. But caution should be exercised so that the path does not become too abstract and overly intellectualized. The path of relationship can help in softening the sometimes hard intellectual edges and in restoring a healthier balance.

Path of Social Action

Those who follow this path to the Divine respond to the needs of others, as representatives of God or as God's children or creations. Social justice concerns are frequently emphasized, and the question of one's moral responsibility to others is seriously considered and acted upon. In Hinduism, this path is called *karma yoga*; Buddhist social activism is called "socially engaged" Buddhism. Without balance with the path of contemplation and its regular periods of quiet and receptivity, however, one may burn out from stress and overwork. Another pitfall is that "works righteousness" may lead to arrogance. It needs to be balanced with the path of contemplative practice.

Path of Contemplative Practice

This path is aimed at helping one to move toward a state of open awareness of the presence of the Divine (or in Buddhist terms, Ultimate Reality). This awareness is possible at all times because the seed of the Divine is always present within us. It is we who make the separation through lack of awareness. Examples of practices with this path are Christian meditative prayer, Buddhist meditation, Hindu meditation and chanting, tai chi or *qigong* (forms of moving meditation), Sufi meditation practices and dervish twirling, and the meditation practices of the Jewish kabbalah.

A potential aberration of this path is excessive self-absorption. This way needs to be balanced with an awareness of and willingness to respond with compassion to others.

Based on a Four Paths model of spiritual journeying developed by members of the program staff of the Shalem Institute for Spiritual Formation (5430 Grosvenor Lane, Bethesda, MD 20814). For a more comprehensive presentation, contact Joan Hickey at the institute.

WHAT IS A SPIRITUAL PRACTICE?

Alongside the frequently asked question about what spirituality means is the related question What is a spiritual practice? Spiritual practice is the regular use of a method that helps us to step out of everyday consciousness and build a relationship with the Divine. A spiritual practice is the vehicle we employ to help us connect with the Other. Aptly named, its most important characteristic is the regular use of a particular spiritual technique. Just as we must practice steadily to develop and maintain our capacity to play a musical instrument or excel at a sport, so too regular spiritual practice develops, maintains, and enhances our relationship with the Divine.

Relationships are not instantly created. A "one-minute meditator" might be applauded for taking at least some time to reconnect with her deeper self, but it's obvious that daily twenty-minute sits would be more beneficial. Relationships need time to grow and develop. Spiritual practice is like setting aside time to spend with a friend. The more time we spend, the more the relationship strengthens and deepens.

But what form should we choose for these appointments with the Divine? There are so many kinds of spiritual practice that deciding where to begin can be overwhelming. There is prayer that uses words and prayer that uses silence; scriptural reading; physical exercises such as tai chi, *qigong,* and yoga; vocalizations such as chanting; and public worship, to name just a few. Within each category, there are numerous forms. For example, prayer seems to be the most frequently used spiritual practice, with many different kinds that may resemble one another but are in fact quite distinct.

Prayer

According to a 1993 Gallup poll commissioned by *Life* magazine, 90 percent of American adults say they pray regularly. Of these, 75 percent say they pray daily and 15 percent pray at least once a week. Almost all of those who pray (98 percent) pray for their family's health and well-being, give thanks (94 percent), ask for the strength and courage to persevere in difficult times (92 percent), and ask for forgiveness for a transgression (92 percent). The same survey found that more than half of those who pray do so conversationally. Only 15 percent say they use formal prayers, like the Our Father or the *Sh'ma* ("Hear, O Israel, the Lord our God, the Lord is One").

In our definition, prayer is a communication with the Divine that can either use words or not. If words are used, they can be said either aloud or silently. These prayers involve praise and adoration, gratitude and thanksgiving, requests and petitions, blessings, confession, and intercession on behalf of others. There's a beautiful description of the myriad kinds of prayers in Friedrich Heiler's book *Prayer: A Study in the History and Psychology of Religion*. He writes that prayer can be "the calm collectedness of a devout individual soul and . . . the ceremonial liturgy of a great congregation." It can be a spontaneous or a mechanical recitation. It can be an emotional outburst or a disciplined, intent focus of concentration. It can appear "as still silent absorption . . . as the flight of the Spirit to the supreme Light, and as a cry out of the deep distress of the heart." He mentions prayers that are childlike entreaties, earnest desires to live a moral and ethical life, and simple requests for the basics in life, such as food, health, and shelter. He describes prayers as "the timed entreaty of the sinner before a stern judge, the trustful talk of a child with a kind father, as the swelling phrases of politeness and flattery before an unapproachable King, and as a free outpouring in the presence of a friend who cares; as the humble petition of a servant to a powerful master, and as the ecstatic converse of the bride with the heavenly Bridegroom."

We might add that prayers can also be intimate conversations with one's Mother, expressions of awe in the face of nature's majesty, and simple thank-yous for the joys, and even the challenges, we encounter in our lives. Some of our prayers are spontaneous. We often exclaim, "Oh my God!" if something particularly good or bad befalls us or, as Anne's mother often repeated, "God help me!" when faced with difficulties. We also particularly like Kathleen Norris's definition. In her book *Amazing Grace*, she says, "Prayer is not asking for what you think you want, but asking to be changed in ways you can't imagine."

Prayers can be said at particular times of the day or in certain ceremonies or services. We like to start our day with a prayer from the Jewish tradition, which captivated us with its spirit of praise and gratitude:

> Blessed art Thou, Lord our God,
> Ruler of the Universe,
> for keeping us alive and preserving us and
> permitting us to behold this day.

We follow it with a twenty-minute centering prayer sit and conclude with a selection from the psalms. Just before bed, Chuck recites a prayer from the *New Zealand Prayer Book* whose sentiments provide a beautiful closure to the day and a gentle entry into the stillness and darkness of night. In this prayer there is a wonderful statement of intention that allows us to release the day's activities and worries and settle into the peace of the night:

> It is night after a long day.
> What has been done has been done;
> what has not been done has not been done;
> let it be.

Many monastic communities build their entire day around periods of prayer. Following the church's canonical hours (matins at midnight, lauds at sunrise, prime at 6 A.M., terce at 9 A.M., sext at noon, none at 3 P.M., vespers at sunset, and compline at 9 P.M.), monks gather to sing, chant, and pray together. Prayer is the skeleton upon which the flesh—work, study, and leisure activities—hangs.

Secular life may not lend itself to such a formal prayer structure but there are ways in which to uphold the spirit and rhythm of the monastic schedule. For example, morning prayers can set the tone for the day. A brief prayer in bed before rising—a simple statement of gratitude for being alive—or a twenty-minute period of meditation before breakfast sets a powerful intention for the day: I want today to be a holy celebration, an opportunity for service, a challenge to remain mindful and open-hearted.

Once at work, a short prayer brings spirituality into the workplace. When Anne works at home, she begins her writing and research by lighting a candle and saying a brief prayer before an altar she put together on a bookshelf in her office. She asks for a blessing on her work—that it be of use to people—and she remembers family and friends who might be ill or having a rough time. The candle serves as a reminder throughout the day of the spiritual intention behind the work.

At mealtimes, saying grace either silently or aloud brings our attention back to soul. Lunch is a reminder of how lucky we are to have sandwiches and bagels, fruit and chips. We Americans are extremely blessed with an abundance of food, so much so that a 1998 article in *Modern Maturity* reported that we are the heaviest people in the world! While that statistic might reflect poor nutritional choices—high-carbohydrate, high-fat diets—nonetheless, food is easily accessible here and relatively inexpensive. Thich Nhat Hanh, a Vietnamese Zen Buddhist monk, frequently uses a story about toothache that has relevance here. When a filling falls out or a tooth breaks or becomes impacted, pain takes over one's consciousness. However, once a dentist takes care of the problem, we are grateful not to have that toothache anymore. What we must remember, Thich Nhat Hanh says, is how wonderful every day is without a toothache. The same can be said about food. We take most meals for granted. Saying grace or simply taking a moment of silence can remind us how wonderful it is to have food to eat.

Additionally, short informal prayers can be scattered throughout the daytime hours. Thich Nhat Hanh recommends using *gathas*, short verses recited when one stops at a traffic light, when dressing or undressing, or when cooking. These simple reminders help maintain mindfulness. For example, in *Present Moment, Wonderful Moment*, he suggests, when the phone rings, to wait a moment before answering it. Become aware of your breathing. Say, "Breathing in, I calm my body; breathing out, I smile." Then answer the phone. Before making calls, he recommends paying attention to inhalation and exhalation, then stating this intention:

"Words can travel thousands of miles. May my words create mutual understanding and love. May they be as beautiful as gems, as lovely as flowers." At night a prayer or religious reading just before bedtime creates a wonderful end-bracket for the day. There are many forms of prayer that can keep us spiritually attuned throughout the day.

Meditation and Contemplation

Prayers without words move along the river of silence in two tributaries: silence in which there is focus of attention and silence in which one attempts to go beyond images, sounds, and emotions to reach an intuitive experience of God. For the sake of this discussion, let us say that meditative practices are those that employ a specific object to help focus attention. These can include the silent repetition of a holy word (mantra), gazing at an image (icon) or symbol (candle), listening to a sound (rhythmic drumming), performing physical movements (yoga, sacred dance, or prostrations), focusing on one's breath, and placing attention on the rising and falling of thoughts and sensations as they pass through your mind and body without attachment to their content or meaning. Similarly, reading scripture or other sacred books, such as the *Tao Te Ching*, can focus your attention as you permit your ordinary mind (and its usual thoughts) to become absorbed in the illumination provided by the texts.

Prayer without a focus of attention is called contemplative prayer. When employing this prayer, one lets go of thoughts, emotions, sensations, worries, and memories. Since the human intellect is limited in its ability to comprehend the Divine, the thinking goes that one must surrender all of one's images, concepts, and feelings regarding God in order to know God. It is the via negativa, the path in which one repeatedly says "neti, neti," God is "not this, nor that" in order to ultimately experience what God really is. The aim is to empty oneself of all things of this world so as to be able to be filled with the presence of God. Zen Buddhists say this differently. They argue that one is indeed seeking emptiness, but that the nature of emptiness contains all things. D. T. Suzuki, an Oriental scholar and the person primarily responsible for seeding Zen Buddhism in the United States, in a dialogue with Trappist monk Thomas Merton, put it this way, "Zen emptiness is not the emptiness of nothingness but the emptiness of fullness in which there is 'no gain, no loss, no increase, no decrease,' in which this equation takes place: zero = infinity."

Contemplative practices rely on intention rather than attention, the intention being to surrender all in order to be in the presence of the Divine. While we can use meditative practices to prepare ourselves for a contemplative experience, we cannot will such union to happen. Just as in love relationships we can't make ourselves love another person or make them love us through an act of will, the experience of divine love comes unbidden (in a manner Christians call *grace*) and in a way we can't rationally explain or control. But when union does come, it is often unforgettable and can change the way we see life. In the Christian religion this state is known as mystical union; in Buddhism, enlightenment. In Hinduism it is called *samadhi*. In the mystical Sufi sect of Islam, one is said to have the experience of becoming one with Allah. In Judaism's mystical kabbalah tradition, one becomes immersed in the glory of God.

Books

Robert Benson, *Living Prayer* (Jeremy P. Tarcher, Perigee, 1998). An autobiographical account of a writer seeking to live a prayerful life.

Marcia Falk, *The Book of Blessings: A New Prayer Book for the Weekdays, the Sabbath, and the New Moon Festival* (HarperSanFrancisco, 1996). Intended for use by inclusive Jewish communities of men and women, Falk presents blessings and poems, prayers and meditations in English, her mother tongue, and in Hebrew, the "language of her blood." Some entries are based on traditional forms, but Falk asks us to entertain radically new images of Divinity and its interactions in our everyday and holy-day lives.

Fannie Flagg and Bernie S. Siegal (forewords), *Daily Word: Love, Inspiration and Guidance for Everyone* (Rodale Press, Inc., 1997). Using the now familiar format for daily meditations popularized in the monthly publication by the same name and in numerous Twelve-Step meditation books, this book provides 365 messages of love, inspiration, and support.

Friedrich Heiler, *Prayer: A Study in the History and Psychology of Religion* (One World, 1932, 1997). Assuming that prayer is the "central phenomenon of all religion—the heartstone of all piety—and the elementary and necessary expression of religious life," Heiler presents an exhaustive exploration of prayer as it has been practiced by primitives in ritual, by great religious personalities, by mystics and prophets, and in public worship. He then distills the essence of all forms (whether silent absorption, artistic poetry, or stammering speech), the drawing down of God into our own small hearts.

Rabbi Lawrence A. Hoffman, editor, *My People's Prayer Book: The Sh'ma and Its Blessings*, vol. 1 (Jewish Lights Publishing Company, 1998). This first book in a seven-volume series explores the oldest and best-known Jewish prayer through ten commentaries by respected teachers.

Timothy Jones, *The Art of Prayer: A Simple Guide* (Ballantine Books, 1997). Jones writes to reassure readers that the beginnings of any authentic prayer life are seeded in the soil of our daily realities—our daily search for bread or blessing or relief from pain or failure. He teaches us to celebrate, to give up all fear of asking, and to move forward confidently even when prayers seem to go unanswered.

Wayne Lee Jones, *Weave a Garment of Brightness: A Gathering of Prayers from Around the World* (Berkley Books, 1997). A collection of prayers of petition, of praise, and of thanksgiving from all traditions and times—from the Incas of Peru, St. Francis of Assisi, the Yoruba people, St. John of the Cross, and Lady Jane Grey on the eve of her execution.

Stephen Mitchell, translator and editor, *A Book of Psalms* (HarperCollins Publishers, 1994). This selection of psalms is translated into contemporary, psychologically oriented language. What it lacks in lyricism, it makes up in an easy, modern, conversational tone. It is not for purists, but for those who wish to hear ancient wisdom in a contemporary voice.

Kathleen Norris (commentary), *The Psalms* (Riverhead Books, 1997). Norris treats the King James version of the Book of Psalms as a continual unfolding of God's revelations to us in the events of our ordinary lives. She finds that modern translations, in their search for accessibility, have sacrificed both music and soul. Norris speaks here in favor of preserving the psalms both as literature and as a manifestation of God's presence.

Elizabeth Roberts and Elias Amidon, *Life Prayers from Around the World* (HarperSanFrancisco, 1996). This collection provides neatly distilled introductions and discussions that precede poems and prayers, gathered from such diverse authors as Vaclav Havel, Marianne Williamson, the Buddha, and Terry Tempest Williams, to bless and invoke God's presence through each of life's turnings—birth, initiation, work in the world, the spiritual dark night, midlife, healing, and death.

Organizations

Fellowship in Prayer (FIP)
291 Witherspoon Street
Princeton, NJ 08542-9945
(609) 924-6863

Incorporated in New York City in 1950, FIP is a nonprofit interfaith organization whose purpose is to promote the practice of prayer and meditation. The organization does this through its bimonthly publication and events as diverse as concerts by Buddhist monks and days of prayer.

Silent Unity
1901 NW Blue Parkway
Unity Village, MO 64065

(816) 246-5400 or (800) 669-7729 (U.S. only) (phone)
www.unityworldhq.org (website)

This organization has been supporting a prayer ministry for more than a hundred years. Daily prayer sessions and a continuous prayer vigil are held. The organization also publishes the *Daily Word*, a pamphlet with inspirational readings for each day of the month.

Periodicals

Praying
P.O. Box 419335
Kansas City, MO 64141
(816) 531-0538 or (800) 333-7373 (phone)
www.natcath.com (website)
8 issues a year; $26.95

Praying, published by the National Catholic Reporter Publishing Company, is a magazine that focuses on spirituality for everyday living. It includes stories, articles, scripture selections, photographs, and interviews with spiritual leaders.

Sacred Journey
291 Witherspoon Street
Princeton, NJ 08542-9945
(609) 924-6863
Bimonthly; $16

This publication from Fellowship in Prayer focuses on the spiritual journey, offering stories of loneliness, confusion, and suffering as well as spiritual illumination.

Weavings
Upper Room
1908 Grand Avenue
P.O. Box 189
Nashville, TN 37202-0189
(615) 340-7254 or (800) 925-6847 (subscriptions) (phone)
(615) 340-7006 (fax)
weavings@upperroom.org (e-mail)
www.upperroom.org (website)
Bimonthly; $24

A Methodist-supported journal whose well-written and lyrical essays reflect aspects of the spiritual journey.

BUDDHIST MEDITATION

In *The Illustrated World Religions: A Guide to Our Wisdom Traditions*, religion scholar Huston Smith begins his chapter on Buddhism with a story:

As the Buddha's message spread across India and he became well known for spiritual wisdom and power, people began to wonder about his nature. One day some people approached and asked if he was a god. He responded, "No." They then wanted to know if he was an angel. "No," he said. "A saint?" "No." "If not a god, an angel, or a saint, then what?" He replied, "I am awake."

This simple story powerfully reflects the essence of Buddhism, a major world religion founded in India in the sixth century B.C. Prince Siddartha Gautama, although wealthy, attractive, learned, and socially and politically prominent, desired spiritual knowledge that would help him deal with worldly conditions, particularly death and suffering. Through many different practices, he was able to reach enlightenment; that is, he was able to wake up to ultimate reality. Buddhist practices are all aimed at this goal.

The oldest lineage, known as Theravada, the Way of the Elders, emphasizes inner practice; another major lineage, known as Mahayana, emphasizes manifesting the fruits of one's practice as a benefit to all beings in the world. Both Zen and Tibetan Buddhism evolved out of the Mahayana tradition. While the goal of Buddhist meditation is to attain enlightenment or nirvana and so be able to step off the Wheel of Life (the cycle of birth, death, and rebirth), Mahayana Buddhists stress the tradition of the bodhisattva, the human being who although at the threshold of complete enlightenment chooses to help others achieve this state. The bodhisattva vow is to remain in the world until all sentient beings enter nirvana.

According to Willard L. Johnson and Richard H. Robinson, authors of *The Buddhist Religion*, all major divisions of Buddhism, from Japan, China, Korea, Vietnam, Tibet, and South Asia, exist in North America today. The October 13, 1997, *Time* cover story, "Americans' Fascination with Buddhism," reported that there are currently 100,000 American-born Buddhists, many of whom have been practicing for decades. Since the seeds of Buddhism were planted at the World Parliament of Religions held in Chicago in 1893, American culture has gradually been shaping Buddhist practice. For example, the *Time* article pointed out that Buddhist centers in America differ fundamentally from their Asian counterparts in that the natural home base for meditation practice in the East is monasteries. In the United States, there are teaching centers, where laypeople gather for communal instruction and practice, which can vary in length from brief evening programs to month-long retreats.

Additionally, feminism has exerted its influence in that women are becoming respected teachers, programs for children and families are being created, more psychological awareness is being brought into the guidance of meditation students by teachers, and more body consciousness is a part of the practice.

Each of the world's major religions has meditative practices, and Buddhism—although some consider it a philosophy rather than a religion because it is not deistic—is no different. In fact, Buddhist meditation can be seen as the heart of American Buddhist practice.

Vipassana

Vipassana (insight) meditation comes from the Theravadan tradition as it developed in Southeast Asia, most notably in Thailand, Sri Lanka, and Burma. According to Jack Kornfield, one of the original American Vipassana teachers, the Theravadan Buddhist tree has two branches in the United States. On the one hand, there is a group of one to two hundred small ethnic monasteries that minister to Thai, Cambodian, Burmese, and Laotian refugees. They teach a form of Buddhism characterized by prayer, devotion, bowing, and ceremony. The other type of Theravadan Buddhism is taught by a handful of American teachers, including Kornfield, Joseph Goldstein, Sharon Salzberg, and Ruth Denison. They practiced in the 1960s and early 1970s in Asia and began to lead retreats in this country in the 1970s. Collaboration among three primary teachers—Kornfield, Goldstein, and Salzberg—resulted in the establishment of two principal centers: the Insight Meditation Society in Barre, Massachusetts, and Spirit Rock in Woodacre, California. Other centers have also grown up, along with a community of approximately 20,000 practitioners.

On the surface Vipassana meditation seems like an extremely simple practice. One need only to sit in a comfortable position, back straight, eyes closed, and focus one's attention on the breath. This can be at the nose where air is coming in and out or on the rising and falling of the chest. When breathing in one mentally says "in," when exhaling one mentally says "out." Should thoughts or emotions arise (and they will), one should simply note their presence and return to following one's breath. Two of the fruits of this practice are mental clarity and equanimity. Because you become mindful of your thoughts and emotions (rather than analyzing or pondering them), over time you acquire a measure of distance from them. After practicing for a while, you begin to recognize how attached you can get to the contents of mind or to feelings, and how strongly identified you are with your feelings. When we *feel* anger, for example, we say "we *are* angry." We get so caught up in the emotion that we forget the feeling will pass, just like a spring thunderstorm. All emotions are eventually transformed into other emotions. The same is true for thoughts. When you are attached to your thoughts, you begin to think that you are only your thoughts and nothing more. Suffering, said the Buddha, is the result of becoming overly attached to thoughts and emotions and in the process losing touch with the real ground of our Being.

Of course, meditation practice is not intended in the long run to be limited to twenty or forty minutes a day of concentrated focus. The whole idea of meditation is to bring what is called mindfulness into daily life. Just as at a certain point in one's meditation practice, one might be at the state of dropping attention on the breath in favor of a wider focus—attention on the rising and falling away of thoughts, physical sensations, and emotions—so too once the meditative period is over, one might bring that mindful awareness into one's life. Of course, it's difficult as life assaults us with traffic jams, phone calls, work assignments, child care, and family responsibilities. But mindfulness does not ask us to change our circumstances; rather it is the discipline of bringing attention to what we are doing, staying aware of what's happening. As a friend puts it, "It's about showing up and staying present in the moment."

Because Vipassana meditation in the United States was introduced and developed by Americans, it has much less of an Asian flavor than either Zen or Tibetan Buddhism, which were transplanted from Asia to America by Japanese *roshis* and Tibetan lamas. As a result, Vipassana has eliminated almost all ritual trappings—bowing, chanting, and costumes. Both practitioners and teachers come to meditation sessions in ordinary street clothes.

Kornfield also points out that though a number of leaders of spiritual communities have been isolated and have gotten embroiled in painful accusations of sexual misconduct, Vipassana teachers often teach in teams. "Most of the retreats are taught by two, three, or more teachers," he explained, which additionally "helps students because they don't confuse the dharma (the teachings) with a particular personality. You hear teachings in three or four different ways. It also helps the teachers because we balance one another."

One valuable practical application of insight meditation has been developed by Jon Kabat-Zinn, founder of the Stress Reduction and Relaxation Program at the University of Massachusetts Medical Center. The program works to help people deal with chronic pain and stress.

There are a number of Vipassana teachers who offer regular classes and silent retreats lasting from a three-day weekend to a month in length. Some teachers intersperse "sitting" sessions with periods of yoga or walking meditation. Most centers and retreats also require the performance of duties, such as washing dishes, sweeping the floor, and cutting vegetables.

Zen

According to several sources, Zen Buddhism traces its legendary origins back to the Buddha's Flower Sermon, which consisted of his simply holding a lotus blossom aloft. While most people in the audience wondered what the

Buddha meant by this, one disciple simply smiled, which indicated to the Enlightened One that he had "gotten" the lesson. The Buddha appointed him his successor.

Zen's primary goal involves being oneself with awareness in the moment. A tenth-century Zen master put it succinctly when he instructed: "When walking, just walk / When sitting, just sit. / Above all, don't wobble." What this boils down to is fully being oneself at all times. The only hitch is that Zen Buddhists don't put much stock in the self. D. T. Suzuki described Zen practice not as "getting rid of the self but realizing the fact that there is no such existence from the first." This precise point was made by the thirteenth-century founder of Japanese Soto Zen, Eihei Dogen Zenji. Albert Low, the director of the Montreal Zen Center, translated Dogen's message this way:

> To practice Zen is to know the self.
> To know the self is to forget the self.
> To forget the self is to be one with all that is.

The means by which one comes to know and then forget the self, realizing the essential unity of all things, is *zazen*, which means "seated meditation." The practice begins with sitting in the lotus position (i.e., legs crossed in front of you) on a meditation cushion (*zafu* or *zabuton*) with back straight and eyes downcast or looking straight ahead, usually at a blank wall. Beginning practitioners start by counting their breaths from one to ten, then returning to one and so on. If a thought appears, one acknowledges its presence, lets it go, and returns to counting the breaths.

Another aspect of Zen is its rich literary legacy of sayings, stories, and koans. A koan is a riddle or conundrum presented to a Zen student for the purpose of leading to an experience of truth without involving logic or the mind. One does not puzzle out or solve a koan. It is a more of an "Aha" experience. One either gets it or doesn't.

Zen itself is a kind of koan, and for that reason it can be difficult to communicate and comprehend. For example, John Daido Loori states in *The Eight Gates of Zen* that *zazen* practice, particularly in a group, is an important part of Zen. Yet he also emphatically declares that *zazen* is not "meditation, contemplation, visualization, or mindfulness. It is not to be found in the *mudra*, chakra, mantra, or koan." Rather, Zen is "to be intimate with the self . . . [and] to realize the whole phenomenal universe is the self."

One branch of Zen Buddhism is activist oriented. Called socially engaged Buddhism, it refers to the active involvement by Buddhists in social, environmental, and political issues. For example, Vietnamese monk Thich Nhat Hanh persistently worked on nonviolent, peace, and reconciliation initiatives during the Vietnam War; poet Gary Snyder is known for his environmental advocacy; and Joanna Macy has tackled ecological and social justice concerns.

Tibetan Buddhism

Tibetan Buddhism, the third major Buddhist path in America, spread from India to Tibet, the "roof of the world," where it blended with the native culture. It has recently received much attention most notably due to the current Dalai Lama, Tenzin Gyatso's receipt of the Nobel Peace Prize in 1989, the series of Hollywood films on the life of the Buddha and on the Dalai Lama, and the efforts of Tibetan supporters worldwide to publicize China's takeover and destruction of the Tibetan culture and religion and exploitation of the country's natural resources.

Comparing Tibetan Buddhism with Zen can be likened to comparing Catholicism with Shaker sensibilities. Whereas Zen naturally inclines toward stark simplicity and a kind of bare-bones elegance, Tibetan Buddhism, like the Catholic Church, brims with "smells and bells." The ceremonies and practices involve chants, *mudras* (gestures or positioning of the hands that symbolize a spiritual truth or aspect of ultimate reality), bells and horns, and elaborate and rich visual imagery as expressed in statues, prayer flags, *thankas* (a scroll on which is painted an icon, generally a Buddha or Bodhisattva), and mandalas.

Many years ago Anne went to an introductory Tibetan meditation lesson, which involved very long, specific, and detailed instructions on building in her mind an image of Tara, the female aspect of the bodhisatva Avalokitesvara. Additionally, Tibetan meditative practices can include focusing on the breath (as in Vipassana and Zen), walking meditation, and prostrations.

Books

Sylvia Boorstein, *Don't Just Do Something, Sit There: A Mindfulness Retreat* (HarperSanFrancisco, 1996). A complete guide to creating a weekend mindfulness retreat on your own.

Joseph Goldstein and Jack Kornfield, *Seeking the Heart of Wisdom* (Shambhala Publications, Inc., 1987). Two preeminent American teachers of insight meditation attempt to distill the wisdom gathered in twelve years of jointly teaching Vipassana retreats. They discuss the obstacles to sitting; the gifts and rewards of practice; and tools for reconciling service and responsible action in the world with the meditative life of nonattachment.

Venerable Henepola Gunaratana, *Mindfulness in Plain English* (Wisdom Publications, 1991). This practical, step-by-step guide to insight meditation by a Theravadan monk who has spent many years teaching in the West offers clear, precise, and simple instruction minus the ritual and philosophical discussion.

Gavin Harrison, *In the Lap of the Buddha* (Shambhala Publications, Inc., 1994). A book that tackles the subject of transforming suffering through insight meditation. It addresses fear, anger, self-hatred, difficult relationships, pain, abuse, faith, freedom, and hope and provides guided meditations for forgiveness, compassion, and equanimity.

Eugen Herrigel, *Zen in the Art of Archery* (Vintage Books, 1953). D. T. Suzuki wrote the introduction to this classic Zen treatise by a German philosopher.

Jon Kabat-Zinn, *Full Catastrophe Living: Using the Wisdom of Your Body and Mind to Face Stress, Pain, and Illness* (Delta, 1990). Ten years of lessons gleaned from the practice of facilitating an eight-week intensive self-directed training program in the art of conscious living. The book is intended for anyone who seeks to transcend limitations and move toward greater levels of health and well-being.

Jon Kabat-Zinn, *Wherever You Go, There You Are: Mindfulness Meditation in Everyday Life* (Hyperion, 1994). This book offers a map for cultivating mindfulness, or wakeful meditation. From the practicalities of posture to the subtle possibilities of changing one's karma, it speaks simply and beautifully of the mind's complexity.

John Daido Loori, Sensei, *The Eight Gates of Zen: Spiritual Training in an American Monastery* (Dharma Communications, 1992). There are eight gates of Zen training; namely, *zazen*, zen study, academic study, liturgy, right action, art practice, body practice, and work practice. This book focuses on doing zen by being it in these areas of training.

Don Morreale, *The Complete Guide to Buddhist America* (Shambhala Publications, Inc., 1998). This compendium of articles and over a thousand resources is a revised, expanded, and updated version of a popular 1988 directory. It introduces readers to the range of Buddhist practices and beliefs in the West and lists retreats, centers, and programs in which to learn and practice Buddhism.

Sharon Salzberg, *A Heart as Wide as the World: Living with Mindfulness, Wisdom, and Compassion* (Shambhala Publications, Inc., 1997). A twenty-five-year student and teacher of meditation and cofounder of the Insight Meditation Center, Salzberg offers teaching stories and anecdotes that reveal our capacity to find happiness by opening our hearts to ourselves and to others. Through insight and lovingkindness meditation, we can embrace all the joys and sorrows of life with wisdom and compassion.

Lama Surya Das, *Awakening the Buddha Within* (Broadway Books, 1997). This book offers an overview of Tibetan Buddhism by an Eastern-trained American-born lama. It includes discussions of karma, rebirth, letting go, living and dying, and the mystical teachings of Dzochen.

Thich Nhat Hanh, *The Miracle of Mindfulness: A Manual on Meditation*

(Beacon Press, 1976). Vietnamese Zen Master Thich Nhat Hanh chooses stories and exercises for teaching the attitude of mind that is perfect rest. He then offers exercises for developing our capacities for detachment, emptiness, and compassion.

Chogyam Trungpa, *Cutting Through Spiritual Materialism* (Shambhala Publications, Inc., 1973). A series of talks offered in 1970 and 1971 in Boulder to new students as an overview of the path and some warnings about the dangers along the way. It is most specifically addressed to the danger of deceiving ourselves into thinking we are developing spiritually when instead we are strengthening our egocentricity through spiritual techniques—a distortion Trungpa names *spiritual materialism*.

Organizations

Barre Center for Buddhist Studies
149 Lockwood Road
P.O. Box 7
Barre, MA 01005
(978) 355-2347 (phone)
bcbs@dharma.org (e-mail)
 The center provides a bridge between study and practice, between scholarly understanding and meditative insight. It also offers study and research opportunities, lectures, classes, seminars, and conferences and engages in publishing and translation activities and interdenominational dialogue.

Buddhist Peace Fellowship (BPF)
Box 4650
Berkeley, CA 94704
(510) 655-6169 (phone)
(510) 655-1369 (fax)
bpf@bpf.org (e-mail)
www.bpf.com/bpf (website)
 The BPF, a membership organization, was founded in 1978 to bring a Buddhist perspective to the peace movement and the peace movement to the Buddhist community. Buddhists of many traditions are invited to explore personal and group responses to political, social, and ecological suffering in the world.

Cambridge Insight Meditation Center
331 Broadway
Cambridge, MA 02139

(617) 419-5070 (phone)

world.std.com/~cimc/index.html (website)

This nonresidential urban center offers daily sittings, weekly dharma talks, ongoing classes and practice groups, teacher interviews, weekend meditation retreats, and library facilities.

Cambridge Zen Center

199 Auburn Street

Cambridge, MA 02139

(617) 576-3229 (phone)

cambzen@aol.com (e-mail)

www.kwanumzen.com/czc (website)

This is a residential meditation center under the direction of Zen Master Seung Sahn. The center offers a variety of programs, including weekly talks, interviews with Zen teachers, morning and evening practice, and monthly retreats.

Dai Bosatsu Zendo

HCR 1, Box 171

Livingston Manor, NY 12758

(914) 439-4566 (phone, 9 A.M.–noon E.S.T. only)

(914) 439-3119 (fax)

A Rinzai monastery and retreat facility affiliated with the New York zendo run by Eido Shamano Roshi.

Dharma Seed Tape Library

Box 66

Wendell Depot, MA 01380

(800) 969-SEED

This nonprofit organization makes available taped talks and instruction given by insight meditation teachers.

Dzochen Foundation

P.O. Box 734

Cambridge, MA 02140-0006

(617) 628-1702 (phone)

(617) 628-1330 (fax)

foundation@dzochen.org (e-mail)

www.dzochen.org/foundation/about.html (website)

Founded in 1991 by Lama Surya Das and a small group of Dzochen practitioners, the foundation aims to preserve Tibetan Dzochen teachings and transmit them to Westerners through programs and retreats led by Dharma teachers, a newsletter and schedule of activities, the translation of texts and oral teachings, and the formation of a long-term retreat center.

Green Gulch Farm Zen Center
1601 Shoreline Highway
Sausalito, CA 94965
(415) 383-3134 (phone)
bodhi.zendo.com/~sfzc (website)
    Green Gulch Farm is a Buddhist practice center in the Japanese Soto Zen tradition, which offers training in Zen meditation.

Insight Meditation Society (IMS)
1230 Pleasant Street
Barre, MA 01005
(508) 355-4378 (phone)
(508) 355-6398 (fax)
www.dharma.org (website)
    Founded in 1975 by Jack Kornfield, Joseph Goldstein, and Sharon Salzberg, the society is a nonprofit retreat center whose purpose is to foster the practice of Vipassana (insight) meditation and to preserve the essential teachings of Theravada Buddhism. The IMS offers a year-round program of intensive meditation retreats.

Karma Triyana Dharmachakra (KTD)
352 Meads Mountain Road
Woodstock, NY 12498
(914) 679-5906 (phone)
(914) 679-4625 (fax)
office@kagyu.org (e-mail)
www.kagyu.org (website)
    This monastery and retreat center is the North American seat of His Holiness the Gyalwa Karmapa, head of the Karma Kagyu school of Tibetan Buddhism. Founded in 1978, the center offers traditional Buddhist training and education as transmitted by meditation masters of the Kagyu lineage since the tenth century.

Karme-Choling Meditation Center
RR 1, Box 3
Barnet, VT 05821
(802) 633-2384 (phone)

(802) 633-3012 (fax)
KarmeCholing@vt.ngs.net (e-mail)
www.kcl.shambhala.org (website)

The center was founded in 1970 by Chogyam Trungpa Rinpoche, a Buddhist meditation master who was formerly the abbot of the Surmang monasteries in Tibet. Chogyam, also known as Vidyadhara, taught throughout Europe and North America and founded the Naropa Institute, Shambhala Training, and Vajradhatu, an international Buddhist church.

Mindfulness Practice
P.O. Box 60
Woodstock, VT 05091
(802) 457-2255 (phone)
(802) 457-9157 (fax)

Founded in 1997 by Thich Nhat Hanh, this center operates as a gathering place and resource center for mindful living. The center offers a variety of programs aimed at parents, educators, health-care professionals, and those dedicated to living mindfully.

Naropa Institute
2130 Arapahoe Avenue
Boulder, CO 80302
(303) 546-3572 (phone)
www.naropa.edu (website)

The Naropa Institute, the only accredited college in North America whose educational philosophy is based on the Buddhist contemplative tradition, offers programs in body psychology, Buddhist studies, dance-movement therapy, contemplative psychotherapy, and transpersonal counseling (art therapy concentration available).

New York Zen Center
2223 East 67th Street
New York, NY 10021
(212) 861-3333 (phone)
(212) 628-6968 (fax)
www.zenstudies.org (website)

This center is affiliated with the monastery Dai Bosatsu (see listing above).

Parallax Press
P.O. Box 7355

Berkeley, CA 94707
(510) 525-0101 (phone)
(510) 525-7129 (fax)
parapress@aol.com (e-mail)
www.parallax.org (website)

A small publishing company that primarily publishes books by Thich Nhat Hanh and other Buddhists.

Plum Village, Meyrac
47120 Loubes-Bernac
France
(011) 33-553-94740 (phone)
(011) 33-533-947590 (fax)

This retreat center, founded by the Vietnamese Buddhist monk Thich Nhat Hanh, is his home base.

Providence Zen Center
99 Pound Road
Cumberland, RI 02864-2726
(401) 658-1464 (phone)
(401) 658-1188 (fax)
kwanumzen@aol.com (e-mail)
www.kwanumzen.com/pzc (website)

Providence Zen Center offers an environment for meditation through practice, retreats, and residencies at its wooded 50-acre facility in northern Rhode Island. Free walk-in meditation instruction is given on Wednesdays at 6:30 P.M. Other programs include daily practice, public talks, introductory workshops, 1- to 90-day retreats, and Christian-Buddhist and Eleventh Step retreats.

San Francisco Zen Center
300 Page Street
San Francisco, CA 94102
(415) 863-3136 (phone)
bodhi.zendo.com/~sfzc (website)

This center offers retreats and workshops at the Beginners Mind Temple in San Francisco, at the Tassajara Zen Mountain Center near Carmel, and at Green Gulch Farm, an affiliated monastic community in Sausalito (see listings, this section).

Southern Dharma Retreat Center
1661 West Road

Hot Springs, NC 28743
(704) 622-7112 (phone and fax)
sdharma@juno.com (e-mail)
www.mindspring.com (website)

Southern Dharma Retreat Center, founded in 1978, is a nonprofit foundation whose purpose is to offer silent group meditation retreats led by teachers from a variety of spiritual paths.

Spirit Rock Center
Insight Meditation West
P.O. Box 909
Woodacre, CA 94973
(415) 488-0164

Spirit Rock Center offers insight meditation retreats that are designed for both beginning and experienced meditators. The center is nonsectarian, although the ethics and traditions of Buddhist psychology offer guidance.

Springwater Center for Meditative Inquiry and Retreats
7179 Mill Street
Springwater, NY 14560
(716) 669-2141 (phone)
(716) 669-9573 (fax)
spwtrctr@servtech.com (e-mail)
www.servtech.com/public/spwtrctr (website)

This center was begun in the early 1980s when Toni Packer, chosen to succeed Philip Kapleau, leader of the Rochester Zen Center, and a group of students broke with their home base. Today Packer no longer considers herself a Zen teacher and the traditional Zen forms have been eliminated. The retreats have agendas and schedules, but all activities except for work assignments—help with meals, cleaning, or grounds work—are optional.

Tara Mandala
P.O. Box 3040
Pagosa Springs, CO 81147
(970) 264-6177 (phone)
(970) 264-6169 (fax)
75402.1127@compuserve.com (e-mail)

Located on 500 acres in the San Juan Mountains, this retreat center sponsors family and teen, Dzochen, and solstice retreats, Chod intensives, and other programs.

Tassajara Zen Mountain Center
39171 Tassajara Road
Carmel Valley, CA 93924
(415) 863-3136 (phone)
(415) 431-9220 (fax)
www.zendo.com/~sfszc (website)

The center, established in 1969, offers various opportunities to study and practice Zen. Its sister organizations are the urban-based temple in San Francisco and Green Gulch Farm in Sausalito.

Tibet House
22 West 15th Street
New York, NY 10011
(212) 807-0563 (phone)
(212) 807-0565 (fax)
mail@tibethouse.org (e-mail)
www.tibethouse.org (website)

Tibet House is dedicated to preserving the living culture of Tibet by means of traveling exhibitions, publications, media productions, a photographic archive, and a resource library.

Upaya Foundation
1404 Cerro Gordo Road
Santa Fe, NM 87501
(505) 986-8518 (phone)
(505) 986-8528 (fax)
upaya@rt.66.com (e-mail)
www.rt66.com/~upaya (website)

Founded by Joan Halifax, Upaya is a Buddhist study and retreat center.

Vipassana Support Institute
4070 Albright Avenue
Los Angeles, CA 90066
(310) 915-1943 (phone)
(310) 391-7969 (fax)
vsi@gte.net (e-mail)
www.shinzen.org (website)

The institute provides information packets as well as tapes and written materials authored by meditation teacher Shinzen Young.

Zen Center of Los Angeles (ZCLA)
923 South Normandie Avenue
Los Angeles, CA 90006
(213) 387-2351 (phone)
(213) 387-2377 (fax)
www.zencenter.org (website)

The ZCLA has both a city and a mountain center. The city center includes a meditation hall and a residential community of about 35 committed Zen practitioners, whose practice is aimed at integrating meditation with family and career life. A 90-day retreat emphasizing everyday life is held during the winter months.

Zen Mountain Center
P.O. Box 43
Mountain Center, CA 92561
(714) 659-5272 (phone)
zmc@primenet.com (e-mail)
www.zmc.org/zmc (website)

The center offers retreats during the spring, fall, and winter months.

Zen Mountain Monastery
Box 197, South Plank Road
Mount Tremper, NY 12457
(914) 688-2228 (phone)
(914) 688-2415 (fax)
zmmtrain@mhv.net (e-mail)
www.mhv.net/~dharma.com (website)

The Zen Mountain Monastery offers a year-round program of weekend and week-long retreats on a wide variety of topics. All retreats are conducted within an ongoing Zen training matrix that includes dawn and evening meditation, Zen Buddhist services, work practice, and talks given by Abbot John Daido Loori, who founded the center in 1980, or by senior Zen students.

Periodicals

Inquiring Mind
A Journal of the Vipassana Community
P.O. Box 9999
North Berkeley Station
Berkeley, CA 94709

Correspondence only by mail
Semiannual; donation
This journal is published in newspaper format and covers topics relevant to Buddhist meditation. It also provides a national listing of meditation retreats.

Journal of Contemplative Psychotherapy
Naropa Institute
2130 Arapahoe Avenue
Boulder, CO 80302
(303) 444-0202
Sporadic; $20
This journal presents psychotherapy from a Buddhist contemplative perspective.

Mindfulness Bell
Community of Mindful Living
P.O. Box 7355
Berkeley, CA 94707
(510) 527-3751 (phone)
(510) 525-7129 (fax)
parapress@aol.com (e-mail)
www.parallax.org (website)
3 issues a year; $18
Each issue includes an article by Thich Nhat Hanh, essays, and accounts of experiences by students and others interested in the practice of mindfulness.

Shambhala Sun
1585 Barrington Street, Suite 300
Halifax, Nova Scotia
Canada B3J 1Z8
(902) 422-8404 (phone)
(902) 423-2701 (fax)
magazine@shambhalasun.com (e-mail)
www.shambhala.com (website)
Bimonthly; $24
Founded in 1978, *Shambhala Sun* is a Buddhist-oriented magazine that presents teachings, political and social commentary, arts and aesthetics, and views on business, lifestyles, and personal development.

Tricycle: The Buddhist Review
92 Vandam Street
New York, NY 10013
(212) 645-1143 (phone)
(212) 645-1193 (fax)
tricycle@well.com (e-mail)
www.tricycle.com (website)

This magazine, the largest Buddhist publication in America, is an independent quarterly dedicated to the ongoing discussion of how Buddhism has and will change when exposed to American democracy, individualism, and feminism.

Audiotapes

Pema Chodron, *Awakening Compassion* (Sounds True). A six-cassette audiotape series with booklet that shows how Tibetan Buddhist teachings can transform difficulties into insights.

Joseph Goldstein and Sharon Salzberg, *Insight Meditation: An In Depth Correspondence Course* (Sounds True). This training course is rooted in the Buddhist style of Vipassana (insight) meditation. The companion book is so clearly organized and well-presented that it can easily stand alone as a solid primer for beginning practitioners.

Jack Kornfield, *The Inner Art of Meditation* (Sounds True). A 90-minute videotape and a six-cassette, 8-hour audiotape series cover the basics of mindfulness meditation for beginners.

Thich Nhat Hanh, *Basic Buddhist Wisdom with Thich Nhat Hanh* (New Dimensions). In an interview, the Vietnamese Zen monk explores concepts such as soul, impermanence, and mindfulness.

Shinzen Young, *The Science of Enlightenment* (Sounds True). A twelve-cassette curriculum on methods of awakening. Although taught by a Vipassana meditation teacher, the tapes explain spiritual practices of the main religious traditions and also examine other spiritual teachings, scientific insights, and practical instruction.

Websites

world.std.com/~metta/index.html
This Access to Insight site contains hundreds of suttras (English translations) from the Pali canon; Theravada text archives: a library of books, articles, and transcribed Dharma talks; the Four Noble Truths: a hypertext exploration of the Buddha's teachings; directories of Theravada meditation centers and practice

groups; books, tapes, electronic texts, and Pali resources on and off the Internet; as well as a discussion of Theravada Buddhism.

www.dharma.org/insight.html

Insight Magazine online carries interviews with teachers such as Kamala Masters and Steve Armstrong, Thanissaro Bhikkhu, Sylvia Boorstein, Ruth Denison, Martine and Stephen Batchelor, and Sharon Salzberg.

www.inet.co.th/cyberclub/bow/main_contents.html

Buddhism On Web (BOW) contains an overview of Buddhism; the life of Gautama Buddha; Tipitaka Buddhist scriptures; Theravada's main doctrines; Buddhist perspective on modern issues; books and articles on Buddhism; Buddhist electronic library; international Buddhist news and reports; a Buddhist question-naire on social concerns; Buddhist discussion forum; and a live chatroom.

www.ncf.carleton.ca/dharma/

This website for Buddhism in the national capital of Canada contains an overview of Buddhism; a hypertext guide to basic Buddhist teachings; meditation instructions; the Five Mindfulness Trainings by Thich Nhat Hanh; the *Dhammapada*; verses of Buddhist wisdom; photographs of renowned Buddhist teachers; answers to frequently asked questions on Buddhism and meditation; and a listing of recommended books.

www.rmi.net/~buddamer

This site features excerpts from Don Morreale's book *The Complete Guide to Buddhist America* (see listing, this section). Of special interest are colorful graphs and charts tracing the growth of Buddhism in North America from 1900 to the present and detailed demographic data on this "fastest growing phenomena on the American spiritual landscape."

CHRISTIAN CONTEMPLATION

The central figure in Christianity is Jesus of Nazareth, a charismatic Jewish healer, spiritual teacher, and socioreligious reformer, whose teachings carried such impact that his followers called him the Anointed One, the Messiah, or in Greek, *Kristos*, the Christ. Other religions, including Islam, recognized him as a great prophet. Born around 4 B.C.E., he took up his ministry about thirty years later. For several years he traveled the countryside, a mendicant preacher performing miracles, healing the sick, exorcising demons, and instructing his followers. His teachings, applicable to individuals as well as communities, urged social, political, and religious reforms, which ultimately brought him into conflict with both Jewish and Roman authorities. The latter executed him for treason.

For a good many years after Jesus' crucifixion, his followers remained observant Jews and were regarded as members of a renewal-minded Jewish sect. Over time and due to many factors, the Jesus movement within Judaism gradually evolved into Christianity, a separate and distinct religion, which despite persecution by the Romans, gained adherents. Early in the fourth century, the Roman Emperor Constantine attributed an important military victory to the Christian cross, the symbol of Christianity. As a result, he converted and legalized Christianity. Thereafter Christians, instead of being executed for treason, could worship publicly and own property.

Because Christianity sprang from Judaism, the two have many similarities, but there are also many differences. Although Jewish texts talked about compassion in general, Judaism emphasized the law, justice, and ethical behavior as articulated in the Torah. Jesus, however, stressed love and compassion as the cornerstone of a spiritual life. Furthermore, although a healer and miracle worker, Jesus was set apart from other prophets and healers of his time not by his powers but by this message of love that captured and inspired not only his contemporaries but people down through the ages. Directives to forgive "seventy times seven," to turn the other cheek, to love your enemies, all comprised an "ethics of love," wrote Archie J. Bahm in *The World's Living Religions*. Jesus' declaration that the most important commandments were to "love the Lord your God with all your heart, and with all your soul, and with all your mind," and to "love your neighbor as yourself" (Matthew 22:37–40) formed the basis for a new vision of how human beings and communities could act.

Another difference between Christianity and Judaism can be found in their perceptions of God. Although in Judaism a personal relationship with God exists, God remains a relatively distant and abstract power as evidenced by the names given to Him: Adonai, Yahweh, the Nameless One, even *Ab*, meaning "Head of the Family." Although covenants were forged and communication took place between God and His people through mediators such as Abraham, Noah, and Moses, God was for the most part envisioned as all-powerful, mighty, and omniscient. Jesus, on the other hand, stressed a more intimate relationship with God. He called God *Abba*, which translates as "Daddy" or "Papa," and likened the relationship of God and human beings to that of a parent and his children. Christians, in seeing Jesus as Divine and as an exemplar and model of spiritual life, carry this image forward. If Jesus is indeed the Son of God, then human beings are the sons and daughters of God, who can experience the same relationship Jesus had with *Abba* by following His teachings. Thus Christianity basically became a religion of relationship based on the love of God and the love of others.

When Christianity became a state-sanctioned religion, many converted for social, political, or economic reasons. The intense devotion of the underground communities was diluted. Those who wanted to lead a life modeled after Jesus Christ sought solitude in the deserts of Northern Africa. These hermits, called the Desert Fathers and Mothers, and their spiritual practices led to the evolution of monastic communities, which became the core of the contemplative Christian tradition.

Today there are several types of Christian meditation popular in the United States that continue that tradition. The most widely known is centering prayer. The others are Christian Meditation (the John Main method), the Jesus prayer (the prayer of the heart), and the Practice of the Presence of God.

Before we talk about each of these methods, we need to clarify our terms. Confusion arises from the fact that the word *contemplation* has come to connote an active mental process, a pondering, ruminating, or reflecting on a subject. In fact, contemplation in the classical sense has the goal of moving beyond one's thoughts, feelings, and sensations.

Contemplation stems from the Latin roots *con* and *templum*. Charles Asher, in his article "Choosing the Contemplative Life" in the Fall-Winter 1995 issue of *Psychological Perspectives*, tells us that in its earliest usage the word "referred to a particular area in the sky, gazed upon by Roman augurs and priests in search of an omen to direct a favorable course of action." Later this sky-gazing activity was redirected to the earth, and contemplation became associated with marking off the land for a temple or worship site. Today, contemplation does exactly that, only inwardly: it is a method by which we clear our inner ground of being of distracting thoughts, feelings, and memories to create a space in which to encounter God.

Centering prayer differs from Buddhist meditation in that the cross-legged sitting posture is not used and instead of observing your breath and your thoughts, you choose a sacred word (e.g., *Abba, Jesus, Mary, Peace, Shalom*), which you silently repeat to yourself whenever you get distracted by feelings, thoughts, or memories. The sacred word is simply a device to bring you back to your intention to be in God's presence. According to one of the cofounders of the centering prayer movement, Cistercian monk Father Thomas Keating, the goal of this method is to increase your intimacy with God by giving up the pretenses of your false self. The process in turn empowers you to be more authentic in your relationship to yourself and others.

Keating is one of the most popular teachers and writers in the area of centering prayer, which was discovered, initially taught, and developed in the 1970s while Keating was the abbot at St. Joseph's Abbey in Spencer, Massachusetts. Involved in reforms resulting from the Second Vatican Council's call for spiritual renewal in the Catholic Church, he had also observed that young Catholics were leaving the Church in droves to join Hindu ashrams and Buddhist *sanghas*. In 1971 he attended a meeting of Trappist superiors in Rome, where, in an address to the monks, the late Pope Paul VI invoked the spirit of Vatican II and declared that unless the Church rediscovered the contemplative tradition, renewal couldn't take place. He specifically called upon monastics to help the laity and those in other religious orders to bring that dimension into their lives.

Keating came away from the meeting determined to make a contribution. He asked the monks at his monastery to search for a contemplative prayer method rooted in the Christian tradition that would be accessible to those outside the monastery. One of the monks found a simple technique in the fourteenth-century classic *The Cloud of Unknowing* and began teaching it to the retreatants at the monastery's guest house. The method eventually came to be known as centering prayer.

Unlike other types of meditation that use a point of focus such as one's breath or the constant repetition of a mantra (a sacred syllable, word, or phrase), centering prayer emphasizes intention rather than attention. Practitioners sit quietly and at first repeat a sacred word to establish their intention to be in God's presence. Once the intention has been established, there is no need to repeat the word. If or when one becomes aware of thoughts, sensations, or feelings that interrupt this process, the sacred word is silently reintroduced. Typically the discipline involves setting aside two twenty-minute periods a day for prayer.

Keating calls this practice Divine therapy because it involves letting go of identification with the false self (a self-image that impedes one's relationship with God) in favor of expressing the true self (our basic core of goodness). Keating believes that we can know God only through our intuitive intellect, not through concepts or images.

Centering prayer has spawned two organizations: Contemplative Outreach, which Keating cofounded and leads, and the Mastery Foundation, with which one of the early pioneers of centering prayer, Father Basil Pennington, is associated. They are dedicated to teaching the method to the laity and to those active in the church ministries, respectively.

Another form of Christian contemplative prayer, designed by the late Canadian Benedictine John Main and called Christian Meditation, is being taught throughout the world under the leadership of Father Lawrence Freeman. In this approach, the word *maranatha* is repeated nonstop for the entire prayer period.

Main described Christian Meditation as "simply being still at the center of your being." The mantra, he explained, roots you in this center by gently leading you "to a depth beyond words and thoughts and images."

Whereas Ram Dass, who followed a Hindu path, urged us to "be here now," and Zen monk Thich Nhat Hanh reminds us to be "in the present moment," John Main used Aristotle's "the perpetual now" to express this same notion: meditation is the doorway to the eternal.

Another Christian contemplative prayer tradition comes from the Eastern Orthodox Church. The practice consists of reciting the name of Jesus over and over like a mantra. According to Cistercian monk Basil Pennington, the beginner would use a long form, "Lord Jesus, Son of David, have pity on me," derived from the Gospel story about a blind beggar who called out those words to Jesus, or "Lord Jesus Christ, Son of the living God, have mercy on me a sinner," found in a parable about a Pharisee and a tax collector. Over time, the phrase is pared down and simplified until the practitioner utters only one word: Jesus.

According to Morton Kelsey, an Episcopal priest and author, the underlying idea behind the Jesus prayer is the belief that the reality of Jesus is tied to His name. Therefore the repetition of Jesus' name acts as an invocation. Pennington tells us that traditionally this prayer was accompanied by prostrations—practitioners either going down on their knees, touching their knuckles to the ground and bowing deeply before an icon, or prostrating their body full length upon the floor.

Apparently this practice was unheard of in the West until 1930 when an obscure manuscript, *The Way of the Pilgrim*, was published. The book, originally written in Russian, tells the story of an anonymous pilgrim who, inspired by the exhortation "Pray without ceasing," found in the Epistle of St. Paul to the Thessalonians, sets off on a search to learn how to do just that.

After meeting and speaking with a host of characters and studying the *Philokalia*, a collection of writings by the Fathers of the Eastern Orthodox Church, the pilgrim teaches a blind man to pray in this way: Visualize your heart in your mind's eye as clearly and vividly as you can. Then listen to its beat. When you have accomplished this, begin to recite this prayer silently. On the first beat of your heart say "Lord." On the second, say "Jesus." On the third, "Christ," on the fourth, "have mercy," and on the fifth beat, "on me." Repeat this over and over again. When you can do this easily, move your attention to your breath. On the inhale, say "Lord Jesus Christ," and on the exhale, "have mercy on me." If any images or thoughts arise, let them go. In time, one may begin to feel a soreness or tenderness in one's heart. This, says the pilgrim, is the love of Jesus Christ beginning to stir.

One other Christian contemplative practice is the Practice of the Presence of God. Articulated by a seventeenth-century lay monastic, Brother Lawrence, the practice is basically an ongoing conversation with God. Specifically, Lawrence urges us to "think of God as often as we can." He recommends "a little lighting up of the heart," "a little remembrance of God, an act of inward worship." In essence, these devotional gestures replace thoughts of earthly matters, turn one's attention to God, and in this way prepare the heart for God.

"The heart must be empty of all other things," wrote Brother Lawrence, "because God will possess the heart alone. . . . [N]either can he act there and do in it what He pleases, unless it be left vacant to Him."

Centering Prayer Guidelines

1. Choose a sacred word as the symbol of your intention to consent to God's presence and action within. Examples of sacred words are *Abba, Jesus, Mary, Love, Yes, Shalom, Jesu,* and *Peace.*
2. Sit comfortably with your eyes closed. Settle briefly, and then silently introduce the sacred word as the symbol of your consent to God's presence and action within.
3. When you become aware of thoughts, sensations, feelings—any perception whatsoever—return gently to the sacred word.
4. At the end of the twenty-minute prayer period, remain in silence with eyes closed for a couple of minutes.

Christian Meditation Guidelines

Sit down. Sit still and upright. Close your eyes lightly. Sit relaxed but alert. Silently, interiorly begin to say a single word. We recommend the prayer-phrase *maranatha.* Recite it as four syllables of equal length. Listen to it as you say it, gently but continuously. Do not think or imagine anything—spiritual or otherwise. If thoughts or images come, these are distractions at the time of meditation, so keep returning to simply saying the word. Meditate each morning and evening for between twenty and thirty minutes.

From *The Way of Unknowing* by John Main (Crossroad Publishing Company, 1990). Used with permission.

Books

Nicholas Herman of Lorraine, *The Practice of the Presence of God, Conversations and Letters of Brother Lawrence* (1824; Oneworld Publications, 1993). A slim volume of fifteen letters and four conversations by a seventeenth-century soldier turned Carmelite lay brother and cook whose one desire was for communion with God. Brother Lawrence offers simple instructions for allowing the soul always to be in silent and habitual conversation with God.

Thomas Keating, *Intimacy with God* (Crossroad Publishers Company, 1994, 1996). A collection of talks given in retreats and workshops over a several-year period of teaching centering prayer. The origins of centering prayer, its theological basis, its psychology, the place of will and intention, and the role of the sacred symbol, sacred word, and the spiritual teacher are all discussed.

John Main, *The Way of Unknowing: Expanding Spiritual Horizons through Meditation* (Crossroads Publishing Company, 1990). The author's depth and simplicity serve to both introduce the newcomer and encourage the veteran meditation pilgrim. The chapters are drawn from talks given to weekly meditation groups.

M. Basil Pennington, *Centering Prayer: Renewing an Ancient Christian Prayer Form* (Doubleday, 1980). Written as a support and an introduction to those wishing to enter into the practice of contemplative prayer, this book strongly encourages spiritual partnership, answers questions about prayer and meditation in a Christian context, and offers guidance in sharing its gifts.

Olga Savin (translator), *The Way of the Pilgrim* (Shambhala Publication, Inc., 1991). A spiritual classic of mysterious origin that advocates ceaseless prayer in pursuit of God and emphasizes the necessity for experienced teachers and full participation in a community of faith.

Clifton Wolters (translator), *The Cloud of Unknowing and Other Works* (Penguin Books, 1961, 1978). This Penguin Classic gathers four anonymously written fourteenth-century mystical tracts recounting the journey of the contemplative soul as it moves through all obstacles to ecstatic union. Each emphasizes the necessity of holding God at the center of all life, knowing God through the limitlessness of love, and expressing that love through continuous prayer.

Organizations

Christian Meditation Center
1080 West Irving Park Road
Roselle, IL 60172
(708) 351-2613 (phone and fax)

This is the central office in the United States for information regarding retreats, meditation groups, and a catalog of books and tapes on Christian meditation by John Main and Lawrence Freeman, the current leader of the Christian Meditation movement.

Contemplative Outreach
10 Park Place, Suite 2B
P.O. Box 737

Butler, NJ 07405

(973) 838-3384 (phone)

www.centeringprayer.com (website)

Contemplative Outreach is a spiritual network of individuals and small faith communities committed to living the contemplative dimension of Christian life through the practice of centering prayer.

Audiotapes

Christian Meditation: The Essential Teaching (Christian Meditation Center). Three 90-minute tapes that include an introduction to Christian Meditation, a discussion about meditation as a Christian practice, and talks for meditators.

Contemplative Prayer (Sounds True). Cistercian monk Thomas Keating offers a 4-hour comprehensive workshop (three cassettes) on centering prayer.

The Contemplative Journey with Father Thomas Keating (Sounds True). This two-volume set of tapes is a guide to the contemplative prayer tradition in Christianity. Using centering prayer as the focus, Keating weaves discussions of the practice with its psychological implications and theological foundation. Each volume contains twelve cassettes.

East and West: The Mystical Connection: An Interview with Father Bede Griffiths (New Dimensions). In this conversation, the monk shares insights about contemplative life.

In the Beginning (Christian Meditation Center). Six 60-minute tapes consisting of a series of 20-minute "how-to" talks. Recommended for group instruction or for individuals who are starting to meditate.

Websites

Christian Meditation

www.cardiff.ac.uk/ccin/main/socecon/roath/church/medit.html

This website includes history of and simple instructions on how to practice Christian meditation.

Firewatch (Merton Research Consortium)

140.190.128.190/merton/merton.html

A website that disseminates the works of Thomas Merton and information on contemplation.

Website of Unknowing

www.anamchara.com/mystics

This site offers information on and excerpts from the writings of the medieval English mystics such as Julian of Norwich, Richard Rolle, and Margery Kempe.

World Community for Christian Meditation
www.wccm.org
This site describes the practice of Chistian meditation as taught by the late John Main OSB.

HINDU PRACTICES

Hinduism is as old as the civilization of India and, unlike Buddhism, Christianity, and Islam, has no sole founder. Rather, this religious tradition is the result of a confluence of cultural streams, the headwaters of which are found in the Indus and Vedic civilizations that produced, over hundreds of years, India's earliest religious texts, including the *Upanishads*, considered to be Hinduism's greatest sacred texts.

Richard Waterstone in his richly illustrated book *India* points out that the Vedas were originally transmitted orally. Because of this, Hindus believe that spiritual power resides not just in the ideas or concepts conveyed in them but in the very sounds of the words themselves. "In fact," writes Waterstone, "Hindus believe that the *Vedas* were revealed or 'heard' (*sruti*), not composed by human beings. . . . Because they [the words] contain certain sacred syllables from which gods and mortals were born, the *Vedas* are thought to have preceded the universe itself, created from the sacred syllable Om." The sound *Om* (aum) is also considered to represent the entire universe.

One core Hindu belief is that the entire universe is united in Self, in God (Brahman). Each individual is a part of that larger Self, although in human beings this divine essence is called Atman, or soul. One distinguishing characteristic of Hinduism is its polytheism. Although it recognizes a single Godhead, it suggests that there are many manifestations of Brahman in the world. For example, the Hindu trinity consists of Brahma, the Creator; Vishnu, the Preserver; and Shiva, the Destroyer. Beyond these there are a host of other gods, including myriad female deities, all manifestations of the goddess Devi. These include Durga, the warrior goddess; Kali, the black goddess of death; Lakshmi, the goddess of abundance; and Parvati/Shakti, Shiva's consort.

The ultimate goal of Hindu spiritual practices is *moksha*, liberation from *samsara*, the cycle of birth, death, and rebirth. Yoga refers to the various paths to this freedom. According to yoga scholar and author Georg Feuerstein, the word *yoga* stems from *yuj*, meaning "to join, unite, or yoke." Paradoxically, by yoking ourselves to a spiritual discipline, we can be free to unite first with Atman (this is known as self-realization) and then with Brahman. Feuerstein, in his book *Sacred Paths*, suggests another interpretation: that yoga yokes attention. He likens a yoga practice to the creation of a laser beam, "which then helps dissolve the barrier between the visible and the invisible and allows us to contact the gods."

There are a number of yogic paths, including *jnana* yoga, the path of knowledge; *bhakti* yoga, the path of devotion and love; *karma* yoga, the path of selfless service and work; and *raja* yoga, the path of meditation and deep concentration. Raja yoga has many different forms. The most familiar and widespread in the West is *hatha* yoga, which utilizes various physical postures (*asanas*), cleansing practices, and breathing techniques. As students become more advanced, the focus moves from concentration on physical postures to concentration on the breathing while performing the postures.

Hinduism's major meditative practice is a "concentration," or attention-based practice, in which a devotee (student) is given a special Sanskrit word (mantra) to repeat over and over silently while sitting in the lotus (cross-legged) position.

Swami Vivekananda is primarily responsible for introducing Hinduism to the United States. A disciple of the highly respected Hindu saint Ramakrishna, Vivekananda captured America's attention at the World Parliament of Religions in 1893 in Chicago. Following that international gathering, he received numerous invitations to lecture across the country. He not only carried the Hindu message but established Vedanta societies, the first of which was founded in New York in 1895.

The next wave of Hindu teachers came in the 1960s and 1970s and included Paramahasa Yogananda, author of the classic *Autobiography of a Yogi* and founder of the Self-Realization Fellowship; Swami Satchidananda, founder of the Integral Yoga Institute; Yogi Bhajan of 3-H-O, the Healthy-Happy-Holy Organization; Maharishi Mahesh Yogi, whose Transcendental Meditation techniques gained wide popularity, were studied by Herbert Benson, M.D., and became integral to his formulation of the Relaxation Response; and Swami Muktananda, the leader of *siddha* yoga, whose successor, Chidvilasananda (Gurumayi), is one of the few major female spiritual leaders in the United States.

The best-known American exponent of Hindu meditation in the United States is psychologist, author, and spiritual teacher Ram Dass (Richard Alpert), whose books on the subject—*Be Here Now, The Only Dance There Is,* and *Journey of Awakening,* among others—have been highly influential since the 1960s and over the past thirty years. Through his writing, lectures, and workshops, Ram Dass became a kind of cultural icon and spiritual frontiersman, moving into spiritual territories just ahead of baby boomer seekers. In the early 1960s, while a professor of psychology at Harvard University, Alpert was introduced by colleague Timothy Leary to *Psilocybe* mushrooms. Leary told him that this substance profoundly affected consciousness and had taught him "more about the human psyche in a few hours than all my years as a psychologist." With that intriguing recommendation, Alpert ingested the mushrooms, experiencing a "blissful unitive feeling." From 1962 to 1967, Alpert experimented hundreds of times with psychedelic substances. The problem, however, was that the effects of the drugs always wore off, and Alpert found himself back in his "separateness and the lonely isolation behind the walls of intellect." In an effort to integrate the consciousness he had tasted into his daily life, Alpert went to India, where after six months he met his guru, Neem Karoli Baba. He received instruction in raja yoga during that first visit, and upon his return he practiced hatha yoga, did breathing exercises, meditated, fasted, chanted, and studied sacred texts.

But it wasn't until much later that Alpert, now called Ram Dass (Servant of God), realized that his guru was steering him toward a path of service. Over the years, Ram Dass did volunteer work with the dying, prisoners, people with AIDS, the homeless, and with environmental groups. Through the Seva Foundation, which he helped to establish, he also worked with Guatemalan refugees and those afflicted with blindness in Nepal and India. He wrote two books about service: the first with Paul Gorman entitled *How Can I Help?* (1985); the second with Mirabai Bush called *Compassion in Action* (1992).

In a more personal vein, he also nursed his aging father before the latter's death. For a couple of years before a stroke left him with significant motor and speech disabilities, Ram Dass began to lecture on the topic of conscious aging.

Another major Hindu figure to attract attention in the United States is Mother Meera, who resides in Thalheim, Germany. Considered to be an avatar by her followers, she teaches through silence and *darshan* (presenting one's self to the guru so as to be seen at every level of one's being). An avatar is God manifest in human form, whereas gurus, saints, the Buddha, and other holy men and women are all humans who attain a state of union with the Divine. Jesus Christ, the Son of God, as part of the Holy Trinity, would be considered by some to be an avatar.

Ayurvedic medical expert Deepak Chopra is an extremely well-known if controversial figure who has created a multimillion-dollar industry based on his books, tapes, and lectures. According to his biographical statement, he is a trained medical doctor, who once taught at Tufts University and Boston University Schools of Medicine and served as chief of staff at New England Medical Hospital. He also founded the American Association of Ayurvedic Medicine and has served on the National Institutes of Health's ad hoc panel on alternative medicine. Beyond his professional credentials, he is a bestselling author (not only have his books sold over ten million copies, according to a 1997 *Newsweek* cover story, but an appearance on *Oprah* in 1993 sold 130,000 copies of his book *Ageless Body, Timeless Mind* in one day). He has written more than two dozen books, including a novel entitled *The Return of Merlin*, produced audio- and videotapes, lectured internationally, and endorsed products ranging from herbal supplements to massage oils. According to *Newsweek*, he is planning to open a chain of Centers for Well Being around the world. Chopra does not advocate meditation per se but ayurvedic medicine and aspects of Hindu philosophy.

Books

Georg Feuerstein, *The Shambhala Guide to Yoga* (Shambhala Publications, Inc., 1996). This book is a clearly written and well-organized introduction to yoga with an emphasis on its history, principles, practices, and spiritual foundation.

Martin Goodman, *In Search of the Divine Mother* (HarperSanFrancisco, 1998). This biography of Mother Meera is set within the spiritual journey of one of her followers. It is a clear-eyed look at the complex relationship between guru and devotee.

Ann Myen and Dorothy Madison, editors, *Living at the Source: Yoga Teachings of Vivekananda* (Shambhala Publications, Inc., 1993). Swami Vivekananda played a pivotal role in the introduction of yoga and Hinduism to America. This book is a collection of his teachings on topics such as the human condition, freedom, and the nature of the mind.

Paramahansa Yogananda, *Autobiography of a Yogi* (Self Realization Fellowship, 1946). This classic book is the story of the spiritual unfolding of a well-known guru, told in his own words.

Organizations

Kripalu Center for Yoga and Health
Box 793, West Street
Lenox, MA 01240-0793
(800) 967-3577 (phone)
(413) 448-3400 (fax)
karen@kripalu.org (e-mail)
www.kripalu.org (website)

This spiritual retreat and program center has been serving people of all backgrounds for over twenty years. Kripalu offers a large number of yoga, self-discovery, holistic health, and spiritual programs that present ancient yogic principles in a contemporary, accessible, and profound way.

Maharishi University of Management
1000 North 4th Street, DB1155

Fairfield, IA 52557-1155
(515) 472-1166 (phone)
(515) 472-1179 (fax)
admissions@mum.edu (e-mail)
www.mum.edu (website)

Integrating traditional academic disciplines with Maharishi's concepts of Vedic science, technology, and consciousness-based education, the university is associated with the practice of transcendental meditation.

Mother Meera
Oberdorf 4A
65599 Dornburg-Thalheim
Germany
(011) 49-064-362-305

Darshan with Mother Meera is held at 7 P.M. on Friday, Saturday, Sunday, and Monday evenings. Those wishing to participate are asked to call and make a reservation. Instructions on where and when to meet are given at that time.

Satchidananda Ashram-Yogaville
Route 1, Box 1720
Buckingham, VA 23921
(804) 969-3121 or (800) 858-9642 (phone)
(804) 969-1303 (fax)
iyi@moonstar.com (e-mail)
www.moonstar/~yoga (website)

Founded in 1979, this spiritual center located in the foothills of the Blue Ridge Mountains in central Virginia sponsors workshops and retreats in hatha yoga, raja yoga, and meditation, teacher training certification, and personal retreat—all based on the Integral Yoga teachings of Sri Swami Satchidananda, founder of the Integral Yoga Institute.

Self-Realization Fellowship (SRF)
3880 San Rafael Avenue
Los Angeles, CA 90065-3298
(213) 225-2471 (phone)
(213) 225-5088 (fax)
www.yogananda-srf.org (website)

Founded in 1920 by Paramahansa Yogananda, this center is part of a worldwide network of fellowship learning centers and retreat centers. SRF has temples, retreats, and more than 500 meditation centers in fifty-four countries.

Self-Realization Fellowship Retreat
215 K Street
Encinitas, CA 92024
(760) 753-1811 (phone)
(760) 753-8416 (fax)

On a 17-acre property overlooking the Pacific Ocean, in the study of the hermitage, Paramahansa Yogananda wrote *Autobiography of a Yogi*. The retreat center currently offers inspirational classes, programs, meditations, and individual and group retreats.

Vedanta Press
1946 Vedanta Place
Hollywood, CA 90068
(213) 465-7114 (phone)
(213) 465-9568 (fax)
vedantas@west.net (e-mail)
www.vedanta.org (website)

The press promotes the teachings of Vedanta philosophy as taught by Ramakrishna and Vivekananda, the harmony of religions, and personal enlightenment.

Vedanta Retreat
P.O. Box 215
Olema, CA 94950
(415) 922-2323 (phone)
(415) 922-1476 (fax)
sfvedanta@juno.com (e-mail)

A 2,000-acre retreat center in northern California. Although no formal meditation programs are given, individuals may use the facilities on a day-long or overnight basis.

Vedic University of America
10509 Caminito Basswood
San Diego, CA 92131
(610) 578-7289

Founded in 1987, Vedic University is a nonprofit institute carrying out research work in the field of Vedic religion and Indian heritage and working for the benefit of Indian families residing in the United States and others who are eager to learn Hindi, Sanskrit, Vedic religion, and yoga.

Vivekananda Retreat, Ridgely
P.O. Box 321
Stone Ridge, NY 12484-0321
(914) 687-4574 (phone)
info@ridgely.org (e-mail)
    Individual retreat and small conference center for serious spiritual aspirants of Vedanta philosophy.

Yoga Research Center
P.O. Box 1386
Lower Lake, CA 95457
(707) 928-9898 (phone)
(707) 928-4738 (fax)
yogaresrch@aol.com (e-mail)
http://members.aol.com/yogaresrch/ (website)
    This nondenominational center, directed by Georg Feuerstein, is dedicated to research and education on all aspects of Hindu, Buddhist, and Jaina yoga. One of its principal projects is the creation of an extensive database of psychological and medical studies on yoga.

Periodicals

Hinduism Today
Himalayan Academy
107 Kaholalele Road
Kapaa, HI 96746-9304
(808) 822-3152 (editorial phone)
(808) 822-4351 (fax)
www.HinduismToday.Kauai.hi.us/ (website)
Monthly; $35
    This magazine covers various topics concerning contemporary Hinduism in the United States.

❀ Islamic Practices and Sufism ❀

By Carl Ernst

    Islam is an Arabic word meaning "submission to God." As a religious and cultural tradition, Islam calls for complete acceptance of the teachings and guidance of God (*Allah* in Arabic). Muslims, followers of the Islamic religion, freely and willingly accept the supreme power of God and strive to organize their lives in accord with the teachings as revealed by the prophet Muhammad in the *Qur'an*, Islam's most sacred text. But acceptance and submission are only one level of Islamic religiosity. Faith in and a direct experience of Allah are two other essential aspects to practicing this religion.

There are an estimated four to six million Muslims now living in the United States, which approaches the number of Jews in America. Of these, half are immigrants who have come within the last generation; the other half are largely African-American, and some European-American, converts.

There is no priesthood in Islam. Every Muslim is required to be educated in the religion. However, some are more educated than others and act as resources for their communities. An *imam* is responsible for leading others in prayer and answering religious questions. His authority is derived from advanced studies of Islam and the *Qur'an*.

In Sufism, Islam's mystical tradition, there is also a lineage of teachers known as *shaykhs*, who have studied under mentors who subsequently appoint them to pass down the spiritual teachings from the Islamic prophet Muhammad, who originated them. *Shaykhs* operate independently of mosques and are able to teach classes if they are capable of attracting students. The best-known Sufi order—a lineage of followers of a particular teacher—in the West is headed by Pir Vilayat Inayat Khan.

There are about forty thousand members of Sufi orders in the United States. They range from liberal to conservative, and from national to international in scope. The basic appeal of Sufism comes from its emphasis on mysticism, its focus on inner work, and its traditional use of poetry, music, and dance as spiritual practices.

When most Westerners think about Sufism, they think of the thirteenth-century Sufi mystic Rumi, who is the bestselling poet in the United States, according to *Publishers Weekly*. Reportedly one collection of Rumi's poems sold fifty thousand copies in a year, which was five times more than the most popular American poetry collection. Westerners are also familiar with the entrancing movements of the whirling dervishes, who perform carefully choreographed movements designed to induce ecstasy in the dancers and, by extension, those who watch them. Rumi himself danced ecstatically, especially after the death of his friend and mentor, Shams of Tabriz. But it was his son who formalized the whirling as an artistic expression to accompany the recitation of his father's poetry. Today the Mevlevi order in Turkey performs this dance all over the world. In their native country, however, they can only present it as a cultural, not a religious, performance for political reasons.

The Sufi orders trace their origin to Divine revelation. In the year 610,

Muhammad, a merchant and family man from a prominent Arab clan, went on retreat in a cave near the town of Mecca. There the *Qur'an* was instantaneously transmitted to his heart. He became known as the Prophet, and over the next twenty-three years, he recited the revelation in 114 chapters. Many individuals who were inspired by his direct mystical experience gradually gathered into informal groups. Over the span of centuries after Muhammad's death, they evolved into the Sufi orders and focused on the inner spiritual experiences of Islam's outer rituals.

To understand the importance of this event with regard to Sufism, it is necessary to know the way the *Qur'an* is studied. In keeping with its inception, this sacred text is frequently memorized in order to internalize it. Those who are especially motivated, in addition to the standard prayer times, continue reciting passages throughout the night. It is probably because of this devotional recitation of the *Qur'an* that an emerging mystical interpretation of the text originated. That is, those who responded to the emotional power of the text probed further to seek its deeper meanings and made a special effort to bring the holy words into their hearts. In fact, the *Qur'an* states that only those who possess "the inner heart" can hold and recall the message. One point that *Qur'anic* passages stress is that there are multiple interpretations corresponding to different levels of listening. Thus Sufis saw their holy book as constantly capable of yielding new meaning relevant to their spiritual quest.

In general, Sufis differ from other Muslims in the emphasis they place on certain spiritual practices. For example, the *zikr*, which is a type of meditation, is used frequently and intensively by those in Sufi orders. For most Muslims, the minimum practice consists of praying five times a day and fasting during the month of Ramadan. Sufis also perform these rituals, but they stress their interiority, the inner and conscious performance of these rituals, over their outer form. Additionally, the inclusion of music, poetry, and dance as spiritual practices is unique to the Sufis in the Islamic world.

Before the twentieth century all Sufi orders in Muslim countries were generally observant followers of Islamic practices. During the twentieth century, however, some groups, in an ecumenical response to religious pluralism, have stopped requiring all of the Islamic rituals and added others. For example, members of the Sufi Order of the West (now known as the Sufi Order International) only peripherally follow Islamic practice, and they incorporate rituals from other religious traditions into their practice. The most distinctive development of Sufism in the West has been in the area of gender. While Muslim societies have typically segregated men and women, in America Sufi women have been able to take on positions of leadership. Interestingly this same phenomenon is taking place among American Buddhist groups.

Spiritual Practices

The principal form of Islamic meditation is known as *zikr* (or *dhikr*), which means "remembrance of the Divine." The meditative practice of *zikr* is a threefold practice of recollection. First one continually repeats the Arabic names of God out loud. After sufficient practice, one begins to repeat God's name constantly and silently in the heart. Eventually one hears God's name at all times in the soul. One can repeat any one of God's ninety-nine names and qualities or phrases such as "There is no God but God" or "Muhammad is the messenger of God." The names fall into two categories: those reflecting God's majesty, power, wrath, authority, and justice and the names that convey beauty, grace, generosity, and compassion. The purpose of repeating God's name—sometimes up to ten thousand or more times daily—is to embed that specific quality in the heart of the practitioner. The choice of the particular quality or name to be repeated is made under the guidance of a Sufi master because some qualities, such as wrathful, require a higher level of development than peace, beauty, or mercy. Some orders recommend that people repeat the words silently while in seclusion; others believe it should be done vocally and in groups to intensify the spiritual experience.

The belief underlying these practices is that we become that which we are conscious of. Spending time on a daily basis creating an atmosphere of peace, beauty or compassion (all names of the Divine) will result in these qualities manifesting in our personality. Beyond this, the Sufis follow these practices hoping to experience the Divine presence, to know God in a particular manifestation (e.g., to know the Compassionate One). They recognize, however, that all anyone can do is to create conditions that are favorable for this experience to occur and that the experience they seek cannot be willed. It is the gift of grace.

The use of meaningful words is a central part of Sufi meditation, as opposed to practices such as centering prayer or Zen forms of Buddhist meditation, where the word carries no meaning but is used only as a vehicle to discipline the mind's ability to focus attention.

Brief passages from the *Qur'an* are recited during five regular periods of prayer each day (dawn, noon, afternoon, evening, and night). On Friday evenings, Sufis frequently go to a mosque (an Islamic place of worship) to say these prayers. There is a prescribed series of movements, including prostrations toward Mecca, the holy city near where Muhammad received his revelation. There are also a series of ablutions (purifying and cleansing rituals) that are performed before saying the prayers.

In Sufism, music and dance accompanied by poetry—most often works of poets such as Rumi or selections from the *Qur'an*—are crafted into spiritual practices. What is emphasized in music and poetry, for example, is the sensitivity of the listener to hearing the arts' inner spiritual quality. For this reason the listener performs ablutions before being able to listen out of a pure longing for God. Devotional music is often accompanied by the recitation of love poetry directed toward God as the Beloved. While listening, some can experience an ecstatic trance. The late Samuel Lewis, a follower of Pir Vilayat Inayat Khan, began an organization known as the Dances of Universal Peace. The group draws on folk and ethnic dancing as well as chants and songs in different languages in an effort to bring about international peace. There are now many branches of the group all over the world.

Since 1994 different Sufi orders have gathered at an annual conference held in northern California under the auspices of the International Association of Sufism.

Carl Ernst is a scholar of Islamic and Indian studies who specializes in Sufism. He is Professor and Chair of the Department of Religious Studies, University of North Carolina at Chapel Hill.

Books

Coleman Barks, translator, et al., *The Essential Rumi* (HarperSanFrancisco, 1997). A collection of ecstatic poetry translated by an outstanding American poet.

Carl Ernst, *The Shambhala Guide to Sufism* (Shambhala Publications, Inc., 1997). This comprehensive introduction to Sufism discusses its origin and development. It also discusses the sacred sources of Sufism; offers an overview of Sufi meditation practices, rituals, and institutions; and covers the spread of the Sufi orders, Sufi poetry and music, and the dilemmas of Sufism in the modern world.

Carl Ernst, translator, *The Unveiling of Secrets: Diary of a Sufi Master* by Ruzbihan Baqli (Parvardigar Press, 1997). An astonishing visionary diary in which a twelfth-century Persian Sufi recorded his encounters with God, the prophets, angels, and saints.

James Fadiman and Robert Frager, *Essential Sufism* (HarperSanFrancisco, 1997). A collection of ancient and modern Sufi prayers and poetry, stories and sayings that all speak from the heart of Islamic mysticism.

Kabir Edmund Helminski, *Living Presence: A Sufi Way to Mindfulness and the Essential Self* (Jeremy P. Tarcher, Perigee, 1992). A practical guide to meditation by an American representative of the Mevlevi Sufi order.

Hazrat Inayat Khan, *Inner Life* (Omega Press, 1997). Three classic essays on the spiritual life by the teacher who brought Sufism to the West.

Pir Vilayat Inayat Khan, *That Which Transpires Behind That Which Appears: The Experience of Sufism* (Omega Press, 1994). A step-by-step guide to the discovery and unfoldment of the soul that includes instructions on methods of meditation and how they can be translated into life in the daily world.

J. Gordon Melton and Michael Koszegi, editors, *Islam in North America: A Sourcebook* (Garland Publishers, 1992). This compendium contains a directory of Sufi orders and other Sufi-related groups.

Idries Shah, *Learning How to Learn: Psychology and Spirituality in the Sufi Way* (Penguin USA, 1996). The most published author on Sufism, Shah presents Sufism in this book not as mystical Islam but as a psychological method for apprehending reality.

Organizations

Abode of the Message, Program Office
5 Abode Road
New Lebanon, NY 12125
(518) 794-8095 (phone)
(518) 791-8060 (fax)
aegis@sufiorder.org (e-mail)
www.sufiorder.org/aegis/ (website)

The Abode of the Message, formerly known as Aegis, was begun with the vision of providing a forum for spiritual studies and for the universal teachings of the Sufi Order of the West. Throughout the years, it has brought teachers from diverse traditions—Christian, Native American, Buddhist, Jewish, Hindu, Muslim, Taoist, and contemporary Universalist—to share their wisdom and offer techniques for enriching life and expanding human awareness.

Bawa Muhaiyaddeen Fellowship
5820 Overbrook Avenue
Philadelphia, PA 19131
(215) 879-6300 (phone)
(215) 879-6307 (fax)
info@bmf.org (e-mail)
www.bmf.org (website)

Muhammad Raheem Bawa Muhaiyaddeen was a Sufi teacher who for seventy years shared his knowledge and experience with people of every race and religion and from all walks of life. The fellowship is a living repository of his teachings, a gathering place where weary travelers on the spiritual path can find direction and focus.

Golden Sufi Center
P.O. Box 428
Inverness, CA 94937

(415) 663-8773 (phone)
(415) 663-9128 (fax)
goldensufi@aol.com (e-mail)
www.goldensufi.org (website)

Although it has no Islamic linkage, the Golden Sufi Center publishes books and tapes on Sufism and holds retreats and other events in the United States and Europe. It emphasizes a psychological approach.

International Association of Sufism (IAS)
25 Mitchell Boulevard, Suite 2
San Rafael, CA 94903
(415) 472-6959

IAS, a nonprofit organization established in 1983, invites teachers, students, and scholars of all schools of Sufism to join in the common purpose of seeking greater knowledge, mutual understanding, and the dissemination of Sufi principles.

Islamic Society of North America (ISNA)
P.O. Box 38
Plainfield, IN 46168-0038
(317) 839-8157

ISNA, a nonprofit membership organization, serves to advance the cause of Islam and Muslims in North America. It provides a range of services to individuals and Islamic centers around the United States, including the Islamic Teaching Center, which offers credit-granting summer classes in the Arabic language and Islamic studies and a correspondence course.

Khaniqah Nimatullahi Publications
306 West 11th Street
New York, NY 10014-2369
(212) 924-7739 (phone)
(212) 924-5479 (fax)
darvish@nimattullahi.org (e-mail)
www.nimatullahi.org (website)

This is the U.S. office of the Nimatullahi Sufi Order, founded at the end of the fourteenth century in Iran. With a focus on integrating the social and spiritual life, this order's practices include reflection, invocation and remembrance of God, self-examination, meditation, and litany.

M. T. O. Shahmaghsoudi (School of Islamic Sufism®)
5225 Wisconsin Avenue, NW, Suite 502

Washington, DC 20015
(202) 364-2609 or (800) 820-2180 (phone)
(202) 364-2608 (fax)
mtos@cais.com (e-mail)
http//mto.shahmaghsoudi.org (website)

Maktab Tarighat Oveyssi Shahmaghsoudi (School of Islamic Sufism), with over 400,000 students worldwide, dates back to the seventh century. The focus of its programs is to present the inner reality of the teachings of the Prophets; seek reasons and provide solutions for religious, ethnic, and gender conflicts; and train individuals to experience true human dignity.

Naqshbandi Sufi Way
c/o Haqqani Foundation
Main Convention and Retreat Center
7007 Denton Hill Road
Fenton, MI 48430-9478
(810) 714-2296 (phone)
(650) 917-9938 (fax)
staff@naqshbandi.org (e-mail)
www.naqshbandi.org (website)

A prominent Islamic scholar and leader of the Naqshbandi Sufi Order in the Americas, Shaykh Hisham Muhammad Kabbani has spent his life spreading the teachings of peace, tolerance, respect, and love. Here in the United States for the last seven years, Shaykh Kabbani has continued to disseminate the light and peace of Islam's spiritual dimension to people of every background, ethnicity, race, and belief.

Peaceworks International Network for the Dances of Universal Peace
444 NE Ravenna Boulevard, Suite 306
Seattle, WA 98115-6467
(206) 522-4353 (phone)
peaceworks@compuserv.com (e-mail)
www.dancesofuniversalpeace.org (website)

A nonprofit membership organization, founded by Samuel Lewis, that links many worldwide dance circles. The Dances of Universal Peace use sacred phrases, chants, music, and movements from many traditions to promote peace and integration within individuals and groups. Contact the center for a listing of regional networkers.

Sufi Order International Secretariat (formerly known as the Sufi Order of the West)
North American Headquarters
P.O. Box 30065
Seattle, WA 98103
(206) 525-6992 (voice mail)
(206) 525-7013 (fax)
sufioffice@compuserve.com (e-mail)
www.sufiorder.org (website)
 Founded in 1910 by Hazrat Inayat Khan, the organization evolved from the spiritual tradition of the Chishti lineage, which originated in the East. Khan sought to make the spiritual legacy of Sufism applicable to the needs of our time.

Sufi Psychological Association
P.O. Box 19922
Sacramento, CA 95819
(800) 338-1467 (phone)
(916) 923-1201 (fax)
sufipsy@ips.net (e-mail)
 In 1996 the association was founded by a group of psychotherapists, psychiatrists, and researchers who had experience with the effects of Sufi practice on the human psyche and who wished to share this knowledge with others. This group publishes a quarterly journal and sponsors different events, including a conference.

Threshold Society
139 Main Street
Brattleboro, VT 05301
(802) 254-8300 (phone)
(802) 257-2779 (fax)
threshold@sover.net (e-mail)
www.sufism.org/threshld (website)
 The society is an educational foundation rooted in the Mevlevi order of the Sufi tradition whose purpose is to facilitate the experience of Divine unity, love, and wisdom in the world. It offers training programs, seminars, and retreats throughout North America, Europe, and the Middle East.

Periodicals

Heart & Wings
P.O. Box 30065

Seattle, WA 98103
(206) 525-6992 (voice mail)
(206) 789-6911 (fax)
sufiorder@aol.com or beauty@compuserve.com (e-mail)
3 times per year; $15
    This newsletter publishes news about the Sufi Order International.

Sufi Magazine
c/o Khaniqah Nimatullahi Publications
306 West 11th Street
New York, NY 10014-2369
(212) 924-7739 (phone)
(212) 924-5479 (fax)
gate.cruzio.com/~darrish (e-mail)
Quarterly; $16
    Published by the Nimatullahi Sufi Order in London, England, this journal is devoted to the study of Sufism. It contains a variety of articles and poetry as well as contemporary fiction and adaptations of early Sufi stories.

Sufi Review
Pir Publications, Inc.
Colonial Green
256 Post Road East
Westport, CT 06880
(203) 221-7595
Quarterly; $9
    This publication discusses contemporary and classical Sufi mystical thought and teachings.

Sufism
P.O. Box 2382
San Rafael, CA 94912
ias@ias.org (e-mail)
www.ias.org (website)
Quarterly; $16
    A journal published by the International Association of Sufism (IAS) whose purpose is to provide lines of communication among Sufis through articles, essays, book reviews, etc.

Websites

homel.gte.net/derdish3/
   The homepage for the Rifa'i Marufi Order, a Turkish Sufi order in Chapel Hill, North Carolina.

world.std.com/~habib/sufi.html
   A great link page to Sufi websites.

www.bawa.org
   A website about the Sri Lankan Sufi master, Bawa Muhaiyaddeen, who is buried in Philadelphia.

www.best.com/~informe/mateen/haqqani.html
   This is a traditional Islamic Sufi group from Cyprus that has a very large following.

www.geocities.com/Athens/9189
   The Tijani home page covers an Africa-based Sufi order (from Senegal) with a strong Islamic orientation and includes information about the Tariqa Tijaiyya, Shaykh Ahmad Al-Tijani (RA), Shaykh Ibrahim Niasse (RA), Shaykh Hassan Cisse, and the African-American Islamic Institute.

www.nimatullahi.org
   This is a Shi'ite Sufi order from Iran that has many centers in the United States. The website contains the principles and practices of the Nimatullahi Sufi Order, books on Sufism, *Sufi* magazine, poetry, and music.

www.sufism.org
   This group has a Turkish orientation but is very universalist. Their publications are quite popular. The website contains information on the Threshold Society, Mevlevi Order, and publications by the Helminskis.

JEWISH MEDITATION

Judaism is an ancient religion with roots extending back to nomadic tribal peoples who wandered the Syro-Arabian desert. It distinguished itself from the religions of neighboring tribes and cultures in three major ways. First, amid polytheistic peoples, the Hebrews worshiped one God. The *Sh'ma* (or *Shema*), a traditional prayer that is frequently recited at the beginning and end of the day, reflects this central tenet and pledges loyalty to this deity: "Hear, O Israel, the Lord our God, the Lord is One." Second, amid gods that seemed amoral, Judaism stressed justice and ethical behavior. Jewish law as presented in the Torah, the five books of Moses, is the cornerstone of Judaism. Lastly, while others' gods and goddesses were not particularly intimate with human beings except carnally, the God of Israel had an intense personal relationship with the Jews. Through dreams, in visions, and through voices, God spoke directly to His Chosen People. The religion itself was shaped through these Divine revelations to prophets and leaders such as Abraham and Moses. But the conversation was not just one way. The psalms, for example, praise, beseech, rejoice in, and even complain to the Divine. Psalm 13 implores: "How long must I suffer anguish in my soul and be so grieved in my heart day and night?" The naked cries of the heart and the soul's exclamations of deep grief and sorrow that are expressed in these verses reflect a beautiful intimacy with the Divine.

The Jewish God concept, however, is a complex one that evolved over time. The deity that Abraham worshiped was called El or El Shaddai—a common Semitic name for God. The God that Moses encountered called Itself YHVH (Yahweh), which translates to "I am who I am." But the actual name of God was considered so holy that it was forbidden to speak it. Thus the Deity is often referred to as Adonai ("Lord") or simply The Name. In mystically minded circles, God is referred to as *Ein Sof*, which means "the Infinite, Without End, No Thingness." It exists beyond all human concepts and representations, although it has been described as white light or the light of pure awareness. Rabbi David Cooper, in his book *God Is a Verb*, talks about *Ein Sof* not as a Being but as "an ever-opening process"—an idea first developed by Rabbi Zalman Schacter-Shalomi of the Jewish Renewal movement. Cooper writes that *Ein Sof* resides not in the past, nor in the future, but only in the ever-present Now. In this way it is reminiscent of Buddhist mindfulness. However, in Judaism *Ein Sof* is regarded as a Deity with which an intimate relationship is possible, whereas Buddhism is nontheistic.

If union with *Ein Sof* is the goal of mystical Judaism, then the question arises: How can a finite human being have a relationship with what is basically an infinite and unknowable God or process? Actively working with that question is what Jewish meditative and mystical practices are all about.

Jewish meditation is a controversial issue within Judaism today. In his article "Unorthodox Jews Rummage through the Orthodox Tradition" in the *New York Times Magazine*, Roger Kamenetz admits that while "Jewish meditation has a long history, many mainstream Jews will state with conviction that it does not exist." Kamenetz attributes this attitude to the fact that meditative practices are found in the Jewish mystical tradition of kabbalah, which was passed on from teacher to student in private (some go so far as to say in secret). Psychologist Barbara Hammer, cofounder and president of the Jewish Psychological Centers in Washington, D.C., leans toward the latter interpretation. She explains that mystics are generally regarded by the mainstream culture as eccentrics—sometimes as benign kooks; other times, as wild-eyed lunatics. Jewish mystics have suffered not only the contempt and scorn of mainstream Jews but also that of Gentiles toward Jews in general. Perle Besserman, author of *The Shambhala Guide to Kabbalah and Jewish Mysticism*, argues similarly. "Whether it was the Romans in the first centuries . . . or the medieval Inquisition or the government programs of modern Europe that motivated their secrecy, the Kabbalists bore the double burden of not only being Jews, but Jews who 'dabbled in magic.'"

The earliest schools of Jewish meditation began around 400 B.C. and included chanting, music, and dance. After the Babylonian exile, however, these schools could no longer function and the practices became the province of an inner circle of rabbis. Kamenetz cites kabbalistic resurgences in thirteenth-century Spain when the *Zohar*, the kabbalistic canon that was once described as a kind of fictional biography of God, was written; in the sixteenth century in Safed, Israel; in the eighteenth century when Hasidism was birthed in the Ukraine; and again today.

Rabbi Wayne Dosick describes this renewal in his book *Dancing with God*. He explains that according to convention there are two periods in Judaism. The first, called Biblical Judaism, was characterized by personal Divine revelations, animal sacrifice, and a central altar located at Jerusalem's Holy Temple. Then, writes Dosick, the "Jews experienced exile and return, religious reformation, religious repression, political persecution, the birth of a powerful new religion, destruction, and once again, exile." As a result of this upheaval, a new period emerged called Rabbinical Judaism. "The Holy Temple was replaced by the synagogue, the cultic priest was replaced by the scholar-rabbi, and animal sacrifice was replaced by prayer." Additionally, direct Divine revelation was superseded by oral law, an extension of Torah law. What this amounted to, explains Dosick, was that Jewish sages no longer saw God's word coming through any individual as it had to the earlier prophets. Rather, the law would be articulated by the sages themselves.

Dosick goes on to argue, as do all kabbalists, that another paradigm shift is about to occur, one that in some ways echoes the first. Dosick calls this new period *Neshamah* (Soul) Judaism, a time characterized by "the intimate, spiritual soul-connection of each person with God, and by its forgers and shapers, precious individual souls." Evidence for such a renaissance can be found in articles in mainstream publications like the *New York Times* and *Time* magazine, in the proliferation of books on Jewish spiritual practices, and in growing participation in Jewish communities that actively embrace a mystical outlook.

The largest mystically oriented Jewish community today is the Hasidic community of Chabad, which was founded in the late 1960s by followers of Rabbi Menachem Mendel Schneersohn. They are best known for their attempts to convince their secularized brethren of the merits of returning to a Torah-based life. Many of Schneersohn's followers believed that he was the Messiah and that after his death, which occurred in 1994, he would be resurrected. There are over 2,500 Chabad communities worldwide, and most metropolitan areas in the United States have at least one Chabad House.

Another type of Jewish mystical community flourishing today is the Jewish Renewal movement, founded by followers of Rabbi Zalman Schacter-Shalomi. The term *Jewish Renewal*, which was coined in 1978 by Rabbi Arthur Waskow, refers to a network of Jews who are deeply involved in bringing an aliveness back to Judaism. More egalitarian and progressive than the Chabad communities, the Jewish Renewal movement is a confluence of Jewish mysticism, feminism, and progressive social concerns. For example, some in the movement are exploring what it would mean to be "eco-kosher," not in the sense of reverting back to traditional dietary laws but in the sense of maintaining an awareness of the environmental implications of food and lifestyle choices. Individuals participate in small groups organized to share spiritual commitments known as *Havurah*. There are also centers for training, healing, and retreat across the country.

With regard to Jewish meditative practices, Rabbi Aryeh Kaplan is frequently cited as the major modern proponent of Jewish meditation. Besserman's book *The Shambhala Guide to Kabbalah and Jewish Mysticism* gives a simple yet comprehensive overview of the various kabbalistic meditative styles and techniques. For example, there is awareness with intention (*kavannah*), which resembles Buddhist mindfulness meditation applied to daily activities. It involves bringing a spiritual attitude and frame of mind to anything and everything we do.

Two other practices are *hitbonenut* and *hitbodedut*. The former translates as "self-understanding," which is acquired by pondering or reflecting on one's place in the ongoing process of creation. According to Rabbi Cooper, out of this meditative process comes the motivation for *tikkun* and *tikkun olam*: repair of the soul and repair of the world. Kabbalistic texts describe all of creation, including human beings, as having inner sacred sparks. Cooper explains that we can repair both our souls and the world by raising these sparks—that is, by raising consciousness—returning them to their Source through meditation, other spiritual practices, and charitable deeds. He emphasizes that "in every moment of existence, we have the potential to raise holy sparks" and therefore that all of humankind has the potential to achieve messianic consciousness with its qualities of lovingkindness, gentleness, calmness, peace, profound understanding, and infinite caring. The other practice, *hitbodedut,* means "self-isolation" and might be compared with classic contemplative Christian practices where there is a separation from and letting go of all internal chatter—thoughts, feelings, memories—an emptying or separating from the everyday self. Sometimes the practice of *hitbodedut* is accompanied by a literal retreat away from distractions of the secular world.

Other Jewish meditative practices include gazing at a specific object such as a hand, water, or holy letters, reciting a mantra such as *yod, heh, vov, heh,* listening attentively to hear the word of God as manifest in life around us, and visualization. Meditation on prayers and on the psalms is the primary spiritual practice used in mainstream synagogues, and some Sabbath rituals incorporate meditative practices. These practices can be quite simple or rather elaborate, but all require consistent focus and commitment in order to unite with God.

Books

Perle Besserman, *The Shambhala Guide to Kabbalah and Jewish Mysticism* (Shambhala Publications, Inc., 1998). A simple yet comprehensive introduction to the philosophy and practice of the Jewish mystical traditions.

David A. Cooper, *God Is a Verb: Kabbalah and the Practice of Mystical Judaism* (Riverhead Books, 1997). Rabbi Cooper tackles a key kabbalistic concept, the notion that God is a continuous process of creation.

Avram Davis, editor, *Meditation: From the Heart of Judaism* (Jewish Lights Publishing, 1997). This is a collection of twenty-two essays by Jewish teachers, scholars, psychologists, and rabbis that address various aspects of meditation from "noble boredom" by Rabbi Jonathan Omer-Man to "mindfulness" by Sylvia Boorstein to "silencing the inner voice" by Rabbi Lawrence Kushner.

Rabbi Lynn Gottlieb, *She Who Dwells Within* (HarperSanFrancisco, 1995). One of the first and most creative women rabbis, Lynn Gottlieb has pulled together a collection of prayers, guided meditations, and rituals in an effort to create a vibrant contemporary Judaism that is gender inclusive.

Roger Kamenetz, *Stalking Elijah* (HarperSanFrancisco, 1998). In this, Kamenetz's seventh book, he shares his search for a connection to a vital Jewish practice through conversations, encounters, and meditations with Jewish teachers across the United States.

Daniel C. Matt, *The Essential Kabbalah: The Heart of Jewish Mysticism* (HarperCollins, 1996). The author, an internationally recognized authority on Jewish mysticism, has chosen selections from traditional texts and kabbalistic teachings to give readers a feeling for the mystical nature of such terms as *Ein Sof, Sefirot,* and *Shekinah.*

Organizations

ALEPH: Alliance for Jewish Renewal
7318 Germantown Avenue
Philadelphia, PA 19119
(215) 247-9700 (phone)
ALEPHajr@aol.com (e-mail)

The Alliance for Jewish Renewal's mission is to provide programs and activities to help enhance participants' spiritual lives while familiarizing them with the Jewish Renewal life paths. ALEPH sponsors retreats, seminars, conferences, and other programs for the general public, as well as nondegree educational programs in Jewish studies.

Elat Chayyim, the Woodstock Center for Healing and Renewal
99 Mill Hook Road
Accord, NY 12404
(800) 398-2630 (phone)
elatchayyi@aol.com (e-mail)

This center conducts week-long retreats in a wooded setting. The programs, run mostly in summer and fall, bring teachers of meditation, sacred text, spiritual philosophy, and the arts to groups of between 50 and 150 participants.

Heart of Stillness Retreats
P.O. Box 106
Jamestown, CO 80455
(303) 459-3431

Heart of Stillness Retreats, founded in 1993, offers individuals, families, and small groups opportunities for spiritual growth and development through silence and meditation.

Kabbalah Learning Center
1062 Robertson Avenue
Los Angeles, CA 90035
(310) 657-5404 (phone)
(310) 657-7774 (fax)
kabbalah@usa.net (e-mail)
www.kabbalah.com (website)

The institute provides research, information, and assistance to those seeking insights of the kabbalah. It offers lectures, classes, seminars, and excursions to mystical sites. There are also other learning centers in the United States (San Diego, New York, and Miami) and abroad.

Metivta: A Center for Jewish Wisdom
Los Angeles Hillel Council
6233 Wilshire Boulevard
Los Angeles, CA 90048
(310) 477-5370 (phone)
(310) 477-7501 (fax)
metivta@metivta.org (e-mail)
www.metivta.org (website)
    This center offers various programs throughout the year that promote studies in Jewish spirituality.

Network of Jewish Renewal Communities
4502 East Paradise Village Parkway South, #1005
Phoenix, AZ 85032
(602) 996-4959 (phone)
admin@jewishrenewal.org (e-mail)
www.jewishrenewal.org (website)
    The network provides listings of communities in the United States and around the world.

Ruach Ami: Bay Area Jewish Healing Center
3330 Geary Boulevard, 3rd Floor
San Francisco, CA 94118
(415) 750-4197 (phone)
(415) 750-4115 (fax)
www.growthhouse.org/ruachami.html (website)
    A group that deals with bereavement and chronic illness.

Sarah's Tent
2461 Santa Monica Boulevard, #319
Santa Monica, CA 90404
(310) 456-2178 (phone)
(310) 456-6578 (fax)
www.mjcs.org (website)
    This organization runs women's meditation retreats.

Periodicals

Lilith
250 West 57th Street, #2432

New York, NY 10107
(800) 783-4903 (subscriptions)
(212) 757-0818 (phone)
(212) 757-5705 (fax)
lilithmag@aol.com (e-mail)
Quarterly; $18
    A scholarly and progressive Jewish feminist magazine.

Meta-Parshiot
7746 Ravenna Avenue NE
Seattle, WA 98115
(206) 522-7012
Monthly; $42
    Teachings on the weekly Torah Readings, with kabbalistic and psychological insights.

New Menorah
ALEPH: Alliance for Jewish Renewal
7318 Germantown Avenue
Philadelphia, PA 19119-1793
(215) 247-9700
Quarterly; $36 includes membership in ALEPH

Sh'ma
440 Park Avenue, 4th Floor
New York, NY 10016-8012
Monthly; $18
    A journal of Jewish responsibility published by the National Jewish Center for Learning and Leadership.

Tikkun
26 Fell Street
San Francisco, CA 94102
(800) 395-7753
Bimonthly; $31
    A Jewish Renewal look at politics, culture, and society.

Websites

www.chadbad.org

This website consists of a huge archive of Chabad literature, from articles teaching basic Judaism to sermons on the weekly Torah readings.

www.havienu.org

The website for Havienu L'shalom, a virtual spiritual congregation, offers Hasidic-based Torah learning and meditative prayer.

www.israel.nysernet.org/Jewish Renewal

This site provides Jewish commentary on holidays and practices.

www.jewhoo.com

A parody of Yahoo, the Internet search engine.

www.Torah.org

This site is a creation of Project Genesis, which teaches Torah and offers many additional features for learning and experiencing the Kabbalah.

🏵 The Hidden Mystics 🏵

By Sophy Burnham

There are only two ways to live your life.
One is as though nothing is a miracle.
The other is as though everything is.

—Albert Einstein

All around us live the hidden mystics. They walk down the streets of New York in shoes with worn-down heels. They beg on street corners. They drive fast cars through Chicago or L.A. They run multimillion-dollar businesses, and when they go home, their heads whirling with figures and finances, they catch their breath at something so simple—the ringing of a bell, the light-struck pigeons flying upward in a flurry of wings, a fragment of music—and in that moment they remember . . . what? They cannot say. Some sign, some glimmering that points beyond themselves to things not of this world.

Some of their mystical experiences are dramatic, passionate events that wash away all prior conceptions, firm ground. Others come as softly as the whisper of silk, a moment of mere harmony. . . . You aren't even certain anything happened there in that time-suspended second, but your spirits lift as you proceed.

Sometimes it is so casual, you step out of your house one morning, and out of the blue, for no reason, you are washed by joy, brushed by an angel's wing. A spiritual event.

Seeing deities, hearing voices, having ecstatic experiences does not make you spiritual. I know brilliant people who have never had a vision, who practice no religion, but are more spiritual than many religious practitioners. They work in the world, saving children, forging social change, or simply raising their own or foster children—most lovingly. No big deal. Just drawing water at the well.

Some people never even think about God. They take a walk, or work on carpentry, or they weave, garden, or cook. Some meditate just by waiting in silence for a few minutes, and some, like Brother Lawrence, simply "practice the presence of God." Are they the truer mystics, these humble, silent ones?

We know certain things of the ecstatic journey. Yet the more we know, the more questions arise. For example, in a survey of Americans' mystical experiences, conducted in 1973,* sociologists Andrew Greeley and William McCready discovered that those admitting to mystical encounters tended to have had happy childhoods, loving parents, and especially a father who expressed religious joyousness. But what does that signify? Since those responding affirmatively were predominately male, the fact of a religiously joyous father might also be interpreted as meaning no more than that the son had received parental permission to testify openly and without embarrassment to his spiritual life. I have only anecdotal evidence to draw upon, but I submit that a happy and a spiritually rich childhood are not prerequisites. Many of the letters I receive are from women who were neglected or abused in childhood, or reared in an atheist or nonbelieving environment, and who nonetheless relate their sweet experiences.

Catherine Brown, for example, from North Carolina, despite her spiritually barren childhood is one of the 5 percent (according to Greeley and McCready) who have been blessed with many ecstasies. "Mystical experiences," she says, "have punctuated my life for over ten years." They began with a request—a prayer made directly to God—and "have continued through meditation and many conscious efforts to remain open to the miraculous in daily affairs." The prayer—that longing of the heart—is important, for God is usually too courteous to barge in uninvited.

My friend Elinor likewise forms an exception to the Greeley-McCready rule,

---

*The survey of 1,460 persons asked one initial question, deriving the narrow wording from Classic Christian mystical experience: "Have you ever felt as though you were very close to a powerful spiritual force that seemed to lift you out of yourself?" Six hundred or about 40 percent of the respondents—"disproportionately" male, black, and college educated—answered yes. For more information, see Sophy Burnham, *The Ecstatic Journey*, pp. 173–178, 192, 229, 254. Or Andrew Greeley, *The Sociology of the Paranormal: A Reconnaissance*. Sage Research Papers in the Social Sciences, v. 3 #90-023. Beverly Hills and London, 1975.

having had a difficult childhood. Her independent mother was distant and busy, her famous father absent, and neither parent indicated any interest in a spiritual dimension. As a grown woman, at the time when we were writing long letters to each other in an effort to understand how the spiritual journey tangled with our marriages, children, and work, she had left her Jewish roots to explore Buddhist and Hindu teachings. At a week-long meditation retreat, as she writes in an as-yet unpublished memoir, she experienced what Hindus call the rising of Kundalini.

On the fifth day of the retreat, her teacher laid both hands on the crown of her head. Elinor turned around, took a few steps through the lawn of meditation cushions, and then:

> A surge of energy was pouring through me. It pounded against my head and forehead, gushed from the center of my heart, sluiced down my arms, and ran out of prickly electric sockets that appeared to have opened in the palm of my hands. My God, I was running and running with the stuff. I was pouring. I was throbbing with it.

What brings on such a mystical encounter? Why does it come at one time and not another? Why must it be invited in, first by the loneliness that aches to be filled, then by surrender, a crying out for help? And why do the mysteries present themselves in such vast and varying forms—wind, light, fire, peace, love, Christ, angels, guides, knowings, or dark nothingness?

It comes like a blow in the night, the mugger sneaking up behind you, and suddenly you are flooded with delights. The writer Joan Borysenko remembers that between the ages of forty-two and forty-six, during a particularly difficult period of her life, she had three and four dreams a night—all of them experiences with light. "I was rewarded by four years of grace. For a time, as the Buddhist saying goes, mountains and rivers were not just mountains and rivers but something spectacular; until slowly the mystical and magical withdrew, and mountains and rivers went back to being mountains and rivers again." There is a Zen saying to the same effect: before enlightenment, chop wood, draw water; after enlightenment, chop wood, draw water.

Many mystics are simply ordinary people, churched or unchurched, born to enjoy these gentle and intuitive altered states of consciousness. They make no dramatic mark in the world. I know another hidden mystic, Bessie, an African-American woman, pretty as a flower, and so filled with the Lord that hardly a phrase can fall from her lips that does not begin or end with "Bless the Lord. Praise the Lord!" So high is her faith and love of God, so vivid are her experiences, that for years she went to night school after work to qualify as a clergywoman of her church.

One day I telephoned her, discouraged. "Rejoice!" she told me, and "Give thanks!" Every morning she wakes up, she says, and her thought is of her Lord, "because I don't own me anymore," she said, and I could hear the lilt in her voice. "I am living for the Lord, going where he wants me to go, needs for me to go." Her relationship is strictly personal, one of intimate simplicity.

She laughed. "'Husband,' I say, 'are we going out tonight?' Sometimes I get angry and tell him what to do: 'Husband, you better pay attention now!' God loves it when I tell him what to do." We laugh into the phone. "God is working things out," she continued. "Don't worry. I can't do nothing, He does everything. 'Show it to me in a dream,' I say and, 'Thank you, Lord!' Letting go and trusting him. If I lose this body today, I wouldn't mind, because I'd be with God." Everything is preordained, she said; her task is only to step out each day in faith.

I put down the phone that morning laughing, my despondency forgotten in her simple trust and gratitude. All through our conversation my pen had been scribbling down her words in the automatic writer's activity, the journalist's reflex. I slipped the paper underneath my desk blotter, and it still sits there to this day. Over the years I have referred to it every now and again, reread her faith and always found my heart uplifted, and as the years have passed I've noticed that sometimes now I talk like this myself to my Beloved, who is husband, mother, sister, brother, father, lover, friend, my very self, it seems.

I have an image: that we spend our lives climbing the winding staircase of a high, glass tower. Sometimes we stand on one step, sometimes on another, and outside the windows, the land spreads gloriously before us, different vistas opening, according to the height of the step we stand on and the direction of the view. We see pine-covered mountains or tropical vegetation, deserts or snows, rivers or seas, flat plains or rolling hills, each step presenting a different sight-line as we circle the tower, sometimes climbing high, sometimes dropping down ten steps on the journey of our lives. With each stair-step the landscape appears mysterious and new, although only the viewing point has changed.

Or perhaps this magical stairway forms a double helix, like two strands of DNA, winding and intertwining, or like a deceptive Möbius strip, so that on our journey we not only move up and down the stairwell but step forward onto the other ribbon as well, twisting in constantly changing circles. We think we've never seen this vista before, while in fact only our position on the stairwell lends the countryside its awe.

Sophy Burnham is the award-winning author of ten books, including two *New York Times* bestsellers, *The Art Crowd* and *A Book of Angels*. She is best known for her speaking and writing on angels, creativity, the search for God, and spirituality. This essay was excerpted from chapter 10 of her most recent book, *The Ecstatic Journey*, with permission from the publisher, Ballantine Books.

9
Psychology and Spiritual Growth

In the fall of 1997, we visited the newly renovated and recently reopened permanent gem exhibit at the Museum of Natural History in Washington, D.C. While the centerpiece of the exhibit is the famous Hope Diamond, it was the metaphorical parallels between the creation of diamonds and soul work that took our breath away.

Diamonds form as the result of an extremely long and hazardous process that begins deep in the body of the earth. When pure carbon is exposed to intense heat (more than 2,000 degrees Fahrenheit) and pressure, its atoms are compressed into the diamond's unique crystalline structure. But the mineral can remain buried for millions, possibly billions, of years before a volcanic eruption sends it hurtling through fissures toward the earth's surface. The journey is dangerous for the diamond because it can be shattered in the explosion, transformed into common graphite if it cools too slowly or vaporized into carbon dioxide if it comes into contact with oxygen too soon. Once on the "surface," it can still be embedded in rock at depths of up to 2,000 feet. Natural elements like wind and water must erode layers of dirt, stone, and detritus before the diamonds can even be mined. When finally extracted, these "diamonds in the rough" are only half as valuable as those whose inner fire has been coaxed out by a precision craftsman.

Soul work is a similar process of forming, finding, and faceting our essential core, which when brilliantly cut and polished displays our inner beauty and spiritual durability. Life's trials and difficulties, painful losses, fearful transitions, trying circumstances, injustices in need of righting, all provide the proper conditions for shaping our souls. Suffering transforms us. In the heat of a personal crisis or pressure from life circumstances, our very essence is molded and shaped. When the situation comes to a head, when it erupts, the diamond soul rides the wild energies of the psyche closer to the surface of awareness. Then other elements—water (emotions) and wind (spirit)—work to free the soul from whatever imprisons it. Once it is relatively accessible, we can utilize techniques—spiritual practices and psychological tools—to clean off the debris of the false self. We drop the mask of who we think we should be and begin to deal with our fears, anger, and mistrust—all the defenses that keep our diamond "in the rough."

We originally approached soul work through psychotherapy. Both of us had had religious training at a young age but we left our root faiths because we could not find people, churches, or programs amenable to our questing and questioning. We groped along dim and narrow pathways and wandered, often far afield, until we finally landed in the psychological realm—Chuck in a psychology Ph.D. program, Anne working for a personal growth center and enrolled in a master's program in body psychotherapy and counseling. In those contexts—albeit in vastly different ways—we found opportunities to begin our mining expedition. As we ferociously dug down, sifting through emotional debris and *materia psychologica*, we both hit lodestones of spiritual yearning. Leery of traditional institutional religion, we participated in a spiritual community called Pathwork for a number of years until muddy interpersonal and organizational dynamics convinced us to leave. Then after several years of practicing Buddhist insight meditation, we found our way back to our Christian roots, all the while staying sometimes more and sometimes less involved in psychological work.

Psychotherapy, for us, gave us entry into our inner world. It helped us sort through emotional conflicts, self-defeating patterns of behavior, and arcane feelings that were coloring present-day interactions. It did not distract us from spiritual pursuits but supported them; after all, as the archetypal psychologists and others point out, psychology, at its root, is the study of the soul. And just as when one is undertaking a long journey it is important to have an astute traveling companion to negotiate the differences in language, customs, and culture, so too on the spiritual path therapy can be useful.

Although for us, soul work was rooted in psychotherapy, for others the soul's quarry may be a religious context. In this chapter, we look at two processes: pastoral counseling, which can help clear away the unnecessary coating of defenses that keep our soul buried in the muck and misery of life, and spiritual direction, which can, among other things, teach discernment, the careful and skillful faceting of our diamond soul so that its inner light shines forth. With both, we look at their relationship to psychotherapy.

Before we move ahead, it may be helpful to clear up several points of confusion about the relationship between psychotherapy and spirituality. First, some believe that because psychotherapy and spiritual practice have different goals and methods, they are incompatible. Typically, spiritual practices are seen as ways to transcend or go beyond self-image, or how we usually imagine ourselves to be. This may seem to contradict one of psychotherapy's goals: that of helping clients achieve and maintain a healthy self-concept. We've already explained that sufficient psychological nourishment eliminates the need for self-preoccupation and self-centeredness. We also believe that it is possible to nourish our sense of self-worth in therapy *and* work through meditation and other practices to transcend our self-concept. The two are not mutually exclusive.

According to Mark Epstein, a psychiatrist, Buddhist meditator, and author of *Thoughts without a Thinker: Psychotherapy from a Buddhist Perspective*, the goal of meditation is to expand awareness, to experience the world through a wider lens than we normally do. Epstein agrees that meditation does not eradicate self-concept; it takes us beyond our sense of identity, allowing us to get a broader view and understanding than was previously possible.

Similarly, many people believe that one surrenders one's ego in spiritual practice and strengthens it in psychotherapy. Epstein softens the harsh dichotomy between these two perspectives. He points out that Western psychotherapists define *ego* quite differently from spiritual teachers and clergy and that this difference causes confusion. Western mental-health clinicians view the ego as our capacity to think and organize our daily lives. In this sense we need our egos in the meditation room too. In meditation we seek to develop the capacity to observe our thoughts and emotions as they arise without getting caught up in them. This process enlists the ego as a neutral observer. What spiritual teachers caution us against is not the ego per se but its negative side, where it functions as the servant and loyal defender of our false self. But the ego can be trained to serve the spiritual process; it can learn to step aside and allow larger forces to inform and direct us. Eliminating the ego would be disastrous for both our mental health *and* our spiritual life.

One other area that bears attention is a defensive tactic known as the "spiritual bypass." This occurs when people try to recast what is really a personal problem into a more universal spiritual issue. For example, a person who is uncomfortable around people might use meditation to avoid intimate relationships or involvement with the world. Meditation is a wonderful path to silence and solitude, but paradoxically it is one that is maximized and enhanced by group practice. Instead of creating isolation from life, spiritual practices should connect us to ourselves, to others, and to that which is larger than we are.

🕸 The Story of Suzanne: An Example of Spiritual Bypass 🕸
By Jeffrey B. Rubin

A woman whom I shall call Suzanne was a long-term Buddhist meditator and esteemed writer on spiritual disciplines. She entered psychotherapy because she sensed that something was "off" in her life. She was successful at work and esteemed by colleagues but felt that something was missing, which she had difficulty pinpointing. After several months of treatment she began to recognize that her divorce a year earlier had been more painful than she had allowed herself to feel. She also realized that she felt removed from life, that she kept others at a distance. This left her feeling deprived and hungry for meaningful emotional connections with other people.

Through meditation Suzanne had developed a heightened ability to pay careful moment-to-moment attention to the texture of her experience. She was able to notice subtle facets of mental and physical sensations with admirable precision. As therapy unfolded, we realized that by concentrating her mind in meditation practice, she had anesthetized herself from the emotional suffering of her painful and unsettling divorce, which resulted in her suppressing and detaching from her pain rather than mourning the loss she was experiencing. Proficiency in categorizing and detaching from highly charged emotional states and experiences had replaced contacting them.

What I realized from Suzanne's experience was that Buddhism has an ambivalent relationship to emotional life. On the one hand, the meditative method counsels acceptance of whatever one experiences, whether anger, desire, greed, lust, or fear. This aids many meditators—like Suzanne—in being more attuned to the subtleties of their experience. On the other hand, the purpose of meditation, according to many Buddhist texts, is to "purify" the mind of "defilements" such as greed, hatred, and delusion. Because purification is only necessary when something is dirty, objectionable, or abject, from this perspective emotions can be seen as obstacles to living. This predisposes meditators to treat whatever they discover about themselves while meditating as weeds that must be eliminated from the mental garden, rather than flowers in disguise. It also compromises a meditator's capacity to use experience as feedback to explore, understand, and work through conflicts, developmental arrests, and interpersonal difficulties. Suzanne could not let go of what afflicted her until she attended to feelings such as sadness and guilt, not in order to transcend them but to understand and eventually integrate them.

While it is important to recognize the possibility of spiritual bypass, it is also fair to say that Buddhism teaches psychotherapy about some of the dangers of self-centeredness, about the suffering and myopia that can occur when one is attached or overinvested in one's particular personal story about oneself. Unhealthy narcissism, as Buddhism aptly notes, is at the root of human suffering and evil. Western culture, in general, and psychotherapy, in particular, arguably foster a self-centered view of self, relationships, and morality, which may feed the alienation and malaise that Western psychotherapies purport to heal.

Western psychotherapies need Buddhism or other spiritual disciplines in order to become less narrow, less self-centered, less focused on the needs and wishes of the separate, sovereign self. The spiritual perspective that Buddhism offers may be a central ingredient in our collective mental health.

Jeffrey B. Rubin, Ph.D., practices psychoanalysis and psychoanalytically oriented psychotherapy in New York City and Bedford Hills, New York. He is the author of *Psychotherapy and Buddhism: Towards an Integration* and *A Psychoanalysis for Our Time: Exploring the Blindness of the Seeing I*.

In chapter 3, we described how spirituality has enriched the psychotherapeutic process; in this chapter, we will look at how psychology has enhanced and supported spiritual processes. The best example is the field of pastoral counseling, which draws on psychotherapy principles and theories to help people who want to be counseled by someone who shares their faith perspective. Spiritual direction is another field that uses some psychotherapeutic methods, not to solve personal problems but to help people develop a relationship with the Divine and understand and integrate spiritual experiences into their lives.

PASTORAL COUNSELING

Although people have always sought out the clergy for guidance, over time the kinds of guidance people have sought have changed dramatically. In the seventeenth century, Christians were primarily concerned with salvation from sin. According to Walter Conn, writing in the journal *Pastoral Psychology*, pastoral care at that time consisted of persuading church members to overcome their faults and vices—perceived to be rooted in innate selfishness—by repenting and seeking forgiveness. In the eighteenth century, Conn continues, the language and concepts changed. Christians desired "rebirth," which was viewed as an "arduous, wrenching experience because it required the breaking of the proud will [and] the suppression of the sinfully assertive self." During this period not only was the will a primary concern of pastoral care, but people equated mental illness and insanity with demonic possession. Other than locking the insane away in asylums and attempting exorcisms, there was very little the clergy could do.

Given these limitations, it is not surprising that during the twentieth century many clergy involved in pastoral care embraced the new Freudian theories about the treatment of mental illness because they promised a new and seemingly effective way of helping those who came to them with serious personal problems. Soon after World War II, pastoral counseling became a specialty of pastoral care and, infused with enthusiasm for psychoanalysis, adopted a more optimistic view of human nature. No longer did the will and selfishness need to be "broken." Instead Conn describes a radical shift, at least among liberal Christian pastoral counselors, toward an empathic, nonjudgmental, receptive attitude meant to encourage counselees to move toward self-realization, not self-abnegation.

The most significant step toward integrating theology and psychotherapy came in the 1950s when the Reverend Norman Vincent Peale, author of the immensely popular *The Power of Positive Thinking*, collaborated with author and psychiatrist Smiley Blanton to form what is now known as the Blanton-Peale Institute, a new kind of psychoreligious clinic and training program. According to Roy Woodruff, Ph.D., executive director of the American Association of Pastoral Counselors (AAPC), the establishment of this clinic marked the formal beginning of the modern form of pastoral counseling. Since that time, clergy have sought mental-health training as a way of responding to requests from their members for help with alcoholism, physical abuse, and depression. But formally and regularly counseling parishioners can add an immense workload to all the other duties required of a pastor. Because of this practical consideration, a counseling specialty—full-time pastoral counseling—has evolved. Their professional organization, the AAPC, was founded in 1963 and today represents eighty different faith groups, including Catholic, Jewish, and Protestant denominations.

Over the years, as the field has expanded, it has diversified. Instead of offering their services to members of a particular church, some clergy trained as pastoral counselors began practicing outside their home congregations. Others started nonsectarian pastoral counseling centers or worked in hospitals, prisons, or homes for the elderly. While their religious affiliation remained intact, the area of expansion and excitement came in learning mental-health techniques. In fact, during the 1960s and 1970s within the more liberal branch of the pastoral counseling field, the psychotherapeutic model largely replaced theology as the main source of insight.

Then the pendulum began to swing in the other direction. Many pastoral counselors realized that the shift to psychotherapy was secularizing the process and began to seek ways to balance spirituality and psychotherapy. Barry Estadt, Ph.D., founding director of the Loyola College program in pastoral counseling and a professor of pastoral counseling, reports that today the field is developing along two parallel lines. One is the strengthening of professional mental-health credentials so that graduates of master's level pastoral counseling programs can become licensed or certified and therefore eligible for third-party insurance reimbursement. At the same time there is an increased emphasis on the experiential aspects of the spiritual journey and its relationship to mental-health factors. At Loyola, for example, some students already have mental-health credentials and have come to study the religious aspects of mental health.

Two other interesting developments are occurring in the field. The first is an increase in participation by laypeople. Today almost two-thirds of the students in the pastoral counseling program at Loyola are lay Catholics or Protestants; one-third are clergy (equal numbers of Catholics and Protestants). The AAPC has encouraged this new development by opening its membership to individuals with mental-health training and certification and a firm and active faith commitment.

The second development counters a criticism of both secular psychotherapy and pastoral counseling; namely, that they focus too narrowly on meeting the needs of individuals and individual families to the detriment of participation in the larger community. Margaret Kornfeld, D.Min., a clinically certified pastoral counselor, has recently written a book, *Cultivating Wholeness: A Guide to Care and Counseling in Faith Communities*, that describes a widening of pastoral counseling through networks of care.

In years past, there was an informal system supporting rituals of care. People offered assistance to individuals and families in crisis. Orphaned children were taken in, people were fed, homes demolished by fire were rebuilt. Today our social systems are organized differently and faith communities cannot assume that the needs of parishioners will be taken care of by those who "always do it." Many of the women who traditionally called on the sick, infirm, and elderly now have jobs. Therefore spiritual communities need to be more organized to minister to the congregation.

In her model, Kornfeld describes how pastoral counselors can consult with the church's clergy and lay counselors, lead educational or support groups and spiritual retreats, and work with congregational groups that provide care for the sick and terminally ill (see her comments below).

Clearly this and other changes indicate a profession in transition. Having begun as a theologically based form of counseling, pastoral counseling is now beginning to move toward incorporating the experiential dimension of religion and shifting from a one-on-one focus to a more encompassing process that includes the larger faith community.

❈ Why Pastoral Counseling? ❈

By Adele M. Pogue

Peter, a man in his thirties, had been sexually molested by a priest when he was young. He came to our pastoral counseling offices because of difficulties with alcohol and relationships. After we began our sessions, I learned that he was feeling alienated from the church and angry at God for allowing the abuse to happen to him. When he spoke of this alienation, he didn't link it to the loneliness, isolation, and despair that pervaded his life. Peter was not eager to talk about his faith or God; he was mired in his anger toward the institutional church.

One day, on a hunch, I wondered aloud whether his loss of faith and sense of being separated from God might be linked to his feelings of meaninglessness. At the time he denied that this was a possibility. Several sessions later, however, while mourning the loss of a girlfriend, he related that in the past week, in a moment of great despair, he had called out to God and had subsequently felt a deep sense of peace. In this moment he recognized that indeed his loss of faith was linked to his other feelings of isolation and loneliness. This was a turning point for Peter, who has since returned to the church and participates regularly in this community.

Perhaps Peter chose a pastoral counselor because subconsciously he realized that a secular therapist might not be open to discussing faith issues, which are important because they are expressions of what people believe and think about God and God's influence in the world. Yet however important it is to be open to the context of beliefs and the beliefs themselves, Peter's experience of calling out to God in despair and finding peace is a spiritual experience that expands beyond the theological.

When I am with clients who have no interest in talking about theology or spiritual issues, I listen carefully because I know that everyone faces existential concerns as part of being alive. I then ask them what has meaning for them and what they see as most worthwhile in life. This raises their curiosity and is similar to asking about their spiritual views, but in a way that seems more neutral. I also find that during the course of therapy most clients eventually bring up these issues if the therapist indicates an openness to hearing them.

Some clients will ask me to pray with them and I do; I will also recommend that we pray together during a session where a difficult decision such as divorce comes up and the client is in chaos. This is a way for both of us to connect to a deeper source of wisdom. Sometimes I recommend biblical passages or other readings when these appear to be relevant.

While I recommend that some clients learn how to meditate, I do not attempt to teach them myself, even though I meditate regularly. I find that meditation enables me to be more open, not only to my clients, but to noticing the movement of God's presence in the session, such as the time the hunch came to me to ask about the link between Peter's anger at God and his despair at having lost his faith.

One of the primary sources of support for my spiritual journey, as well as for my husband's, has been our participation for the last thirty years in Celebration House Church, a group affiliated with the Church of the Brethren. I have felt sustained by our membership in the group, where we study the scriptures together; go on retreats; and love, confront, and help one another in life crises. We also participate in the church's outreach efforts to the larger community, which keeps us aware of the world beyond ourselves.

Adele M. Pogue, M.A., L.I.C.S.W., a lay pastoral counselor and clinical social worker who received her clinical training at the Institute of Pastoral Psychotherapy in Washington, D.C., practices pastoral counseling with the Pastoral Psychotherapy Group in Washington, D.C. She is a member of the American Association of Pastoral Counselors.

❈ Community Pastoral Care ❈
By Margaret Kornfeld

In the early 1980s, a small congregation largely composed of young adults and small families felt as if it had been hit by a plague. In a six-month period, five young women—mainstays of the community—were diagnosed with breast cancer. The women, their families, and the religious community were totally unprepared. Prior to diagnosis, most of the women had only been in a hospital to have their tonsils removed or babies delivered. Not only did they not know how to *think* about cancer, they could not even formulate the questions about their condition that would give them the information they needed to make decisions about proposed surgery and treatment. As one after another was diagnosed, the congregation went into denial. No one wanted to believe it was happening. Soon, however, the congregation woke up.

In the next two years, because of community involvement, the women, their families, and the congregation had a crash course in the etiology of cancer and its treatment. The women learned to talk to physicians without being intimidated. They learned how to be patients; their families learned how to maximize their care in the hospital. They and the congregation learned about ways to support health through diet and nutrition, visualization and relaxation techniques, and meditation. All learned about the possibilities for alternative treatments. Some of the women's families worked with a family therapist to resolve issues and tensions so that healing could be enhanced. The community listened to the women as they struggled to make meaning of their cancers. The women asked questions such as "I've been healthy; I've lived reasonably. Why has this happened?" "Is it my fault?" "What's going to happen to my children?" "The treatment doesn't seem to be working. Do I have the right to say no to more treatment?"

The community held healing services. They also organized parties where those who were ill were celebrated. At these parties, friends shared memories—the kinds of things usually reserved for eulogies at memorial services.

Within three years, all five women died. Still the community continued to gather together. They learned about mourning and about being healed from grief. In gratitude, the family of one of the young women established a memorial fund to be used to share what the congregation had learned about caring for those with cancer. This money was used to staff a weekly cancer support group.

Through their involvement with these women, members of the congregation felt that they had been given a gift, and they wanted to continue their involvement as a pastoral counseling ministry for the wider local community. They had learned that *to be healed* did not necessarily mean being *cured* of cancer. Although the women had died, each had become more *whole*. Through their experience, the congregation had learned how to be with and care for those with cancer. They had knowledge to share. Because of their friendships with hospice nurses and physicians, they had a referral network. They let these professionals know that they were forming a new group and invited them to send people to it.

This support group was led by an oncology nurse who had become aware of the congregation through the concern they had shown to her patient, a parish member. She had begun to attend their services and was delighted when the board asked her to lead the support group. She was assisted by members of the congregation, who by now had become knowledgeable about cancer care and could share their knowledge as well as prepare nutritious lunches. Church members also taught relaxation and visualization techniques and led meditation and prayer periods.

In these weekly meetings, group members talked about their fears and concerns. They were able to ask the leader questions about cancer and its treatment and to get coaching—both from the nurse and each other—about coping with the side effects of treatment. They learned about ways to be healthy even with cancer. They learned about the special stress caused by cancer and its treatment and the beneficial role of diet and supplements. They learned visualization techniques to support healing.

Two of the new group members went into remission but stayed in the group to support others. Several members died. The group had helped them prepare for dying as they listened to their concerns and supported them in prayer and meditation. Even though they had cancer themselves, several members visited them in the hospital and comforted them by being quiet, loving presences.

The cancer support group remains a small community within the larger community of the congregation. The original leader has taken a break, but other members are there to step in. While there is no cure for cancer, the group has found that there is a cure for the isolation—and sometimes, stigma—that accompanies cancer. That cure comes through the loving support of knowledgeable friends.

Margaret Kornfeld, D.Min., is a pastoral psychotherapist who practices in New York City, teaches at the Blanton-Peale Graduate Institute and Union Theological Seminary, and is a consultant to pastoral counseling centers and faith communities.

This essay was adapted from her book *Cultivating Wholeness: A Guide to Care and Counseling in Faith Communities* by Margaret Zipse Kornfeld. Copyright © 1998 by Margaret Zipse Kornfeld. Reprinted by permission of the Continuum Publishing Company.

Books

Margaret Kornfeld, *Cultivating Wholeness: A Guide to Care and Counseling in Faith Communities* (Continuum, 1998). Written by a practicing pastoral counselor, this book aims to help congregations become networks of care in which the needs of individual parishioners, the congregation as a whole, and the other communities that interface with them may be met.

Elaine Ramshaw, *Ritual and Pastoral Care* (Fortress Press, 1987). This readable and useful book illustrates how ritual can provide care for the individual, the community, and the world. She shows how communities can develop new life-cycle rites as well as rituals that address needs in special circumstances such as grieving because of divorce, still-birth, or news of terminal illness.

Organizations

American Association of Pastoral Counselors (AAPC)
9504A Lee Highway
Fairfax, VA 22031
(703) 385-6967 (phone)
(703) 352-7725 (fax)
info@aapc.org (e-mail)
www.metanoia.org/aapc/ (website)

The AAPC was founded in 1963 as an organization that certifies pastoral counselors, accredits pastoral counseling centers, and approves pastoral counseling graduate training programs. Its members belong to more than eighty different denominations, including the Protestant, Catholic, and Jewish faiths.

Blanton-Peale Institute
3 West 29th Street
New York, NY 10001
(212) 725-7850 (phone)
(212) 689-3212 (fax)

The institute has been a healing resource to individuals, couples, families, and religious communities for over sixty years. Founded by the Reverend Norman Vincent Peale and Smiley Blanton, M.D., to train clergy to counsel in their congregations, it has expanded its scope and now offers advanced professional train-ing for ministers, rabbis, nuns, priests, and lay and professional caregivers in pas-toral care, psychotherapy, marriage and family therapy, and the spiritual dimen-sion of therapy. It offers counseling and provides services such as educational programs, consultation in conflict resolutions, crisis management, and communal organization. Its Clergy Consultation Service, a nationwide service to clergy of all faiths, assists with personal and professional problems and provides supervision of pastoral care and counseling.

Stephen Ministries
2045 Innerbelt Business Center Drive
St. Louis, MO 63114-5765
(314) 428-2600 (phone)
(314) 428-7888 (fax)

This interdenominational system of training has for many years trained teams of laypersons from congregations to provide effective caring ministry to the hospi-talized, the terminally ill and their families, people who are homebound, in a job crisis, inactive in their congregation, separated or divorced, lonely, and those with disabilities and their families.

SPIRITUAL DIRECTION

Cartoons often depict a wizened and bearded holy man sitting atop a mountain listening to those who have made the arduous pilgrimage seeking his wisdom. Inevitably the guru offers an amazingly simple solution and the last cartoon panel shows the pilgrim, wide-eyed and shocked, unable to believe that he has traveled so far for that obvious answer. We throw our heads back in laughter because we recognize that through the ages people have gone to great lengths to seek out those known to have deep spiritual wisdom. Yet in most cases after long, perilous, and difficult travels, they find that the answer was much closer to home; in fact, within themselves.

In India and other Southeast Asian countries, spiritual teachers who have gained a reputation for being Divinely inspired or gifted attract disciples by teach-ing at centers, known as ashrams, or traveling around the country to teach. Some of these teachers have come to the United States, where they have been eagerly sought out, because American organized religion has not until relatively recently focused on the experiential dimensions of religion.

In the last several years, however, this situation has been changing, and the art of spiritual direction, which had been preserved in the monasteries, has been revived. The model of spiritual direction is quite different from the Eastern teacher-disciple relationship. Spiritual direction is more of a dialogue between equals. Instead of being taught by the spiritual director, the directee is assisted in developing a relationship with God through conversations and suggestions for enhancing spiritual practice.

There is also an increasing focus on spiritual guidance in the search-for-God/spiritual renewal movement in Reform Judaism. Carol Ochs and Rabbi Kerry Olitzky wrote *Jewish Spiritual Guidance: Finding Our Way to God* to bring to light the tradition of Jewish spiritual guidance with the hope that people will not only consider receiving such guidance but perhaps offer to guide others. "Frequently we need the help of someone other than ourselves," they explain, "to understand our own heart's desire."

Thus if you yearn to better understand the workings of God in your life or to build an ongoing relationship with the Divine, you might want to consider the regularly scheduled series of conversations known as spiritual direction or guidance.

Issues That Draw People into Spiritual Direction

Jeffrey Gaines, executive director of Spiritual Directors International, says that people frequently seek a spiritual director because they have had an encounter with God or the holy and want to be able to wrap words around the experience so that they can comprehend and integrate it. Others want to deepen their relationship with God or are curious about the subject and feel engaged by it. Still others feel called to pray; they are looking for a doorway to a deeper inner life that will provide spiritual grounding for their lives.

Although the terms *spiritual director* and *directee* seem to denote determination of a course of action, these words are misleading. A spiritual director is more of a companion, someone with more spiritual experience, who listens as you tell your story and helps you more clearly hear, see, and notice urgings from your soul and the movement of spirit in your life. This process of discernment is the key factor in spiritual direction. It helps you determine whether a problem or experience in your life is a signal from the Divine.

The general arrangement is that you meet with a director for an hour or more on a monthly basis. Usually the director listens quietly and shares his or her own experience when it is relevant. The director should be sensitive to your need for time to reflect in silence or to pray or meditate during the session. Sometimes a director will suggest reading scripture together or recommend other readings or spiritual practices such as visualizations, journal writing, or a retreat. However, it is very important that the director remain sensitive to the movement of the Divine in your life and not seek to impose her or his spiritual journey on you.

How to Choose a Director

In a large urban area, it is sometimes difficult to plug into an informal network to learn where to find those people who have well-earned reputations for helping others discern the movement of the holy in their lives. In such situations it is best to ask someone you trust or admire for a referral or to ask a member of the clergy. You can also call local retreat centers or a spiritual direction training center for a recommendation. You may also call Spiritual Directors International, which, while it does not endorse or recommend any particular director, will give you the name of one of their regional contacts who may know spiritual directors in your locale. (See organization listings at the end of this section.)

Once you find someone, it is advisable to meet for several sessions to determine if the relationship feels right. If it does, you might then agree to meet for a predetermined length of time. If it does not feel right or comfortable, try another director.

According to Lucy Abbott Tucker, who teaches at the Institute for Spiritual Leadership in Chicago, spiritual direction has a long history within the Christian community, tracing its origins back to the Desert "abbas and ammas" (literally translated as daddies and mommies) of the fourth and fifth century. At that time, those desiring a relationship with God would go into the desert for solitude, prayer, and discipline. "The rigors of the desert made spiritual guidance by an elder dweller essential," explains Tucker. Newcomers would receive instruction from the elders about their daily activities, prayer life, and spiritual practices. In some cases, these desert dwellers and the tradition of spiritual guidance they established evolved into monastic communities in which the abbot bore primary responsibility for guiding the souls of the monks under his care.

In the twelfth century, Tucker continues, the religious communities founded by Dominic (Dominicans) and Francis (Franciscans) extended spiritual guidance to laypeople. "This soul care was a kind of spiritual direction intended to calm, console, and advise individuals, helping them grow in a life of prayer," says Tucker. Both men and women, religious and laypeople participated in this form of soul care. From the brilliant mystic Hildegard of Bingen (1098–1179), founder and abbess of a Benedictine monastery as well as composer, herbalist, and writer, to Catherine of Siena (1247–1300), a laywoman and spiritual guide to a circle of friends, women participated in this form of spiritual leadership.

By the fifteenth century, Tucker points out, the confessional had gained popularity as a devotional tool in the Catholic Church. While that development broadened the reach of spiritual guidance, it narrowed the ranks of spiritual directors to male clerical confessors. In time the focus of spiritual direction became limited to confession and vocational advice.

It was not until the Second Vatican Council in the early 1960s that religious education and spiritual development again became a focal point for renewal within the Church. Jesuit-led "directed retreats" were the first to include time for individuals to sit with clergy to talk about their spiritual life. Later the practice became standard operating procedure for most retreatants. From that practice of sitting down and talking about one's spiritual life with someone knowledgeable and experienced in the journey evolved the form of spiritual direction practiced today.

While spiritual direction originated and developed as a Roman Catholic tradition, over the last few years it has spread to other denominations, including Episcopalians, Methodists, and Presbyterians. According to Gaines, there are now 182 spiritual direction training centers in the United States. Some are attached to churches, some to retreat centers, and a few are independent fee-for-service arrangements. Surprisingly, relatively few theological seminaries teach courses in spiritual direction.

One emerging development in the field is group spiritual direction. Rose Mary Dougherty, S.S.N.D., director of spiritual guidance at the Shalem Institute for Spiritual Formation in Bethesda, Maryland, believes that there are three essential conditions necessary for group spiritual direction. Members must agree to commit themselves to an honest relationship with God, to participate wholeheartedly in the group process through prayerful listening and response, and to open their spiritual journey to others. She sees these as necessary conditions because the depth of sharing necessary in group spiritual direction demands a level of trust not often found in other types of groups. According to Dougherty, one main ingredient draws people into a spiritual direction group: having been touched by God's desire to love them, they now want their desire for God to become the determining factor in their life choices, and they recognize that they need help to do this. For this reason she believes that the group's primary task is to make this shared desire explicit and hold one another in it.

Of course a process is needed to help people do what they have come to do. First she recommends that the group consist of no less than three and no more than five members. Second, she suggests that different faith perspectives be included because such diversity tends to enrich the collective wisdom. Third, there should be time for the participants to become acquainted with one another and familiar with each other's faith language before actually beginning the group direction. Fourth, groups might consider the benefits of having an outside facilitator in the beginning. Fifth, once the group decides to meet, it should agree to meet for two and a half hours at four- or five-week intervals for a period of one year. Once that point is reached, the group needs to decide if it seems right to continue. The format Dougherty recommends is to begin with twenty minutes of silence. Someone then shares for ten to fifteen minutes followed by three to four minutes of silence. This is followed by group member responses for about ten minutes, and then another five minutes is devoted to praying for the person who has just spoken. This sequence of sharing-silence-response-silence is repeated (with a short break midway) until all members have shared. The group ends with ten minutes of shared reflection on the whole time together, and finally the group prays for any member who could not be present; members are also asked to pray for one another between group meetings.

How Spiritual Direction Differs from Psychotherapy

The practice of spiritual direction has traditionally been understood as a gift or vocation, a calling as opposed to an acquired skill or profession. That perspective is one reason why many spiritual directors do not charge for sessions and do not make it a career. It is seen as a service to be offered.

The other characteristic that distinguishes spiritual direction from psychotherapy is the type of relationship each supports. In general, a therapist focuses on the client's relationship with him- or herself or the client's relationships with significant others. But transference, the concept that the client replicates a primary relationship in therapy, projecting qualities of that person onto the therapist, is observed and worked on in the client-therapist relationship. A spiritual director, on the other hand, acts as a midwife through which a client's relationship to the Divine is birthed. If psychotherapy aims to develop psychological integrity and a healthy adaptation to life, then spiritual direction's aim is to assist in the search for a healthy relationship with the sacred.

Some spiritual directors have been influenced by Jung's depth psychology and use psychological techniques such as active imagination, guided visualization, active listening, focusing, dream work, art work, and movement during sessions. Still, these tools are employed as aids to noticing the action of the spirit in the directee's life. Most spiritual directors will recommend psychotherapy if and when it seems appropriate.

🏵 Varieties of Spiritual Companionship 🏵
By Gerald May

Spiritual direction's recent rise in popularity has been accompanied by a corresponding increase in confusion. Most people would agree that spiritual direction means companionship with another person or group through which the Holy One shines with wisdom, encouragement, and discernment. Some, however, expect this companionship to be of a professional nature, with a trained, supervised, and perhaps even certified spiritual director. At the other extreme are those who see it as a spontaneous and gifted calling, and strongly resist any signs of professionalization.

In truth, spiritual guidance can happen authentically in a vast variety of forms. To give a sense of the range of these possibilities, I list some examples below. The list is neither exclusive nor exhaustive; some forms of guidance might combine aspects of more than one category, and I may have neglected to mention other forms. Further, while I describe them as one-to-one relationships, most of the examples can also be applied to groups. I have divided them into two major groups: Formal Spiritual Direction and Informal Spiritual Companionship.

Formal Spiritual Direction

These relationships are explicitly defined as spiritual direction, with a clear separation of roles between director and directee. Meetings are usually scheduled in advance on a regular basis, and a directee normally has only one formal director.

Professional ("expert") spiritual direction is in large part patterned after contemporary psychotherapeutic models. It is a highly structured relationship in which the director is seen as providing a professional service to the directee. The focus of meetings is firmly on the directee, and the director seeks to remain caring but unattached. Mutuality and relationships outside of direction are discouraged. The director is viewed as an expert: skilled, trained, and experienced. Directors are usually supervised and may be certified. Fees for service are common. The "locus of discernment" (where discernment happens) varies according to the director's style; as in counseling, some directors make assertive discernments for their directees, while others are more nondirective, helping directees come to their own discernments.

Gifted ("charismatic") spiritual direction is also a formal relationship in that meetings are held regularly and the focus is primarily on the directee. The director, however, is seen more as gifted and called than skilled and trained. Many such directors claim no expertise, do not consider themselves professionals, and place their primary emphasis on remaining attentive to the Holy Spirit as the true Director. This kind of direction is not usually seen as a service, but as God's gift to the director as well as the directee. Fees are therefore not normally charged. Mutuality and extra-direction relationships occur more readily than in professional direction. Here again the locus of discernment varies, but is more commonly placed in the directee.

Master/disciple relationships are a special kind of charismatic direction in which the director is seen as a uniquely transparent window of the Divine. As in the Desert tradition of Christianity and in many Hindu and Buddhist paths, the locus of discernment generally resides in the master. Mutuality is not generally acknowledged. It is a formal relationship in terms of the identification of roles, but meetings are seldom regularly scheduled. Offerings are common, fees virtually nonexistent.

Institutional direction. In some religious communities, a representative of the community assumes an official role as spiritual director and may exercise institutional authority over the directee. Mutuality is uncommon in such relationships, and the locus of discernment is usually assumed to be in the director.

Mentoring, disciplining, and eldering are identified formal relationships that usually focus on moral and educational guidance within a particular faith community. They can, however, include dimensions of spiritual direction.

Informal Companionships

These relationships are characterized by a lack of structure and role definition. They are not considered exclusive, and most people have several such companionships. Meetings tend to be irregular and spontaneous. There is nearly always some atmosphere of mutuality, and each person retains his or her own locus of discernment. There is no notion of providing a service, and fees are out of the question.

Wisdom sharing. My maternal grandmother was a wisdom figure in our extended family. People seemed naturally drawn to her, presumably because of her prayer, love, and insight, but this was not identified or discussed openly. People listened carefully to her words but always felt free to express their own opinions and make their own decisions. They also felt a desire to support her, often visiting simply to pay their respects.

Spiritual friendship. Most people have friends with whom it feels natural to discuss their life with God. They communicate as friends do, according to their desire and as time and circumstance allow. Some of these friendships may be lifelong, others very transient. All, however, are recognized as opportunities for mutual support and discernment.

Soul mates. Here a deep inner connectedness is mutually recognized between people, and their interactions are of profound spiritual significance for both. Their prayer and life experience blend powerfully, and it is common for such relationships to include deep love that lasts a lifetime.

Occasional encounters. These are chance meetings, in spiritual settings or elsewhere, in which some kind of spiritual guidance happens for one or both parties. Although it is certainly possible for these to grow into ongoing friendships, they are usually one-time events.

It seems to me that professional standards are appropriate for directors who see themselves as providing an expert service, especially if they charge fees. Those who practice spiritual direction in this way would rightly avail themselves of specialized training programs, formal supervision, perhaps even certification. Ethical standards of conduct are decidedly important here, especially in relationships where the director assumes responsibility for making discernments for the directee.

In contrast, people who are called to more gifted or informal companionships, especially those who believe the locus of discernment should remain in the directee, may feel uneasy if they attempt to fit themselves into a professional model. Enrichment programs that foster a simple, contemplative availability to God are likely to suit them better than training programs that focus on skills and methods. Shared support and prayerful accountability may make more sense than formal "clinical" supervision. Communal confirmation and affirmation would take the place of certification for such spiritual guides, and mutual reverent respect rather than standards of practice would form their basis of ethical conduct.

Though this listing may be misleadingly arbitrary, I hope it will be helpful in clarifying your own sense of authenticity as a spiritual companion.

Gerald G. May, M.D., is Director of Research at the Shalem Institute of Spiritual Formation in Bethesda, Maryland, and author of numerous books, including *Addiction and Grace* and *Care of Mind, Care of Spirit*.

This article was reprinted from the *Shalem News*, Winter 1998, by permission of the Shalem Institute for Spiritual Formation, 5430 Grosvenor Lane, Bethesda, MD 20814.

Books

William A. Barry and William J. Connolly, *The Practice of Spiritual Direction* (HarperSanFrancisco, 1995). A classic introduction to the art of spiritual direction that contains all the essential elements of this relationship.

Rose Mary Dougherty, *Group Spiritual Direction: Community for Discernment* (Paulist Press, 1995). A resource for people wishing to explore the possibilities of spiritual community within the context of group spiritual direction. The author provides detailed information for establishing spiritual direction groups and practical suggestions for fostering a contemplative stance in groups for spiritual direction.

Tilden Edwards, *Spiritual Friend* (Paulist Press, 1980). In addition to presenting a history of spiritual direction, the author covers practical aspects, including a chapter on group spiritual direction and a discussion of the differences among psychotherapy, pastoral counseling, and spiritual direction.

Kathleen Fischer, *Women at the Well* (Paulist Press, 1988). In this book the author uses a feminist lens through which to explore spiritual direction.

Margaret Guenther, *Holy Listening* (Cowley Publications, 1992). Using the image of hospitality, the author offers a very feminine and poetic approach to spiritual direction.

Thomas Kelly, *Testament of Devotion* (HarperSanFrancisco, 1941, 1996). This book has become a devotional classic for those who wish to center their lives on God's presence. In plain spoken language, the author offers five essays, which invite readers to "an internal simplification of the whole of one's personality" so that one can hear the voice of the "Eternal Now" in every aspect of life, thus bringing together personal devotion and social consciousness.

Kenneth Leech, *Soul Friends* (Harper & Row, 1977). The author traces the history of spiritual direction since the beginning of Christianity and advocates for sharing your life journey with another person.

Gerald May, *Care of Mind, Care of Spirit* (HarperSanFrancisco, 1992). An excellent resource for spiritual directors as well as therapists. In it the author distinguishes among the roles of therapist, pastoral counselor, and spiritual director, giving each its due.

Carol Ochs and Rabbi Kerry M. Olitzky, *Jewish Spiritual Guidance: Finding Our Way to God* (Jossey-Bass, Inc., Publishers, 1997). Written by two leaders in the search-for-God/spiritual renewal movement, this book describes aspects of spiritual guidance, a neglected element of the Jewish tradition.

Organizations

Institute for Spiritual Leadership (ISL)
P.O. Box 53147
Chicago, IL 60653-0147
(773) 752-5962 (phone)
(773) 752-5964 (fax)
ISLUSA@aol.com (e-mail)

The institute, founded in 1974, recognizes that forming competent, compassionate spiritual leaders involves both personal transformation and professional development. ISL annually offers an intensive program focusing on personal spiritual growth and companioning skills.

Shalem Institute for Spiritual Formation
5430 Grosvenor Lane
Bethesda, MD 20814
(301) 897-7334 (phone)

(301) 897-3719 (fax)
info@Shalem.org (e-mail)
www.Shalem.org (website)

Founded in 1978, Shalem is an ecumenical center that offers a variety of resources for contemplative living, including group spiritual direction. In addition, it offers programs for leaders of spiritual formation groups and a two-year program for spiritual directors.

Spiritual Directors International (SDI)
1329 Seventh Avenue
San Francisco, CA 94122
(415) 566-1560 (phone)
(415) 566-1277 (fax)
info@sdiworld.org (e-mail)
www.sdiworld.org (website)

SDI is an ecumenical association whose purpose is to serve the growing network of spiritual directors and those people who train them. The network offers regional networking opportunities, an annual symposium for trainers, and a conference for directors. It also acts as a clearinghouse by connecting individuals with directors in their locale.

Periodicals

Presence
Spiritual Directors International
1329 Seventh Avenue
San Francisco, CA 94122-2507
(415) 566-1560 (phone)
(415) 566-1277 (fax)
Kesecker-Dotson@sdiworld.org (e-mail)
www.sdiworld.org (website)
3 times a year; $19.95

Grounded in the Christian faith and the belief that God's active presence is revealed in human experience, this journal invites dialogue within the Christian community and with other spiritual traditions. *Presence* provides a forum for the exploration of present and future trends in spiritual direction, both as an art and as a profession.

Weavings
Upper Room

P.O. Box 189
1908 Grand Avenue
Nashville, TN 37202-0189
(615) 340-7254 (phone)
(615) 340-7006 (fax)
Weavings@upperoom.org (e-mail)
www.upperroom.org (website)
Bimonthly; $24

This journal has a Protestant flavor and often covers topics relevant to spiritual direction. Its essays are sensitively and eloquently written.

The best way of viewing the relationship between psychotherapy and spiritual practice is to see them as allies. Both meet inner needs in ways that are quite complementary. In this last section we present three different spiritual voices: Buddhist meditation teacher Jack Kornfield, Sufi leader Pir Vilayat Inayat Khan, and medical intuitive Caroline Myss. Kornfield and Khan compare and contrast aspects of psychotherapy and spirituality. Myss talks about the dark night of the soul, one aspect of the inner journey that can't be helped by psychotherapy. Although not clinical depression, it is sometimes mistaken for it. The dark night is soul territory where you acutely experience the absence of God.

❀ In Conversation with Jack Kornfield: ❀
The Promises and Perils of Integrating Psychotherapy and Spiritual Practices

I don't like to make a distinction between what is spiritual and what is psychological because I believe it's a false distinction. It's one of the many compartments by which we create delusion and pain in our culture. I would like to change the language and not speak about psychological and spiritual but rather about what's *personal* and what's *universal* because both are dimensions of spiritual life.

In teaching meditation, what I learned from Western clinical psychology has helped enormously. Half of the people in any group of one or two hundred that come to a meditation retreat are grieving, suffering from the trauma of abuse, or dealing with divorce, codependence, or conflict in their lives. Western psychology describes these problems and provides tools with which one can deal with them. The Buddhist principles and guidelines—to be compassionate and forgiving—are good, but how one can understand and apply these principles to one's own grief and pain has been the work of the best of Western psychology for many years.

Likewise, meditation has influenced my psychotherapy work. The root of the counseling I do—and of the meditation too—is to have people experience a shift of identity. Instead of being identified with their wounds, they become able to sense a much greater reality, you could call it their Buddha nature, their true nature. So a key in both meditation and counseling is to understand that our consciousness is much greater than what we normally take it to be.

In meditation, one learns to hold all of life with compassion and understanding, even in the face of death. In counseling, it's the same. We look at what we take to be our identity and discover something greater. Now many people have tried to do that by skipping over what's personal. That doesn't work. Many who come to me for therapy or counseling also have spiritual practices. A number of them have entered spiritual life in a very committed way—spent years in an ashram, temple, or monastery—and have in their background an alcoholic family or a history of being abused. Often they do not know that's what they have to heal. They think that they are working solely in a spiritual realm.

Many things are so painful, frightening, or difficult that they are rarely able to be healed, opened to, or released in meditation alone. Instead, meditation can be used to bypass them, which is easy when you concentrate on meditation because the nature of a focused mind is to move you away from conflict. It does this automatically. But the conflict rearises when the meditative state subsides. This is where psychotherapy can help. When people touch the places that are their most secret fears and most hidden feelings of unworthiness, they often need someone else to hold their hand. They need the consciousness of another heart to hold those places with them so that they can see, "Yes, this too can be held in compassion; yes, this too is not really who I am."

I've wanted in my teaching over the years to redefine spiritual practice from the way it was initially presented in America. I want people to understand that while spiritual practice can offer a profound awakening of every dimension of life, it doesn't happen automatically and you can't skip steps.

Rather than try to avoid personal conflict or pain, I work with it and say this is part of that limited identity that needs to be healed, to be faced with compassion, to be expressed, to be given voice, to be held with an understanding heart. Great pain, when it is honored from the heart, opens into great understanding.

I've sent people away from meditation retreats if I felt they were using meditation practices to reinforce their defenses. With people who have a great deal of emotional trauma, there are certain meditations that can help and certain ones that are not helpful at all. For example, a woman came to me in my capacity as a meditation teacher. She said that she was feeling the selflessness of the world, which is a Buddhist term that refers to the emptiness of self. As I talked to her, she seemed disheveled and depressed. I asked her to show me her walking meditation and to describe what her experience was. As she did, we discovered together that what she was experiencing wasn't emptiness, it was deadness. She had been practicing meditation for three or four years with a teacher but was depressed when she started. She had been meditating, feeling her deadness, and saying, "Oh, this is emptiness." She was empty, but empty of any well-being. So I told her to stop meditating and to work with a counselor who could help her look at her issues around food addiction. It made a huge difference; she came back to life. The meditation she was doing was the wrong medicine.

Other times people will come who have done many years of psychotherapy and say, "I've told my story, I know about my parents." I'll say, "It is time for you to do a retreat. Do a month." If they do a month of loving-kindness meditation and deep insight practice, they'll dissolve the whole small sense of their life and open to wonderful dimensions of the spirit. They'll go back home, their life informed in ways that could never happen just through exploring the story of their childhood.

The principle in both psychotherapy and meditation is to be present with what is—to be present with the heart, the mind, and the body together, and not make compartments. When therapy is most beneficial, it is like a joint meditation. In fact, the best of modern therapy is much like a process of shared meditation, where therapist and client sit together learning to pay close attention to those aspects and dimensions of the self that the client may be unable to touch on his or her own.

> Jack Kornfield, Ph.D., has played a seminal role in bringing, rooting, and cultivating Buddhism in America. He cofounded the Insight Meditation Society in Barre, Massachusetts, and ten years later he helped to establish Insight Meditation West, the Spirit Rock Center in Woodacre, California. He has authored and coauthored a half-dozen books on Buddhist topics and conducts meditation retreats across the country.

> This essay was adapted from an interview with Jack Kornfield that ran in *Common Boundary* magazine.

Books on Buddhism and Psychotherapy

Mark Epstein, *Going to Pieces Without Falling Apart: A Buddhist Perspective on Wholeness* (Broadway Books, 1998). The author challenges the Western notion that happiness comes from building up the self-image and makes a case that happiness really comes from learning how to surrender, as in falling in love, opening to the creative gesture, or letting go into the moment. He believes that both therapy and meditation can teach us how to let go.

Paul R. Fleishman, *The Healing Spirit: Explorations in Religion and Psychotherapy* (Paragon House, 1989, 1990). This book compares psychological and spiritual needs and presents case histories of clients that demonstrate how certain core human needs are met psychotherapeutically and spiritually. Although the author is a psychiatrist who practices Buddhism, the book adopts an interfaith perspective.

Jack Kornfield, *A Path with Heart: A Guide Through the Perils and Promises of Spiritual Life* (Bantam Books, 1993). A comprehensive and compassionate overview and instruction manual for the spiritual seeker. Kornfield considers the interconnections between physical disciplines, psychotherapeutic techniques, and meditative practice, the distinctions between codependence and true generosity and compassion, and the necessary pains and betrayals of life in spiritual community.

Jeffery Rubin, *Psychotherapy and Buddhism: Towards an Integration* (Plenum Publishing, 1996). The author argues that Buddhist meditation practices can sometimes "transcend" certain negative experiences so that they remain submerged and not integrated. He also maintains that Buddhist meditation provides a needed corrective to psychotherapy's tendency to foster a self-centered view of self, relationships, and morality.

❁ In Conversation with Pir Vilayat ❁ Inayat Khan: Nitty-Gritty Spirituality

Many psychotherapists are in search of a further dimension, one that might be called spiritual, something beyond. Let's say transpersonal. Spiritualists, on the other hand, need to be much more aware of human problems. I know that many psychotherapists accuse spiritualists of what they call a *spiritual bypass*, which means that spirituality can be used to keep you high, keep you from dealing with human problems. Of course, one must be aware that there is also something called a *psychological bypass*. I find, for example, that therapists try to heal the wounds in the psyche of people who have undergone trauma: people who have been abused or rejected or have developed resentment, despondency, or guilt. The curious thing is that the people who imagine that they have been damaged—because it is really in the mind—will use these past experiences as an excuse for not becoming what they could become. On the one hand, they want to be cured; on the other, they don't. By "curing" them, you take away their excuse. They like their lives to develop into what, in England, one calls "tempests in their teacups."

When people overly focus on these "tempests," they fail to participate in the cosmic celebration. I can talk from personal experience because as a young man I had a terrible trauma. I was involved in a motorcycle accident with my fiancée, and she was killed. There was a defect in the machine; the stand jammed against the back wheel. It was not a collision or anything like that, but she fell on the road and suffered brain damage. There was no way of predicting that this could happen, and it was very difficult to understand how God could wish it to happen. I was totally broken.

I cured myself by playing the entire Bach Mass every evening and was totally cured after three months. Now I am not sure that this would cure everybody the way it cured me, but I attributed it to the fact that the glorification of the music put my personal problems in the shade, so to speak. That is why I say that when we get caught up in "tempests in our teacups," we fail to participate in the cosmic celebration.

For a long time I used to think that one should be able to transform suffering into joy. Now, I believe that joy is in discovering that it is OK to suffer. One can be happy at the same time one is suffering! It's OK for there to be a wound. It's part of being human, to have little bits and pieces that are cracked. I play the cello. Some of the eighteenth-century cellos are very badly cracked, but they play more beautifully than the perfectly made modern ones. It's perfectly appropriate to entertain a wound as long as you don't get caught up in that little bit of suffering, and as long as you are able to exult in joy and glorification.

People suffer because they haven't turned out the way they wanted themselves to turn out. People's greatest disappointment is not becoming what they would have liked to become. At one of her seminars many years ago, Dr. Elizabeth Kübler-Ross said that when people are about to die, there are two things that they regret most: the first is not having achieved what they wanted to achieve; the second is not having become what they would have liked to become, what they feel they could have been.

What I am doing is helping people unfold their personality as well as work toward a state of *samadhi*. We start with *samadhi* because by so doing, one is freed from one's self-image. We follow the alchemical process outlined by Jung in the book called *Psychology and Alchemy* in which one goes through two phases. The first is to dissolve, to break down; the other, to coagulate, to rebuild. In the first half of my retreats and seminars, I try to break down assumptions. We go through a dark night of the soul. The late R. D. Laing, an English psychiatrist, spoke about the breakdown that becomes a breakthrough. That is how one progresses in life: by going through crises, overcoming them, and going through other crises. Of course, a psychotherapist needs to know how to carry a person through crises so that the breakdown becomes a breakthrough. In a retreat, we start people questioning their self-image and questioning their assessment of their problems. Personal assessment of problems is not reliable. In fact, people spend more time trying to sort out their concepts of their problems than tackling them. Categories and concepts are static in comparison to a dynamic flow of thinking. A lot of psychotherapists understand that. Eugene Gendlin, author of the books *Focusing* and *Let Your Body Interpret Your Dreams*, for example, asks people to get in touch with their feelings rather than their thoughts and concepts about a problem. Dr. Kübler-Ross, too. She says, "I'm not interested in what you think about your problem, I want to feel what you feel about the problem."

People are convinced that they are only what they think they are. There is no way of changing a person if they only identify themselves with their self-image. Changing self-image requires a kind of jolt. Once you realize that your self-image is the product of your imagination, all of a sudden something clicks. You lose your hold on your self-image. Of course, you have to replace that self-image with a more realistic one, as Jung said, by shifting to the center of one's being. This consists of working with qualities that are already present within. Just as every cell of the body has within it the code of the whole body and, in fact, the entire universe but displays only a very small fraction of what is present within it, our personality carries within it a divine inheritance. But we manifest very little of this bounty because we limit ourselves by believing in who we *think* we are. Instead of saying, "I'd like to have more power or more mastery or more insight," one needs to say, "I am beginning to discover the mastery that is present within me and that I have not been using because I didn't believe in it."

It is terribly constraining to think that you are born a certain way and limited by the way you were born. It's very exciting to realize that there is nothing that one cannot become if one so wishes. In this connection, I like to quote the Tibetans, who feel very strongly about this and who meditate on deities. These deities represent certain aspects of Divine qualities. We Sufis do the same thing, but instead of meditating on deities, we meditate on masters. We imagine a master like Abraham or Melchizedek, like Jesus, Shiva, or Buddha.

The first stage is imagining what it would be like to be Abraham. In doing so, you discover qualities about yourself that you never thought you possessed. However, this is only half of the process. If imagining a master were all of it, one would just model oneself on a master, and that is exactly what we deplore in some of the charismatic groups—that people limit themselves by aping the guru. The second step I am suggesting is where you project forward how you would be if *you* became who you could be.

For example, I consider meditation a kind of rehearsal. If you are not being completely truthful with someone, then you can rehearse in meditation. You can work on that part of you that is truthful. Instead of working on truth vaguely, you imagine meeting this person. In your rehearsal you say, "I am going to have the courage to tell this person something. It is absolutely devastating; it will undermine me. Perhaps I'll be fired, but I will do it." From the moment that one resolves to do something, a kind of power begins to come through. One feels an ecstasy. There is no use working with these qualities unless you are serious about them and translate them into the nitty-gritty details.

Other areas that we deal with that are relevant to psychotherapy are guilt, resentment, and poor self-image. All three are linked, of course. With guilt, you first need to admit it to yourself—that is, if there is guilt. You have to be careful not to accuse yourself of something that you are not responsible for—this is indulging a guilt complex. On the other hand, one has to be very careful about using justifications as cover-ups for whatever you did. Now having admitted your guilt, there is the problem of what to do about it. I advise people to get into the consciousness of the victimized person. There is a technique that we use in meditation that allows you to get into the consciousness of other people in order to discover what it is like to be another person. After that, I suggest doing whatever you can do to repair the harm. Sometimes, there is no way that you can, totally. In other circumstances, you can.

Then comes the issue of how to forgive yourself. To stay aware, you must forgive yourself. If forgiving yourself is more than you can do now, look to God. But once you ask for Divine grace and you still wallow in guilt, then you are not graciously accepting Divine grace. You're showing a lack of gratitude. Mind you, it is preposterous to have harmed someone and then ask to be let off the hook. This is not taking responsibility.

Now thinking in terms of a higher self and a lower self is thinking simplistically. I try to avoid that. The simplistic response would be to say, "Well, the shadow part of my being is what I inherited from my ancestors. I had an irate grandfather, so I have a bad temper. But my *real* being is sublime." My father, Hazrat Inayat Khan, spoke about the Divine perfection in each being that suffers from human limitation. You identify with the Divine in you but you are also aware of the limitations to that perfection. Another description that I find very, very meaningful talks about the aristocracy of the soul and the democracy of the ego— the greatest pride existing with the greatest humility at the same time. Instead of inflating into megalomania or deflating into an inferiority complex, one needs to reconcile the irreconcilable, which is a great thing.

Now we also work very intensely with resentment—I find it is the scourge of humanity. I often say to people, just imagine Christ knocking at your door today. And what does he say? He says, "I beg you, overcome your resentment of people. You're afraid of war. Do you know that wars stem from the collective revenge of the people?" You might think to yourself, "What does he mean? Does he mean I should invite the person who has ruined my life for a cup of tea?" Yes, that is what it means. When I say this to people, some say they feel like that's going too far; they can't do it. Yet it's the message of Christ. If you don't, you remain the way you are. If you want to change, that is the way to go about it. I am not saying forgive a person. I am saying get into the consciousness of the person who harmed you. See where the action came from, because resentment is looking at things from one point of view only. It doesn't mean condoning the person that did you harm. But you need to get into the consciousness of the person whose need became a compulsion and who could not control their action.

Kübler-Ross once visited a prison where she asked to see the worst of the prisoners—one of these really tough guys. It was one of the worst penitentiaries, where the inmates were just brutes. She asked to see the worst of them. He had killed—I don't know—eleven people. Now if she had been a priest, she would have said, "You have to repent, you're a sinner." And that would have just made him angry; it wouldn't have accomplished anything. People don't like to be called sinners. What she said was, "Tell me something about your childhood." He said that he had been brought up by a stepfather who had beaten him, put vinegar on his wounds and spit at him, locked him in his room for three days at a time without food, and then one day threw him out of the house. He took up with some robbers and then a gang who perpetrated armed robberies. Then she said, "Is that why you kill people? Because you wanted to rob them?" "Yes," he said, "why otherwise?" "Are you sure?" she asked. "Well," he said, "as a matter of fact, I hate people." "Now tell me," Dr. Ross said, "do you know something about your stepfather's childhood?" "Yes. My stepfather was brought up by his stepfather, who beat him and did the very same things." So she said, "Can you see that the reason why you're shooting people is not because you want to rob them but because you're taking out your hatred of your stepfather on them? And the reason why your stepfather was the way he was is because of his hatred for *his* stepfather? Do you see that?"

Well, the man broke down. You know, when a very obnoxious person breaks down, he becomes very lovable. It takes Dr. Kübler-Ross to do that, you see. And that's what psychology is doing. In traditional spirituality, you've got to repent. But instead of telling someone to forgive, you need to get into the consciousness of the person who has done you harm and understand how the act took place. Then you can love them; you can't hate them anymore. It's not forgiving; it's understanding, it's loving. Forgiving seems to be such a smug kind of thing. The key is having room in your heart for people who are destroying you. And if there is any meaning in spirituality, that for me is it.

Pir Vilayat Inayat Khan is an eighty-two-year-old meditation teacher, workshop and retreat leader, and head of the Sufi Order International. Pir (which means teacher) Vilayat has carried forward the spiritual legacy inherited from his father, Hazrat Inayat Khan, who initiated his eldest son and appointed him his successor in 1926 when Vilayat was just ten.

This essay was adapted from an interview with Pir Vilayat Inayat Khan that ran in *Common Boundary* magazine.

❀ In Conversation with Caroline Myss: ❀ Will Power and Dark Night of the Soul

We all have three levels of consciousness: Arian, Piscean, and Aquarian. Each represents a different level of perception. One is external (Arian/sensory); one is internal (Piscean/ psyche); and one is transcendent or archetypal (Aquarian).

The Arian level is represented by the five senses. Therefore decision-making in this system is based only on what you can see, hear, and touch. Additionally, the Arian mindset is very tribal; it's a "we're-all-in-this-together" mentality. Therefore there's more latitude in avoiding responsibility by saying, "Look, I didn't do this; this is the way my tribe taught me." In the Arian system, individuals don't have a self, instead there is a group soul. At this level, God is seen as both a loving and a vengeful force. When you are rewarded with pleasure and prosperity, the tribal mind says, "God is blessing me." When you lose that, the tribal mind says, "God is punishing me."

And Jesus comes along and says, "This is nonsense. Let me show you what God is really like." Calling God "Abba," which is interpreted as "Daddy," not "Father," he describes a very intimate relationship with God, who is not punishing but loving and approachable.

But just as Jesus provided a map to manage our emotional system, the Buddha offered one to manage our mental system. The Buddha told us to challenge the way our five-sensory mind perceives things. "Life is illusion," he said. What appears before you is an illusion not because your five senses cannot perceive it but because your five senses cannot access the entire spectrum of reality in order to understand what is going on. From this point of view, you have to detach from what you see and from becoming part of the ongoing manufacture of this illusion.

When Jesus said, "Father, forgive for they know not what they do," he was referring to the fact that nobody understands God's design. For example, say you are fired from a job. Your five senses say, "This is awful. How am I going to pay the bills? How am I going eat? How am I going to maintain my house?" You go into a panic/survival mode. But two years later the most spectacular offer comes to you. What if during that two-year period you take the position that your job wasn't the right thing for you, and you let it go. The next thing that happens is inevitably that another door opens, and that door will be something that your five senses could not have foreseen.

The teachings of Jesus and the Buddha are Piscean. They take us into our internal world to discover the power and virtue of our internal resources. This is the process of individuation, the process of becoming a self. You have to manage your own heart and forgive. If your tribe doesn't forgive, you are not off the hook.

At this level, you begin to experience the anguish in your own soul. It is much easier to experience tribal anguish because you can sit around and support each other. But if you find yourself attached to something—a personal memory or grief pattern—you are on your own because nobody else has that memory. You have to develop some inner mechanism for handling it. So a whole new inner dimension has to be developed within the person. Whereas the five-sensory world is the world in front of our eyes, the Piscean world is the world behind our eyes, the one in which we have the ability to recognize that we are interpreting and shaping events to suit ourselves.

To mature at this level of consciousness, we have to redefine how we understand will power. Under tribal law, will power is the ability to control others and to amass goodies that give you control and authority. Wealth gives you control and authority; so does power. In the Piscean level, we investigate what our heart wants and when we discover what that is we move toward it. But the Arian side says, "How are you going to support yourself?" Jesus says, "Look, get your heart, soul, mind, and consciousness moving in this direction and my Father will provide. Everything will be taken care of." But we still cling to the illusion that we can physically provide for ourselves. We think our will is to be used to manipulate other people on behalf of our physical security. We need to see that everyone who defines and experiences the world through will power fails again and again.

Genuine power does not lie in our capacity to control someone else but in our capacity to control ourselves. Controlling one's addictions through the Twelve-Step and other recovery programs represents what I am talking about: the tools that show you that control comes from within. Your tribe cannot stop your drinking, this is your responsibility; *you* have to do it. But in order to do it, you have to develop an internal system in which you realize that there's got to be something more than internal will power. We are involved in an evolutionary process that ultimately leads us to recognize that there is no other enlightened choice but to release our will to the Divine flow of God's intelligence and compassion. No matter what we choose, it doesn't work out the way we want. If it does, it's because of the X factor; the thing that makes it work out in the right way is something that happened that we don't see coming.

Will power is an illusion. But we have to deal with it in stages. First you have tribal will, in which the choices are made by a group; no one has individual responsibility. Then you evolve to the point where you start recognizing the "I." You start taking responsibility for the choices you have made. You have to learn to manage your emotions and your responses to people. That inevitably leads you to recognize, "Actually, I don't have will in the way I thought I did. My will is only in my ability to release my will; that's the highest choice I can make."

The dark night is a process that leads to a more intimate, deeper spiritual relationship. It is as if you are being called to God. It is not depression. Depression can be caused chemically or because of circumstances—because you've lost a job, because you feel alone, because you feel abandoned. It's an entirely different level of suffering. In a depression, there are things you can do. You can go into treatment. You can't do that in a dark night. Heaven calls the shots. The dark night is genuine soul territory. Those going through it recognize that what they are experiencing is the absence of God. You cannot "move through" it, you can only *endure* it. There's a huge difference. There are, of course, spiritual practices such as prayer that can help you to endure. You can turn to very intense journal keeping. And those experiencing a dark night would benefit enormously from a spiritual director—someone to go to once a week or once a month, someone who asks you, "How have you known God this month? What have you experienced? Let's talk about prayer." But spiritual direction is not aimed at ending the dark night; it's to get everything you can out of it. You can't be moved through a dark night; it ends when God says so.

We have to go back to the classical understanding of the dark night and we've got to stop using the term so loosely as to suggest that a dark night is merely a bad day in earth school because a romance fell apart. That's not when a dark night strikes. A dark night generally hits a person when they are experiencing the best time in their life because that's when paradox is established: I have everything I need. I have money, I have a family, I have status, and I have a job. I'm feeling that I'm finally safe and secure and then it hits. God says, "Oh you think you're safe? Come over to me." What happens is that a person shifts from being externally oriented to being internally oriented. You have so much, but although you thought all of it would make you happy, you can't relate to any of it. You start asking, "What is the meaning of life?" It starts out from the position of "I have all of this, but I don't feel filled or fulfilled."

Now granted, there are other ways that lead a person to God. Trauma does, the loss of a job does, but it's not the same path as the dark night. The difference is that one is based on an occurrence, something that happened to you; the other is the perception that there's nothing meaningful in your life. If I'm depressed and suddenly someone says, "Look, here is the romance of your life; here's the most perfect job," my lights will go on. But if you tell that to someone in a dark night, they will just look at you. They know that no matter what jewel you offer them, it's not going to help.

You could have a very deep connection to God and all of a sudden it's not enough. Suddenly it feels empty. The dark night can be brought about even though you have deep faith in God. You simply feel this absence and ask, "Where did God go in my life? How come I can't feel God anymore? I have no sense of Presence." There are two levels here. There is the spiritual path that is based on asking God for support in order to get through life. But some people go further in their journey. Thomas Merton is a perfect example. One might get the impression that everyone who enters a monastery is at the same level spiritually, that they come to know God in the same way. That's an illusion. The fact is that Merton was a mystic; the rest weren't. He's the one who goes through the dark night. The others go into a depression every now and again.

Look at the Buddha. He sat under the bodhi tree for years. That was his dark night. You don't get where you're going without your spirit being pulled completely into your soul so there's no distinction anymore. That's what the dark night does. It turns the lights off on everything external so you have no place to go for contentment or support but inside. The lights are even dark on the inside. You feel spiritually abandoned; you have no alternative but to pray.

I've been there. I know what it's like to say, "I don't have a damn bit of faith in you and yet I am praying to you to get me out of this." Both are true simultaneously. What kept me going was anger. I was so angry at God's choreography of my life that I could barely contain myself. This anger lasted about twelve to fifteen years. It was not a weekend experience; a seminar could not get me out of it. I knew it was a dark night; I knew that from within. In some way God's grace was present, giving me a sense that this period would end if only I could endure it.

I felt as if there was a kind of Divine sedative at work. Every now and again, I would have a day that would feel incredibly sweet. It was like the gods let me come up for air. Sometimes it would last two days, sometimes a week, but no longer than that, and down I would go again. Those brief experiences gave me peace and the will to keep going.

Let's take away the glamour of the dark night. I am not through with knowing God. Am I enlightened? No. Are my difficult days with God over? No! Let's make sure that this experience is not seen as nirvana because it is not. But having gone through it, I have a more mature sense of the presence of divine compassion and a deep, deep knowing that everything happens for a reason. We cannot access that reason and the wiser choice is not even to try. We need to seek guidance, to have faith, to hold onto the truth that everything we see is truly an illusion. I don't think this is true, I know it is. The physical world is indeed an illusion, and based upon that truth, I try to manage my emotional and psychological responses to life. I no longer base my emotional responses on information from the physical world. I come from the spiritual. I pray a lot.

Do I think that everybody needs to endure such a thing? Maybe. I suspect that to get to an intimate relationship with God, where you no longer question His presence and where you are truly able to release your will, yes, maybe that does take a dark night. What I suggest is to leave the phenomenal, five-sensory world alone. Go with what's simple: love, forgiveness, and the recognition that all things are an illusion. This is the Aquarian level of consciousness.

Caroline Myss, Ph.D., is an international lecturer and pioneer in the field of energy medicine. She is the author of the *New York Times* bestseller *Anatomy of the Spirit*. Her latest book is *Why People Don't Heal and How They Can*.

10
Reading the Future

Back in the 1970s while working on her master's thesis, Anne studied with Joan Kellogg, an art therapist who created the MARI® (Mandala Assessment Research Instrument) Card Test, a therapeutic projective tool that offers a visual and metaphorical picture of psychological and emotional processes.

In 1975 Joan had not yet developed the cards. She had been working with Stanislav Grof at Maryland Psychiatric Research Center in Catonsville, Maryland, where the Czech psychiatrist was conducting LSD research with cancer patients. Gathering information from study participants before their ingestion of the psychoactive substance was easy, but after their "trip," debriefing was a bit problematic. To get some sense of whether the journey had reached closure, Joan had participants draw mandalas.

Mandala is the Sanskrit word for "circle." In Buddhism these circles contain elaborate representations of enlightenment, replete with precisely placed bodhisattvas and buddhas, animals and flowers, decorative motifs and forms that represent natural elements such as earth, water, wind, and fire, or qualities such as wisdom or bliss. Many mandalas are intricate maps of heavenly realms, a sacred precinct surrounded by levels of gates, guardians, and guideposts. Mandalas from other religious traditions circumscribe very simple forms. But whether simple or complex, the mandala is both a meditative aid and a visual path that leads us to the sacred.

Perhaps one of the best-known mandalas today is the labyrinth found in Chartres Cathedral. Thanks to the efforts of the Rev. Lauren Artress, canon for special ministries at San Francisco's Grace Cathedral and author of *Walking a Sacred Path: Rediscovering the Labyrinth as a Spiritual Tool*, individuals all over the world have been able to "walk the labyrinth" (by way of a reproduction) and experience its calming, centering, and deepening benefits.

Joan Kellogg, while quite respectful of the religious uses of the mandala, agreed with C. G. Jung who saw them as potent psychological tools, "protective circles" that, among other things, served as a "traditional antidote for chaotic states of mind." Joan used the mandala with the research participants to take a reading of their process. Subjects created mandalas by using a pencil and a paper plate to draw a circle on a large piece of white paper. Taking the plate away, participants saw a circle about the size of their heads. It was as if they were gazing into a mirror, a reflective space. She would suggest that they move their attention to a box of oil pastels and allow their intuition to choose a color or colors. Then she suggested that they color their mandala, again letting their intuition direct the shapes, pressure on the page, whether to stay within the confines of the circle, and so on. In this way the unconscious poured itself onto the blank page into the safety of the circle.

For therapeutic or personal growth purposes, you could draw these mandalas regularly, collecting a series that over time would show specific themes emerging. Thus one could, in effect, "read" one's process or journey in the personal symbols, shapes, and colors that move around the circle.

Anne had clients draw mandalas both before and after sessions for a period of about four to six months. Not infrequently, Joan was able to "read" the mandalas, describing the concerns and issues Anne's clients had. What was astounding, however, was that Joan might describe an issue a full six months before the client articulated the concern. Therefore mandalas in our mind offer a sense of not only what is but what is to come.

Just as Joan Kellogg helped Anne see the journey her clients were on by reading their mandalas, we have been reading trends in the psychology, spirituality, and healing fields and see certain distinct patterns emerging. For example, the fields of holistic and alternative medicine have struck a nerve with the general public and are gradually gaining in credibility as well as popularity. A survey conducted for Landmark Healthcare, Inc., found that in 1997, 42 percent of adults in this country visited an alternative therapy practitioner. The same survey, which was national in scope, also found that 70 percent of health maintenance organizations reported receiving an increase in requests for alternative medical therapies by their plan members. The most frequently used methods, according to the 1998 report, were herbal therapy, chiropractic, and massage therapy.

According to James S. Gordon, M.D., director of the Center of Mind-Body Medicine in Washington, D.C., holistic medicine "is a comprehensive approach, an attitude of thoughtful openness to all the techniques which modern science and empirical use, in our own and other cultures, have revealed to be helpful, a force for revitalization and synthesis in medicine."

Holistic medicine—we use the term interchangeably with alternative, mind-body, or complementary medicine—does not necessarily mean the use of unconventional therapies. "Holistic medicine is not so much a field of medicine as an attitude," explains Alan R. Gaby, M.D., past president of the American Holistic Medical Association. "Many holistic doctors embrace alternative therapies, others use conventional drugs and surgery but treat all aspects of the patient: body, mind, and spirit."

Other critical elements of holistic or alternative medicine that separate it from conventional Western practice are the involvement of the patient and the notion that healing is inherent in the person, that it does not occur entirely because of treatments and protocols. In the 1800s French chemist Louis Pasteur and German physician Robert Koch discovered that tiny microbes caused disease. The heady era of medical wonder drugs followed. With the development of antibiotics and insulin, science became the source of all cures. "It didn't matter if you believed in the treatment, it didn't matter if the doctor handing the drug to you laughed out loud and uproariously at the prospect of it working, it didn't matter if the relationship between the two of you was hostile and scornful, the treatment worked!" writes Herbert Benson, M.D., in his book *Timeless Healing*. "Modern medicine came to expect that all healing could be accomplished with specific applications."

This trend accelerated as ever more sophisticated technologies and medications were developed. Lab tests and CAT scans replaced house calls and bedside manner. With a dizzying amount of information to master, physicians increasingly chose to specialize. Patients, reduced to ever smaller body parts, began to skip over the general practitioner as an unnecessary middle man and head straight for the specialist. A person with a stomach problem sought help from a gastroenterologist. Someone with depression went to a psychiatrist. The backache sufferer called the orthopedist. Often these physicians neither communicated with one another nor understood what mental, emotional, and social factors might be contributing to the patient's condition. The general practitioner, as symbolized by TV's soothing Marcus Welby, M.D., became a quaint anachronism.

Also buried was the belief in the human organism's own power to heal, an ability evolved over millennia to protect the species. This power, which Benson calls "remembered wellness," was written off as the placebo effect, a meddlesome obstacle that interfered with researchers' efforts to test the efficacy of "real" therapies such as drugs. Rather than appreciating and figuring out how to foster this amazing innate ability to heal, medical researchers and practitioners shunted it aside. The more science offered, the more dependent the individual became upon the medical establishment to fix every ill.

Holistic medicine acknowledges the relationship of mind, body, and spirit as well as the healing properties of alternative medical therapies gathered from around the globe and across the centuries. These include everything from ancient Oriental practices such as acupuncture and *qigong* to physical manipulations such as chiropractic and massage to herbal medicine, nutrition, meditation, and exercise. Such therapies generally are not taught in U.S. medical schools (although this is changing) and, with a few exceptions, are not covered by health insurance. Nevertheless, one in three American adults seeks these unconventional approaches to medicine, according to a much-cited survey by Harvard researcher David M. Eisenberg, M.D., and his team, published in the January 28, 1993 *New England Journal of Medicine*. Based on a national sample of 1,500 adults, the researchers estimated that 425 million visits were made to alternative practitioners in 1990, compared with 388 million visits to primary care physicians.

Most of those in the study who ventured outside the mainstream sought help for chronic conditions that were not alleviated by conventional medicine, including back pain, allergies, arthritis, insomnia, and headache. Interestingly, a significant portion also sought help not because they were ill, but because they apparently wished to stay healthy. "A full third of the respondents who used unconventional therapy in 1990 did not use it for any of their principal medical conditions," the study found. "From this fact we infer that a substantial amount of unconventional therapy is used for nonserious medical conditions, health promotion, or disease prevention."

Thus despite access to one of the most sophisticated medical systems in the world, many health-care consumers are seeking a new approach to healing. Simultaneously researchers are discovering a biological basis for holistic health. Among the research findings supporting this medicine are the following:

- A five-year multidisciplinary study at the University of Maryland is using homeopathy, acupuncture, and other alternative therapies to treat pain.
- Numerous studies have found that religious commitment contributes to a reduction of many disorders, including high blood pressure, depression, and substance abuse.
- The immune system appears to be influenced by an individual's circle of friends and family—the more supportive the personal relationships, the better the immune system functions. This has been shown in lonely teenagers, in breast cancer patients, in medical students, and in elderly caregivers of people with Alzheimer's disease.

Advances in the field of psychoneuroimmunology are showing at the cellular level how our behaviors, attitudes, and hormones affect our bodies' resistance to disease. The mind-body split has been proved to have no basis in fact. Neuroscientists such as Candace Pert have discovered that neuropeptides, including endorphins, the body's natural painkillers, are found not only in the human brain but throughout the body. Our thoughts and emotions trigger these chemicals, which act as messenger molecules to our cells. Other research unexpectedly found nerve fibers in the immune system, further blurring, if not erasing, the line dividing mind and body.

"The implications of these discoveries are really profound," says Pert. "How you feel, how you react to stress, the emotions that you repress are all going to play a role in your health. This is very radical. It has the potential to change the face of medicine."

Congress is supporting this type of research through the Office of Alternative Medicine (OAM), a part of the National Institutes of Health (NIH). With small but growing funding—OAM's $2 million initial budget passed in 1992 had grown to $12 million by 1997—the office funds studies aimed at determining the efficacy of alternative therapies. Grants have been awarded to study the potential for treating unipolar depression, osteoarthritis, and attention deficit disorder with acupuncture; substance abuse with prayer; AIDS and bone marrow transplant patients with massage therapy; and Parkinson's disease with Ayurvedic herbs, to name a few. In addition to awarding research grants, the office funds ten specialty research centers and disseminates information through its clearinghouse. Although OAM's budget and activities represent a mere toehold in the medical establishment, its presence and steady growth signal a certain level of acceptance and support for alternative medical therapies.

Another important medically related development is still in its infancy. While managed care in general is squeezing the reimbursement pipeline, some health insurers are taking a more enlightened approach. As of January 1997, Oxford Health Plans, a health maintenance organization based in New York City, began offering a plan that includes treatments from a network of chiropractors, acupuncturists, and nutritionists as well as a mail-order operation for herbs and natural medicines. *Time* magazine also reported in fall 1996 that American Western Life of Foster City, California, had begun a wellness program that covers many alternative treatments, and more than twenty insurers now cover Dean Ornish's heart disease prevention and recovery program, which includes yoga, meditation, and nutritional elements.

But the real cutting edge of alternative medicine is energy medicine, also called the subtle energies field. Subtle energies are a manifestation of the life force that flows through the body and psyche and that may be directed by various mind-body techniques (some of them spiritually based). Working with subtle energies can be physically and emotionally therapeutic and can induce nonordinary states of consciousness.

This energy, described by a host of diverse cultures—forty-nine in all, according to bestselling author Joan Borysenko—has been called variously *chi*, *prana*, *ruach*, *ha*, *foat*, *mana*, etheric energy, orgone, odic force, homeopathic resonance, and animal magnetism.

Both new and old therapies, including acupuncture, qi gong, Polarity, Reiki, Therapeutic Touch, and other modalities, work with subtle energies. The idea is to keep the energy flowing smoothly through movement, breathing, meditation, and special techniques of pressure and touch. Practitioners and patients describe these energies as sensations of warmth, weight, vibration, and expansiveness. In energy-based medicine, concepts of flow, balance, and harmony are essential to good health. Disease is seen as the result of energy being blocked or dammed and becoming stagnant.

"Traditional Chinese medicine acknowledges that there are germs and pathogens, things that can come into the body that are harmful, but what is regarded as far more important is the internal energetic environment of the body and how it deals with what comes in," explains Glenn Johnson, Ph.D., a member of the International Society for the Study of Subtle Energies and Energy Medicine (ISSSEEM).

Energy medicine also examines phenomena such as self-regulation and other mind-body approaches. "Today we have strong evidence that any aspect of bodily functions, once brought to awareness, can be deliberately altered to some extent, for healing or the development of new abilities," writes Michael Murphy in *The Future of the Body*. It has been documented, for example, that individuals are capable of generating and controlling electrical forces that seem to influence their physiological and psychic systems. Conversely, low-level changes in magnetic, electrical, electromagnetic, acoustic, and gravitational fields have profound effects on both biological and psychic functioning, suggesting that energy emitted from the environment influences humans and animals in a variety of ways.

Many religious traditions, particularly those of the East, believe that expansions of consciousness are related to changes in subtle energies. The most advanced research in the field, which has taken place at the Menninger Foundation in Topeka, Kansas, suggests that subtle energies may not be part of the known physical fields as we understand them.

Because of the difficulty of measuring subtle energies, Western medicine in general has been reluctant to acknowledge these therapies and their value. Acupuncture has been an exception to that rule. It has not only been the subject of considerable research but has also been quite successful in gaining advocates. The former *New York Times* reporter James Reston was an early booster. Stricken with appendicitis when covering Nixon's trip to China in 1972, Reston had his appendix removed by Chinese doctors who treated his postsurgical pain with acupuncture. Once home, Reston described his experience in highly favorable terms—and in print. Twenty-five years later, the NIH has endorsed the ancient Chinese healing art. In November 1997, a twelve-member panel convened by the NIH reported that acupuncture did indeed provide benefits for a variety of medical conditions, including easing nausea experienced as a result of pregnancy, chemotherapy, or surgery. They also recommended its use as a complementary method in the treatment of addictions, headache, menstrual cramps, asthma, carpel tunnel syndrome, and other conditions.

Once the basic concept of *chi*, or life energy, is accepted, other subtle-energy therapies should presumably become more widely recognized. In the meantime, these therapies are being used to treat many conditions, especially those that are stress or pain related. Therapeutic Touch, for example, is used in hospitals to ease anxiety and to treat pain in patients of all ages, from newborns to the elderly. Others, such as Reiki or qi gong, may be especially useful in promoting an overall sense of well-being.

Of course, the answer does not lie in substituting acupuncture for Advil but in fundamentally changing who is responsible for health. "It's very difficult for people in the healing profession and clients alike to move away from the biomedical model which is so tenacious," says Elliott Dacher, M.D. "So for instance the current preoccupation with alternative therapies, although they have been valuable in adding pluralism of choice and in breaking the dominance of the medical model, almost without exception, are external remedies. We have yet to move toward a fundamental change that empowers the individual and shifts authority away from professionals. Once we do that, it is the intention of individuals to work with their own life, mind, body, and spirit that becomes foremost."

Acupuncturist Bob Duggan agrees. "It's a very pivotal moment," he says. "My fear is that the alternative medicine folks will all professionalize, make themselves experts, and create new dependencies."

"The way to health lies within each of us," he adds. "We've disempowered everybody from knowing common-sense things, about food, about how we hold tension, about spirituality. My prayer is that people won't suddenly come to an acupuncturist. I'd rather they went to church, to the theater, to exercise. The patients themselves will bring the change."

Strategies for Reducing Stress

Today most health complaints stem not from germs but from our inability to manage the stresses of daily living. The American Institute of Stress, based in Yonkers, New York, estimates that 75 to 90 percent of visits to physicians are for stress-related disorders, including hypertension, diabetes, headache, backache, ulcers, and allergies. According to testimony by Michael O. Smith, M.D., presented at a U.S. Senate hearing on alternative medicine in May 1993, only 16 percent of common symptoms have an organic cause, such as a broken bone or a bacterial infection.

"Humankind has seen the development of new and very different adversities, which have resulted in the emergence of a uniquely new category of modern-day ailments, particularly stress-related diseases, acute and chronic, that are directly linked to personal attitudes and lifestyle," says Elliott Dacher. "As a result, the limitations of a medical model that cannot effectively incorporate psychological, psychosocial, or spiritual factors—factors that are at the source of these ailments—have become increasingly evident."

Stress reduction and the important role relaxation can play in keeping our immune, cardiovascular, and other systems healthy are the most important and well-researched aspects of mind-body healing. Research increasingly shows the physiological benefits that flow from a relaxed state and, conversely, the harm caused by high levels of stress.

Stress is our body's response to an event or condition—known as the stressor—and is thus specific to each individual. "What's distressing to one person may be pleasurable for another," says Paul Rosch, M.D., president of the American Institute of Stress. For example, a roller-coaster may be a white-knuckle ride of terror for one person and a sheer delight for another. Performing in public can be a thrilling and exhilarating experience for some people, while others blanch at the mere suggestion of getting up in front of an audience. "It's not external events; it's how you perceive them," says Rosch.

The scientific basis for our understanding of stress dates back to Walter Cannon, M.D., of Harvard Medical School, who at the turn of the century identified the "fight-or-flight" response, the adrenaline rush that is hardwired in humans and other organisms. Canadian researcher Hans Selye, M.D., expanded on this work by studying how animals respond to long-term stressful conditions. Selye described the "general adaptation syndrome," a three-stage process of alarm, resistance, and exhaustion, which helped explain the relationship between chronic stress and disease.

Just as our primitive ancestors reacted when a tiger leapt down from a tree, so do modern humans respond to less dramatic threats to their well-being, such as a tyrannical boss, rush-hour traffic, or a troubled marriage: our hearts beat faster, our blood pressure rises, our muscles tense, and our minds race. While these changes can aid us in bringing all our resources to bear during an emergency, a chronic state of stress can have profound ill effects on our bodies. When we face constant tension, the immune system becomes suppressed, blood cholesterol levels rise, and our bones begin to lose calcium.

It is not surprising then that researchers have correlated stress-related illness to major life change events, such as death of a spouse, divorce, personal injury, or losing a job. Studies suggest a relationship between such events and the onset of heart disease, tuberculosis, skin disease, and a general decline in health. It seems that no system is invulnerable to the perils of stress. For example, a four-year prospective study of three thousand factory workers by researchers at the

University of Washington found that back injuries were more likely to happen to those employees who were unhappy in their jobs. "These findings . . . help explain why past prevention efforts focusing on purely physical factors have been unsuccessful," the study found. A study reported in the *New England Journal of Medicine* found a relationship between psychological stress and susceptibility to the common cold. In a controlled trial, nose drops containing cold viruses were given to volunteers; those who were under psychological stress were much more likely to come down with a cold.

Fortunately, a wide array of techniques such as guided imagery, biofeedback, massage, meditation, hypnosis (including self-hypnosis), and exercise, among others, can mitigate the ill effects of stress. For example, Herbert Benson, M.D., associate professor of medicine at Harvard Medical School and Deaconess Hospital and founder and president of the Mind/Body Medical Institute, pioneered the relaxation response, through which individuals train themselves to slow their frenetic internal pace.

In a relaxed state, our bodies use less oxygen, a condition called hypometabolism. "The body responds to techniques that elicit the relaxation response by downshifting your metabolism, by allowing your internal perpetual-energy machine to ease off working so hard," writes Benson in *Timeless Healing*. "Your heart need not beat so quickly, your blood need not be pumped as forcefully. Your breathing can be slower and deeper, and your muscles relaxed and requiring less blood." As a result, all of the organs in the body are given a respite.

Many techniques have been developed to elicit the relaxation response. Benson's method involves repeating a word, phrase, or simple action and setting aside intrusive thoughts.

Another method, progressive muscle relaxation, described in the 1920s by physiologist Edmund Jacobson, teaches people how to be aware of tension by flexing and relaxing isolated parts of the body from head to toe. Autogenic training, developed by German physician Johannes H. Schultz, is another technique, in which the person lets go of tension by concentrating on breathing and allowing the limbs to feel heavy and warm.

Although it would seem to have the opposite effect of relaxation, exercise can also reduce stress, depending on the individual and the type of exercise performed. The physiological benefits of exercise are well documented: the cardiovascular system improves, lung capacity grows, and bone density increases, leaving us less prone to heart disease and osteoporosis. In addition, exercise promotes psychological and emotional well-being, acting as a buffer against stress. Many people feel a psychological lift as well as a curtailment of anxiety from regular exercise.

In a particularly stressful period, Anne was having trouble sleeping. Working out at our health club helped enormously. The physical exertion "cleaned out" the tightness and cleared the mind. Instead of going to bed dog-tired, feeling like a crumpled, discarded rag, an hour on the treadmill produced a natural fatigue, which allowed her to fall asleep more quickly and to sleep more deeply.

When we learn how to relax consciously (as opposed to simply watching TV or reading a book), our heart rate, blood pressure, respiration rate, and muscle tension all decrease. There are also psychological benefits as well such as decreased anxiety and depression.

Yet stress reduction strategies notwithstanding, many people are taking more drastic measures. They are revising their lifestyles, scaling down expenditures so that they can scale back work hours, and looking for ways to make prayer and spiritual practice the center of their lives. A movement called simple living has sprung up, producing at least half a dozen books and a handful of newsletters, websites, and organizations that coach harried individuals on how to simplify life. One major culprit that gobbles up time and applies varying degrees of pressure is work. We all need to earn money, but the problem is that the more time we spend *making* a living, the less we are in fact living. Not long ago a local Washington, D.C., news program aired a segment on work habits. Not only are increasing numbers of workers not taking a lunch hour—choosing instead to do errands during that time or simply nibbling on a sandwich while working straight through at the computer—but the length of the workday has been extended. One man said he rose at 4:30 A.M. so that he could be at his desk by 5:30 A.M. so that he could be home with his family by 7 P.M.! Other professionals routinely arrive at the office at 7:30 A.M. and leave twelve hours later. These are not one-time or short-term situations created by the crunch of a deadline. These are steady, regular hours. And it's not just professionals. Blue-collar and office workers frequently take a second job or work overtime "just to make ends meet."

The result is a desperate sense of being chronically and breathlessly busy. The saddest modern ritual is calling a friend for lunch and volleying dates back and forth until finally finding a mutually available time usually weeks away. When trying to set a meeting time, the problem magnifies exponentially the more people are involved.

This is a far cry from the days when people just naturally dropped by for a cup of coffee or sat on their porches in the evening chatting with neighbors who happened to pass by. Now in many urban settings it has become rude or awkward to just stop by.

This stress-ridden, lack-of-time scenario is fraught with paradox. For example, *U.S. News & World Report* reported in 1995 that while most Americans report feeling stressed out, they are in fact making more money, enjoying more leisure time, spending more money on recreation, and using more labor-saving appliances and technology than their parents or grandparents did. Part of the problem is that the revolution in communications technology allows—or forces—us to respond to each other virtually always and everywhere. Cellular phones, faxes, and e-mail travel with us, so that travel time is no longer allotted on business trips. Instead of sitting back and enjoying the flight or train ride, one generally opens up the laptop, activates the cell phone, and continues to conduct business as usual. Vacations are no longer sacrosanct unless strict boundaries are set.

No wonder people are exploring this new concept of simple living, a lifestyle built on the notion that "less is more" and that combines more environmental awareness and less acquisitiveness with communal resource sharing and mutual support. From the movement's Bible, a book by Duane Elgin called *Voluntary Simplicity: Toward a Way of Life That Is Outwardly Simple and Inwardly Rich* to Janet Luhr's *The Simple Living Guide: A Sourcebook for Less Stressful, More Joyful Living*, many authors are stepping forward with not only the rationale but ways to slow down and simplify. Some proponents such as David Yount, author of *Spiritual Simplicity*, suggest voluntarily changing careers or jobs. Yount and his wife report making 60 percent of their former income but feel that their "spiritual standard of living has risen beyond anything we have experienced since childhood." Others abandon the hectic pace of urban living for more tranquil and community-oriented small towns.

Still others suggest that it may not be necessary to change where you live or what you do. According to Jacob Needleman, the point is to focus on the now. "The answer to the problem of time is not more time, not more efficiency, not even in itself more biological life," he writes in *Time and the Soul*. "The answer to the problem and the sorrow of time is one thing and one thing only: *the experience of meaning*. And this experience occurs only when the Self touches the self, when the soul touches the ego—when the two worlds meet."

Over and over in the literature, authors repeatedly emphasize that in divesting ourselves of distractions, work pressures, social obligations, and unnecessary activities, we come back to ourselves. Janet Luhrs says it this way: "Simplicity is the first step we can take to quiet that loud, outer voice. We can't hear the inner pleas when we work 40 and 60 hours a week at a job we'd rather leave, when we're busy maintaining our expensive cars and houses, when we spend countless hours shopping for more outer trappings, when we zoom from one appointment and commitment after another, and when we drop, exhausted at night in front of the TV because we have nothing left. We can't hear anything then." Luhrs says that "Simple living is about living deliberately . . . living consciously . . . being fully present, fully aware."

Thus just as alternative medicine was the portal to the inner journey, so too dealing with stress can lead to simple living, a form of soul work that leads us back to ourselves, to what is important, to a spiritual awareness. Sarah Ban Breathnach, author of *Simple Abundance*, explains that she "began writing about eliminating clutter and ended up on a safari of the self and spirit." According to this bestselling author, "*Simple Abundance* has enabled me to encounter everyday epiphanies, find the sacred in the ordinary, the Mystical in the mundane, and fully enter into the sacrament of the present moment."

Gerald Celente of the Trends Research Institute of Rhinebeck, New York, forecasts that by the year 2000, a full 15 percent of baby boomers will be incorporating elements of simple living and that the trend will grow throughout the twenty-first century. We would simply add that along with the economic adjustments simple living engenders, parallel strides in spirituality will occur. We see individuals becoming more and more interested in aspects of contemplative living: daily prayer, meditation, and spiritual reading; retreats that involve either informal time at home or in one's garden or formal programs in monasteries and retreat centers; and structured or unstructured time in nature. Certainly the baby boomers who are negotiating the shoals of their middle years are primed for such a change.

Religious Voices of Women

According to a 1995 survey in *New Woman* magazine, only 30 percent of adult female respondents practice the religious traditions in which they were raised. For some, weekly church attendance simply lost its appeal; for others the political rigidity and lack of inclusiveness of patriarchal systems drove them away. Still, many women estranged from their childhood religions feel a deep longing for spiritual connection and practice. They appreciate the texture and meaning that ritual, story, and community can give to their lives. Somewhere along the way, however, the liturgy, rituals, and traditions of their root traditions ceased to speak to their hearts. They got tired of feeling like outsiders looking in.

With the emergence of the feminist movement in the 1960s and 1970s and the dramatic shifts in perspective ushered in by the feminization of psychology, many women became aware of the subtle and not-so-subtle negation of their experiences. Because men far outnumbered women in religious leadership positions, it was men's voices that were heard in worship and prayer, in the development and interpretation of tradition, and in the rituals and celebrations. Women, on the other hand, were frequently seen as inherently flawed, more susceptible to temptation and sin, lacking in higher spiritual understanding, and apt to seduce men into their evil ways.

Just as the overall feminist credo was that women were the experts on their own experience, so did the feminist spiritual revolution claim women's experience as central and primary to any discussion of Divine revelation. As this discussion gained ground through the 1970s, many women argued that what feminist scholars, writers, and teachers were calling "women's experience" was actually the experience of white, middle-class, heterosexual women of western European descent. To be a woman of color, they said, or to be economically disenfranchised or to be lesbian implied entirely new and more complex concerns. These women called for increased attention and sensitivity to the diversity of female experience, claiming that to collapse all women's experience under one definition was limiting.

In the past thirty-five years, women have undertaken the monumental task of reexamining all aspects of traditional religion, from scripture, liturgy, and ritual to questions of ethics. But the feminism of the heady early years has undergone a change. No longer are women banging on the cathedral or synagogue doors, demanding entry. Today, while the goals have remained the same, women ministers and rabbis—as well as female Buddhist meditation teachers—are operating in a different arena. Many are now working from the inside, their very presence at the altar, at the front of the meditation hall, or at Jerusalem's Wailing Wall an affirmation of women's spiritual leadership.

For too long theology was approached "from the top down." In other words, one started with a theory or statement and structured subsequent beliefs, traditions, and moral decrees around it. And although the theory generally emerged from male experience, the resulting theology was assumed to reflect human experience. Feminist theologians are turning that formula on its head by doing theology "from the bottom up," by examining human experience, particularly the experience of women, in order to learn about the nature of the Divine.

Thus today we have scholars looking to bring women's experience into traditional religious contexts. Such women include the Jewish pioneer Lynn Gottlieb and Christian authors and scholars such as Carol P. Christ and Elisabeth Schüssler Fiorenza, among others. Additionally, eclectic women's spirituality groups focus on celebrating the goddess, female images of the Divine, and Wiccan traditions. Groups vary, from those that intersperse intellectual explorations with experiential exercises to those that focus solely on ritual such as new moon ceremonies.

Both feminist theology and women's spirituality groups today are seeking a shift from hierarchy to models of relationship, community, and cooperation. Some feminists believe that the existing structures in most religions are so entrenched in male-dominated traditions, rituals, stories, language, and doctrines that it is impossible to rescue them for women. For these women, the only solution is to break away from the old religious traditions and start new ones. Others, however, look for kernels of truth within the religious traditions they were born into and seek to correct the distortions from the inside out. According to Christian feminist theologian Rosemary Radford Ruether, three steps are necessary to correct existing biases in religious traditions:

1. Acknowledge that the bias found in the tradition is a misstatement of the original message. God is not a sexist, but perhaps the early religious leaders were.
2. Look beyond the existing tradition to find new (or perhaps very old) sources of spiritual enlightenment.
3. Reconstruct or re-create the theological tradition—including stories, rituals, and other elements—so that it reflects the unbiased message.

Women in various traditions and denominations are actively working with all three levels. For example, women have done important work with regard to the first step—identifying where women have been subordinated in and eliminated from sacred texts or where biases exist in the practice of a faith. Lynn Gottlieb opens her book *She Who Dwells Within* with a story of taking a course—her third—with the distinguished Jewish scholar and Holocaust survivor Elie Wiesel. At the start of the class, Wiesel began reciting the names of the "heroes of the Bible," the course's subject. But his litany failed to include even one woman. Gottlieb pointed this out and was given the task of "doing" Eve. But when she offered her *midrash*—questioning and expanding on the sacred text using methods more philosophical and imaginative than historical, which focused on Eve's "quest for wisdom and her desire to know from the sight of her own eyes, the taste of her own tongue, and the touch of her own hands," Weisel countered with his own interpretation: that the snake seduced Eve with her own words. He then added that if Adam had been there to watch over "his foolish wife" perhaps the unfortunate event would not have occurred! He went on to say that Eve's seemingly endless tears were the reason Adam reluctantly ate the fruit. "Who can refuse a tearful wife?" Gottlieb quotes Wiesel as saying. The fact that such a personage as Wiesel would carry—and impart—such stereotypical tripe is a startling reminder of how prevalent bias and patronizing patriarchal attitudes still are.

New Testament historian and scholar Elisabeth Schüssler Fiorenza, author of *In Memory of Her*, sees scripture as a valuable spiritual and historical resource and tool. Dismissing the Bible, she argues, deprives women of their rightful history as active members of the Jesus movement and early Christian church. Therefore her work seeks to reclaim scripture for women. Through research, she has uncovered evidence that women held central roles and leadership positions both in Jesus' circle of disciples and in the earliest work of the Christian community. It was subsequent teachings, traditions, and theology that by selectively focusing on certain details and ignoring certain facts created the false impression that women had always been marginal, their leadership nonexistent.

For example, Fiorenza cites the Gospel of Mark, where the evangelist writes about the days just before the crucifixion. Fiorenza sees those passages as having three major protagonists: Judas Iscariot, who betrayed Jesus; Peter, who denied

Jesus; and an unnamed female disciple, who anointed him. Even though in the Gospel Jesus says, "Truly I tell you, wherever the good news is proclaimed in the whole world, what she has done will be told in remembrance of her" (14:9), Fiorenza points out that not only is her action ignored, but her name is lost. "The name of the betrayer is remembered," writes Fiorenza, "but the name of the faithful disciple is forgotten because she is a woman."

In Buddhism, the concept of *emptiness* implies that nothing has independent existence; each seemingly separate entity is actually connected in the web of life. Thus specifics such as gender are illusory. Furthermore, Buddhism teaches that all sentient beings including animals and plants possess an indwelling Buddha-nature and the potential to achieve enlightenment. Rita Gross, author of *Buddhism After Patriarchy: A Feminist History Analysis and Reconstruction of Buddhism*, has persuasively used these and other Buddhist principles to point out the gap between Buddhist teachings and its general practices. For example, if nothing exists independently, asks Gross, how can such an illusory aspect as femininity be used to prove women ineligible for leadership in Buddhist practice? And if all sentient beings equally possess the potential for Buddhahood, then women's different levels of achievement relative to those of men can be attributed only to a weakness in Buddhist institutions, which did not train them as well as they trained men.

Many of those involved in the tradition, especially in its native lands, fail to recognize these and other discrepancies between doctrine and practice. While dedicated Buddhist women may become nuns, they have traditionally held a much lower status and enjoyed considerably less education than male monks, who greatly outnumber nuns. The Vajrayana Buddhist folk wisdom tradition still considers female birth unfortunate; a woman can only hope to be reborn in the next life as a man, if she does well in her practice in this lifetime.

But while there are unfortunate discrepancies in status and opportunities for Buddhist monks and nuns in Eastern cultures, Vipassana practitioner and teacher Sharon Salzberg suggests that the outlook is much more optimistic for laywomen in the East as well as the West and improving in monastic settings worldwide as Westerners get more involved. Salzberg, who received her initial training in India in the early 1970s, says she felt that an egalitarian relationship existed between the sexes. "I've never felt that I, as a woman, have encountered a situation where I was receiving less profound instruction or mediated or compromised transmission," she reports. "I know that such things exist, because friends of mine have encountered them. But not with the teachers I had." Consequently, strains of Buddhism that center around laypeople rather than monastics tend to be more open and accessible for Western women.

Because Buddhism was imported to North America by monks who were themselves products of their Asian cultures, their cultural biases permeated both the practices and the community. One notable exception is Vipassana, or insight meditation, a derivative of the Theravada tradition of Southeast Asia, which was introduced to the United States largely by Americans, including Jack Kornfield, Joseph Goldstein, and Sharon Salzberg.

Given this situation—the invisibility of women or their second-class status—many women are themselves reclaiming their spiritual heritage. For example, ancient Jewish mystical texts refer to a divine feminine presence called Shekinah. Derived from the Hebrew verb meaning "to dwell" or "to abide," *Shekinah* has been translated as "She who dwells within" and has proved to be a powerful source of inspiration, strength, and encouragement for Jewish feminists seeking to incorporate feminine language and images into their spiritual tradition.

In its earlier usage, Shekinah was used interchangeably with HYVH (Yahweh) and Elohim, the articulated names of God. According to Lynn Gottlieb, the evolution and persistent appearance of the term demonstrate the natural human desire to relate to the Divine as both masculine and feminine. *Shekinah* is related to the word *mishkan*, which was the tent that God commanded the Israelites to build to house their sacred relics. After the destruction of the first temple at Jerusalem in 586 B.C. and through the following periods of oppression, themes of exile and redemption continued to develop the meaning of *Shekinah*. The Jewish mystical tradition of kabbalah came to envision Shekinah as God's wife, lover, and daughter. Unfortunately, the kabbalah imposed a hierarchical distinction between male and female images of the Divine, resulting in Shekinah's association with "lower" aspects of the Divine, such as passivity and receptivity and relationship to the material world. Drawing on themes of feminist spirituality in general, Gottlieb has explored some traditional images of Shekinah as particularly fruitful for Jewish women seeking to feel their experiences echoed in their faith tradition: Shekinah as the Being Who Connects All Life; Shekinah as the Longing for Wholeness; and Shekinah as the Cry for Justice.

Buddhism is a nontheistic religion, so it does not have the same problems for feminists as monotheistic religions do, such as masculine names and images of the Divine. Indeed, Mahayana and Vajrayana (or Tantric) Buddhism have well-developed systems of feminine symbolism, including a variety of both male and female figures that are not really gods but more like guides intended to help practitioners attain enlightenment. Furthermore, Tantra, sacred sexual practices found in both Hinduism and Buddhism, profoundly appreciate the female body and sexuality, and sexual and sensual pleasure in general—something that most feminists seek to nurture in Western religious reform. Although many scholars have claimed that women in Tantric practices were mere objects for the pleasure and spiritual advancement of men, scholar and teacher Miranda Shaw, in her book *Passionate Enlightenment: Women in Tantric Buddhism*, offers a well-documented account of women's dignity and even their leadership in Tantra. She also offers bold images of enlightened females, who "dance, leap, and soar in exuberant poses that reveal the body in all its female glory, without shame or fear. Their limbs glisten with vitality; their eyes brim with ecstasy and ferocious intensity as they gazes into the depths of reality. Energy bursts around them."

In the Christian tradition, many women have found role models in figures such as that twelfth-century Renaissance woman the mystically inclined yet pragmatically grounded abbess Hildegard of Bingen. Scholar Karen Jo Torjesen's book *When Women Were Priests* also furthers the cause of recognizing women's place in the early years of Christianity. Her main point is that early Christians met in homes, where women played prominent roles, but gradually, with the formal institutionalization of the Church, the setting of worship changed along with the locus of power. "Understanding why and how women, once leaders in the Jesus Movement and in the early church, were marginalized and scapegoated as Christianity became the state religion is crucial if women are to reclaim their rightful, equal place in the church today," writes Torjesen. "Jesus' message and practice were radically egalitarian in their day and constituted a social revolution that likely provoked his crucifixion. It is high time that the church, which claims to embody his good news to the world, stop betraying its own essential heritage of absolute equality."

Torjesen cites examples of women's leadership such as evidence of an inspirational speech and sermon given by Mary Magdalene, who was called in some texts "Apostle to the Apostles," artwork that depicts a female bishop, and an inscription at a Greek burial site that identifies the deceased as a female priest.

Ruether's third step—reenvisioning traditional rituals, stories, and prayers—is also an exciting and fruitful area for women. The rabbinical practice of midrash is particularly well suited to feminist investigation because it attempts to get behind the text itself to discover the deepest meaning for present times. For example, the myth of Lilith is the result of rabbinical attempts to reconcile the two very different creation stories found in Genesis 1 and 2. Lilith is Adam's first wife, created by God simultaneously with the man, and she believes she is Adam's equal. In the traditional midrash, Lilith is an evil character, banished from Eden, who terrorizes women and children. Judith Plaskow has written a feminist midrash of the Lilith story in which Lilith is a strong, courageous woman who leaves Adam because she refuses to be his slave. Plaskow's story addresses the questions What happens when women share their stories with one another? What happens when women recognize and define their own power? Most important, Plaskow's new myth shows how Jewish feminists can expose the biases of the existing traditions and reclaim their inherent power.

Although there are biblical accounts of other significant women, such as

Sarah, Rebecca, Rachel, and Leah, their stories are traditionally told in relation to their husbands and sons. Jewish feminists are working to develop these women's stories so that present and future generations can come to know them in their own right and in their relationships with women.

While revising texts that have been corrupted by sexism is important, Jewish feminists are also focusing their energies on present-day rituals and ceremonies. Of special importance are those that welcome young girls into the community of the faithful while reaffirming the place of all women in that community. The Rosh Hodesh, or New Moon, ceremony has received much attention as a model for female-centered rituals. Outlined in the Torah as a holiday of great importance, it lost significance over the centuries but has been reclaimed and revitalized by Jewish feminists. This monthly celebration, corresponding with the lunar cycle, has always had a special connection to women, who also renew their cycles monthly through menstruation.

Various branches of Judaism have increased the openness of rituals and celebrations that used to be the sole province of men. The bar mitzvah—a celebration marking a Jewish boy's coming of age at thirteen—has had a girls' counterpart, the bat mitzvah, since 1922. By the 1970s, the girls' ceremony was virtually universal among all Jewish denominations with the exception of the Orthodox Jews. However, even Orthodox girls now frequently celebrate a bat mitzvah, although the ceremony is limited to the women's section of the synagogue with only women present and no regular prayer service held.

In addition, since 1985 groups of women have joined together in Jerusalem to pray aloud at the Kotel (Wailing Wall). Jewish psychologist and author Phyllis Chesler was one of about seventy women from Europe, North America, Australia, Asia, South America, and the Middle East who gathered in ritual garments for prayer and Torah reading at the Wall on December 1, 1988, during the first International Jewish Feminist Conference in Jerusalem. "We prayed at the Kotel but only on the women's side, behind a high barrier that separated men from women and women from the Torah," recalls Chesler. "The service was disrupted by verbal and threatened physical assaults from some ultra-Orthodox men and women at the site." The prohibition of women's spoken prayer at the Wall appears to originate in the rabbinical belief that women's voices are dangerous to male listeners. Eve tempted Adam verbally; and some Orthodox men even today believe that if a man hears a woman's voice while he is engaged in prayer, it will distract him, interfering with his ability to pray. Although the Israeli Supreme Court ruled in 1994 that it is illegal for women to pray aloud at the Kotel, groups of women continue to gather at or near the Wall for prayer. "Once you've got this kind of energy moving among the people," states Chesler, "there's no way of stopping it."

In Buddhism, the majority of the feminist critique focuses not on the religion's doctrines, which are relatively gender neutral, but on the state of the Buddhist practice, initiation, and transmission of the dharma. Despite its core teachings, Buddhism is a tradition that originated in the East and therefore reflects many of that culture's values and practices. Until quite recently, the practice of American Buddhism mirrored its Asian counterpart in several areas that made it especially challenging for women. For example, a serious dharma student was expected to spend long hours meditating with other practitioners in a meditation hall, which created child-care problems for those who were parents. Practice was largely seen as something that took place in retreats and communal religious centers, not something that one did at home as part of the daily routine.

Vipassana meditation teacher Kamal Masters sometimes tells her students a story about her early experience studying Buddhist practice in Hawaii. She was a single mother with three children, working two jobs. Her teacher, Munindra, was staying at her house, and he used to tell her that she needed to "sit"—to meditate in a formal way for a prescribed period of time—every day. She couldn't possibly find the time. Finally, Munindra asked her, "What activity do you do more than any other?" After some thought, she responded, "I wash dishes." So he brought her to the sink and they began to practice a washing-dishes meditation. From then on, every time Masters washed the dishes, she practiced mindfulness.

Happily, large numbers of American women of all religious persuasions are incorporating spirituality into their daily lives and making their spiritual practice more home centered. Not long ago Kathleen Stanley, writing in the *Washington Post* Home section, described "soul" as a new trend in interior decorating. But as usual, reality was skewed and twisted by cynicism. "Today's notion of soul," Stanley wrote, "must look good at all costs. This is about stuff, not reverence." She couldn't be more wrong. Of course, there are those who want to market soulful products and those who want to "buy a look," but the trend that Stanley is picking up on is a real change in the venue of practice. No longer are many people satisfied to confine worship to Saturday in the synagogue or Sunday in the church. Today, homes are becoming spiritual bases. Home altars and meditation or quiet rooms are in evidence; housewarmings now include blessings for the structure as well as its occupants; and feng shui, a Chinese system that recognizes and works with the flow of energies, is being used to bring harmony to the home. Morning and evening prayers and/or meditation periods, grace at mealtime, even concerted efforts to have family meals, all provide evidence of the growing desire to bring spirituality into daily life. They are characteristic of the widening view of practice that stresses its integration with daily life rather than renunciation of the world.

However, home-based practice is far from replacing the foment within institutional arenas. Just as in Judaism, many Christian feminists are choosing to focus their energies on reforming sexist aspects of the church. Women have fought long and hard to become ministers, and in most denominations they have succeeded. (Significant exceptions are Roman Catholicism and Eastern Orthodoxy.) However, it is not enough for women to be allowed to recite the gender-biased liturgies of traditional Christianity; Christian feminists are seeking to revamp the entire way congregants participate in worship, celebration, and theology. As is usually the case, changes can be seen in local churches long before they are formalized in the national institutions, and in most metropolitan areas today, local worshippers know where to find the services where the preachers use feminine pronouns, new songs are sung, and new rituals are enacted.

Unfortunately, there are few recorded rituals, songs, or myths that reflect early Christian women's expressions of their spiritual experiences, so contemporary women are inventing their own. Simply gathering together and telling one another stories of their own experiences as women is an important way for present-day feminists to understand and nurture their relationship with the sacred. In addition, some groups have created rituals to address the needs of women that have been ignored or silenced by the traditional church, including healing rites for lesbians, victims of rape and incest, and women who have experienced divorce or abortion.

Not surprisingly, traditions in which women have been the most oppressed have spawned some of the strongest and most organized revisionary efforts. For example, the influential movement Women-Church originated out of Roman Catholic women's frustration with their limited roles in their church. Introduced at a major conference in 1983 in Chicago, Women-Church rejects Catholicism's hierarchical structure of ministry in favor of a community-oriented structure in which participants minister to one another. The movement welcomes men and non-Catholics and seeks to reclaim the true biblical tradition. However, recognizing that the Bible is tainted with sexism, Women-Church communities are also open to spiritual resources outside of the traditional Christian texts. Rosemary Radford Ruether, one of Women-Church's most vocal proponents, says that Women-Church is not an offshoot of the true church but rather *is* church. Believing that the traditional institution got off track, Women-Church hopes and prays for a unification of the church, when the word *women* will no longer need to be appended to the title because their presence will once again be an integral part of the ongoing tradition.

Whether undertaken from within the traditional world religions or from nontraditional feminist spirituality movements, the new feminist revision of spirituality calls for nothing less than a massive paradigm shift. Feminist reform is not simply a nice addition but a restructuring essential to preserving the integrity of religion's core meanings. The feminist critique of spirituality is aimed at overhauling all aspects of religious life, including ritual, liturgy, language, theology, ethics, story, and symbol. It cannot be any other way, as these are all intercon-nected. As Rita Gross writes, "Wherever it starts, feminism eventually changes every part of the interwoven fabric of religion. In the complex interweaving of myth and ritual, of theory and praxis, of theology and liturgy, if you pull on one thread, it affects all the other criss-crossed threads." Although progress may seem glacial at times, we see continual strides being made due in large part to the fierce dedication and determination of legions of women.

The Media as Messenger

Soul work, along with alternative medicine, is definitely getting more and better press coverage. Bill Moyers, the popular host of PBS television specials, has over the years introduced millions of viewers to aspects of soul work through his inter-views with mythologist Joseph Campbell, religious scholar Huston Smith, African-American scholar and singer Bernice Johnson Reagon, poet Robert Bly, choreographer and dancer Bill T. Jones, and others, as well as through programs that tackled specific topics such as the Books of Genesis, the mythic journey, spirit and nature, addictions, and, of course, *Healing and the Mind*, a series on the mind-body relationship. In a speech to the Religion Newswriters Association, he declared that "the most interesting stories of our time are emerging in the inter-section between the secular and the spiritual, between God and politics." And although recognized as one of the first, Moyers is no longer the only journalist to notice the spiritual renaissance in the country.

In the past several years, print and broadcast outlets have made staff commit-ments to the coverage of religion. For example, National Public Radio (NPR) made Lynn Neary its first full-time religion reporter, and Newhouse News pur-chased Religious News Service with the intention of increasing its coverage of spirituality and ethics. In fall 1997 PBS aired a thirteen-part series entitled *Religion and Ethics*, and in spring 1998 PBS's *Frontline* presented a four-hour pro-gram, *From Jesus to Christ: The First Christians*, which traced the development of Christianity in its first three hundred years.

In the newspaper world, the *Dallas Morning News* debuted a weekly six-page religion section staffed with an editor and three full-time reporters; the Washington bureau chief for Knight-Ridder newspapers inaugurated a religion, culture, and values beat; and papers like the *Detroit Free Press* and *Washington Post* promised to increase efforts at reporting news related to religion, values, and ethics. While there is hardly a land rush to stake out the religion beat—the *Washington Post*'s religion section is nearly impossible to find, and most religion sections consist of one page on Saturday devoted to church announcements and hours of services—we believe that more high-profile, high-placed journalists are seeing the value of addressing subjects related to people's exploration of the sacred. They are moving beyond traditional and politically linked religion stories, such as abortion, denominational events, and papal visits, to fresh stories about religious rituals, spiritually assisted dying, and even dreamwork.

Peter Jennings, the senior anchor and editor of ABC's *World News Tonight*, for example, writes about coming back in the mid–1980s from an overseas posting. "I was struck by how many Americans in the midst of such plenty were hungry for something more than our vaunted consumer society could provide them. And very slowly I began to realize the most obvious fact—that people's faith and religious beliefs were connected in so many ways to everything going on around me." He recalls how, once this observation was made, potential religion stories began appearing everywhere. In 1994 *ABC World News Tonight* became the first television network news program to hire a full-time religion correspondent. We see more and more editors, producers, and reporters "getting it," seeing how central spirituality is to the fabric of our lives.

Managing Managed Care

Another issue affecting the psychology field today is managed care. Ten years ago if you had health insurance, all you had to do was pick a psychotherapist of your own choice and your insurance company would reimburse you for between 50 and 80 percent of the cost as long as your therapist was properly certified and licensed as a clinical social worker, psychiatrist, or psychologist. You could be in therapy as frequently and for as long as you and your therapist wished. This arrangement is going the way of the dinosaur as an increasing number of health insurance companies add cost-cutting measures such as gatekeepers who must review your case before allowing for reimbursement; a requirement that you pay more per session if you select a therapist "outside the network" of preselected providers who contract with the insurance company to offer their services for a fixed and usually discounted rate; a limit on the number and frequency of sessions that are reimbursed (it can be as low as six to ten sessions); and a requirement that the therapist submit lengthy, complex, and frequent reports justifying ongoing treatment.

As more and more insurance companies adopt these cost-saving mechanisms, the practice of psychotherapy is changing. First, in order to continue caring for clients whose insurance has run out and who cannot afford current session fees, therapists may need to decrease their fees, see the clients less frequently, or refer them to a less costly therapist, including those working for government-sponsored clinics. Therapists may also offer less costly forms of therapy such as group therapy, which usually costs a little more than half of what individual therapy costs. In terms of client response to managed care requirements, many will go outside the conventional health-care system and seek counseling within a less costly educational model and context. This is the trend emerging in the marriage counseling field. Clients may also seek less expensive treatment from government agencies, college guidance centers, or pastoral counseling centers, as well as organize or join self-help groups.

There are, however, those in the field—James Hillman, Thomas Moore, and other archetypal psychologists—who prefer to view psychotherapy as belonging more to the arts and humanities than to science and medicine. For this reason they believe that the future of psychotherapy may lie in the province of art and literature, myth, storytelling, and poetry. In this context, reimbursement is not an issue.

The current limits placed on psychotherapy by managed care programs may force it out of the health-care context and back into the healing arts from which it came. Already people are paying millions of dollars out of pocket for alternative medical care. In our experience, many therapists have never joined networks of preferred providers or health maintenance organizations, nor do they deal with health insurance companies. Still they have thriving practices, especially when the economy is strong. Others whose practices have suffered are moving into consultation, teaching, and supervision. Additionally, therapists are specializing in therapies such as Eye Movement Desensitization Reprocessing and forms of body-work and body psychotherapy. Many consumers are clearly voting with their pocketbooks and continuing therapy without receiving reimbursement.

No More Whine

Although we are not quite sure where this movement is going, it is notable that there seems to be an impatience with emotional woundedness and inklings of a return to moral exhortation. Popular radio talk show host, author, and marriage and family therapist Laura Schlessinger, Ph.D., is the perfect example of this trend. Her internationally syndicated talk show is heard by more than ten million people and ranks second only to Rush Limbaugh's in popularity. Her strong and forceful views on the need for personal ethical conduct seem to be part of her appeal.

At a taping of a lecture, the slim, energetic, fiftyish Dr. Laura, as she is called, paces back and forth across the stage slashing the air with her arms. The audience is subdued but listening intently. Rhetorically she asks, "Why bother being moral?" then launches into her answer by pointing out that people (like other animals) are not innately moral—only potentially so. Sometimes she says, "We have to go against the 'survive and reproduce' laws of nature in order to obey another set of laws—the moral laws." This, she emphasizes, is what "elevates us above the termites."

To add drama, she stops her perpetual movement for a few seconds and declares that happiness doesn't come from having fun or acquiring things. Instead, she tells her rapt audience, feeling good about yourself comes from having character, courage, and commitment. These qualities, she continues, require us to discipline our self-indulgence, rise above temptation, and make sacrifices. As an example, she tells a story about a single father who told her that he was considering fulfilling his childhood dream of going to medical school, even though it would mean spending less time with his children. Dr. Laura's response to this man's dream was not just "Get over it" but "Stuff it."

Why do her strident harangues about morality draw such big crowds? One possible answer is that she fills the gap created by the breakdown of commonly shared values and the weakened moral authority of our social institutions. Dr. Laura is not shy about jumping into the void and prescribing traditional remedies. She believes, for example, that if people have children, the children should be the first priority in their lives, not their careers or lifestyle needs.

Although a licensed counselor, she is not a fan of the psychotherapy profession, saying that it encourages a national allegiance to the "do-it-if-it-feels-good" and "let-it-all-hang-out" mentalities. This allegation highlights an old question: Do people feel good about themselves because they do good, as Dr. Laura maintains, or do people do good because they feel good about themselves, as most psychotherapists would contend?

Speaking from the psychotherapist's point of view, well-known author and psychologist Eugene Gendlin believes that people have something inside them that organizes and directs their lives. Thus they do not need to have moral values imposed from the outside, as Dr. Laura suggests. Instead he believes that therapists can help clients nurture their own inner source of moral and ethical direction.

Pastoral counselor Robert Randall, in a *Christian Century* book review, speaks to the issue of what kind of change process best helps people improve their ethical behavior. He begins by making a distinction between those who believe that the starting point for change is to be stripped of self so as to be emptied of pride and selfishness and those who believe that pride is more often a symptom of feeling empty and a defense against loss of self. People, he writes, "in order to be moral need to find, not strip, themselves. Being broken is not the solution; it is the problem." Randall believes that ethical behavior is the result of having inner wounds healed. He states that in twenty-five years of psychotherapy practice, he has not known anyone who was "able to sustain new behavior without first finding care for his beleaguered soul."

Whether the "get-over-it" position of Dr. Laura or the focus on inner work will win in the cultural arena is still an open question. Having read *Soul Work*, we're sure you sense our bias. To us, the more courageous stance is to trust in the innate goodness of human beings, ever mindful of the difficulties of staying connected to this core and fully aware that many people are either not interested in or unaware of their cores. Somerset Maugham once said, "There is an heroic courage with which man confronts the irrationality of the world, a beauty greater than the beauty of art." We also believe that it is heroic and courageous to connect with the mysteries of life. The process of keeping connected is precisely the journey we see so many people on today.

More and more of us are being exposed to soul work and eagerly, though not without trepidation, immersing themselves in the work. How can we not? For once we taste the juicy sweet meat of meaning, we are urged on by something much larger than ourselves. Albert Einstein once said that "the most beautiful thing we can experience is the mysterious." That experience—whether stumbled upon or worked toward—is the siren's call that spurs us forward in our journey. Our hope is that this book has served and will continue to serve as a field guide—orienting, encouraging, informing, advising, and guiding you along the way. And perhaps like Laurens van der Post, you too will have the experience of living your life "not by conscious plan or prearranged design but as someone following the flight of a bird."

Resources

One of the ironies in preparing *Soul Work* was the need to separate and categorize. Given the interconnectedness of the holistic field, this task was a particularly challenging one. For example, when working on the dance therapy section in chapter 6, we had to grapple with the perplexing reality that dance could be utilized as a form of body psychotherapy, as an arts therapy, and as a somatic therapy.

A similar conundrum occurs in compiling a list of resources because many organizations defy simple and easy classification but are nonetheless important resources for engaging in soul work. This appendix was conceived of as a catchall collection of centers, institutes, foundations, publications, and programs whose common element is that they can aid and abet inner work.

RETREAT CENTERS

One of the downsides of our increasingly hectic lives is a sense that feeling frazzled is a way of life, that it is the norm, not the exception. Up unconscionably early to get the kids off to school and to do battle with daily commuter traffic, and home much too late at night, we intersperse the weekday grind with weekends primarily devoted to chores that keep our home life on track: grocery shopping, cleaners, shoe repair, laundry, yard work, and on and on. Though most of us wouldn't trade in our children or jobs, a change of pace is definitely in order.

Retreats offer the opportunity for rejuvenation, personal exploration, and firsthand experience of a spiritual practice. They provide a rest stop on the highway of life. They can refresh the body, revive the mind, and renew the spirit. Vacations can accomplish similar goals, but retreats add the structure and resources for intentionally focusing inward, on our souls.

Retreat centers have become astoundingly popular as people seek opportunities not only to remove themselves from the daily distractions, stresses, and strains of life but also to gain deeper perspective. Only five years ago, one could call a monastery or retreat house and sign up for virtually any weekend. No longer. We have seen our favorite retreat sites begin to book months in advance, some up to a year! Despite the need to plan well in advance, the retreat experience remains well worth it. Chuck cavels about the camaraderie of kindred spirits, the nourishing food, and the natural settings. Anne is called by contact with the natural world and the deeply nourishing silence.

Some people shy away from long periods of silence because they thrive on social contact and see silence as a form of isolation. Some fear that being alone with only their thoughts would be torture. For this reason, we highly recommend that you pick a retreat program that has the amount of silence you feel comfortable with. Some retreats observe strict silence even at mealtimes, while others have periods throughout the day when silence is observed, such as before breakfast or just after evening prayers or meditation. In between the silent periods, some retreat centers offer opportunities for individual or group spiritual guidance, scripture reading, or different forms of worship services. Often it is possible to take walks in nature and to spend time reading or writing in your journal.

Listed here are some of the most popular retreat centers in the United States. The length of retreats and the types of programs vary considerably, as do the fees. Check with the individual center and ask whether it offers work exchange or scholarship programs. Also note that some holistic conference centers provide special retreat programs as well.

You may also want to consult one of the guidebooks listed at the end of this section for more detailed information. Please note that some retreat centers are listed in chapter 4 in the meditative practice sections. Here we list some of the best-known and most popular retreat centers that draw people from more than one local region.

Campion Renewal Center
319 Concord Road
Weston, MA 02193
(781) 894-3199 (phone)
(781) 894-5864 (fax)
Founded in 1972, this Jesuit center is committed to adapting the spiritual exercises of Saint Ignatius to help people of all faiths grow in a contemplative relationship with God.

Center for Spiritual Awareness
P.O. Box 7
Lakemont, GA 30552
(706) 782-4723 (phone)
(706) 782-4560 (fax)
csmainc@stc.net (e-mail)
www.csa.davis.org (website)
The center offers meditation retreats in the northeast Georgia mountains from May to September. The director, Roy Eugene Davis, teaches in the Kryla yoga tradition.

Center for Spiritual Development
96 Milton Road
Rye, NY 10580
(914) 967-7328 (phone)
(914) 967-7387 (fax)
The center offers various programs in spirituality.

Dayspring Silent Retreat Center
11301 Neelsville Church Road
Germantown, MD 20876
(301) 428-9348
Established forty years ago, the center offers ecumenical Christian silent retreats guided by mature, experienced leaders. Dayspring also makes its space available for group or personal retreats conducted within its framework of silence.

Feathered Pipe Ranch
P.O. Box 1682
Helena, MT 59624
(406) 442-8196 (phone)
(406) 442-8110 (fax)
fpranch@initco.net (e-mail)
The Ranch offers retreat-style workshops on topics such as astrology, yoga, women's wisdom, and shamanism.

Grailville
932 O'Bannonville Road
Loveland, OH 45140-9742
(513) 683-2340
Grailville is an education and conference center offering programs related to ecology, spirituality in various traditions, feminism, the arts, and social justice. The Grailville newsletter, published three times a year, is available for a $10 donation.

Heartwood Institute
220 Harmony Lane
Garberville, CA 95542
(707) 923-2021
Heartwood provides resources for attaining higher physical, psychological, and spiritual well-being. Heartwood conducts various personal growth retreats, often within an educational framework.

Hollyhock
Box 127
Manson's Landing
Cortes Island, BC VOP 1KO
Canada
(800) 933-6339 (phone)
(250) 935-6424 (fax)
hollyhock@oberon.ark.com (e-mail)
www.hollyhock.bc.ca (website)
Located at the edge of British Columbia's vast coastal wilderness, Hollyhock provides a warm, supportive environment for experiential learning and creative self-expression. The remote setting affords a healing and regenerative encounter with the natural world. One-month intensives and work-study opportunities are available.

Karmê Chöling
Buddhist Meditation Center
RR 1 Box 3
Barnet, VT 05821
(802) 633-2384 (phone)
(802) 633-3012 (fax)
KarmeCholing@Shambala.org (e-mail)
www.kcl.shambala.org (website)
Founded in 1970 by Chögyam Trungpa, this meditation center offers courses in Buddhist meditation; Shambala training; psychology and health; and calligraphy, ikebana, and Dharma art.

Lama Foundation
P.O. Box 240
San Cristobal, NM 87564
(505) 586-1269 (phone)
(505) 586-1964 (fax)
76375.2726@compuserve.com (e-mail)
Incorporated in 1968, Lama is a nonprofit educational center and spiritual community dedicated to the awakening of consciousness. Lama offers a program of summer retreats and two hermitages. It also operates a small cottage industry: making prayer flags that bear symbols from many spiritual paths.

Mountain Light Retreat Center
Route 2, Box 419
Crozet, VA 22932
(804) 978-7770 (phone)
(804) 978-7559 (fax)
Located in the Blue Ridge Mountains outside of Charlottesville, the retreat center is home to the Mountain Light Zen Center. Individuals and groups can rent the center for retreats or workshops or join the center's Zen activities.

Mount Madonna Center for the Creative Arts and Sciences
445 Summit Road
Watsonville, CA 95076
(408) 847-0406 (phone)
(408) 847-2683 (fax)
programs@mountmadonna.org (e-mail)
www.infopoint.com/orgs/mmc (website)
The Mount Madonna Center is a community designed to nurture the creative arts and the health sciences within a context of spiritual growth. Personal and group retreats as well as weekend programs are available. The center also maintains a work-study program.

Pecos Benedictine Monastery
Pecos, NM 87552
(505) 757-6415 (phone)
(505) 757-2285 (fax)
guestmaster@juno.com (e-mail)
www.pecosabbey.org (website)
This Benedictine monastery is of the Olivetan Congregation and so consists of one family in two distinct communities—one of men, one of women.

Retreatants are offered a variety of programs, including dream interpretation in the biblical tradition, enneagram study with contemplative prayer, healing the family tree, and other offerings that combine the psychological and the sacred.

Phoenicia Pathwork Center
P.O. Box 66
Phoenicia, NY 12464
(914) 688-2211 (phone)
(914) 688-2007 (fax)
info@pathworkny.org (e-mail)
www.pathworkny.org (website)
The Pathwork is a contemporary path of self-transformation, integrating psychological insight with spiritual wisdom. The Phoenicia Pathwork Center, the founding center of the Pathwork worldwide, offers weekend seminars, yearlong programs, and an extensive body of teachings detailing a practical and inspired process for rediscovering one's real self.

Resources for Ecumenical Spirituality
3704 Highway 13
Dunnegan, MO 65640-9620
(417) 754-2562
Founded in 1987, this Missouri-based, nonprofit organization fosters mutual understanding among religious faiths through shared spiritual practice and dialogue. It sponsors retreats, colloquia, publications, and other projects related to spiritual practice and study.

Saint Benedict Center
P.O. Box 5070
Madison, WI 53705
(608) 836-1631 (phone)
(608) 831-9312 (fax)
Saint Benedict Center is the home of a woman's ecumenical monastic community and a retreat and conference center. Open to all, Saint Benedict Center provides a welcoming place for personal retreats, group meetings, spirituality programs, public prayer, and enjoying God in creation.

Shenoa Retreat and Learning Center
P.O. Box 43
Philo, CA 95466
(707) 895-3156 (phone)
(707) 895-3236 (fax)
Shenoa is a Findhorn-inspired retreat center for groups, families, and individuals. Located two and a half hours north of San Francisco and thirty minutes from the Pacific Coast, Shenoa offers a variety of meeting spaces, an outdoor pool, and miles of hiking and biking trails.

Spiritual Life Institute
1 Carmelite Way
Crestone, CO 81131
(719) 256-4778
The Spiritual Life Institute, founded in 1960, is a small ecumenical Roman Catholic monastic community of men and women who embrace a life of contemplative solitude according to the Carmelite ideal. Hermitages are open for private retreats

SYDA (Siddha Yoga Dham) Foundation
P.O. Box 600
South Fallsburg, NY 12779
(914) 434-2000 (phone)
www.siddhayoga.org (website)
The *siddha* yoga movement, which traces its lineage to Bhagwan Nityananda, an Indian holy man, had its foundations laid by Swami Muktananda and its reach extended globally by Swami Chidvilasananda. *Siddha* yoga is aimed at profoundly altering consciousness through the guru-disciple relationship, chanting, *shaktipat* (a transmission of energy from guru to devotee), and other spiritual practices.

Temenos Institute
29 East Main Street
Westport, CT 06880
(203) 227-4388
The Temenos Institute offers workshops, lectures, films, and courses that represent different models of depth psychology.

Temenos Retreat Center
1564 Telegraph Road, Route 162
West Chester, PA 19382
(610) 696-8145 (phone)
(610) 696-7335 (fax)
Established in 1986, Temenos is a service of the Swedenborgian Church. Regular offerings include dream sharing, family relationships and communication, couples retreats, creative expression, holotropic breathwork, universal peace dances, and Swedenborgian spiritual perspectives.

Whidbey Institute for Earth, Spirit, and the Human Future
P.O. Box 57
Clinton, WA 98236
(206) 467–0384 (toll-free from Seattle)
(360) 341–1884 (phone)
(360) 341–1899 (fax)
whidinst@whidbey.com (e-mail)
www.whidbey.com/Whidbey_Institute (website)
The Whidbey Institute (formerly known as Chinook Learning Center) offers programs designed to connect the inner life of the self with the outer world of society, including retreats, conferences, special classes and consultations, an intergenerational Folkschool, and "Power of Hope," an ongoing program for youth. Please inquire about work-study and internship opportunities.

Guidebooks to Retreat Centers

Artists' and Writers' Colonies (1995)
By Gail Hellund Bowler
Blue Heron Press
24450 Northwest Hansen Road
Hillsboro, OR 97124
(503) 621-3911

The Complete Guide to Buddhist America (1998)
Edited by Don Morreale
Shambhala Publications, Inc.
Horticultural Hall
300 Massachusetts Avenue
Boston, MA 02115

Healing Retreats and Spas Newsletter
2022 Cliff Dr., Suite 339
Santa Barbara, CA 93109

Healthy Escapes: Spas, Fitness Resorts, and Cruises (1997)
Fodor's Travel Publications
201 East 50th Street
New York, NY 10022

A Place Apart: Houses of Prayer and Retreat Centers in North America (1995)
Compiled by Janet Joy
Source Books

P.O. Box 794
Trabuco Canyon, CA 92678

Renewing Your Soul (1995)
By David Cooper
HarperSanFrancisco
353 Sacramento Street, Suite 500
San Francisco, CA 24111

Sanctuaries: A Guide to Lodgings in Monasteries, Abbeys, and Retreats: The Complete United States (1996)
By Jack and Marcia Kelly
Bell Tower, Harmony Books, Crown Publishers, Inc.
201 East 50th Street
New York, NY 10022

Silence, Simplicity, and Solitude: A Guide for Spiritual Retreat (1992)
By David Cooper
Bell Tower, Harmony Books, Crown Publishers
201 East 50th Street
New York, NY 10022

Transformative Adventures, Vacations and Retreats: An International Directory of 300+ Host Organizations (1994)
By John Benson
New Millennium Publishing
P.O. Box 3065
Portland, OR 97208

Whole Heaven Catalogue: A Resource Guide to Products, Services, Arts, Crafts, and Festivals of Religious, Spiritual, and Cooperative Communities (1998)
By Marcia and Jack Kelly
Bell Tower/One Spirit, Crown Publishers
201 East 50th Street
New York, NY 10022

CONFERENCE CENTERS

Conference centers are a wonderful mix of retreat and educational opportunities. Often located in lovely natural settings, these centers open up possibilities for growth at every level: intellectual, emotional, psychological, physical, and spiritual. They offer a vast array of programs either throughout the year or during the summer months. Some can be likened to adult summer camps; others are more professionally oriented. In addition to offering personal transformation programs, conference centers allow those in the helping professions to take part in meaningful dialogues with their colleagues and expand their knowledge of other healing methods. Conference centers often provide work-exchange, internship, and scholarship programs. The centers listed here are a sampling of the best-known and most popular that draw participants from more than one local region.

Avalon Institute
3985 Wonderland Hill
Boulder, CO 80302
(303) 443-4363 (phone and fax)
Avalon offers contemplative retreats and summer education programs. It also offers training programs in Jungian and archetypal psychotherapy.

Breitenbush Hot Springs Retreat and Conference Center
P.O. Box 578
Detroit, OR 97342
(503) 854-3314
Breitenbush offers workshops and individual retreats.

Center for Action and Contemplation
P.O. Box 12464
Albuquerque, NM 87195-2464
(505) 242-9588 (phone)
(505) 242-9518 (fax)
The center offers forty- and twelve-day internships, retreats, conferences, workshops, and liturgies that focus on the integration of social action and contemplative prayer. The guest house is available for private retreats.

Claymont Society
Route 1, Box 279
Charles Town, WV 25414
(304) 725-4437
The Claymont Society was founded in 1975 as a community and school to promote the principles of continuous education and integrated human development. In 1985 Claymont Court Seminars, sponsored by the society, was established to host and facilitate retreats, workshops, and seminars.

Esalen Institute
Highway 1
Big Sur, CA 93920
(408) 667-3000 (phone)
(408) 667-2724 (fax)
www.esalen.org (website)
Founded in 1962 as an educational center devoted to the exploration of unrealized human capacities, Esalen can be experienced in several ways: an overnight visit, a long-term stay, a weekend or five-day workshop, a twenty-eight-day work-study module, long-term training, or participation in the Ongoing Residence Program.

Full Circle Center for Holistic Studies
1332 Talbot
Huntington Woods, MI 48070
(248) 541-3033
Full Circle Center brings people of all ages and cultural, ethnic, and spiritual backgrounds together to develop a deeper understanding of the interrelationship between spirituality, psychology, ecology, and creativity.

Hope Spring
P.O. Box 2948
Summerville, SC 29484-2948
(800) 342-9655 or (803) 873-6463 (phone)
(803) 832-3018 (fax)
www.hopespring.org (website)
Hope Spring is a center for holistic studies in the coastal South Carolina low country. Topics for programs include creative writing, drawing, herbal healing, and alternative medicine.

International Transpersonal Center
38 Miller Avenue, Suite 160
Mill Valley, CA 94941
(415) 388-7788
The center is still in its conceptual phase but plans to be an international community dedicated to facilitating the application of new scientific paradigms that recognize the unity underlying all of humanity and the material world.

Kalani Honua Conference and Retreat Center
RR 1, Box 4500
Pahoa, HI 96778
(808) 965-7828 (phone)
(808) 965-9613 (fax)
kalani@kalani.com (e-mail)
www.kalani.com (website)
Kalani Honua was founded in 1980 as an intercultural conference center devoted to supporting physical, spiritual, and emotional healing, the arts, and traditional Hawaiian culture. This multicultural, shared-living community presents a spectrum of educational events, including workshops, conferences, and retreats.

Kanuga Conferences
P.O. Drawer 250
Hendersonville, NC 28793
(704) 692-9136
Affiliated with the Episcopal Church, the center sponsors conferences, educational programs, retreats, and summer camps.

Kirkridge
RR 3, Box 3402
Bangor, PA 18013-9359
(610) 588-1793
Founded in 1942, Kirkridge derives its name from the Scottish word for church, kirk, and the center's location on the Appalachian ridge. It offers ongoing workshops, lectures, seminars, and retreats.

Mercy Center
2300 Adeline Drive
Burlingame, CA 94010
(650) 340-7474 (phone)
(650) 340-1299 (fax)
www.mercy-center.org (website)
Mercy Center fosters a contemporary spirituality rooted in the Christian tradition and enriched by scripture, spiritual practice, the social sciences, and other faith traditions. Training programs in spiritual direction and meditation, private and directed retreats, conferences, Taize and centering prayer, and a wide range of workshops are offered throughout the year.

Merritt Center
P.O. Box 2087
Payson, AZ 85547
(520) 474-4268 or (800) 414-9880 (phone)
(520) 474-8588 (fax)
Merritt Center was created to provide a climate conducive to the renewal and empowerment of individuals and organizations. To this end, the center sponsors Elderhostel wellness, adult journey, and relationship renewal programs; empowerment workshops; and various weekend and weeklong seminars.

National Havurah Committee (NHC)
P.O. Box 2621
Bala Cynwyd, PA 19004-6621
Havurah, meaning "fellowship" in Hebrew, is a dynamic form of Jewish community that attempts to bridge the differences between Reformed, Reconstructionist, Conservative, and Orthodox Judaism. The NHC conducts national summer institutes and weeklong gatherings for intensive study, discussion, celebration, and community living.

New York Open Center
83 Spring Street
New York, NY 10012
(212) 219-2527 (phone)
(212) 226-4056 (fax)
nyocreg@aol.com (e-mail)
www.opencenter.org (website)
The New York Open Center, a nonprofit holistic learning center founded in 1984, offers workshops, lectures, in-depth and long-term programs in various disciplines (polarity therapy, prana yoga, reflexology, esoteric and feminine spirituality), and opportunities for study and retreat abroad. The center publishes Lapis, a journal that covers many of the topics addressed at the center.

Ojai Foundation
P.O. Box 1620
Ojai, CA 93024
(805) 646-8343
Ojai offers weekend workshops, group retreats, educational programs, and ceremonies for youth and adults to heal the split between work in the world and spiritual practice.

Omega Institute for Holistic Studies
260 Lake Drive
Rhinebeck, NY 12572
(800) 944-1001 (phone)
(914) 266-4828 (fax)
www.omega-inst.org (website)
Founded by the Sufi master Pir Vilyat Inayat Khan, the Omega Institute has been providing programs in mind, body, and spiritual education for more than twenty years. Omega is a vibrant learning community offering more than 250 workshops, retreats, and professional trainings in holistic health; psychological development; spiritual practice; the arts; relationships; work, business, and society; and sports.

Openway
RR 10, Box 105
Charlottesville, VA 22903
(804) 293-3245 (phone)
(804) 971-5815 (fax)
openway@rle.net (e-mail)
Founded in 1983, Openway is a nonsectarian center for healing and education dedicated to teaching students, and facilitating for clients, the Integral Healing Method—a synthesis of psychology and energy techniques.

Peace Valley
HC 65, Box 73B
Caddo Gap, AR 71935
(501) 356-2908 (phone)
(870) 356-4841 (fax)
pvnet@cswnet.com (e-mail)
www.cswnet.com.~pvnet/ (website)
Peace Valley offers workshops and retreats, which provide a healing place for awakening unconditional love and reverence for all life.

Plymouth Institute Conference and Retreat Center
N4683 Silver Spring Lane
Plymouth, WI 53073
(800) 377-7513 (phone)
(920) 528-8488 (call to fax)
www.execpc.com/'highwind/Plymouth (website)
The Plymouth Institute, dedicated to developing models and ideas of sustainability, offers year-round conference and retreat facilities. Work exchange or intern opportunities are available.

Rowe Camp and Conference Center
Kings Highway Road
Rowe, MA 01367
(413) 339-4954 (phone)
(413) 339-5728 (fax)
retreat@rowcenter.org (e-mail)
www.rowecenter.org (website)
Rowe Camp and Conference Center offers weekend retreats in the spring, fall, and winter that provide a wide variety of spiritual, psychological, political, health, and vacation opportunities. In the summer Rowe Camp comes into full operation, offering opportunities for teenagers, families, singles, men, women, gay men, people in recovery, and preteens to enjoy the camping experiences designed specifically for them.

Sevenoaks Pathwork Center
Route 1, Box 86
Madison, VA 22727
(540) 948-6544 (phone)
(540) 948-3956 (fax)
sevenoaksp@aol.com (e-mail)
www.pathwork.org (website)
Sevenoaks Pathwork Center offers workshops and trainings in the Pathwork, a contemporary path that stresses the exploration and transformation of our shadow side as well as the cultivation and celebration of our innate divinity. Sevenoaks offers workshops on healing, shamanism, meditation, and earth-centered spirituality.

Taos Institute
Box 4628, Camino de la Placita
Taos, NM 87571
(505) 751-1232
The Taos Institute, a center for dialogue, inquiry, and consultation aimed at achieving more humane and ecologically viable forms of relationship—from daily intimacies to local communities and organizations, and onward to the global community—offers conferences, consulting, and workshops.

Vallecitos Mountain Refuge
P.O. Box 1507
Taos, NM 87571
(505) 751-0351 (phone)
(505) 751-1775 (fax)

refuge@vallecitos.org (e-mail)
www.vallecitos.org (website)
The Vallecitos Mountain Refuge, a remote wilderness ranch located in the mountains of the Carson National Forest west of Taos, New Mexico, is a retreat center and refuge for career activists seeking personal and spiritual renewal.

INDEPENDENT TRAINING PROGRAMS

Sometimes, instead of "retreating" from our daily routine, we need to spend time in educational activities that not only stimulate our intellects but also provide opportunities to learn experientially. Or we want to find programs that allow us to pursue a particular topic or technique in depth over time. The following organizations offer training, educational resources, seminars, and so on, that can advance personal transformation and inner growth and/or enhance your professional skills.

Academy for Guided Imagery
P.O. Box 2070
Mill Valley, CA 94942
(415) 389-9324 or (800) 726-2070 (phone)
(415) 389-9342 (fax)
www.healthy.net/ag (website)
Drawing on related disciplines, including Eriksonian hypnosis, Jungian psychology, psychosynthesis, self-actualization, and ego-state psychology, the academy teaches professionals in the counseling and health fields to use imagery in their practices.

Aletheia Heart Institute
1068 East Main Street
Ashland, OR 97520
(503) 488-0709
Founded in 1958, Aletheia supports programs and research that synthesize the findings of science, the perspectives of philosophy and psychology, and the revelations of spirituality. All of the programs emphasize the mind-brain-body connection and assist the participant in applying tools to his or her daily life.

Alternatives for Simple Living
3617 Old Lakeport Road
Sioux City, IA 51106
(712) 274-8875 (phone and fax)
(800) 821-6153 (toll-free)
Alternatives's mission is to equip people of faith to challenge consumerism, live justly, and celebrate responsibly by offering workshops and a nationwide speakers' bureau. *Whose Birthday Is It Anyway?* is produced annually to help families resist the pressures of overconsumption at Christmas time.

American Imagery Institute
P.O. Box 13453
Milwaukee, WI 53213
(414) 781-4045 (phone, call to fax)
Founded in 1983, the institute organizes workshops, primarily in the field of imagery, for counselors, nurses, psychologists, physicians, social workers, and educators. The institute sponsors a biannual conference and serves as a resource for books, tapes, and literature on imagery and its applications.

American Society of Alternative Therapists
P.O. Box 703
Rockport, MA 01966
(978) 281-4400 (phone)
(978) 282-1144 (fax)
asat@asat.org (e-mail)
www.asat.org (website)
Founded in 1990, the society offers courses in holistic health counseling and a diploma in CORE counseling.

Barbara Brennan School of Healing
P.O. Box 2005
East Hampton, NY 11937
(516) 329-0951 (phone)
(516) 324-9745 (fax)
bbshoffice@barbarabrennan.com (e-mail)
www.barbarabrennan.com (website)
Founded in 1982 by Barbara Brennan, author of *Hands of Light* and *Light Emerging*, the School of Healing is an internationally recognized educational institute dedicated to the evolution of the human spirit. Students learn techniques of healing to create health on physical, emotional, mental, and spiritual levels while experiencing their own transformational journey.

Biofeedback Training Institute (BTI)
Stens Corporation
6451 Oakwood Drive
Oakland, CA 94611
(510) 339-9053 or (800) 257-8367
BTI is the largest accredited biofeedback training program in the United States and offers certification classes in Atlanta, Berkeley, Chicago, Dallas, Denver, New York, San Francisco, and various locations in Florida, New Jersey, and Ohio. Special biofeedback courses in pain management and eeg/neurofeed-back are also offered.

Body Wisdom Inc.
669A 24th Street
Oakland, CA 94612
(510) 814-9584 (phone)
bodywisdom.simplenet.com (e-mail)
Body Wisdom is a nonprofit corporation codirected by Cynthia Winton-Henry and Phil Porter and devoted to the reintegration of body and spirit through performance, teaching, and writing.

Cape Cod Institute
1308D Belfer
Albert Einstein College of Medicine
1300 Morris Park Avenue
Bronx, NY 10461
(718) 430-2307
The Cape Cod Institute offers a summer series of in-depth, weeklong courses taught by professionals such as Thomas Moore, Herbert Benson, Margaret Wheatley, James Spira, and Harville Hendrix.

Center for Action and Contemplation
P.O. Box 12464
Albuquerque, NM 87195-2464
(505) 242-9588
Founded in 1987 by Richard Rohr, the center is interested in social change through a Christian faith perspective. Program topics include contemplation and liberation theology, Myers-Briggs/enneagram workshops, activist dialogues, and spiritual direction. Forty- and twelve-day "come to the desert" residential internships are also available.

Center for Attitudinal Healing
33 Buchanan Drive
Sausalito, CA 94965
(415) 331-6161 (phone)
(415) 331-4545 (fax)
cah@well.com (e-mail)
www.healingcenter.org (website)
Attitudinal healing is based on the belief that it is possible to choose peace rather than conflict, and love rather than fear. The center was established in 1975 by Gerald Jampolsky, and supplements traditional health care with an environment in which children, youths, and adults faced with life-threatening illness actively participate in the attitudinal healing process. Similar independent centers are located around the United States; contact the center for more information.

Center for Journal Therapy
Dept. 0-3, P.O. Box 963
Arvada, CO 80001
(303) 421-2298 or (888) 421-2298 (phone)
(303) 421-1255 (fax)
journaldoc@aol.com (e-mail)
www.journaltherapy.com (website)
Founded in 1985 by Kathleen Adams, the center teaches the art of journal writing to individuals, groups, and mental health professionals.

Center for Sandplay Studies
254 South Boulevard
Upper Grandview, NY 10960
(914) 358-2318 (phone)
(914) 358-5824 (fax)
ljcarey@spyval.net (e-mail)
Sandplay therapy was developed by Dora Kalff, a Swiss psychologist and collaborator with Carl Jung. The therapy combines aspects of play therapy, art therapy, and verbal therapy to enhance and often accelerate the therapeutic process. The center offers training and workshops onsite and worldwide.

Center for Spirituality and Psychotherapy
National Institute for the Psychotherapies (NIP)
330 West 58th Street
New York, NY 10019
(212) 582-1566 (phone)
(212) 586-1272 (fax)
NiPinste/oaol.com (e-mail)
psychospiritualtherapy.com (website)
The Center for Spirituality and Psychotherapy was

recently formed to train psychotherapists in spirituality, train religious professionals in psychotherapy, and explore the psycho-spiritual realm with the general public. The center will hold a yearly conference, offer continuing education programs in spirituality and psychotherapy, and, starting in 1999, offer two comprehensive, multi-year training programs in spirituality and psychotherapy, one for psychotherapists and one for religious professionals.

Center for Studies of the Person
Carl Rogers Institute of Psychotherapy, Training, and Supervision
1125 Torrey Pines Road
La Jolla, CA 92037
(619) 459-3974 (phone)
(619) 459-5237 (fax)
The Center for Studies of the Person is a place where a group of professionals carry out their commitment to person-centered values based on the principles developed through the research and practice of the late psychologist Carl R. Rogers. The center maintains the Carl Rogers Memorial Library.

Concord Institute
Box 82
Concord, MA 01742
(978) 371-3206 (phone and fax)
This educational organization was founded in 1990 to help professionals expand and deepen their work within a comprehensive spiritual context. It offers a range of training in individual and group work and is collaborating with kindred training organizations in Russia and Europe on the development of a global spiritual psychology.

Dialogue House Associates
80 East 11th Street, Suite 305
New York, NY 10003-6008
(212) 673-5880
The late Ira Progoff, Ph.D., developed the Intensive Journal method in the mid-1960s and founded Dialogue House to make the method available to the general public.

The Educational Center
6357 Clayton Road
St. Louis, MO 63117
(314) 721-7604 (phone)

(314) 721-2388 (fax)
TheEdCenter@aol.com (e-mail)
Established in 1941, the Educational Center houses Centerpoint, a unique study of the psychology of Carl G. Jung; Centerquest, an issue-centered, story-based program for all ages; and the Bible Workbench, a lectionary-based Bible study program.

Eupsychia
3930 W. Bee Caves Road, Suite J
Austin, TX 78746
(512) 327-2795 or (800) 546-2795 (phone)
(512) 327-6043 (fax)
eupsychia@aol.com (e-mail)
www.jacquelynsmall.com (website)
Eupsychia, founded by Jacquelyn Small in 1975, is a holistic education institute that offers programs for health professionals and others seeking knowledge and experience of personal psycho-spiritual transformation.

Foundation for *A Course in Miracles*
1275 Tennanah Lake Road
Roscoe, NY 12776-5905
(607) 498-4116 (phone)
(607) 498-5325 (fax)
www.facim.org (website)
The foundation was founded in 1983 to offer workshops and educational programs on *A Course in Miracles*, a three-volume curriculum of spiritual development channeled by Helen Schucman, Ph.D., and transcribed by William Thetford, Ph.D. The foundation's principal goal is to help students deepen their understanding of the *Course's* thought system, so that they may be more effective instruments of the Holy Spirit's teaching in their own lives.

Foundation for Community Encouragement, Inc. (FCE)
P.O. Box 17210
Seattle, WA 98107
(206) 784-9000 (phone)
(206) 784-9077 (fax)
inquire@fce-community.org (e-mail)
The FCE, a nonprofit educational foundation founded by M. Scott Peck, teaches the principles and values of community to individuals, groups, organizations, and businesses.

Foundation for Inner Peace
P.O. Box 598
Mill Valley, CA 94942-0598
(415) 388-2060 (phone)
(415) 388-9010 (fax)
info@acim.org (e-mail)
www.acim.org (website)
The foundation is currently translating A *Course in Miracles* into numerous languages, including Chinese, Russian, Japanese, and Swedish.

Four-Fold Way Training
P.O. Box 2077
Sausalito, CA 94966
(415) 331-5050 (phone)
(415) 331-5069 (fax)
Founded by Angeles Arrien, these educational programs explore indigenous wisdom, cross-cultural values, and experiential practices gleaned from ancient and modern ways.

Friends Conference on Religion and Psychology
3091 Connecticut Avenue, NW, #109
Washington, DC 20008
fcrp@quaker.org (e-mail)
www.quaker.org/fcrp (website)
This conference meets each Memorial Day weekend at Lebanon Valley College in Annville, Pennsylvania. Attendees seek ways to strengthen the inner life of the Spirit through the integration of the insights of Friends and depth psychology, with an emphasis on the teachings of Carl Jung. A Washington-area miniconference meets each February at Wellspring Center.

Grof Transpersonal Training
20 Sunnyside Avenue, Suite A-314
Mill Valley, CA 94941
(415) 383-8779 (phone)
(415) 383-0965 (fax)
www.holotropic.com (website)
In 1976 Christina and Stanislav Grof developed holotropic breathwork, a comprehensive approach to self-exploration that helps people access many levels of human experience, including unfinished issues from postnatal history, sequences of psychological death and rebirth, and the entire spectrum of transpersonal phenomena. The program has two

tracks—either to become a certified practitioner or simply to experience and study this practice in a more in-depth format.

Guild for Psychological Studies (GPS)
2024 Divisadero Street, Suite 2
San Francisco, CA 94115
(415) 931-0647 (phone)
(415) 913-1273 (fax)
guildst@aol.com (e-mail)
Since 1952, the GPS has offered seminars on the process of becoming a "value-centered" individual. Religious, psychological, mythological, and literary texts are emphasized.

Heartwood Institute
220 Harmony Lane
Garberville, CA 95542
(707) 923-2021 (phone)
(707) 923-5010 (fax)
enroll@heartwoodinstitute.com (e-mail)
www.heartwoodinstitute.com (website)
The institute sponsors programs in hypnotherapy, transformational studies, addiction counseling, and interdisciplinary somatic therapies.

Helen Palmer Workshops
1442A Walnut Street, Suite 377
Berkeley, CA 94709
(510) 843-7621 (phone)
(510) 540-7626 (fax)
The center's objective is to articulate and document the bridge between personality type and the spectrum of higher consciousness. The curriculum is rooted in the enneagram system and practices that support spiritual progress for different types of people. The center also offers a professional training program.

Hippocrates Health Institute
1443 Palmdale Court
West Palm Beach, FL 33411
(561) 471-8876 (phone)
(561) 471-9464 (fax)
hippocrates@worldnet.att.net (e-mail)
www.hippocratesinst.com (website)
Founded in 1981, this six-month certificate program offers educational experiences in five areas of personal and career development: lifestyle and nutritional education, apprenticeship experience, self-

actualization, opportunities in holistic disciplines, and career placement opportunities.

Institute for Dialogical Psychotherapy
Executive Plaza Bldg.
225 Stevens Ave., Suite 101
Solana Beach, CA 92075-2058
(619) 481-8744
The institute, founded in 1984, arose out of the desire of a number of psychotherapists to apply Martin Buber's philosophy of dialogue (the I-thou relationship) to the practice of psychotherapy.

Institute for the Study of Imagination
c/o Jean Lall
4803 Yellowwood Avenue
Baltimore, MD 21209
(410) 367-3219 or (410) 367-1961
The institute is a nonprofit organization founded in Massachusetts in 1987 to encourage imagination in all areas of life. It sponsors seminars, conferences, lectures, readings, and occasional publications in archetypal psychology and in the history, theory, and practice of imagination. Centers are located in various regions.

Institute of Imaginal Studies
47 Sixth Street
Petaluma, CA 24252
(707) 765-1839 (phone)
(707) 765-2351 (fax)
institut@imaginal.edu (e-mail)
www.imaginal.edu (website)
The Institute of Imaginal Studies offers M.A. and Ph.D. programs in psychology designed to meet the educational requirements for clinical psychology and MFCC licenses. Imaginal psychology is dedicated to the reclamation of the soul as psychology's primary concern and to care of the soul by giving close attention to the image we inhabit.

Institutes of Religion and Health
Blanton-Peale Graduate Institute
3 West 29th Street
New York, NY 10001-4597
(212) 725-7850 (phone)
(212) 689-3212 (fax)
The American Foundation of Religion and Psychiatry was founded in 1937 when the late Smiley Blanton, a New York psychiatrist, was contacted by the famous Rev. Dr. Norman Vincent Peale for help with the people coming to him for counseling during the Depression years. The Academy of Religion and Mental Health, started by the Rev. George Christian Anderson, Paul Tillich, Gordon Allport, and William C. Menninger in 1954, was created to provide a forum for interested clergy, psychiatrists, and other medical, social, and behavioral scientists to discuss the relationship of health and behavior and its relevance to issues of faith and wholeness. The two organizations were merged in 1972 to form the Institutes of Religion and Health, which includes the Blanton-Peale Graduate Institute.

Jewish Women's Caucus
1300 University Drive, #6
Menlo Park, CA 94025
(415) 327-2051
This group grew out of the Association for Women in Psychology (AWP) in 1989 in order to specifically address the issues of Jewish women in the mental health professions. The group sponsors preconference gatherings for Jewish feminists and workshops at AWP gatherings and independent events.

Journey School
4219 Magnolia Street
New Orleans, LA 70115
(504) 899-2335 (phone)
(504) 827-1265 (fax)
journey@mail.sstar.com (e-mail)
Founded in 1988, the Journey School offers weekend workshops that focus on the mythology of the "ancient mysteries" and their relationship to psychological and spiritual truths.

Ma'yan: The Jewish Women's Project
15 West 65th Street
New York, NY 10023
(212) 580-0099 (phone)
(212) 580-9498 (fax)
A program of the Jewish Community Center on the Upper West Side (New York City), this group serves, educates, and empowers Jewish women to make change in the Jewish community. Operating from a feminist perspective, Ma'yan organizes inclu-

sive rituals, including a monthly Rosh Hodesh and a large annual feminist seder as well as workshops and annual conferences.

Miracle Distribution Center
1141 East Ash Avenue
Fullerton, CA 92831
(714) 738-8380 (phone)
(714) 441-0618 (fax)
The center, a nonprofit organization founded in 1978, serves as an international contact point and teaching center for *A Course in Miracles*. Its services include worldwide study group listings; a bimonthly publication, *The Holy Encounter*; lectures; retreats; prayer ministry; and counselor referral service.

Monroe Institute
Route 1, Box 175
Faber, VA 22938
(804) 361-1500 (phone)
(804) 361-1237 (fax)
monroeinst@aol.com (e-mail)
www.monroeinst.org/ (website)
Founded by the late Robert Monroe, the institute offers programs in the Hemi-Sync learning system, a sound-based technology that teaches techniques to enhance perception beyond the five senses.

Mosaic Multicultural Foundation
P.O. Box 364
Vashon, WA 98070
(206) 463-9387 (phone)
(206) 463-9236 (fax)
mosaic@wolfenet.com (e-mail)
A nonprofit foundation established and directed by Michael Meade to organize, sponsor, and support programs and events that encourage greater understanding between men and women and elders and youths from diverse cultural and spiritual backgrounds.

Mystery School
P.O. Box 3300
Pomona, NY 10970
(914) 354-4965 (phone)
(914) 354-4295 (fax)
www.waking.com/myst_school.html (website)
Founded and directed by Jean Houston, Ph.D., the Mystery School offers various weekend and yearlong trainings that incorporate sacred psychology, his-

tory, music, theater, anthropology, philosophy, theology, science, and metaphysics.

Naropa Institute
School of Continuing Education
3285 30th Street
Boulder, CO 80301
(303) 402-1109 (phone)
(303) 402-1642 (fax)
The School of Continuing Education offers credit and noncredit courses in the arts, psychology, religion, and the environment. The Naropa Institute is a private, nonsectarian, liberal arts college inspired by a unique Buddhist heritage.

New Seminary
7 West 96th Street, Suite 19B
New York, NY 10025
(212) 866-3795 (phone and fax)
rebjhgt@aol.com (e-mail)
www.interfaith.org (website)
This institution offers Jewish spiritual guides, rabbinical ordination, correspondence programs, interfaith ministry, and Kabbalistic healing and visual meditation.

New Warrior Network
P.O. Box 230
Malone, NY 12953-0230
(800) 870-4611 (phone)
(514) 624-2527 (fax)
drury@nwn.com (e-mail)
www.nwn.org (website)
New Warrior training programs are located in twenty-four cities in the United States, Canada, and England. The network aims to reclaim the sacred masculine through initiation, training, and action. Centers are involved in mentoring disaffected youth, working with gangs and incarcerated young men, building shelters for the homeless, and creating programs for Vietnam-era veterans.

Nine Gates
437 Sausalito Street
Corte Madera, CA 94925
(415) 927-1677 (phone)
(415) 927-3418 (fax)
gayluce.com (e-mail)
www.ninegates.com (website)

Founded and directed by Gay Luce, Ph.D., the Nine Gates training program incorporates concepts developed from the ancient mystery schools.

Pendle Hill
Box B
338 Plush Mill Road
Wallingford, PA 19086
(610) 566-4507 or (800) 742-3150
Founded in 1930 by members of the Religious Society of Friends, this Quaker center roots its educational philosophy in equality, simplicity, harmony, and community.

Spiritual Emergence Network
930 Mission Street, #7
Santa Cruz, CA 95060
(408) 426-0902 (phone)
sen@cruzio.com (e-mail)
lcelfi.com/sen (website)
The network's training program, which encompasses the full spectrum of spiritual emergence syndromes, recognizes, understands, and works with individuals moving through spiritually transformative experiences. Affiliated trainings are offered through JFK University, California Institute for Integral Studies, and the Institute for Transpersonal Psychology.

Servant Leadership School
Church of the Savior
1640 Columbia Road, NW
Washington, DC 20009
(202) 328-7312 (phone)
(202) 328-7483 (fax)
The Servant Leadership School was founded as a combined seminary/school of social work to enable people to explore and develop their potential for service to the poor. The school hopes to train servant leaders who will contribute to social transformation and social justice, and it offers various ecumenical, multiracial, and multicultural workshops and classes.

Taoist Mountain Retreat Center
P.O. Box 1727
Nederland, CO 80466
(303) 258-0971
The Taoist Mountain Retreat Center, directed by Ken Cohen, one of the original spokespersons for

qigong in the United States, offers qigong training and research both at the center and in various other centers around North America. Advanced training, which leads to certification, takes approximately three years.

Transformational Arts Institute
1380 Pacific Street
Redlands, CA 92373
(909) 798-4453
Founded by Hugh and Nancy Redmond in 1980, the institute focuses on integrating the psychological, spiritual, and creative realms of human experience within a transformational context.

Unergi Center
Box 335
Pt. Pleasant, PA 18950
(215) 297-8006 (phone)
(215) 297-8199 (fax)
Unergi@aol.com (e-mail)
www.LifeEnrichment.com (website)
The Unergi method, a holistic system of touch (Alexander Technique), psycho-physical movement (Feldenkrais), verbal dialogue (Gestalt therapy), art therapy, chakra attunement, and spirituality is taught three times per year, six days each, in Virginia.

Veriditas: The World Wide Labyrinth Project
Grace Cathedral
1100 California Street
San Francisco, CA 94198
(415) 749-6356 (phone)
(415) 749-6357 (fax)
veriditas@gracecathedral.org (e-mail)
www.gracecathedral.org (website)
Veriditas is committed to reintroducing the labyrinth in its many forms as a spiritual tool and establishing labyrinths in churches, retreat centers, retirement homes, hospitals, prisons, and community spaces around the world. Rev. Lauren Artress, the director of Veriditas, lectures and leads training programs in the use of the labyrinth. Weekend retreats are also offered.

Wainwright House
260 Stuyvesant Avenue
Rye, NY 10580

(914) 967-6080 (phone)
(914) 967-6114 (fax)
registrar@wainwright.org (e-mail)
www.wainwright.org (website)
Wainwright House is a nonsectarian learning center dedicated to awakening consciousness in the mind, body, spirit, and the community as a whole. With special focus on interdisciplinary programming, the center provides seminars, conferences, and ongoing courses in spirituality, psychology, personal growth, health, the arts, global issues, and business leadership.

Wise Woman Center
P.O. Box 64
Woodstock, NY 12498
(914) 246-8081 (phone and fax)
The center offers herbal medicine and spirit-healing workshops with Susan Weed, Vicki Noble, Z Budapest, and other notable herbalists, priestesses, witches, and healers. It offers one-, two-, and three-day workshops, intensives, live-in apprenticeships, and correspondence courses.

ASSOCIATIONS, ORGANIZATIONS, AND INSTITUTES

Association for Past-Life Research and Therapies (APRT)
P.O. Box 20151
6825 Magnolia Avenue, Suite D
Riverside, CA 92506
(909) 784-1570 (phone)
(909) 784-8440 (fax)
pastlife@empirenet.com (e-mail)
The APRT, founded in 1980, is an international association of practitioners and laypersons interested in researching and promoting the use of alternative healing therapies, particularly past-life regression therapy. The association sponsors two educational conferences per year, and occasionally presents seminars and training workshops.

Association for Research and Enlightenment (ARE)
P.O. Box 595
Virginia Beach, VA 23541-0595
(804) 428-3588 (phone)
(757) 422-6921 (fax)
are@are-cayce.com (e-mail)
www.are-cayce.com (website)
The ARE was founded in 1931 to preserve, research, and make available the readings of Edgar Cayce, most of which have to do with psychic issues, meditation, dreams, reincarnation, and prophecy. The association also offers conferences, lectures, and seminars; publishes a magazine, *Venture Inward*; and sponsors academic degree programs through its affiliation with Atlantic University.

Association for the Study of Dreams
P.O. Box 1600
Vienna, VA 22183
(703) 242-0062 (phone)
(703) 242-8888 (fax)
ASDreams@altum (e-mail)
www.ASDreams.org (website)
The Association for the Study of Dreams is dedicated to the investigation of dreams and dreaming. Its purposes are to promote an awareness and appreciation of dreams in both the professional and public arenas; to encourage research into the nature, function, and significance of dreaming; to advance the application of the study of dreams; and to provide a forum for the eclectic and interdisciplinary exchange of ideas and information.

Association of Holistic Healing Centers
109 Holly Crescent, Suite 201
Virginia Beach, VA 23451
This membership organization founded in 1990 is dedicated to providing opportunities for individuals and groups involved in the healing arts to work together toward a more integrated health care methodology that bridges and complements traditional practices.

Center for Advancement in Cancer Education
300 East Lancaster Avenue, Suite 100
Wynnewood, PA 19096
(610) 642-4810 (phone)
(610) 896-6339 (fax)
www.lifeenrichment.com/cancer (website)
The center is a nonprofit information, counseling, and referral agency that offers resources for cancer prevention and nontoxic, holistic approaches as adjuncts or alternatives to conventional cancer treatments.

Center for Visionary Leadership
3408 Wisconsin Avenue, NW
Washington, DC 20016
(202) 237-2800 (phone)
(202) 237-1399 (fax)
cvldc@visionarylead.org (e-mail)
www.visionarylead.org (website)
The Center for Visionary Leadership is a nonprofit educational center providing spiritual insights and innovative whole-systems solutions to social problems. It offers public programs, consulting, and values-based leadership training as well as citizen dialogues to help heal the issues that divide us as a nation.

Center for Women and Religion
c/o Graduate Theological Union
2400 Ridge Road
Berkeley, CA 94709
(510) 649-2490 (phone)
(510) 649-1730 (fax)
cwr@gtu.edu (e-mail)
www.gtu.edu/Centers/cwr.html (website)
Part of the Graduate Theological Union in Berkeley, California, the center sponsors lectures, conferences, and other programs for those interested in women's issues in diverse religious traditions.

Chopra Center for Well Being
7630 Fay Avenue
La Jolla, CA 92037
(619) 551-7788 or (888) 424-6772 (phone)
(619) 551-7811 (fax)
info@chopra.com (e-mail)
www.chopra.com (website)
Formerly a research institute studying the effectiveness of Ayurvedic and Western medicine and the mind-body connection, the center now offers programs based on the principles and practices of mind-body medicine. Half-day, full-day, three-day, and seven-day packages are available, as are evening and weekend workshops and study groups.

Common Boundary
4905 Del Ray Avenue, Suite 210
Bethesda, MD 20814
(301) 652-9495 (phone)
(301) 652-0579 (fax)
connect@commonboundary.org (e-mail)
www.commonboundary.org (website)
Since 1980 Common Boundary has held conferences in the Washington area on topics that explore the interface between psychology, spirituality, creativity, and ecology. Common Boundary sponsors educational programs and acts as a clearinghouse for information on graduate and professional education programs. Common Boundary and the Institute of Noetic Sciences jointly sponsor an annual award of $1,000 for the outstanding dissertation/thesis on the interface between psychotherapy and spirituality. In cooperation with the Simple Abundance Charitable Fund, Common Boundary offers a $5,000 annual Green Dove Award for projects integrating ecology, spirituality, and psychology.

Creation Spirituality Network
2141 Broadway
Oakland, CA 94612-9944
(510) 836-4392 or (800) 973-2228 (phone)
(510) 835-0564 (fax)
csmag@hooked.net (e-mail)
www.csnet.org (website)
The network is a gathering point for those interested in learning about and studying creation spirituality, as articulated by Matthew Fox.

Fetzer Institute
9292 West KL Avenue
Kalamazoo, MI 49009-9398
(616) 365-2000 (phone)
(616) 372-2163 (fax)
www.fetzer.org
The Fetzer Institute is a nonprofit, private operating foundation that supports research, education, and service programs that explore body, mind, and spirit. The institute has a special interest in how individuals and communities are influenced by the interactions between the physical, psychological, social, and spiritual dimensions of life, and how understandings in these areas improve health, foster growth, and better human conditions.

Foundation for Global Community
222 High Street
Palo Alto, CA 94301
(650) 328-7756 (phone)

(650) 328-7785 (fax)
info@globalcommunity.org (e-mail)
www.globalcommunity.org (website)
The foundation is a nonprofit educational organization. Through the Center for the Evolution of Culture, it offers education and action programs that attempt to answer the questions: What must change if we are to survive and evolve as a species? How does the individual participate in this process of change?

Friends World Committee for Consultation
Section of the Americas
1506 Race Street
Philadelphia, PA 19102
(215) 241-7250 (phone)
(215) 241-7285 (fax)
The committee oversees the Elizabeth Ann Bogert Memorial Fund, which provides grants of up to $500 to individuals involved in the study and practice of Christian mysticism.

Institute for Ecumenical and Cultural Research
P.O. Box 6188
Collegeville, MN 56321-6188
Founded in 1967, the institute is committed to research, study, prayer, reflection, and dialogue in a community shaped by the Benedictine tradition of worship and work. It encourages constructive and creative thought not only in theology and religious studies but also in the humanities, natural sciences, and social sciences as they relate to the Christian tradition.

Institute for Engaged Spirituality (IES)
P.O. Box 237
Stinson Beach, CA 94970
(415) 868-2088 (phone)
(415) 868-2087 (fax)
wtmuller@aol.com
The IES is dedicated to examining how spiritual practices—meditation, contemplation, and quiet wisdom—may take form as loving kindness, sympathetic joy, and compassion in the world. One goal of IES is to deepen the dialogue between individual practice and tangible service. To this end, IES sponsors a four-day summer conference in Santa Fe, New Mexico.

Institute for the Study of Health and Illness (ISHI)
Commonweal
P.O. Box 316
Bolinas, CA 92924
(415) 868-2642 (phone)
(415) 868-2230 (fax)
ishi@igc.org (e-mail)
www.commonwealth.org (website)
The ISHI is a professional development institute for physicians and other health professionals who wish to take a more relationship-centered approach to the practice and teaching of medicine and to reclaim a deeper sense of personal meaning and satisfaction in their work.

Institute for the Study of Human Knowledge (ISHK)
P.O. Box 176
Los Altos, CA 94023
(415) 948-9428 or (800) 222-4745 (phone)
(800) 223-4200 (fax)
ishkorders@aol.com (e-mail for orders)
www.sufis.org (website)
The ISHK works at the frontier of psychological research, especially where there is a need to explain new discoveries and their practical applications. The institute offers seminars, a book service, tapes, and a newsletter, and the continuing education it provides in the field of psychology is accredited by the American Psychological Association.

Institute of Noetic Sciences (IONS)
475 Gate Five Road, Suite 300
Sausalito, CA 94965
(415) 331-5650 or (800) 383-1394 (phone)
(415) 331-5673 (fax)
www.noetic.org (website)
The IONS, founded in 1973, is a research foundation, an educational institution, and a membership organization. The institute is committed to the development of human consciousness through scientific inquiry, spiritual understanding, and psychological well-being. The IONS provides seed grants for cutting-edge scientific and scholarly research; organizes lectures; sponsors conferences; and publishes books, journals, and research reports. It also supports a variety of networking opportunities, member research projects, and local member group activities.

Islamic Research Foundation for the Advancement of Knowledge (IRFAK)
7102 Shefford Lane
Louisville, KY 40242-6462
(502) 634-1395
The IRFAK, a nonprofit educational, research, and charitable organization, encourages free thinking and opposing viewpoints in order to help reestablish the tenets of Islamic civilization. It funds awards and grants to research projects relevant to Islamic traditions.

Joseph Campbell and Marija Gimbutas Library
Pacifica Graduate Institute
249 Lambert Road
Carpinteria, CA 93013
(805) 969-2626, ext. 118 (phone)
(805) 565-1932 (fax)
reference@pacifica.edu (e-mail)
www.pacifica.edu (website)
The Joseph Campbell and Marija Gimbutas Library is dedicated to the preservation of a unique collection of manuscripts, books, and memorabilia. In addition to the collections of the mythologist Joseph Campbell and the archeologist Marija Gimbutas, the library houses the papers of the psychologist James Hillman.

Monterey Institute for the Study of Alternative Healing Arts (MISAHA)
3855 Via Nona Marie, Suite 102-C
Carmel, CA 93923
(408) 625-9617 (phone and fax)
misaha@aol.com (e-mail)
www.whps.com/misaha/ (website)
The MISAHA is a scientific research organization dedicated to broadening knowledge of alternative healing methods and mind-body connections in order to make them more acceptable to conventional medical practitioners.

National Institutes of Health
Office of Alternative Medicine (OAM)
Building 31, Room B1-C35
Bethesda, MD 20892
(301) 402-2466 (phone)
(301) 402-4741 (fax)
DRT@CU.NIH.GOV (e-mail)

www.nih.gov (website for Medline research)
The OAM was established by Congress in 1992. Areas of investigation include, but are not limited to: diet, nutrition, and lifestyle changes; mind-body control, such as biofeedback and guided imagery; traditional and ethnomedicine, including acupuncture, Native American medicine, and traditional Oriental medicine; energetic therapies, including therapeutic touch and *qigong;* and bioelectromagnetic applications. The office organizes occasional conferences and publishes a free newsletter, *Alternative Medicine*.

New Dimensions Radio
P.O. Box 569
Ukiah, CA 95482
(707) 468-5215 (phone)
ndradio@igc.org (e-mail)
www.newdimensions.org (website)
Since 1973, New Dimensions Radio has been inviting radio listeners to tune into weekly interviews with leading thinkers in psychology, mythology, human values, business, spirituality, health, science, politics, ecology, philosophy, and the arts. In addition to membership fees, the foundation supports its work with revenue generated from the sale of audiotapes of its radio interviews.

Parapsychology Foundation (PF)
228 East 71st Street
New York, NY 10021
(212) 628-1550 (phone)
(212) 628-1559 (fax)
www.parapsychology.org (website)
The Parapsychology Foundation was established in 1951 to encourage and support impartial scientific inquiry into the psychical aspects of human nature such as telepathy, clairvoyance, precognition, and psychokinesis. It sponsors a grant program to support scientists, universities, laboratories, and individuals in their parapsychological research; a scholarly incentive program to encourage authors and students; a publishing program for the proceedings of international conferences; and a scholarly monograph series.

Park Ridge Center
211 East Ontario, #800

Chicago, IL 60611
(312) 266-2222 (phone)
(312) 266-6086 (fax)
The center studies the interaction between health, faith, and ethics.

Spindrift
P.O. Box 5134
Salem, OR 97304-5134
Spindrift is a private, nonprofit corporation dedicated to education and research in the area of spiritual healing.

John Templeton Foundation
P.O. Box 8322
Radnor, PA 19087-8322
(610) 687-8942 (phone)
info@templeton.org (e-mail)
www.templeton.org (website)
The foundation encourages scholarly research on matters of both spiritual and scientific significance, including theology and the natural sciences; religion and medical science; and religion and the behavioral sciences. The foundation offers the world's largest prize (more than $1 million) every year to a person or organization that has made an important contribution to these fields.

Women Church Convergence
205 West Monroe
Chicago, IL 60606
(312) 641-5151
A coalition of organizations united in their work to attend to women's voices in the church. This "Catholic-rooted" organization meets twice a year, sponsors occasional conferences, and facilitates the trading of newsletters among its member organizations. Member organizations include WATER, Women's Ordination Conference, Catholics for Free Choice, and others.

Women's Ordination Conference
P.O. Box 2693
Fairfax Circle Center
Fairfax, VA 22031
(703) 352-1006 (phone)
(703) 352-5181 (fax)
A grassroots organization of Roman Catholic women and some men (and some people from other Christian traditions) who are working toward the ordination of women in the church. The group sponsors occasional conferences and is joining with similar groups in other countries to form a network of organizations called Women's Ordination Worldwide.

INTERDISCIPLINARY RESOURCES

American Anthropological Association
Society for the Anthropology of Consciousness (SAC)
4350 North Fairfax Drive, Suite 640
Arlington, VA 22203
(703) 528-1902, x3005 (phone)
(703) 528-3546 (fax)
www.ameranthassn.org (website)
The SAC is an interdisciplinary group concerned with cross-cultural, experimental, experiential, and theoretical approaches to the study of consciousness. Its primary areas of interest include (altered) states of consciousness, religion, possession, trance, and dissociative states; ethnographic studies of shamanistic, mediumistic, mystical, and related traditions; indigenous healing practices; linguistic, philosophical, social, and symbolic studies of consciousness phenomena; and psychic (psi) phenomena.

American Holistic Nurses Association (AHNA)
P.O. Box 2130
Flagstaff, AZ 86003-2130
(800) 278-2462 (phone)
(520) 526-2752 (fax)
ahna.org.@flaglink.com (e-mail)
www.ahna.org (website)
The AHNA works to create opportunities for nurses to empower themselves and others through integrating holism in their lives and in their work and so promotes the education of nurses and the public in the concepts and practices of health for the whole person. The association offers seminars and conferences and an AHNA certification program in holistic nursing.

Brahma Kumaris World Spiritual University (BKWSU)
1609 West Chase Avenue

Chicago, IL 60626

(312) 262-2828

Over the last fifty years, the BKWSU has expanded from its beginnings in Pakistan to become an international organization with some fifteen hundred centers. Activities include sponsoring major projects to promote the International Years of Youth and Peace and organizing conferences, concerts, lectures, and training workshops in hospitals, schools, universities, prisons, and youth and community centers.

Center for a New American Dream
6930 Carroll Avenue, Suite 900
Takoma Park, MD 20912
(301) 891-3683 (phone)
(301) 891-3684 (fax)
newdream@newdream.org (e-mail)
www.newdream.org (website)
This center is for people who believed that the "American Dream" was having it all and who are waking up to the realization that more is not necessarily better. The center offers Simple Living Action Kits, a clearinghouse on research and conferences, and a quarterly newsletter.

Center for Psychology and Social Change
1493 Cambridge Street
Cambridge, MA 02139
(617) 497-1553 (phone)
(617) 497-0122 (fax)
cpsc@igc.apc.org (e-mail)
The focus of the center, which is affiliated with the Harvard Medical School at Cambridge Hospital, is to explore the role human consciousness plays in building a sustainable world peace.

Center for Women, the Earth, and the Divine (CWED)
114 Rising Ridge Road
Ridgefield, CT 06877
CWED is dedicated to exploring the parallels between the imagined and the actual treatment of women and the earth, and how images of the divine relate to the experiences of women and the earth. CWED makes its work available to the public through talks, workshops, written materials, and retreats.

Children: Our Ultimate Investment (COUI)
P.O. Box 1868
Los Angeles, CA 90068
(213) 461-8248 (phone)
(213) 461-8470 (fax)
This organization, founded in 1977 by Laura Huxley, is dedicated to the nurturing of the possible human by educating the public about the preparation for conception, pregnancy, birth, and the first five years of life. COUI sponsors two social programs. Teens and Toddlers endeavors to discourage teen pregnancy; Project Caress brings together toddlers and senior citizens to help break down age barriers and reestablish bonding between elders and the young.

Circle Sanctuary
P.O. Box 219
Mount Horeb, WI 53572
(608) 924-2216 (phone)
(608) 924-5961 (call to fax)
circle@mhtc.net (e-mail)
www.circlesanctuary.org (website)
Circle Sanctuary, founded in 1974, provides spiritual resources for Wiccans, pagans, and other nature-religion practitioners worldwide.

Consciousness Directory
P.O. Box 99
Chatfield, TX 75105
(903) 345-2267 (phone)
(903) 345-2301 (fax)
info@thecd.com (e-mail)
www.thecd.com (website)
The Consciousness Directory is an Internet directory providing resources in the exploration of meaningful living and acknowledging the men and women whose teachings, ideas, and actions inspire and create the possibility of a conscious universe. It provides a list of speakers, teachers, writers, organizations, retreat facilities, and tour providers.

Covenant of the Goddess (CG)
P.O. Box 1226
Berkeley, CA 94704
Wicca, or Witchcraft, is a life-affirming, earth- and nature-oriented religion that sees all of life as sacred and interconnected. Established in 1975, CG func-

tions as an umbrella organization to increase cooperation and mutual support among Wiccans and to secure legal protections enjoyed by members of other religions.

Earth Ministry
1305 NE 47th Street
Seattle, WA 98105-4498
(206) 632-2426 (phone)
emoffice@earthministry.org (e-mail)
www.earthministry.org (website)
Earth Ministry works with individuals and congregations to connect faith with care for the environment by exploring environmental ethics, simple living, and environmental justice.

EarthSpirit Community (ESC)
P.O. Box 365
Medford, MA 02155
The ESC is a Boston-based collective that coordinates a nationwide network of people following earth-centered spiritual paths. Their spiritual practices are rooted in the ancient traditions of pagan, pre-Christian Europe, at the core of which is a respectful awareness of the sacredness of the earth.

Ecopsychology Institute at California State University, Hayward Campus
P.O. Box 7487
Berkeley, CA 94707-0487
The institute's function is publishing a newsletter twice a year. The editors are Melissa Nelson and Theodore Roszak. The newsletter (available for $10/year) offers news, articles, and a listing of conferences and resources that explore the interface between psychology and ecology.

Forge Institute for Spirituality and Social Change
Hunter College Program in Religion
695 Park Avenue
New York, NY 10021
(212) 772-4987 (phone)
ForgeInst@aol.com (e-mail)
Founded in 1992 to develop a coalition of leaders, movements, and participants within the modern spirituality movement, the Forge Institute is also dedicated to developing procedures, networks, and an infrastructure for this effort. The institute offers ongoing weekend, residential retreats and conferences to encourage dialogue among people from a variety of spiritual traditions and professions.

Gaia Institute
Cathedral of Saint John the Divine
1047 Amsterdam Avenue at 112th Street
New York, NY 10025
(718) 885-1906 (phone)
(718) 885-0882 (fax)
gaiainst@aol.com (e-mail)
The Gaia Institute is a center for research, development, design, and education. On the belief that the integrity of the earth as an abode for life begins in our backyards, our cities and parks, even around landfills, toxic dumps, and storm sewers, the Gaia Institute is developing technologies that behave like natural systems, turning wastes into resources, improving diversity and quality of life in the process.

Institute for Bio-Spiritual Research (IBSR)
6305 Greeley Hill Road
Coulterville, CA 95311-9501
The IBSR is an international network of parents, counselors, health-care providers, hospice volunteers, clergy, teachers, therapists, and spiritual guides. The institute's mission is to develop a transcultural psychological foundation for healthy spiritualities that are solidly grounded in the body's processes. The institute offers training programs, publications, audio- and videotapes, focusing retreats, six-day intensives, and an annual conference.

Institute of Cultural Affairs (ICA)
Lifestyle Simplification Series
5911 Western Trail
Greensboro, NC 27410
(910) 605-0143 (phone)
(910) 605-9640 (fax)
ICAGboro@igc.apc.org (e-mail)
ICA offers participatory workshops for individuals and families concerned about developing a simpler, sustainable lifestyle. Materials include self-guided workbooks and a process to explore sustainable lifestyle options in dialogue with others so as to develop new images and rationales and a collegial context.

International Association for Near-Death Studies (IANDS)
P.O. Box 502
East Windsor Hill, CT 06028-0502
(860) 528-5144 (phone)
(860) 528-9169 (fax)
www.iands.org (website)
The IANDS is the world's only organization devoted to scientifically grounded exploration of the near-death experience. Its membership includes researchers and professionals interested in near-death experience. It publishes the quarterly *Journal of Near-Death Studies* and sponsors conferences.

International Network for Attitudinal Healing (INAH)
P.O. Box 390129
Kailua-Kona, HI 96739
(888) 222-7205 (toll-free phone)
(808) 322-8894 (fax)
NetAttHeal@aol.com (e-mail)
www.attitudinalhealing.org (website)
In 1975 Gerald Jampolsky, a pediatric and adolescent psychiatrist who was an exponent of *A Course in Miracles*, developed a process known as attitudinal healing. He originally used it as a way of helping children and others face loss, bereavement, and life-challenging illness. Eventually it became more of a process of letting go of painful and fearful attitudes. In 1994 the network was formed to provide a framework for individuals, groups, and centers to exchange information, ideas, and support.

Interspecies Communication (IC)
273 Hidden Meadow Lane
Friday Harbor, WA 98250
IC was founded in 1978 to promote a better understanding of what is communicated between human beings and other animals (especially dolphins and whales) through music, art, and ceremony. Its methods consist of integrating the arts and the sciences with a strong emphasis on environmental preservation.

Isthmus Institute
2701 State Street
Dallas, TX 75204
(214) 220-9158 (phone)
(214) 220-0195 (fax)

The institute's mission is to provide an educational forum for participants to explore the interactions between scientific and spiritual approaches to reality. It holds an annual conference.

Lindisfarne Association
22 Orchard Street
Amherst, MA 01002
Lindisfarne is an association of individuals devoted to the study and realization of a new planetary culture. It offers conferences, concerts, lectures, exhibitions, poetry readings, and public workshops.

National Hospice Organization (NHO)
1901 North Moore Street, Suite 901
Arlington, VA 22209
(800) 658-8898 (phone)
(703) 525-5762 (fax)
drsnho@cais.com (e-mail)
www.nho.org (website)
The NHO offers referrals to more than nineteen hundred local hospice groups, most of which incorporate a spiritual framework into their work.

Northwest Earth Institute
921 SW Morrison, Suite 532
Portland, OR 97205
(503) 227-2807 (phone)
(503) 227-2917 (fax)
nwei@teleport.com (e-mail)
One of the projects of the institute is the teaching and promotion of voluntary simplicity study circles. Its study guide and other educational materials are very helpful to support groups of people trying to escape from the trance of consumerism.

Sacred Dance Guild
Joann Flanigan
1004 Brookridge Circle SE
Huntsville, AL 35801
(205) 881-8171 (phone)
(205) 880-8628 (fax)
JoannSDG@aol.com (e-mail)
Founded in 1958, the guild is dedicated to dance as a spiritual expression—as a language of faith and celebration. It sponsors a national festival; publishes the *Sacred Dance Guild Journal;* and organizes regional and chapter workshops.

San Francisco Center for Meditation and
Psychotherapy (SFCMP)
1719 Union Street
San Francisco, CA 94123-4406
(415) 567-8404 (phone)
(415) 567-3374 (fax)
The SFCMP is an association of individual psychotherapists who share an interest in the practice of meditation and a commitment to exploring the relationship between psychotherapy and spirituality. In addition to offering various types of psychotherapy, the SFCMP hosts a weekly meditation group and sponsors seminars and training workshops relevant to the interface between psychology and spirituality.

Spiritearth
43 Spaulding Lane
Saugerties, NY 12477-2399
(914) 247-0816
Spiritearth is a nonprofit center for spirituality in the ecological age. It publishes a newsletter and offers workshops by such leaders as Elizabeth Dobson Gray, Miriam Therese MacGillis, Thomas S. Toolan, and Thomas Berry.

Women's Alliance for Theology, Ethics, and Ritual (WATER)
8035 13th Street, Suites 1, 3, and 5
Silver Spring, MD 20852
(301) 589-2509 (phone)
(301) 589-3150 (fax)
water@hers.com (e-mail)
www.hers.com/water (website)
WATER is a feminist educational center that began in 1983 as a response to the need for serious theological, ethical, and liturgical development for and by women. It offers programs, projects, publications, workshops, retreats, and counseling.

World Research Foundation
P.O. Box 10187
Marina Del Rey, CA 90295
(310) 827-0070 (phone)
Lavernewrf@netvip.com (e-mail)
www.wrf.org (website)
Research request contact:
41 Bell Rock Plaza
Sedona, AZ 86351

(520) 284-3300 (phone)
(520) 284-3530 (fax)
Founded in 1984, the foundation locates, gathers, codifies, evaluates, classifies, and disseminates information dealing with health and the environment, including both ancient and current data from traditional and nontraditional medicine. Library searches focus on complementary, alternative, nontraditional, and natural therapeutics.

PERIODICALS

This section includes periodicals that are relevant to the subjects outlined in this field guide but are too general or multidisciplinary to fit within any one section or chapter.

Journals

Corona
c\o Linda Sexson
Dept. of History and Philosophy
Montana State University
Bozeman, MT 59717
(406) 994-5200 (phone)
(406) 994-3768 (fax)
Annual
Corona is an annual, interdisciplinary journal whose presiding metaphor is "the edge": the place of play, of connection, of beginnings that are ends and boundaries that are entrances. *Corona* informs and is shaped by the emergent myth "that will retell the tale of who we are."

Creative Downscaling
P.O. Box 1884
Jonesboro, CA 30237-1884
(770) 471-9048 (phone)
kilgo@mindspring.com (e-mail)
www.mindspring.com/~kilgo/index.html (website)
Ten times per year; $10 (sample copy $2)
This newsletter advises simple living advocates on the best steps for downscaling and publishes practical articles on simple and thrifty living.

Dreaming
Association for the Study of Dreams
P.O. Box 81

Kelly, WY 83011
Quarterly; $70 ($44 student)
This journal investigates all topics germane to dreams and dreaming.

The Empty Vessel: A Journal of Contemporary Taoism
996 Ferry Lane
Eugene, OR 97401-3349
(503) 345-8854 or (800) 574-5118 (phone)
solala@abodetao.com (e-mail)
www.abodetao.com (website)
Quarterly; $20
This publication, dedicated to the exploration and dissemination of Taoist philosophy and practice, contains articles on the practical applications of Taoist thought, internal arts, tai chi, Chinese medicine, and *qigong*.

Everyman: A Men's Journal
Box 4617, Station E
Ottawa, ON K1S 5H8 Canada
(613) 832-2284 (phone)
www.everyman.org (website)
Annual; $15
This journal focuses on men's inner work (soul journeys) and men's outer issues (gender politics) and attempts to build bridges between the mythopoetic and men's rights movements.

Holistic Education Review (HER)
Holistic Education Press
P.O. Box 328
Brandon, VT 05733-0328
(802) 247-8312 or (800) 639-4122 (phone)
holistic@sover.net (e-mail)
www.sover.net/~holistic/ (website)
Quarterly; $35
HER aims to stimulate discussion and application of person-centered educational ideas and methods. Articles explore how education can encourage the fullest possible development of human potentials and planetary consciousness.

Image: A Journal of Arts and Religion
P.O. Box 674
Kennett Square, PA 19348
(610) 444-8065 (phone)
73424.1024@compuserv.com (e-mail)
Quarterly; $30

Image provides interviews, poetry, reviews, full-color visual reproductions, and scholarly discussions of the religious in art and art in the living practice of religion.

Journal of Feminist Studies in Religion (JFSR)
Scholars Press
P.O. Box 15399
Atlanta, GA 30333-0399
(404) 727-2320 or (800) 221-9369 (phone)
(212) 647-1898 (fax)
info@plenum (e-mail)
www.@plenum.com (website)
Annual; $18
JFSR is a channel for the dissemination of feminist scholarship in religion and a forum for discussion and dialogue among women and men of differing feminist perspectives.

Journal of Near-Death Studies (JNDS)
Human Sciences Press
P.O. Box 735
Canal Street Station
New York, NY 10013-1578
(212) 620-8000 or (800) 221-9369 (phone)
(212) 647-1898 (fax)
info@plenum.com (e-mail)
www.@plenum.com (website)
Quarterly; $36
JNDS publishes articles on near-death experiences and related phenomena, such as out-of-body experiences, deathbed visions, and comparable experiences under other circumstances.

Journal of Religion and Health
Institute of Religion and Health
Plenum Publishing
233 Spring Street
New York, NY 10013-1578
(212) 620-8000 (phone)
(212) 807-1047 (fax)
plenum@panix.com (e-mail)
Quarterly; $56
This publication primarily covers Judeo-Christian aspects of religion and psychology. It is published by one of the earliest pastoral training and counseling programs, the Institute of Religion and Health, which was founded in 1937 by the Rev. Norman Vincent Peale and the psychiatrist Smiley Blanton.

Journal of Sandplay Therapy
Sandplay Therapists of America
P.O. Box 4847
Walnut Creek, CA 94596
Semiannual; $25
The journal carries theoretical, clinical, and research articles on sandplay, a symbolic of nonverbal therapy developed by the Jungian analyst Dora Kalff; case studies, book reviews, and essays on symbols and the therapeutic process are regular features.

METIS: A Feminist Journal of Transformative Wisdom
California Institute of Integral Studies
9 Peter Yorke Way
San Francisco, CA 94109
(415) 674-5500, ext. 454 (phone)
www.ciis.edu/community/bookstore.html (website)
Annual; $10 (individual)
Named for Metis, goddess of wisdom and mother of Athena, this interdisciplinary journal seeks to further feminist consciousness and theory by publishing articles that reflect embodied, critical, and creative scholarship and language and by integrating passion and analysis in well-crafted writing.

MYTHOSPHERE: A Journal for Image, Myth, and Symbol
P.O. Box 11005
Tuscaloosa, AL 35486-0002
(205) 348-8685 (phone)
(205) 348-9642 (fax)
myth@woodsquad.as.ua.edu (e-mail)
Quarterly; $36
MYTHOSPHERE is an interdisciplinary and cross-disciplinary journal presenting and analyzing myth, ritual, symbols, and imagery in folk and popular culture. Contributors to early issues included prominent thinkers in religion, mythology, and depth and archetypal psychology.

PanGaia: Exploring the Pagan World
P.O. Box 641
Point Arena, CA 95468
(707) 882-2052 (phone)
(707) 882-2793 (fax)
info@sagewoman.com (e-mail)
www.pangaia.com (website)
Quarterly; $18

Formerly *The Green Man, PanGaia* contains eighty pages of science, magic, eco-action, and global paganism.

Pilgrimage: Reflections on the Human Journey
Pilgrimage Press
Route 1, Box 188M
Highlands, NC 28741
5 issues a year; $24
This journal is mainly written for and by therapists and people in therapy. The publication began as a pastoral counseling journal but has widened its scope in recent years to include the personal experience in psychotherapy.

Psychoscience: The Journal of Theoretical Psychiatry
P.O. Box 7176
Loma Linda, CA 92354-0689
(909) 799-7651
Semiannual; $15
Psychoscience is considered a new theory of mind and was propounded in part by the late physicist David Bohm, who was in turn influenced by Jiddu Krishnamurti.

Re-Imagining
122 West Franklin Avenue, Room 4A
Minneapolis, MN 55404-2470
Quarterly; $25 ($15 limited income, $35 dual)
The publication of the Re-Imagining Community, this journal features essays, poetry, and other writings by and for people interested in the ecumenical reassessment of various women-oriented themes in the Christian tradition. Subscription is included in membership in the Re-Imagining Community.

ReVision: Journal of Consciousness and Change
Heldref Publications
1319 18th Street, NW
Washington, DC 20036-1802
(202) 296-6267 or (800) 365-9753 (phone)
(202) 296-5149 (fax)
Quarterly; $28
Since 1978, *ReVision* has provided a unique forum for new paradigm thinkers, countercultural intellectuals, philosophically inclined spiritual seekers, transpersonally oriented social activists, undogmatic exponents of the perennial wisdom, constructive postmodernists, and other kindred minds.

Studia Mystica
Edwin Mellen Press
P.O. Box 450
Lewiston, NY 14092-0450
(716) 754-2788
Annual; $49.95
This annual journal offers scholarly articles on and translations of mysticism and visionary literature and essays that explore connections between mysticism, the arts, and the humanities.

Voices: The Art and Science of Psychotherapy
P.O. Box 1611
New Bern, NC 28563
(919) 634-3066 (phone)
(919) 634-3067 (fax)
aapoffice@aol.com (e-mail)
Quarterly; $40
Published by the American Academy of Psychotherapists, *Voices* emphasizes the experience and personhood of the therapist.

Women and Therapy
Haworth Press
10 Alice Street
Binghamton, NY 13904-1480
(800) 429-6784 (phone)
(800) 895-0582 (fax)
starley@haworthpressinc.com (e-mail)
www.haworthpressinc.com (website)
Quarterly; $40 (individual)
This journal is intended for feminist practitioners as well as individuals interested in the practice of feminist therapy.

Magazines and Newsletters

While some conventional magazines like *New Woman* and *Self* are now offering topics similar to those published in the magazines listed here, they are seldom written about with the same depth. The following is a sampling of publications that examine various dimensions of soul work.

Alternative Medicine
National Institutes of Health
Office of Alternative Medicine
Building 31, Room B1-C35

Bethesda, MD 20892
(301) 402-2466 (phone)
(888) 644-6226 (toll-free call for faxed info)
altmed.od.nih.gov (e-mail)
Bimonthly; complimentary subscription
Alternative Medicine is the official bimonthly newsletter of the Office of Alternative Medicine.

Brain Mind and Common Sense
Interface Press
P.O. Box 4221
4717 North Figueroa Street
Los Angeles, CA 90042
Monthly; $45
Founded by Marilyn Ferguson, author of *The Aquarian Conspiracy*, this several-decades-old newsletter reports on research dealing with the mind-body interface.

Business Spirit Journal
4 Camino Azul
Santa Fe, NM 87505
(505) 474-7604 (phone)
(505) 471-2584 (fax)
message@nets.com (e-mail)
www.spiritinbiz.com (website)
Bimonthly; $29
This newsletter offers information, inspiration, and resources for those wanting to broaden the definition of the "bottom line" to include spirit at work.

Christian Meditation USA
Christian Meditation Center
1080 West Irving Park Road
Roselle, IL 60172
(630) 351-2613 (phone and fax)
pademarco@snet.net (e-mail)
Quarterly; $20
This newsletter is published to promote a Christian way of prayer as it was initially taught by John Main.

Common Boundary
4905 Del Ray Avenue, Suite 210
Bethesda, MD 20814
(301) 652-9495 (phone)
(301) 652-0579 (fax)
(800) 548-8737 (subscriptions only)
connect@commonboundary.org (e-mail)

www.commonboundary.org (website)
Bimonthly; $24.95
Common Boundary magazine explores the relationship of psychology, spirituality, creativity, and ecology. It includes feature articles, interviews, essays, and departments that cover psychospiritual trends and innovations; reviews of books and audiotapes; and first-person accounts of spiritual journeys.

Communities
138-G Twin Oaks Road
Louisa, VA 23093
(540) 894-5798 (phone)
www.ic.org (website)
Quarterly; $18
Published by the Fellowship for Intentional Community, the magazine is a main source for the latest information, issues, and ideas about intentional communities and cooperative living. It covers, among other things, ecovillages, cohousing, and growing older in a community.

Crone Chronicles: A Journal of Conscious Aging
P.O. Box 81
Kelly, WY 83011
(307) 733-5409
Quarterly; $18
Founded in 1989 to "activate the archetype of the Crone," this grassroots publication is written by and for wise, older women who are challenging cultural stereotypes.

Convergence
1 Sanborn Road
Concord, NH 03301
(603) 225-3720 (phone)
(603) 225-2059 (fax)
staff@convergence-web.com (e-mail)
www.convergence.com (website)
5 issues a year; $15
This publication describes itself as a magazine for "personal and spiritual growth and holistic health."

Enneagram Monthly
117 Sweetmilk Creek Road
Troy, NY 12180
(518) 279-4444 (phone)
(518) 279-3019 (fax)

EnneaMonth@aol.com (e-mail)
www.ideodynamic.com/enneagram-monthly (website)
Monthly; $30
This publication researches, gathers, and disseminates information on the enneagram. It includes interviews with prominent teachers and writers in the field and a national calendar of teaching, training, and conference opportunities.

Gnosis
Lumen Foundation
401 Terry Francios Boulevard, Suite 110
San Francisco, CA 94107
(415) 974-0600 (phone)
gnosis@well.com (e-mail)
www.lumen.org (website)
Quarterly; $20
Gnosis explores the Western transformational paths, spiritual approaches, and esoteric pathways, inside and outside of the Judeo-Christian-Islamic traditions.

Healing Arts Report
P.O. Box 1728
Winchester, VA 22604
(800) 915-9335 (phone)
(304) 728-0089 (fax)
www.healingartsreport.com (website)
Monthly; $39.95
This newsletter offers reports on new developments in holistic health and integrative medicine. Recent stories have covered music therapy for healing chronic illness, healing and energy transfer, and magnetic deficiency syndrome.

Hope
P.O. Box 160
Naskeag Road
Brooklin, ME O4616
(207) 359-4651 (phone)
(207) 359-8920 (fax)
info@hopemag.com (e-mail)
www.hopemag.com (website)
Bimonthly; $24.95
Hope aims to inspire a sense of informed hope among readers by encouraging deeper understanding of the human experience at its best and at its worst.

Intuition
275 Brannan Street
San Francisco, CA 94107
(415) 538-8171 (phone)
(415) 538-8175 (fax)
intuitmag@aol.com (e-mail)
Quarterly; $19.95
This magazine presents articles, profiles, and interviews on topics relevant to the development and application of intuition.

Magical Blend
133 ½ Broadway
P.O. Box 600
Chico, CA 95927
(888) 296-2442 (phone)
magical.inreach.com (e-mail)
www.magicalblend.com (website)
Bimonthly; $19.95
Magical Blend's purpose is to chart the course of the fundamental transformation taking place in society and to assist the individual in coping with this process. The magazine does not endorse one path to spiritual growth but attempts, in its exploration of many alternative possibilities for transforming the planet, to "embrace the hopes, transform the fears, and discover the magical."

Natural Health (formerly *East-West Journal*)
17 Station Street, Box 1200
Brookline, MA 02146
(617) 232-1000 (phone)
(617) 232-1572 (fax)
naturalhealth@bcpress.com
Bimonthly; $24
This magazine provides information on alternative approaches to health and encourages readers to rely on remedies that facilitate the body's natural healing capacities.

New Age Journal
42 Pleasant Street
Watertown, MA 02172-2333
(617) 926-0200 (phone)
(617) 926-5562 (fax)
editor@newage.com (e-mail)
Bimonthly; $14.95

Founded nearly twenty-five years ago by Peggy Taylor, Eric Utne, and others, this publication is a natural lifestyle magazine for the conscious consumer. Issues include a mix of features and departments on natural health and wellness, personal growth, the environment, spirituality, and social change.

The Other Side
300 West Apsley Street
Philadelphia, PA 19144
(215) 849-2178 or (800) 700-9280 (phone)
tos.pa@ecunet.org (e-mail)
www.theotherside.org (website)
Bimonthly; $24
The Other Side is a nonprofit ministry whose mission is to uphold a Christian vision that nurtures those who thirst for deeper spiritual rooting, long for justice, and are working toward a transformed world.

Parabola: The Magazine of Myth and Tradition
656 Broadway
New York, NY 10012
(212) 505-6200 (phone)
(212) 979-7325 (fax)
orders@parabola.com (e-mail)
www.parabola.org (website)
Quarterly; $24
Parabola is published by the Society for the Study of Myth and Tradition, an organization devoted to the dissemination and exploration of materials relating to myths, symbols, and rituals. Each issue of *Parabola* has a theme such as humor, forgiveness, hospitality, addiction, sadness, the body, and pilgrimage, around which the essays, stories, poems, and other materials are organized.

Sagewoman: Celebrating the Goddess in Every Woman
P.O. Box 641
Point Arena, CA 95468
(707) 882-2052 (phone)
(707) 882-2793 (fax)
info@sagewoman.com (e-mail)
www.sagewoman.com (website)
Quarterly; $21
Sagewoman writes about aspects of the wisdom of the Divine Feminine.

Simple Living: The Journal of Voluntary Simplicity
Simple Living Network, Inc.
P.O. Box 233
Trout Lake, WA 98650
(509) 395-2323 (phone)
(509) 395-2128 (fax)
slnet@slnet.com (e-mail)
http://slnet.com (website)
Quarterly; $16
This twenty-four-page magazine provides a forum on topics such as saving money at the supermarket, finding cheap long-distance rates, being inwardly rich, and living deliberately.

The Sun
107 N. Roberson Street
Chapel Hill, NC 27516
(800) 875-2997
Monthly; $32
The Sun is a literary magazine that frequently covers psychospiritual subjects.

What Is Enlightenment?
Moksha Press
P.O. Box 2360
Lenox, MA 01240
(413) 637-6000 or (800) 376-3210 (phone)
(413) 637-6015 (fax)
moksha@moksha.org (e-mail)
www.moksha.org/wie (website)
Quarterly; $11
Because there is "so much confusion, misunderstanding, and misinformation" as to what enlightenment actually is and what it really means, this publication investigates the possible answers to the question.

Yes! A Journal of Positive Futures
P.O. Box 10818
Bainbridge Island, WA 98110
(206) 842-0216 or (800) 937–4451 (for U.S. orders) (phone)
(206) 842-5208 (fax)
yes@futurenet.org (e-mail)
www.futurenet.org (website)
Quarterly; $24
This journal supports active citizen engagement in creating a more just, sustainable, and compassionate world. Each issue of *Yes!* focuses on a theme such as

"Moving Beyond the Consumer Culture," "Democracy: The New Stories," "Money: Print Your Own!," and "A Millennium Survival Guide."

Yoga Journal
2054 University Avenue, Suite 302
Berkeley, CA 94704
(510) 841-9200 (phone)
(510) 644-3101 (fax)
info@yogajournal.com (e-mail)
www.yogajournal.com (website)
Bimonthly; $19.97
Founded in 1975, this magazine defines yoga as practices that aspire to unite us with a higher power, greater truth, or deeper source of wisdom, as well as to increase the harmony of body, mind, and spirit. The focus is on mind-body approaches to personal and spiritual development.

SMALL PRESSES

Walk into any bookstore—from small independent shops to the superstores replete with armchairs, lattés, and regularly scheduled lectures and book signings—and the likelihood of finding titles published by HarperCollins, Bantam, Doubleday, or Ballantine is very high. What you may or may not be able to find are books by small, more narrowly focused publishers. The following is a list of companies whose books might be of interest.

Anthroposophic Press
3390 Route 9
Hudson, NY 12534
(518) 851-2054 (phone)
(518) 851-2047 (fax)
anthropres@aol.com (e-mail)
www.anthropress.org (website)
Dedicated to the encouragement of cultural renewal and an ever-wider exposure for the works of Rudolph Steiner, the independent and nonprofit Anthroposophic Press publishes Steiner's work as well as books by other authors on topics including anthroposophy, Waldorf education, health, and social renewal.

Bear & Company
P.O. Drawer 2860
Santa Fe, NM 85704
(800) 932-3277 (phone)
(505) 989-8386 (fax)
This publishing company offers spiritual and new age books on a variety of topics.

Conari Press
2550 Ninth Street, Suite 101
Berkeley, CA 94710
(510) 949-7182
Conari specializes in contemporary and feminist spirituality.

Council Oak Books
1350 East 15th Street
Tulsa, OK 74120
(918) 587-6454 or (800) 247-8850 (phone)
(918) 583-4995 (fax)
oakie@ionet.net (e-mail)
Council Oak publishes Native American and metaphysical titles.

Crossing Press: Tools for Personal Change
P.O. Box 1048
Freedom, CA 95019
(800) 777-1048 (phone)
(408) 722-2749 (fax)
Spirituality, health, dreams, self-help, and the body are the main areas covered by the Crossing Press.

Dove Publications
Pecos Benedictine Monastery
Pecos, NM 87552
(505) 757-6597 (phone)
(505) 757-2285 (fax)
dovebooks@juno.com (e-mail)
www.pecosabbey.org (website; click on BookNook for a listing of books)
Dove publishes pamphlets, cassettes, and books on prayer, depth psychology, and healing, much of which comes directly from material presented in retreats at the monastery.

Element Books
42 Broadway
Rockport, MA 01966
(978) 546-1040 (phone)
(978) 546-9882 (fax)
This spirituality/psychology publisher focuses on alternative health and world religions.

Gateways Books and Tapes
P.O. Box 370
Nevada City, CA 95959
(800) 869-0658 (phone)
(916) 272-0184 (fax)
Gateways' offerings are in the areas of spirituality and gestalt.

Hay House, Inc.
P.O. Box 5100
Carlsbad, CA 92018-5100
(800) 654-5126 (phone)
(800) 650-5115 (fax)
Founded by Louise Hay, this publishing company focuses on spiritually oriented self-help books.

Healing Arts Press
1 Park Street
Rochester, VT 05767
(802) 767-3174 or (800) 246-8648 (phone)
(802) 767-3726 (fax)
The press's imprint, Inner Traditions, offers titles in alternative medicine and holistic health that combine contemporary thought and innovative research with the accumulated knowledge of the world's great healing traditions.

Inner City Books
Box 1271, Station 2
Toronto, ON M4T 2P4 Canada
(416) 927-0355 (phone)
(416) 924-1814 (fax)
Inner City Books publishes studies by Jungian analysts, including Marion Woodman, Sylvia Brinton Perrera, James Hall, Edward Edinger, Nancy Qualls-Corbett, and Marie Louise Von Franz.

Larson Publications
4936 Route 414
Burdette, NY 14818
(607) 546-9342 (information) or (800) 823-2197 (orders)
(607) 546-9344 (fax)
larson@lightlink.com (e-mail)
www.lightlink.com/larson/ (website)

Larson Publications specializes in books that bring together the wisdom of the East and West and of ancient and modern spirituality in order to nourish the new, creative, universal outlook that draws upon all sacred traditions and transcends each one.

Life Rhythm
P.O. Box 806
Mendocino, CA 95460
(707) 937-1825 (phone)
(707) 937-3052 (fax)
This small company publishes books by John Pierrakos (core energetics) and Malcolm Brown (organismic body psychotherapy) and works in other areas of alternative healing.

Lindisfarne Books (LB)
3390 Route 9
Hudson, NY 12534
(518) 851-2054 (phone)
(518) 851-2047 (fax)
www.Lindisfarne.org (website)
LB publishes titles intended to encourage the recovery of the sacred in our lives and to transform the pursuit of knowledge from a science based on competition to one founded on contemplation and compassion.

Message Company
4 Camino Azul
Santa Fe, NM 87505
(505) 474-0998 (phone)
(505) 471-2584 (fax)
message@nets.com (e-mail)
www.bizspirit.com (website)
The Message Company publishes and distributes books, videos, and audiotapes focusing on practical and leading-edge information in new business paradigms (primarily spirituality in business), managing change, New Science, and simple living.

Newcastle Publishing Company
13419 Saticoy Street
North Hollywood, CA 91605
(818) 787-4378 (phone)
(818) 780-2007 (fax)
This company publishes self-improvement titles with an emphasis on spirituality and creativity.

New Harbinger Publications
5674 Shattuck Avenue
Oakland, CA 94609
(510) 652-0215 or (800) 748-6273 (phone)
(510) 652-5472
nhhelp@newharbinger.com (e-mail)
www.newharbinger.com (website)
New Harbinger offers books, audiotapes, and videotapes on self-help psychology and personal growth, as well as health and professional titles.

Nicholas Hays, Inc.
P.O. Box 612
York Beach, MN 03910-0612
(207) 363-4395 (phone)
(207) 363-5799 (fax)
Distributed by Samuel Weiser, Inc.
The titles from this publisher mainly cover Jungian and spiritual psychology, mythology, and symbolism.

North Atlantic Books
P.O. Box 12327
1450 Fourth Street
Berkeley, CA 94701
(510) 559-8277 (phone)
(510) 559-8279 (fax)
Offerings from this publisher include books on mind/body, whole foods, Jungian psychology, Oriental medicine, Buddhist women, Kahlil Gibran, and Zen koans.

Papier-Mache Press
627 Walker Street
Watsonville, CA 95076-4119
(408) 763-1420 (phone)
www.ReadersNdex.com/papiermache (website)
Titles focus on social work and women's studies.

Parallax Press
Community of Mindful Living
P.O. Box 7355
Berkeley, CA 94707
(510) 525-0101 (phone)
(510) 525-7129 (fax)
parapress@aol.com (e-mail)
www.parallax.org (website)
This publisher's book list is dedicated to books and tapes for mindful living by Thich Nhat Hanh

and other prominent teachers of meditation and engaged Buddhism.

Quest Books
c/o National Book Network
4720 Boston Way, Suite A
Lanham, MD 20706
(800) 462-6420 (phone)
(301) 459-2118 (fax)
Although Quest Books comes out of the theosophical tradition, its offerings cover a broad range of spiritual topics.

Samuel Weiser, Inc.
P.O. Box 512
York Beach, MN 03910-0612
(207) 363-4393 or (800) 423-7087 (phone)
(207) 363-5799 (fax)
weiserbooks@worldnet.att.net (e-mail)
This publisher is committed to making available the best in esoteric studies.

Station Hill Press
Station Hill Road
Tarrytown, NY 12507
(914) 758-5840 (phone)
(914) 758-8163 (fax)
This publisher's list includes books on new age topics and self-healing, poetry, and some literary commentary.

Wisdom Publications
199 Elm Street
Somerville, MA 02144
(617) 776-7416 or (800) 272-4050 (for orders)
Wisdom focuses solely on Buddhist spirituality.

RECORDING COMPANIES

The following companies offer audiotapes (often recorded at workshops, conferences, or lectures) covering topics such as psychology, spiritual traditions, relationships, mythology, creativity, holistic health, and methods of healing.

AGC Educational Media
1560 Sherman Avenue, Suite 100
Evanston, IL 60201

(847) 328-6700 (phone)
(847) 328-6706 (fax)
agc@mcs.net (e-mail)
www.agcmedia.com (website)
Affiliated with the Menninger Foundation, this company provides educational material on mental health.

Audio Renaissance
Cassette Production Unlimited—East
6 Commerce Way
Arden, NC 28704
(800) 452-5589 (phone)
audiobooks@earthlink.net (e-mail)
www.audiosource.com/audio/ (website)
Audio Renaissance tapes include fiction, self-help, and inspirational titles.

Big Sur Tapes
P.O. Box 4
Tiburon, CA 94920
(800) 688-5512 (phone)
info@bigsurtapes.com (e-mail)
www.bigsurtapes.com (website)
Big Sur recordings include Stanislav Grof, Anne Armstrong, Ram Dass, Joseph Campbell, Angeles Arrien, and other teachers who have made presentations at the Esalen Institute over the last two decades.

Dharma Communications
P.O. Box 156DC, South Plank Road
Mount Tremper, NY 12457
(914) 688-7993 (phone)
dharmacom@zen-mtn.org (e-mail)
www.zen-mtn.org (website)
Dharma Communications provides resources pertinent to the challenges and opportunities encountered by spiritual practitioners within Buddhist and other religious traditions.

Dharma Seed Tape Library
P.O. Box 66
Wendell Depot, MA 01380
(800) 969-SEED (phone)
world.std.com/~metta/ (website)
The Dharma Seed Tape Library originated in 1983 to provide meditative instruction, guidance, and inspiration by teachers who conduct retreats at the Insight Meditation Society in Massachusetts.

Dolphin Tapes
P.O. Box 71
Big Sur, CA 93920
Dolphin Tapes records psychospiritual topics by various teachers, including Jack Kornfield, Huston Smith, Carl Rogers, and Angeles Arrien.

Hanuman Foundation Tape Library
524 San Anselmo Avenue, Suite 203
San Anselmo, CA 94960
(415) 457-8570 (phone)
rdtapes@aol.com (e-mail)
www.Ramdasstapes.org (website)
The foundation distributes audiocassettes and videotapes of workshops, lectures, and meditations by Ram Dass and other spiritual teachers.

Image Paths Inc.
891 Moe Drive, Suite C
Akron, OH 44310
(800) 800-8661 (phone)
(330) 633-3778 (fax)
info@healthjourneys.com (e-mail)
www.healthjourneys.com (website)
Image Paths produces and distributes the psychotherapist Belleruth Naparstek's Health Journeys—guided imagery audiotapes and more than twenty-five books designed to help with physical and emotional challenges such as stress, cancer, weight loss, and depression.

Mystic Fire Audio
P.O. Box 422
Prince Street Station
New York, NY 10012
(800) 292-9001 (phone)
mysticfire@echonyc.com (e-mail)
www.mysticfire.com (website)
Mystic Fire's offerings include tapes on healing, consciousness, and new age topics.

New Dimensions Radio (NDR)
P.O. Box 569
Ukiah, CA 95482
(707) 468-5215 (phone)
ndradio@igc.org (e-mail)
www.newdimensions.org (website)
NDR tapes feature dialogues with leading social innovators, teachers, and thinkers who provide practical knowledge and perennial wisdom to inspire a healthy life of mind, body, and spirit.

New Medicine Tapes (NMT)
1308 Gilman Street
Berkeley, CA 94706
(800) 647-1110 (phone)
www.nemed.com (e-mail)
NMT offers audio- and videotapes of presentations made at conferences and retreats on transformative topics and by presenters such as Thich Nhat Hanh, Angeles Arrien, David Whyte, Ram Dass, and others.

New World Library
58 Paul Drive
San Rafael, CA 94903
(800) 972-6657 (phone)
escort@nwlib.com (e-mail)
www.nwlib.com (website)
Originally associated with Shakti Gawain, this company's titles cover self-help, spiritual growth, and enlightened business subjects.

Oral Tradition Archives
P.O. Box 51155
Pacific Grove, CA 93950
(800) 779-1116 (phone)
oraltrad@oraltraditions (e-mail)
Oral Tradition specializes in tapes of live presentations by Michael Meade, James Hillman, Robert Bly, Marion Woodman, and Malidome and Sobunfu Some, among others.

Parabola Audio Library
656 Broadway
New York, NY 10012
(800) 560-MYTH (phone)
orders@parabola.org (e-mail)
www.parabola.org (website)
Parabola's forte is its storytelling, mythology, and spirituality tapes.

Quest Audio
P.O. Box 270
Wheaton, IL 60289
(800) 669-9425 (phone)
questbooks@aol.com (e-mail)
www.theosophical.org (website)

Metaphysical, holistic, spiritual, and psychological tapes are issued by Quest.

Sound Horizon Audio and Video Publishing (*See* Words of Wisdom).

Sounds True
735 Walnut Street
Boulder, CO 80302
(800) 333–9185 (phone)
Soundstrue@aol.com (e-mail)
Sounds True has more than three hundred audio-tapes from speakers such as Clarissa Pinkola Estés, Sogyal Rinpoche, Marion Woodman, Stephen Levine, and Thomas Moore. In addition to single cassettes, the company issues multi-cassette educational programs. Sounds True also records many of the conferences in the field, including all the Common Boundary conferences since 1989.

Source Books
P.O. 292231
Nashville, TN 37229-2231
(615) 773-7652 or (800) 531-9283 (phone)
sourcebk@ix.netcom.com (e-mail)

www.sourcebooksinc.com (website)
The Source Books list includes tapes on "acoustic brain research," relaxation, and stress management.

Words of Wisdom (formerly Sound Horizons)
250 West 57th Street, Suite 517
New York, NY 10107
(212) 219-2527 (phone)
SndHorizons@aol.com (e-mail)
This tape collection consists of recordings made during New York Open Center workshops by teachers such as Jeanne Achterberg, Shakti Gawain, Robert Bly, Deepak Chopra, and Thich Nhat Hanh.

World Research Foundation (WRF)
41 Bell Rock Plaza
Sedona, AZ 86351
(520) 284-3300 (phone)
info@wrf.org (e-mail)
www.wrf.org (Tape from website!)
WRF offers audio- and videotapes on the theme of "New Directions for Medicine." Examples include *qigong*, Ayurvedic medicine, and wellness.

Index

ANNE A. SIMPKINSON is an award-winning journalist and editor of *Common Boundary* magazine. She has a master's degree in counseling and body psychotherapy and served on the board of directors for the Association for Transpersonal Psychology for five years.

CHARLES H. SIMPKINSON is the publisher of *Common Boundary* and a practicing clinical psychologist. He has had a faculty appointment at the Johns Hopkins Medical School in the department of Psychiatry and Behavioral Science and is an adjunct faculty member at the Union Institute in Cincinnati, Ohio.

Together they coedited two anthologies, *Sacred Stories: A Celebration of the Power of Stories to Transform and Heal* and *Nourishing the Soul* (with Rose Solari). Charles also coedited the *Common Boundary Graduate Education Guide*. They live in Chevy Chase, Maryland.